Bloom's Modern Critical Views

African American
  Poets: Wheatley–
  Tolson
African American
  Poets: Hayden–
  Dove
Edward Albee
Dante Alighieri
American and
  Canadian Women
  Poets, 1930–
  present
American Women
  Poets, 1650–1950
Hans Christian
  Andersen
Maya Angelou
Asian-American
  Writers
Margaret Atwood
Jane Austen
Paul Auster
James Baldwin
Honoré de Balzac
Samuel Beckett
Saul Bellow
The Bible
William Blake
Jorge Luis Borges
Ray Bradbury
The Brontës
Gwendolyn Brooks
Elizabeth Barrett
  Browning
Robert Browning
Italo Calvino
Albert Camus
Truman Capote
Lewis Carroll
Willa Cather
Cervantes
Geoffrey Chaucer
Anton Chekhov

Kate Chopin
Agatha Christie
Samuel Taylor
  Coleridge
Joseph Conrad
Contemporary Poets
Julio Cortázar
Stephen Crane
Daniel Defoe
Don DeLillo
Charles Dickens
Emily Dickinson
John Donne and the
  17th-Century Poets
Fyodor Dostoevsky
W.E.B. DuBois
George Eliot
T.S. Eliot
Ralph Ellison
Ralph Waldo Emerson
William Faulkner
F. Scott Fitzgerald
Sigmund Freud
Robert Frost
William Gaddis
Johann Wolfgang von
  Goethe
George Gordon, Lord
  Byron
Graham Greene
Thomas Hardy
Nathaniel Hawthorne
Robert Hayden
Ernest Hemingway
Hermann Hesse
Hispanic-American
  Writers
Homer
Langston Hughes
Zora Neale Hurston
Aldous Huxley
Henrik Ibsen
John Irving

Henry James
James Joyce
Franz Kafka
John Keats
Jamaica Kincaid
Stephen King
Rudyard Kipling
Milan Kundera
Tony Kushner
D.H. Lawrence
Doris Lessing
Ursula K. Le Guin
Sinclair Lewis
Norman Mailer
Bernard Malamud
David Mamet
Christopher Marlowe
Gabriel García
  Márquez
Cormac McCarthy
Carson McCullers
Herman Melville
Arthur Miller
John Milton
Molière
Toni Morrison
Native-American
  Writers
Joyce Carol Oates
Flannery O'Connor
Eugene O'Neill
George Orwell
Octavio Paz
Sylvia Plath
Edgar Allan Poe
Katherine Anne
  Porter
Marcel Proust
Thomas Pynchon
Philip Roth
Salman Rushdie
J.D. Salinger
José Sarramago

Bloom's Modern Critical Views

Bloom's Modern Critical Views

ROBERT LOUIS STEVENSON

Edited and with an introduction by
Harold Bloom
Sterling Professor of the Humanities
Yale University

CHELSEA HOUSE
P U B L I S H E R S
A Haights Cross Communications Company
Philadelphia

Printed and bound in the United States of America.

10 9 8 7 6 5 4 3 2 1

Library of Congress Cataloging-in-Publication Data
Robert Louis Stevenson / Harold Bloom, ed.
    p. cm. — (Modern critical views)
  Includes bibliographical references (p.   ) and index.
  ISBN 0-7910-8128-1 (alk. paper)
  1. Stevenson, Robert Louis, 1850-1894—Criticism and interpretation. I. Bloom, Harold. II.
Series.
  PR5496.R568 2004
  828'.809—dc22
                                    2004013050

Contributing Editor: Jesse Zuba

Cover designed by Keith Trego

Cover photo: © Bettman/CORBIS

Layout by EJB Publishing Services

Contents

Editor's Note

My introduction attempts an evaluative overview of Robert Louis Stevenson, drawing some of its material from his letters, while touching upon such varied achievements as his short fiction, his poetry, and his major novelistic romance, *The Master of Ballantrae*.

Gilbert Keith Chesterton, sublimely Falstaffian poet-critic-prose romancer and Catholic polemicist, surveys Stevenson's style, acutely finding in it "a sort of fastidiousness that has still something of the fighting spirit".

The late Leslie Fiedler centers upon Stevenson's lifelong Jekyll-Hyde split, which he sees as culminating in *The Master of Ballantrae*, while Robert Kiely emphasizes the writer's retention of a child's imagination. Douglas Gifford then shows the place of *The Master of Ballantrae* in the history of Scottish fiction.

The unfinished *Weir of Hermiston* is analyzed by K.G. Simpson, while William Veeder interprets *Dr. Jekyll and Mr. Hyde* as a hidden study in the resentment of patriarchy.

Henry James and Stevenson are juxtaposed by George Dekker, after which Stephen Arata confronts *Jekyll and Hyde* as a "dissociation of writing from selfhood", and Alan Sandison provides a very useful account of *Treasure Island*.

The poet-critic John Hollander movingly illuminates *A Child's Garden of Verses*, while Vanessa Smith concludes this volume by a incisive analysis of Stevenson's tales of "the island world of the Pacific".

HAROLD BLOOM

Introduction

1

There is no single clue or formula that will enable readers to hold together the varied literary achievements of Robert Louis Stevenson, born in Edinburgh, Scotland in 1850 and dying in Samoa in December, 1894. Like the very different but equally tragic D.H. Lawrence, also dead at forty-four from the consequences of hereditary tuberculosis, Stevenson searched incessantly for a climate to sustain him, while composing profusely in nearly every literary genre. Lawrence, however was a nonconformist prophet, in the tradition of Milton and Blake, while Stevenson was essentially a Romantic storyteller. Their one common element was the influence of Walt Whitman, subtly muted in Stevenson, but triumphantly transformative in Lawrence.

It is no kindness to Stevenson to juxtapose him with Lawrence, a writer now eclipsed by political correctness, but certain to become canonical, when authentic aesthetic and cognitive standards return, as eventually they will, though perhaps not in my own lifetime. Lawrence's shorter fiction, his poems and prophecies, and his finest novels have major reverberation. Stevenson is far more than an entertainer, but his scope and substance are of the eminence of Rudyard Kipling's rather than of Thomas Hardy's and D.H. Lawrence's.

The best introduction the common reader can have to Stevenson is the volume of his *Selected Letters*, edited by Ernest Mehew (New Haven, 1997). The humor, endurance, and narrative genius figure constantly. As a letter-writer, Stevenson sustains comparison with Henry James, a friend and frequent correspondent, if not quite with John Keats and Lord Byron. The daemonic genius of Stevenson does not however inform his letters, or his essays and travel-writings. Unfortunately, it is also absent from his poetry, which in consequence is minor though accomplished. The immensely and perpetually popular fictions have achieved the status of myth, because they were composed by his daemon: *Treasure Island, Kidnapped, The Master of Ballantrae*, and above all *Strange Case of Dr. Jekyll And Mr. Hyde*. These always will be the essential Stevenson, works that seem to have been there even before first he wrote them.

2

Stevenson married a motherly woman a decade older than himself, and became a kind of elder brother to her young son, who eventually was to be co-author, with Stevenson, of *The Wrong Box*. Rather deliberately, Stevenson resisted growing up. Three months before dying, Stevenson wrote an extraordinary letter to his cousin Bob. An only child, Stevenson first found a brother in Bob, who led him into a break with his Calvinist parents. Musing on their common ancestors, the author confessed his inability to get beyond first childhood:

> What a singular thing is this undistinguished perpetuation of a family throughout the centuries, and the sudden bursting forth of character and capacity that began with our grandfather! But as I go on in life, day by day, I become more of a bewildered child: I cannot get used to this world, to procreation, to heredity, to sight, to hearing; the commonest things are a burthen; the sight of Belle and her twelve-year-old boy, already taller than herself, is enough to turn my hair grey; for as Fanny and her brood, it is insane to think of. The prim obliterated polite face of life, and the broad, bawdy, and orgiastic—or maenadic—foundations, form a spectacle to which no habit reconciles me; and 'I could wish my days to be bound to each' by the same open-mouthed wonder. They *are* anyway, and whether I wish it or not.

The quotation from Wordsworth's "My heart leaps up" is exactly relevant to Stevenson's dilemmas. He suffered not only the bewilderments of a dying child, but a longing for continuity with an earlier self that evaded him. This is the burden of one of his last and most famous poems:

> Sing me a song of a lad that is gone,
>   Say, could that lad be I?

Merry of soul he sailed on a day
   Over the sea to Skye.

Mull was astern, Rum on the port,
   Eigg on the starboard bow;
Glory of youth glowed in his soul:
   Where is that glory now?

Sing me a song of a lad that is gone,
   Say, could that lad be I?
Merry of soul he sailed on a day
   Over the sea to Skye.

Give me again all that was there,
   Give me the sun that shone!
Give me the eyes, give me the soul,
   Give me the lad that's gone!

Sing me a song of a lad that is gone,
   Say, could that lad be I?
Merry of soul he sailed on a day
   Over the sea to Skye.

Billow and breeze, islands and seas,
   Mountains of rains and sun,
All that was good, all that was fair,
   All that was is gone.

Memorably poignant and rather deliberately slight, this is almost self-elegy. Contrast the opening of the "Preface" to *The Master of Ballantrae*:

Although an old, consistent exile, the editor of the following pages revisits now and again the city of which he exults to be a native; and there are few things more strange, more painful, or more salutary, than such revisitations. Outside, in foreign spots, he comes by surprise and awakens more attention than he had expected; in his own city, the relation is reversed, and he stands amazed to be so little recollected. Elsewhere he is refreshed to see attractive faces, to remark possible friends; there he scouts the long streets, with a pang at heart, for the faces and friends that are no more. Elsewhere he is delighted with the presence of what is new, there tormented by the absence of what is old. Elsewhere he is content to be his present self; there he is smitten with an equal regret for what he once was and for what he once hoped to be.

That "regret" is persuasive in Stevenson, including the best of his shorter fictions: "The Bottle Imp", "The Merry Men", and properly the most famous, *Strange Case of Dr. Jekyll And Mr. Hyde*. Conceived in a Stevensonian nightmare, this story might be even more effective had he not allowed his wife to talk him out of a now destroyed first version, in which Dr. Jekyll had been a wicked genius who outered the persona of Mr. Hyde as a mere disguise. A lapsed Calvinist, Stevenson always entertained the doctrine of Predestination in his inmost being.

Critical opinion remains divided upon the eternally popular R.L.S. Borges, in his veneration for Stevenson, converted many who had become skeptical. Unlike the equally popular Poe, Stevenson was a superb stylist, and I continue to reread him with pleasure; if also with a certain reserve, wondering at his selfsameness (to employ a Shakespearean term). I am content to allow Italo Calvino the last word here:

> There are those who think him a minor writer and those who recognize greatness in him. I agree with the latter, because of the clean, light clarity of his style, but also because of the moral nucleus of all his narratives.

G.K. CHESTERTON

The Style of Stevenson

Before writing this chapter I ought to explain that I am quite incapable of writing it; at least as many serious literary authorities think it ought to be written. I am one of those humble characters for whom the main matter of style is concerned with making a statement; and generally, in the case of Stevenson, with telling a story. Style takes its own most living and therefore most fitting form from within; as the narrative quickens and leaps, or the statement becomes warm or weighty, by being either authoritative or argumentative. The sentence takes its shape from motion; as it takes its motion from motive. And the motive (for us outcasts) is what the man has to say. But there is a technical treatment of style for which I have a profound respect, but it is a respect for the unknown, not to say the unintelligible. I will not say it is Greek to me, for I know the Greek alphabet and I do not know the alphabet of these grammars of cadence and sequence; I can still even read the Greek Testament, but the gospel of pure and abstract English brings me no news. I salute it from afar as I do musical harmony or the higher mathematics; but I shall not introduce into this book a chapter on any of these three topics. When I speak of the style of Stevenson I mean the manner in which he could express himself in plain English, even if it were in some ways peculiar English; and I have nothing but the most elementary English with which to criticise it. I cannot use the terms of any science of language, or even any science of literature.

From *Robert Louis Stevenson* in *The Collected Works of G.K. Chesterton*, volume XVIII. © 1991 by the Ignatius Press.

Mr. Max Beerbohm, whose fine and classic criticism is full of those shining depths that many mistake for shallowness, has remarked truly enough on the rather wearisome repetitions in the newspapers, which did great harm to the Stevensonian fame at the time of the Stevensonian fashion. He notices especially that a certain phrase used by Stevenson about his early experiments in writing, that he has 'played the sedulous ape' to Hazlitt or to Lamb, must be permanently kept in type in the journalistic offices, so frequently do the journalists quote it. There are about a thousand things in Stevenson much more worth quoting, and much more really enlightening about his education in letters. Every young writer, however original, does begin by imitating other people, consciously or unconsciously, and nearly every old writer should be quite as willing to admit it. The real irony in the incident seems never to have been noticed. The real reason why this confession of plagiarism, out of a hundred such confessions, is always quoted, is because the confession itself has the stamp not of plagiarism but of personal originality. In the very act of claiming to have copied other styles, Stevenson writes most unmistakably in his own style. I think I could have guessed amid a hundred authors who had used the expression 'played the sedulous ape.' I do not think that Hazlitt would have added that word 'sedulous.' Some might say he was the better because the simpler without it; some would say that the word is in the strict sense too *recherché*; some might say it can be recognised because it is strained or affected. All that is matter for argument; but it is rather a joke when so individual a trick is made a proof of being merely imitative. Anyhow, that sort of trick, the rather curious combination of two such words, is the thing I mean by the style of Stevenson.

In the case of Stevenson, criticism has always tended to be hyper-criticism. It is as if the critic were strung up to be as strict with the artist as the artist was with himself. But they are not very consistent or considerate in the matter. They blame him for being fastidious; and so become more fastidious themselves. They condemn him for wasting time in trying to find the right word; and then waste more time in not very successful attempts to prove it is the wrong word. I remember that Mr. George Moore[42] (who at least led the attack when Stevenson was alive and at the height of his popularity) professed in a somewhat mysterious manner to have exposed or exploded the whole trick of Stevenson, by dwelling at length on the word 'interjected': in the passage which describes a man stopping a clock with interjected finger. There seemed to be some notion that because the word is unusual in that use, it showed that there was nothing but artificial verbalism in the whole tragedy of *Jekyll and Hyde* or the fun of *The Wrong Box*. I think it is time that this sort of fastidiousness about fastidiousness should be corrected with a little common sense. The obvious question to ask Mr. Moore, if he objects to the word 'interjected,' is, 'what word would you use?' He would immediately discover that any word would be much weaker and even much less exact. To say 'interposed finger' would suggest by its very sound a much clumsier and less precise action; 'interjected' suggests by its very sound a sort of jerk of neatness; a mechanical neatness correcting mechanism. In other words, it suggests what it was meant to suggest. Stevenson used the word because it was the right word. Nobody else used it, because nobody else thought of it. And that is the whole story of Stevensonian style.

Literature is but a language; it is only a rare and amazing miracle by which a man really says what he means. It is inevitable that most conversation should be convention; as when we cover a myriad beautiful contrasts or comedies of opposites by calling any number of different people 'nice.' Some writers, including Stevenson, desired (in the old and proper sense) to be more nice in their discrimination of niceness. Now whether we like such fastidious felicities or no, whether we are individually soothed or irritated by a style like that of Stevenson, whether we have any personal or impersonal reason for impatience with the style or the man, we ought really to have enough critical impartiality and justice to see what is the literary test. The test is whether the words are well or ill chosen, not for the purpose of fitting our own taste in words, but for the purpose of satisfying everybody's sense of the realities of things. Now it is nonsense for anybody who pretends to like literature not to see the excellence of Stevenson's expression in this way. He does pick the words that make that picture that he particularly wants to make. They do fix a particular thing, and not some general thing of the same sort; yet the thing is often one very difficult to distinguish from other things of the same sort. That is the craft of letters; and the craftsman made a vast multitude of such images in all sorts of materials. In this matter we may say of Stevenson very much what he said of Burns. He remarked that Burns surprised the polite world, with its aesthetes and antiquarians, by never writing poems on waterfalls, ruined castles or other recognised places of interest; the very fact, of course, which showed Burns to be a poet and not a tourist. It is always the prosaic person who demands poetic subjects. They are the only subjects about which he can possibly be poetic. But Burns, as Stevenson said, had a natural gift of lively and flexible comment that could play as easily upon one thing as another; a kirk or a tavern or a group going to market or a pair of dogs in the street. This gift must be judged by its aptness, its vividness and its range; and anybody who suggests that Stevenson's talent was only one piece of thin silver polished perpetually in its napkin does not, in the most exact and emphatic sense, know what he is talking about. Stevenson had exactly the talent he attributes to Burns of touching nothing that he did not animate. And so far from hiding one talent in one napkin, it would be truer to say that he became ruler over ten cities; set in the ends of the earth. Indeed the last phrase alone suggests an example or a text.

I will take the case of one of his books; I deliberately refrain from taking one of his best books. I will take *The Wrecker*, a book which many would call a failure and which nobody would call a faultless artistic success, least of all the artist. The picture breaks out of the frame; indeed it is rather a panorama than a picture. The story sprawls over three continents; and the climax has too much the air of being only the last of a long string of disconnected passages. It has the look of a scrap-book; indeed it is very exactly a sketch-book. It is merely the sketch-book of Loudon Dodd, the wandering art student never allowed to be fully an artist; just as his story is never allowed to be fully a work of art. He sketches people with the pen as he does with the pencil, in four or five incongruous societies, in the commercial school of Muskegon or the art school of Paris, in the east wind of Edinburgh or the black squall of the South Seas; just as he sketched the four fugitive murderers gesticulating and lying in the Californian saloon. The point is (on the strict principles of *l'art pour l'art*, so dear to Mr. Dodd) that he sketched devilish well. We can take the portraits of twenty social types in turn, taken from six social worlds utterly shut out from each other, and find in every case that the strokes are at once few and final; that is, that the word is well chosen out of a hundred words and that one word does the work of twenty. The story starts: 'The beginning of this yarn is my poor father's character'; and the character is compact in one paragraph. When Jim Pinkerton first strides into the story and is described as a young man 'with cordial, agitated manners,' we walk through the rest of the narrative with a living man; and listen not merely to words, but to a voice. No other two adjectives could have done the trick. When the shabby and shady lawyer, with his cockney culture and underbred refinement, is first introduced as handling a big piece of business beyond his *metier*, he bears himself 'with a sort of shrinking assumption.' The reader, especially if he is not a writer, may imagine that such words matter little; but if he supposes that it might just as well have been 'flinching pride' or 'quailing arrogance' he knows nothing about writing and perhaps not much about reading. The whole point is in that hitting of the right nail on the head; and rather more so when the nail is such a very battered little tintack as Mr. Harry D. Bellairs of San Francisco. When Loudon Dodd merely has to meet a naval officer and record that he got next to nothing out of him, that very negation has a touch of chilly life like a fish. 'I judged he was suffering torments of alarm lest I should prove an undesirable acquaintance; diagnosed him for a shy, dull, vain, unamiable animal, without adequate defence—a sort of dishoused snail.' The visit to an English village, under the shadow of an English country house, is equally aptly appreciated; from the green framework of the little town, 'a domino of tiled houses and walled gardens,' to the reminiscences of the ex-butler about the exiled younger son; 'near four generations of Carthews were touched upon without eliciting one point of interest; and we had killed Mr. Henry in the hunting field with a vast elaboration of painful circumstance and buried him in the midst of a whole sorrowing county, before I could so much as manage to bring upon the stage my intimate friend, Mr. Norris.... He was the only person of the whole featureless series who seemed to have accomplished anything worth mentioning; and his achievements, poor dog, seemed to have been confined to going to the devil and leaving some regrets.... He had no pride about him, I was told; he would sit down with any man; and it was somewhat woundingly implied that I was indebted to this peculiarity for my own acquaintance with the hero.' But I must not be led away by the large temptation of quoting examples of the cool and collected and sustained irony, with which Loudon Dodd tells his whole story. I am only giving random examples of his rapid sketches of very different sorts of societies and personalities; and the point is that he can describe them rapidly and yet describe them rightly. In other words the author does possess a quite exceptional power of putting what he really means into the words that really convey it. And to show that this was a matter of genius in the man, and not (as some of his critics would imply) a matter of laborious technical treatment applied to two or three prize specimens, I have taken all these examples from one of the less known works, one of the least admired and perhaps of the least admirable. Whole tracts of it run almost as casually as his private correspondence; and his private correspondence is full of the same lively and animated neatness. In this one neglected volume of *The Wrecker* there are thousands of such things; and everything to show that he could have written twenty more volumes, equally full of these felicities. A man who does this is not only an artist doing what most men cannot do, but he is certainly doing what most novelists do not do. Even very good novelists have not this particular knack of putting a whole human figure together with a few unforgettable words. By the end of a novel by Mr. Arnold Bennett or Mr. E.F. Benson I have the sense that Lord Raingo or Lord Chesham is a real man, very rightly understood; but I never have at the beginning that feeling of magic; that a man has been brought to life by three words of an incantation.

This was the genius of Stevenson; and it is simply silly to complain of it because it was Stevensonian. I do not blame either of the other two novelists for not being somebody else. But I do venture to blame them a little for grumbling because Stevenson was himself. I do not quite see why he should be covered with cold depreciation merely because he could put into a line what other men put into a page; why he should be regarded as superficial because he saw more in a man's walk or profile than the moderns can dig out of his complexes and his subconsciousness; why he should be called artificial because he sought (and found) the right word for a real object; why he should be thought shallow because he went straight for what was significant, without wading towards it through wordy seas of insignificance; or why he should be treated as a liar because he was not ashamed to be a story-teller.

Of course there are many other vivid marks of Stevenson's style, besides this particular element of picked and pointed phrase, or rather especially the combination of picked and pointed phrases. I might make much more than I have made out of something in his rapidly stepping sentences, especially in narrative, which corresponds to his philosophy of the militant attitude and the active virtues. That word angular, which I have been driven to use too often, belongs to the sharpness of his verbal gestures as much as to the cutlasses and choppers of his pasteboard pirates. Those early theatrical figures, from the sketch-book of Skelt, were all of them in their nature like snapshots of people in swift action. Three-Fingered Jack could not have remained permanently with the cudgel or the sabre swung about his head nor Robin Hood with the arrow drawn to his ear; and the descriptions of Stevenson's characters are seldom static but rather dynamic descriptions; and deal rather with how a man did or said something than with what he was like. The sharp and shrewd Scottish style of Ephraim Mackellar or David Balfour seems by its very sound exactly fitted to describe a man snapping his fingers or rapping with his stick. Doubtless so careful an artist as Stevenson varied his style to suit the subject and the speaker; we should not look for these dry or abrupt brevities in the dilettante deliberations of Loudon Dodd; but I know very few of the writer's works in which there are not, at the crisis, phrases as short and sharp as the knife that Captain Wicks rammed through his own hand. Something should also have been said, of course, of the passages in which Stevenson deliberately plays on a somewhat different musical instrument; as when he exercised upon Pan's Pipes in respectful imitation of Meredith upon a penny whistle. Something should have been said of the style of his poems; which are perhaps more successful in their phraseology than their poetry. But these again teem with these taut and trenchant separate phrases; the description of the interlacing branches like crossed sword in battle; the men upholding the falling skies like unfrowning caryatids; the loud stairs of honour and the bright eyes of danger. But I have already explained that I profess no scientific thoroughness about these problems of execution; and can only speak of the style of Stevenson as it specially affects my own taste and fancy. And the thing that strikes me most is still this sense of somebody being pinked with a rapier in a particular button; of a sort of fastidiousness that has still something of the fighting spirit; that aims at a mark and makes a point, and is certainly not merely an idle trifling with words for the sake of their external elegance or intrinsic melody. As a part of the present criticism, such a statement is only another way of saying, in the old phrase, that the style is the man; and that the man was certainly a man and not only a man of letters. I find everywhere, even in his mere diction and syntax, that theme that is the whole philosophy of fairy-tales, of the old romances and even of the absurd libretto of the little theatre—the conception that man is born with hope and courage indeed, but born outside that which he was meant to attain; that there is a quest, a test, a trial by combat or pilgrimage of discovery; or, in other words, that whatever else man is he is not sufficient to himself, either through peace or through despair. The very movement of the sentence is the movement of a man going somewhere and generally fighting something; and that is where optimism and pessimism are alike opposed to that ultimate or potential peace, which the violent take by storm.

NOTE

42. George Moore (1852–1933) was an Irish novelist and critic.

LESLIE A. FIEDLER

R.L.S. Revisited

Originally the Introduction to *The Master of Ballantrae*
by Robert Louis Stevenson, Rinehart, 1954

"That angel was a devil ..."

One hundred years after the birth of Stevenson, the question of his worth as a writer remains still very much at issue. Unless we are willing to surrender him completely to children or to indulge a sneaking fondness for him as unanalytically as if we were ourselves children, we must make a really critical assessment of his work. We must meet the question: Is a liking for *Treasure Island*, a literary enthusiasm or a minor subliterary vice, like reading detective stories? The enthusiasm of the first generation of Stevensonians found a critical approach to what seemed to them all charm and magic impertinent, but today we are inclined to be suspicious of the easy triumphs of the R.L.S. style; and the genre of Romance to which Stevenson's reputation is tied has been relegated among us to the shelves of the circulating library. David Daiches has recently attempted to redeem Stevenson for our time by showing him progressing from the lesser form of the Romance to the Novel proper; but this approach concedes too much by assuming a derogatory evaluation of the Romance as such (to which I am not prepared to subscribe), and leads to a failure to understand the intent of the conclusion of *The Master of Ballantrae* and of the proposed ending to the *Weir of Hermiston*.

From *No! in Thunder*. © 1960 by Leslie A. Fiedler.

13

If we remember that Long John Silver appeared for years in the "Katzenjammer Kids," we will, I think, begin to see the possibilities of a quite different approach. Imagine Anna Karenina or Stephen Dedalus appropriated by the comic strips! It could be done only in vulgar burlesque; but the Sea-Cook can be kidnapped without impertinence. Like other Stevensonian characters (Jekyll and Hyde, for instance), he exists, as it were, in the public domain—along with Thor and Loki, Hansel and Gretel. The characters of Stevenson seem to have an objective existence, a being prior to and independent of any particular formal realization. They are, in short, not merely literary creations, but also embodiments of archetypal themes—and it is in the realm of myth, which sometimes overlaps but is not identical with literature, that we must look for clues to the meaning and unity of Stevenson's work.

Modern prose fiction has handled the myth in two quite different ways, one sophisticated, one naïve; the former, that of James Joyce, for instance, leads from the inward novel of character, through psychological naturalism, to symbolism and beyond to the conscious manipulation of the mythic; the latter begins with the outward Romance of incident, the boys' story or thriller, and moves through allegory, often elusive, to the naïve or unconscious evocation of myth. To the latter group belong such varied writers as Melville, Arthur Conan Doyle, Graham Greene—and Robert Louis Stevenson. They are possessed of a double ambiguity: on the one hand, they are likely to deny point-blank the symbolic intent which the critic can not help seeing in them; and on the other, they tend to define a wavering line between literature, and subliterature—falling sometimes to the side of achieved formal statement and sometimes to that of a shoddy and cheaply popular evocation of archetypal themes.

Sophisticated exploiters of the mythic (Joyce, Mann) are inevitably limited in their appeal, and in their work the traditional "story" plotted in time tends to be replaced by the timeless movement of archetypes in the psyche. Such naïve exploiters of the mythic as Greene and Stevenson, on the contrary, preserve the "story" and its appeal intact; in them the picturesque never yields completely to the metaphysical—and they can always be read on one level as boys' books or circulating—library thrillers.

To understand and examine Stevenson as a writer of this kind is at once to take him seriously and to preserve the integrity of his Romances qua Romances. More than that, such an understanding may lead to the more general appreciation of an honorable alternative to realism, somewhat out of fashion but by no means exhausted in its possibilities, a genre in which the serious contemporary fictionist may find a strategy for closing the distance between himself and the large audience of novel readers ordinarily immune to serious literature. It is well to realize, however, the difficulties inherent in such a strategy; and when we have come to see Stevenson's development as a writer of fiction, in terms of a struggle to exploit ever more deeply the universal meanings of his fables, with the least possible surrender of their structure and appeal as "howling good tales," we shall be able to understand, perhaps better than their author ever did, certain contradictions of tone and intent in the later books.

Over and over again since his reputation was first questioned, critics have asked: Is there in Stevenson's work a single motivating force, beyond the obvious desire to be charming, to please, to exact admiration—that seems to us now a little shallow and more than a little coquettish? Frank Swinnerton, who led the first reaction against the uncritical adulation of R.L.S. found in only one book, *Jekyll and Hyde*, a "unifying idea." But "idea" is a misleading word; a single felt myth gives coherence, individually and as a group, to several of Stevenson's long fictions—and it is the very myth explicitly stated in *Jekyll and Hyde*. The books besides the latter are *Treasure Island, Kidnapped, The Master of Ballantrae* and the *Weir of Hermiston*; the organizing mythic concept might be called the Beloved Scoundrel or the Devil as Angel, and the books make a series of variations of the theme of the beauty of evil—and conversely the unloveliness of good. The Beloved Scoundrel makes his debut as Long John Silver in *Treasure Island*, a tale first printed, it is worth noticing, in a boys' magazine, and written to explain circumstantially a treasure map drawn for a child's game that Stevenson had been playing with his young stepson.

There can be little doubt that one of Stevenson's motives in marrying was to become a child—and finding himself at the age of thirty at long last a child enabled him unexpectedly to become for the first time a real creative writer; that is, to sustain a successful long fiction. All of Stevenson's major loves had been older, once-married women—which is to say, mothers. There was his "Madonna," Mrs. Sitwell, who in the end married his friend Sidney Colvin, and to whom he used to sign his letters of passionate loneliness "Your Son"; there was the agreeably alien and mature Mme. Garischine, whom he assured "what I want is a mother"; and there was, at last, the woman he actually wed, Fanny Osbourne, some eleven years older than himself, the mother of three children.

His marriage to Mrs. Osbourne not only gave him a mother to replace his own, from whom he felt estranged and to whom he could not utterly commit himself without feelings of guilt toward his father, but provided him for the first time with a brother in the form of his twelve-year-old stepson,

Lloyd. An only child and one isolated by illness, Stevenson had never been able to feel himself anything but a small adult (his parents observed him, noted down his most chance remarks with awful seriousness); against the boy Lloyd he was able to define himself as a boy. Together they *played* at many things; toy soldiers, printing (they founded the Davos Press to publish accounts of their mock warfare)—even writing. Before Lloyd had fully matured, he and Stevenson had begun their collaboration with *The Wrong Box*. Writing to R.L.S. seemed always a kind of childish sport; "to play at home with paper like a child," he once described his life's work, a glance over his shoulder at his disapproving forebears, good engineers and unequivocal adults. But there is in such a concept of art, not only the troubled touch of guilt, but the naïve surge of joy; and Stevenson's abandonment to childhood meant his first release as an artist—produced *Treasure Island, Kidnapped* and *A Child's Garden of Verses*.

Long John Silver is described through a boy's eye, the first of those fictional first-person-singulars who are a detached aspect of the author. It is Jim Hawkins who is the chief narrator of the tale, as it is Jim who saves the Sea-Cook from the gallows. For the boy, the scoundrel par excellence is the Pirate: an elemental ferocity belonging to the unfamiliar sea and uncharted islands hiding bloodstained gold. And yet there is an astonishing innocence about it all—a world without sex and without business—where the source of wealth is buried treasure, clean gold in sand, for which only murder has been clone, but which implies no grimy sweat in offices, no manipulating of stock, none of the quiet betrayals of capitalist competition. The very embodiment of this world, vain, cruel, but astonishingly courageous and immune to self-deprecation, able to compel respect, obedience—and even love—is John Silver; and set against him for a foil is Captain Smollett, in whom virtue is joined to a certain dourness, an immediate unattractiveness. Not only Jim, but Stevenson, too, finds the Pirate more lovable than the good Captain. In one of his *Fables* written afterwards, he sets before us Alexander Smollett and John Silver, debating with each other while their author rests between Chapters XXXII and XXXIII; and Captain Smollett" is embarrassed by the Sea-Cook's boast that their common creator loves him more, keeps him in the center of the scene, but keeps the virtuous Captain "measling in the hold."

Kidnapped, like *Treasure Island*, was written for a boys' magazine, and in both all important relationships are between males. In *Kidnapped*, however, the relation of the Boy and the Scoundrel, treated as a flirtation in the earlier book, becomes almost a full-fledged love affair, a pre-sexual romance; the antagonists fall into lovers' quarrels and make up, swear to part forever, and remain together. The Rogue this time is Alan Breck Stewart, a rebel, a deserter, perhaps a murderer, certainly vain beyond forgiveness and without a shred of Christian morality. The narrator and the foil in this book (certainly, technically the most economical—perhaps, in that respect, the best of Stevenson) are one: David Balfour is Jim Hawkins and Captain Smollett fused into a single person. David must measure the Scoundrel against himself, and the more unwillingly comes to love that of which he must disapprove. Here good and evil are more subtly defined, more ambiguous: pious Presbyterian and irreverent Catholic, solid defender of the status quo and fantastic dreamer of the Restoration—in short, Highlander and Lowlander, Scotland divided against itself. It is the Lowlander that Stevenson *was* who looks longingly and disapprovingly at the alien dash, the Highland fecklessness of Alan through the eyes of David (was not Stevenson's own mother a Balfour?); but it is the Highlander he *dreamed* himself (all his life he tried vainly to prove his father's family were descended from the banned Clan MacGregor) that looks back. The somber good man and the glittering rascal are both two and one; they war within Stevenson's single country and in his single soul.

In *Dr. Jekyll and Mr. Hyde*, which Stevenson himself called a "fable"—that is, a dream allegorized into a morality—the point is made explicit: "I saw that of the two natures that contended in the field of my consciousness, even if I could rightly be said to be either, it was only because I was radically both." It is the respectable and lonely Dr. Jekyll who gives life to the monstrous Mr. Hyde; and once good has given form to the ecstasy of evil, the good can only destroy what it has shaped by destroying itself. The death of evil requires the death of good. *Jekyll and Hyde* is a tragedy, one of the only two tragedies that Stevenson ever wrote; but its allegory is too schematic, too slightly realized in terms of fiction and character, and too obviously colored with easy terror to be completely convincing; while its explicit morality demands that evil be portrayed finally as an obvious monster.

In *The Master of Ballantrae*, Stevenson once more splits in two for dramatic purposes what is in life one: unlovely good and lovely evil, restoring to the latter the glitter and allure proper to his first vision. *The Master* is a splendid book, Stevenson's only truly embodied tragedy—and the wittiest of his works, in its device of placing the narration of the tragic action in the mouths of comic characters, a story told turn and turn about by the comic alter ego of the graceless good man and that of the winning scoundrel, the burlesque Scotsman and the burlesque Irishman, MacKellar and the Chevalier Burke—comic both of them, it is worth noticing, by virtue of their cowardice. To Stevenson, as to all small boys, cowardice is the laughable vice—as courage is the unimpeachable virtue. And yet for this book, the boys' scoundrel, one-legged Pirate or Kilted Highland Rebel will not do; there must be an adult villain, though he must live and die in terms of a "howling good tale." That villain is James Durrisdeer, the Master of Ballantrae.

He is, like John Silver or Alan Breck, absolutely brave and immediately lovable, though unscrupulous and without mercy, two-faced and treacherous, inordinately proud and selfish. But he is all these conventionally villainous things in an absolute sense; he is the very maturity, the quintessence of evil. He is for a time like Long John a Pirate, like Alan a Rebel (and like the later Frank Innes a Seducer), but these are for him mere shadowy forms of what he is ideally. Stevenson, as if to make sure we understand, brings the Master face to face first with the protagonist of *Kidnapped*, "Alan Black Stewart or some such name," and next with Teach himself, the infamous Blackbeard— surely a fit surrogate for Silver and all his crew—and shows each of these in turn shamefully outwitted by the Master. Alan's conduct in their encounter is described as "childish," and Teach, called first "a wicked child," meets his defeat at the Master's hand "like a wicked baby." Beside ultimate villainy, the Pirate and the Highland Rebel seem scarcely adult; theirs is the rascality of the nursery, laughable rather than terrible—and they serve at last only to define the Master's "deadly, causeless duplicity," that final malevolence which must be called "beautiful," the "nobility of hell."

In a letter in which he first discusses his plans for the book, Stevenson writes, "*The Master* is all I know of the devil," and later to Henry James, "The elder brother is an INCUBUS!" One of the happiest strokes of invention in *The Master* is the presentation of elemental good and evil as brothers: Esau and Jacob in their early contention, Cain and Abel in their bloody ending. It is an apt metaphor of their singleness and division.

Henry, the younger brother of the Master, James, is patient, loyal, kind though not generous, at first more than reasonably pious and humble. He has, however, the essential flaw of Stevenson's virtuous men: the flaw of Alexander Smollett, who was "not popular at home," perhaps even of R.L.S. himself appealing to his "Madonna" to assure him that he is not "such cold poison to everybody." Henry does not compel love, not his father's nor that of Alison, the woman who marries him believing that her real beloved, his malefic brother, is dead. He feels his lack of appeal as a kind of guilt, and when his wife is morally unfaithful to him (he is, like the hero of *Prince Otto*, in everything but physical fact a cuckold), he can reproach only himself.

Ephraim Mackellar, called "Squaretoes," the Steward of Durrisdeer and the loyal supporter of Henry, is everything that his Lord is—exaggerated toward the comic—and a pedant and a coward to boot. It is through his dry, finicky prose (with the exception of two interpolated narratives by the

Chevalier Burke, the comic alter ego of James) that the story unfolds, and it is in his mind that the conflict of feeling—repulsion and attraction—toward the Master is played out.

There is no question of James Durrisdeer having some good qualities and some bad; it is his essential quality, his absolute evil, that is *at once* repellent and attractive. The Master *is* evil, that imagined ultimate evil which the student Stevenson naïvely sought in the taverns and brothels of Edinburgh, another Mackellar, his notebook in hand! It is the quality that, Stevenson found, women and unlettered people instinctively love—the dandiacal splendor of damnation that even a Mackellar must call at one point "beautiful!" The study of such double feeling is not common in the nineteenth century, which preferred melodrama to ambivalence; and it is the special merit of Stevenson to have dealt with a mode of feeling so out of the main stream of his time.

From the beginning of the book, the diabolical nature of the Master is suggested, at first obliquely and almost as if by inadvertence. "I think you are a devil of a son to me," the old father cries to James; it is merely a commonplace, a figure of speech, but later it becomes more explicit. Henry, veiledly telling his young son of his duel with the Master, speaks of "a man whom the devil tried to kill, and how near he came to kill the devil instead." They are the words of one already half-mad with grief and torment, but the eminently sane Mackellar is driven to concur in part: "But so much is true, that I have met the devil in these woods and have seen him foiled here." All leads up to the moment of recognition and unwilling praise, when Mackellar says of James: "He had all the gravity and something of the splendor of Satan in the 'Paradise Lost.' I could not help but see the man with admiration...."

But if James is in any real sense the Devil, he must be immortal; his defeats and deaths can be only shows—and this, indeed, the younger brother comes to believe: "Nothing can kill that man. He is not mortal. He is bound upon my back to all eternity—to all God's eternity!" Actually—which is to say according to the account of Mackellar—at the point where Henry breaks forth into near hysteria at the news of yet another presumed death the Master has been falsely thought dead twice. "I have struck my sword throughout his vitals," he cried. "I have felt the hilt dirl on his breastbone, and the hot blood spirt in my very face, time and again, time and again! But he was never dead for that.... Why should I think he was dead now!" And truly, he is to rise once more. Which account is then true? Mackellar's dry literal report, or the younger brother's hallucinated sense of the moment of strife, the unreal death repeated again and again through all time—James and Henry, Esau and Jacob, Cain and Abel?

It is Stevenson's difficult task to juggle both truths: to contain in a single tale the eternally re-enacted myth and the human story, the historical event—and to do it in "Mackellarese"! Small wonder if he felt his problem almost impossible, and if, to some degree, he failed. I do not think he understood the precise nature of his difficulty ever (there is a price to pay for choosing to be a child), but he sensed its presence. "My novel is a tragedy ...," he wrote to Henry James. "Five parts of it are bound [sound?], human tragedy; the last one or two, I regret to say, not so soundly designed; I almost hesitate to write them; they are very picturesque, but they are fantastic; they shame, perhaps degrade, the beginning. I wish I knew; that was how the tale came to me however.... Then the devil and Saranac suggested this *dénouement*, and I joined the two ends in a day or two of feverish thought, and began to write. And now—I wonder if I have not gone too far with the fantastic? ... the third supposed death and the manner of the third re-appearance is steep; steep, sir. It is even very steep, and I fear it shames the honest stuff so far...."

The "honest stuff," the "sound, human tragedy" is the story of the hatred of two brothers and its genesis: the love of Alison for the Master; his supposed death at Culloden; her marriage to Henry, who has all the while loved her; and the Master's reappearance. It is an episode doubtless suggested in part by the actual experience of Stevenson's wife, whose first husband, presumed dead, had reappeared to his supposed widow. Indeed, Samual Osbourne seems to have been in his own right a scoundrel worthy of sitting for James Durrisdeer. This aspect of his novel Stevenson has handled with great psychological accuracy: the Master's reappearance causing the disconcerting transformation of what had been a touching loyalty to the dead into a living infidelity; the Master's two faces, graceful charm for Alison and his father, careless scorn for Henry and the Steward; the timid rage of Mackellar mounting toward the climactic moment at sea when he discovers he is not quite the coward—or the Christian—he has thought himself, and prays blasphemously in the midst of a storm for a shipwreck that will destroy him and the Master together.

But the "steep" denouement that joined itself to the soundly human story, one freezing night at Saranac, impelled the original material toward allegory, in the direction of the mythical. In that remote place, Stevenson had remembered a story told him by an uncle many years before: a tall tale of an Indian fakir who could, by swallowing his tongue, put himself into a state of suspended animation that would permit his being buried alive and later exhumed without any permanent ill effects. The last presumed death of the Master was to be such a deliberate East Indian sham, translated to the Province of Albany. To justify so "fantastic" a conclusion in terms other than the merely picturesque, Stevenson would have had frankly to abandon ordinary standards of credibility, to make the Master *really* a devil, and to risk the absurdity of a myth of the deathlessness of evil. But that would have impugned the *human* tragedy he had already blocked out, and he dared be in the end only fantastic enough for a yarn; that is to say—far from too fantastic—not fantastic enough. Even in *Jekyll* Stevenson had felt bound to explain the transformation to Hyde in the "scientific" terms of a graduated glass and a compound of salts—and that story he considered an outright "Fable"—immune to the human limitations of the novel.

Stevenson will have the fabulous, but he will have it rationally explicable too. The Master must be provided with an Indian servant, must indeed have been in India himself; and there must even be an interpolated narrative to give us a glimpse of him there. The voice which frankly terms him supernatural, which asserts, "He's not of this world.... He was never canny!" must be that of a man nearly mad. If *The Master* seems to pull apart a little at the seams, it is this timidity on the part of its author that is the cause, rather than the fact, customarily insisted upon, that the book was begun in upstate New York and only completed after a lapse of inspiration in Honolulu. After all, the beginning and the end, whenever actually written, were *conceived* together. Perhaps the real trouble was that Stevenson, unlike his characters, did not really believe in Hell.

And yet the ending is effective all the same. The Master, who had seemed to die at Culloden, and had turned up again only to be apparently killed in a duel with his younger brother, is carried off by smugglers, healed, and returns once more to pursue his brother on two continents; but Henry, finally tormented out of humility and reason, turns on James, who, at last trapped by the cutthroats his younger brother has hired to kill him, "dies" and is buried in the midwinter American wilderness. Dug up by his Hindu servant under the eyes of his brother, the Master revives for a moment, just long enough to cause the death by heart failure of the onlooking Henry, and to ensure their burial under a single marker in that remote waste.

The point is the point of *Jekyll*: evil will not die until it has corrupted the good to its own image and brought it down by its side to a common grave. "He is bound upon my back to all eternity—to all God's eternity!" Henry had prophetically cried; and Mackellar, noting the universal meaning of his degeneration, its relevance to that struggle of us all—in which combating evil we come to resemble it—said, "I was overborne with a pity almost approaching the passionate, not for my master alone but for all the sons of man."

Toward the end of his life, Stevenson seems to have lost faith in the worth of *The Master*, though the book had received great critical acclaim, and he had begun with a sense of its being "top chop," "a sure card!" One of his last recorded remarks about the book is that lacking "all pleasureableness," it was "imperfect in essence"—a strange judgment surely, for it is precisely a pleasurable story, a work of real wit: a tragedy seen through the eyes of a comic character. Much more just seems to us the comment of Henry James, written out of his first enthusiasm: "A pure hard crystal, my boy, a work of ineffable and exquisite art." The word "crystal" is peculiarly apt; it is a winter's tale throughout, crystalline as frost, both in scene, from the wintry Scottish uplands to the icy, Indian-haunted Albanian forest; and in style, the dry, cold elegance of "Old Squaretoes"—preserved in a subzero piety in which nothing melts. The quality of the writing alone—the sustained tour de force of "Mackellarese," that merciless parody of the old maid at the heart of all goodness and of Stevenson himself, which makes style and theme astonishingly one in this book—is the greatest triumph of Stevenson's art.

In the unfinished *Weir of Hermiston*, alone among his important novels, R.L.S. attempts to write in the third person, in his own voice—and consequently, there is in that book, as there is never in *The Master*, downright bad writing. Stevenson's instinctive bent was for first-person narrative; and when in his last book he attempts to speak from outside *about* his fiction, his style betrays him to self-pity (we *know* Archie is really the author, and the third-person singular affects us like a transparent hoax), sentimentality and the sort of "fine" writing he had avoided since *Prince Otto*.

The *Weir* is the first of Stevenson's books to deal at all adequately with a woman and with sexual love. (Alison in *The Master* becomes quickly a background figure; and the earlier efforts along these lines in *Catriona* and *Prince Otto* were failures, sickly or wooden); but even here the most successfully realized character is not the Ingenue, young Kirstie, but Old Kirstie, the epitome of all Stevenson's foster mothers from his nurse, Cummy, to his wife. The division of the desired sexual object into two, the blonde and the dark, the young and the old, joined with a single name: a relatively frank mother-projection and the more conventional image of the young virgin is an intriguing example of what the psychologists like to call "splitting"—but in the *Weir*, despite this unconscious camouflage, sex is at last openly touched upon and a further meaning of Stevenson's sexually immature or impotent heroes is revealed. To possess the desired woman can be for Stevenson only to possess the Mother, to offend the Father and court death. He desires to *be* a father, for to inherit a son is harmlessly to emulate his own admired begettor, but himself to *beget* a son is to become his father's rival, to commit symbolic incest. I do not think it is an accident that R.L.S. had no children of his own, was in fact a foster father.

In his books, Stevenson's protagonists are often foster sons, orphans in search of a spiritual father: Jim looking to Long John, David leaning on Alan, Loudon Dodd turning from Jim Pinkerton to Captain Nares. In one sense, all the Beloved Villains *are* Fathers, physically prepossessing, obviously strong, sexually vigorous—but by the same token they are bad sons, betrayers of their own fathers, possessors of the Mother—those who have, as in Stevenson's harrowing fable, *The House of Eld*, cast off the gyve that is loosed only by patricide. They are almost always shown as murderers, but in the earlier books and the books written in collaboration they themselves are spared by the pseudo-son who feebly contemplates their death (Herrick of Attwater, Jim of John Silver). The unloved virtuous are dutiful sons, sexless or impotent, because they had flinched before the killing of the Father, but they are racked by guilt, for the Beloved Villain is an externalization of what they have dreamed but not dared; and the Father, seeing deep, is offended none the less.

Parallel to the series of books I have been chiefly describing are the books written by Stevenson in collaboration with his stepson, especially *The Wrecker*, in which the father–son relationship is more openly treated, in the surprisingly contemporary terms of the relationship between the son as the insecure artist and the father as the assured bourgeois. The pursuit of the muse is felt as a device of Oedipus; and the making of fictions as a prolonged betrayal.

In the *Weir* the two themes at last coalesce, in what might have been, if Stevenson had lived to overcome the stylistic difficulties of its opening portion, the most complex and adult of his fables. Even in the fragment we have, read with the projected conclusion, we can assess Stevenson's achievement, his realization of a solution to the archetypal plight of sonship, placed between the alternatives of murder–incest and impotence–cowardice. Once R.L.S. had dared to confront face-to-face the sexual crisis underlying his fictions, that crisis ceased to be an ultimate explanation, became merely another symbolic level from which he could push on toward more ultimate and more metaphysical explications of the problem with which he had begun: the grace of evil and the unloveliness of good. In the *Weir*, the Lovable Rogue makes a final appearance, this time as the Seducer, Frank Innes, a school friend of, and foil to, the protagonist Archie Weir, the prototype of all those "good" Stevensonian characters who are somehow unworthy of love. The Master, who contains in himself all of Stevenson's lesser scoundrels, had already foreshadowed the Seducer, is intent upon his brother's wife, and in fact upon the village girl Jessie Broun, casually abandoned after a brief and brutal amour by the older brother, but provided for by the kindness of the younger. Young Kirstie in the *Weir* is something of Alison and something of Jessie, a Cressida at heart, neither untouchable nor yet a harlot.

In the book as originally planned, Young Kirstie, baffled by the principled coldness of Archie, who loves her but whom she cannot understand, was to be got with child by Frank Innes, who would then be killed by Archie, and Archie in turn would be condemned to die on the gallows by his own father, a hanging judge of terrible integrity. It is the ending of *Jekyll* and *The Master* all over again—good destroying itself in the very act of destroying evil—but Stevenson relented. In the projected ending reported by his amanuensis and much deplored by most of his critics, Archie was to have broken prison just before the day of his execution and to have escaped with Kirstie to America, making her his wife and taking as his own the child she was carrying, the by-blow of the Scoundrel he has killed.

It was to be a complete merging of good and evil, not as before in mutual destruction and the common grave, but in the possession of a single woman able to love—though in different senses—both; and in the seed which virile evil is able casually to sow, but which only impotent virtue can patiently foster. To cavil at this as an unmotivated "Happy Ending," and to wish that Stevenson had survived once more to change his mind, is to miss utterly the mythic meaning of the event: a final resolution of man's moral duality this side of the grave.

ROBERT KIELY

The Aesthetics of Adventure

For many years Robert Louis Stevenson was a man to be dealt with, both while he lived and after he died. "It has been his fortune," wrote Henry James in 1900, "... to have had to consent to become, by a process not purely mystic and not wholly untraceable—what shall we call it?—a Figure."[1] Whether you liked him or not, whether you read him or not, his personality and his books somehow demanded attention and definition. He seemed bound to remain a kind of literary enigma, changing his style, his face, his habitation, his genre, taunting his readers and daring his critics to give him a name that would cover all situations. Of course the critics took him up on it. They called Robert Louis Stevenson a child.

As might be expected, Stevenson's close friend and correspondent, Henry James, gave the consensus its most graceful and intelligent expression. In an article which Stevenson read in proof in 1887 and approved, James wrote:

> The part of life that he cares for most is youth ... Mingled with his almost equal love of a literary surface it represents a real originality ... The feeling of one's teens, and even of an earlier period ... and the feeling for happy turns—these, in the last analysis ... are the corresponding halves of his character .. In a

word, he is an artist accomplished even to sophistication, whose constant theme is the unsophisticated.[2]

Apt as James' statement is—and his two essays on Stevenson remain the finest criticism written about that author—there is the tendency already in 1887, when Stevenson had seven of his most productive years still ahead of him, to come to "the last analysis," to put his literary character "in a word," to label and have done. Perhaps now, seventy years after his death, it would be worthwhile to investigate again the nature of his "real originality," to pursue the man who, Chesterton said, had "barricaded himself in the nursery ... [because there] dwelt definite pleasures which the Puritan could not forbid nor the pessimist deny."[3]

2

The most consistent characteristics of Stevenson's elusive and quixotic disposition are, as James suggests, his devotion to the art of letters and to the less sophisticated, though not necessarily childish, life of adventure. The two do not seem to go together, but if we are to take him as he was and if we are to avoid the invariably awkward acrobatics of juggling form in one hand and matter in the other, we shall have as often as possible to talk about both simultaneously. Stevenson, it is true, was capable of taking the adventure story in its conventional, almost sub-literary, sense as a mode in which change for its own sake was uppermost; motion counted more than direction, physical action overshadowed interior motivation—a concatenation of faraway places, bizarre characters, sea voyages, mysterious benefactors, abductions, duels, endless flights from hostile pursuers, and seemingly endless quests for unattainable goals.

But to stop here is to stop short of Stevenson's full understanding of adventure. He spent much of his life thinking about outlandish enterprises, writing about them, and occasionally succeeding in embarking upon them. In a very real sense, adventure was the material of his mind, and it is unlikely that over a period of forty-four years it would not have taken on some of the peculiar shape and coloring of that mind. Of course, this might be said of the material of even the most indifferent writer if he spent long enough at his business, but Stevenson's concept of adventure was also part of a highly serious and carefully developed theory of fiction.

In the early 1880s, when Stevenson rose to the defense of the romantic novel in three of his most famous critical essays, Scott, Marryat, and Kingsley were dead, and Charles Reade was an old man. The novel of romance had all but gone out of vogue, and what George Saintsbury called the "domestic and usual novel" had taken its place. "It is certain that for about a quarter of a century, from 1845 to 1870, not merely the historical novel, but romance generally, did lose general practice and general attention ... Those who are old enough ... will remember that for many years the advent of a historical novel was greeted in reviews with a note not exactly of contempt, but of the sort of surprise with which men greet something out of the way and old fashioned."[4] It was the period when Anthony Trollope and George Eliot were at their height in England and Émile Zola was clamoring that naturalism was "the intellectual movement of the century."[5]

But in the decade of the 1880's there were signs of a small but vigorous countermovement in Great Britain. *Treasure Island* (1883) and H. Rider Haggard's *King Solomon's Mines* (1885) were received with a popular acclaim and serious critical attention which neither their authors nor publishers could have predicted. William Ernest Henley, who was instrumental in getting both books published, served the "revival" as poet, critic, and, on occasion, as agent. Another even more versatile defender of romance was Andrew Lang, the Scottish classicist, poet, folklorist, literary critic, and journalist. His graceful praises of Scott, Dumas, Mrs. Radcliffe, and later of Stevenson and Haggard, gave wit and authority to the small current which was running steadily against the tide of literary realism. In an essay entitled "The Supernatural in Fiction," he wrote:

> As the visible world is measured, mapped, tested, weighed, we seem to hope more and more that a world of invisible romance may not be far from us ... I can believe that an impossible romance, if the right man wrote it in the right mood, might still win us from the newspapers, and the stories of shabby love, and cheap remorses, and commonplace failure.[6]

It is thoroughly characteristic of Stevenson that, in the midst of a general enthusiasm for literary domestication and realism, he should join the dissenters and raise his voice in behalf of romance. In 1882 he wrote a sentence in "A Gossip on Romance" which has been quoted so often that its meaning has worn thin: "Drama is the poetry of conduct, romance the poetry of circumstance" (XIII, 329). Stevenson always associated drama with drawing-room realism, partly because of the kind of play being written in the seventies and eighties, but also because properties, costumes, and stage sets could duplicate the concrete paraphernalia of everyday life in a way that the novel obviously could not. But Stevenson also meant to emphasize something much more serious and general than this obvious distinction between dramatic and narrative literature.

He was using aesthetic armament to fight a philosophical and moral battle against an epoch which seemed to him to be making an idol out of the scientific method. Émile Zola was the most persuasive and vociferous evangelist of the new gospel as it applied to literature. For him, conduct and circumstance needed no longer to be regarded as separate because, through experimentation, man would eventually learn how to control circumstance and make of it a predictable consequence of conduct.

> This, then, is the end, this is the purpose in physiology and in experimental medicine: to make one's self master of life in order to be able to direct it ... Their object is ours; we also desire to master certain phenomena of an intellectual and personal order, to be able to direct them. We are, in a word, experimental moralists, showing by experiment in what way a passion acts in a certain social condition. The day in which we gain control of the mechanism of this passion we can treat it and reduce it, or at least make it as inoffensive as possible. And in this consists the practical utility and high morality of our naturalistic works, which experiment on man, and which dissect piece by piece this human machinery in order to set it going through the influence of the environment.[7]

It is in juxtaposition to a statement like this that Stevenson's attitude toward all art, particularly the art of writing, becomes clear. He neither believed nor hoped that man would discover the mystery of his existence by regarding himself as a machine to be dismantled and analyzed. Zola had said, "The metaphysical man is dead; our whole territory is transformed by the advent of the physiological man." And again later: "I insist upon [the] fall of the imagination."[8]

But Stevenson, too, was capable of stinging and memorable phrases: "I would not give a chapter of old Dumas ... for the whole boiling of the Zolas" (*Letters*, II, 85). And in 1883 he wrote to Will H. Low: "Continue to testify boldly against realism. Down with Dagon, the fish god! All art swings down toward imitation, in these days, fatally. But the man who loves art with wisdom sees the joke ... The honest and romantic lover of the Muse can see a joke and sit down to laugh with Apollo" (*Letters*, II, 171).

Although Stevenson's concept of the imagination was more limited than that of the earlier English Romantics, he spent his life trying to prove to himself and a skeptical age that every man possessed a creative power of mind which science could not (and should not) reach. (It was not until later in his career that he began seriously to probe the possibility that the source of nonrational mental activity might produce destructive as well as creative effects.) It was this instinctive and unself-conscious element in man which Stevenson saw as participating in and responding to the rhythm of natural circumstances without being able to "regulate" or "direct" them like a machine. The language he uses, in contrast to that of Zola, is deliberately nonscientific. He repeatedly emphasizes the pleasure and value of mood, emotion, atmosphere, intuition, coincidence.

Stevenson passionately believed that the greater part of life was chance! And although his own published statements on the subject usually came as unsystematic responses to the pronouncements of his contemporaries, they arose from a consistent, even tenacious, conception of art. Stevenson has been accused of frivolity in his criticism and fiction—and, in a sense, justifiably so. He often resorted to frivolity—an impulse he regarded as more purely artistic than that of "practical utility"—in order to liberate fiction from the impingement of sociology, genetics, and political science. In doing this, Stevenson may not at first have been able to avoid the hazards of aesthetic indulgence, but that should not obscure his salutary efforts to distinguish art from propaganda.

The concept of chance seemed to provide some of the mystery and imaginative range found by artists of other periods in revelation or inspiration. Chance, as Joseph Conrad's Marlow was to argue, might be the one remaining escape hatch in a modern and closed universe. It was also a byword for a young Edinburgh writer who was convinced that so long as art was treated primarily as an instrument of reform, it was incapable of fulfilling its highest function. Chance and frivolity were Stevenson's ammunition against the stultifying threat which determinism and utility posed to literature. Those artists who I shared his fears—however different they were from Stevenson in other respects—responded to his essays with surprising fervor.

Gerard Manley Hopkins found an almost Shakespearian freedom from prevailing biases in Stevenson's definition of romance, and rallied to its defense as to an ally newly discovered:

> [Stevenson's] doctrine, if I apprehend him, is something like this. The essence of Romance is incident and that only ... no moral, no character-drawing ... As history consists essentially of events likely or unlikely, consequences of causes chronicled before or what may be called chance, just retributions or nothing of the sort, so Romance, which is fictitious history, consists of

event, of incident. His own stories are written on this principle: they are very good and he has all the gifts a writer of fiction should have, including those he holds unessential.[9]

In the great century of biography and character portrayal, Stevenson stressed the importance of event. And at the dawn of science's confident claim that it could predict and perhaps form behavior, he emphasized the random nature of the human adventure. Neither Hopkins nor Stevenson thought of man as a puppet totally manipulated by unknown forces, but they also did not like to think of him as the plaything of his own scientific and political "schools." The unpredictability of incident, if nothing else, could save him from that, and it became paradoxically a kind of protective talisman. Stevenson uses the words "active" and "passive" in "A Gossip on Romance" not to indicate the degree of physical and mental participation in an event, but the degree to which the individual willingly brings about or controls the circumstances in which he finds himself. In this sense, much of Jim Hawkins' experience in *Treasure Island* is "passive" since things keep happening to him which he cannot foresee or prevent; whereas a character like Madam Merle, who exerts little physical energy, plays a relatively "active" role in the events of James's *Portrait of a Lady*. Since Stevenson believed that much of life is ungovernable circumstance, he would argue that Hawkins is the more representative of the two characters.

In 1883 Stevenson continued his defense and definition of romance in "A Note on Realism." He rejects the claim that the French naturalists have found a way of representing a larger truth than that possible in a stylized romance. He argues that all art which is "conceived with honesty and executed with communicative ardour" has a claim to veracity. The disagreement is rather one of method. "The question of realism, let it be clearly understood, regards not in the least degree the fundamental truth, but only the technical method, of a work of art."[10] The realist has made the mistake of confusing detail with truth, while the romantic novelist persistently keeps his eye on the whole and admits detail into his narrative only as it contributes to a total vision.

Over thirty years later, Joseph Conrad wrote to Stevenson's friend Sidney Colvin that although he (Conrad) had been called a "writer of the sea, of the tropics, a descriptive writer, a romantic writer," his real concern had always been "with the 'ideal' value of things, events, and people."[11] In 1883, Stevenson anticipated Conrad's claim by making a similar one for himself and for all serious writers of romance:

The idealist, his eye singly fixed upon the greater outlines, loves ... to fill up the interval with detail of the conventional order, briefly touched, soberly suppressed in tone, courting neglect. But the realist, with a fine intemperance, will not suffer the presence of anything so dead as convention; he shall have all fiery, all hot-pressed from nature, all charactered and notable, seizing the eye ... The immediate danger of the realist is to sacrifice the beauty and significance of the whole to local dexterity, or ... to immolate his readers under facts ... The danger of the idealist is, of course, to become merely null and lose all grip of fact, particularity, or passion ... But though on neither side is dogmatism fitting ... yet one thing may be generally said, that we of the last quarter of the nineteenth century, breathing as we do the intellectual atmosphere of our age, are most apt to err upon the side of realism than to sin in quest of the ideal.[12]

3

Significantly enough, Stevenson's most important single piece of criticism is an essay in response to James's "The Art of Fiction," in which truth to life was emphasized as the essential criterion for judging a novel's value. James's emphasis is clearly very different from that of Zola, yet he too upholds a method which Stevenson rejects:

As people feel life, so they will feel the art that is most closely related to it. This closeness of relation is what we should never forget in talking of the effort of the novel. Many people speak of it as a factitious, artificial form, a product of ingenuity, the business of which is to alter and arrange the things which surround us, to translate them into conventional, traditional moulds ... Catching the very note and trick, the strange irregular rhythm of life, that is the attempt whose strenuous force keeps Fiction upon her feet. In proportion as in what she offers us we see life *without* rearrangement do we feel that we are touching the truth; in proportion as we see it *with* rearrangement do we feel that we are being put off with a substitute, a compromise and convention.[13]

In his reply, "A Humble Remonstrance," published in *Longman's Magazine* in 1884, Stevenson praises much that James has to say, but disagrees with his basic premise that the function of art is to come as close as possible to resembling life. Stevenson takes a directly opposite position:

> No art—to use the daring phrase of Mr. James—can successfully "compete with life"; ... To "compete with life," whose sun we cannot look upon, whose passions and diseases waste and slay us—to compete with the flavour of wine, the beauty of the dawn, the scorching of fire, the bitterness of death and separation—here is, indeed, a projected escalade of heaven ... Life is monstrous, infinite, illogical, abrupt, and poignant; a work of art, in comparison, is neat, finite, self-contained, rational, flowing and emasculate. (XIII, 347–350)

Stevenson argues that art should not try too hard to be like life because the copy is bound to appear pale and spurious beside the real thing. At first glance, he would seem to be working from Coleridge's famous distinction between "imitation" and "copy." Imitation, according to Coleridge, is always the more beautiful and successful in its own terms because, unlike the detailed waxwork copy, it begins by acknowledging the essential difference between it and the object being imitated.

> In all imitations two elements must coexist, and not only coexist, but must be perceived as coexisting. These two constituent elements are likeness and unlikeness ... If there be likeness to nature without any check or difference, the result is disgusting.[14]

Stevenson, early a reader of Romantic prose, particularly Coleridge, Hazlitt, and Wordsworth, evidently has the general argument, if not this precise statement of it, in mind. But he carries the point to a rather un-Romantic conclusion by stressing that aspect of art which is most unlike nature, rather than seeking, as Coleridge did, a balance between sameness and difference. If art cannot hope to compete with life, then, suggests Stevenson, let it cease the effort, and accentuate instead those characteristics in which it is most obviously and peculiarly itself. In content as well as form, let it be openly and unashamedly "neat, finite, self-contained, rational, flowing, and emasculate."

The ultimate implications of this aesthetic for fiction are extreme; yet on and off, until the later years of his life, he reiterated his position and attempted in his creative work to put the theory into practice. As a doctrine it is worth exploring, partly because it is in itself a unique and refreshing combination of familiar critical assumptions; moreover, it provides an insight into aspects of Stevenson's intelligence which we are not normally aware of in his fiction and poetry. Eventually, in his increasing inability or unwillingness to follow his own literary rules, we discover a mind in rebellion against itself—a philosophy, a morality, and a way of writing undergoing change in spite of early and earnest attempts to establish a permanent orthodoxy.

The tenets of that orthodoxy as set forth in "A Humble Remonstrance" must be understood before we can discover, through analyzing the fiction, how and why he gradually came to modify his own "dogmas," and to disregard some of them altogether. First, the novel or story is to be "neat" and "finite," that is to say, without loose ends—no unexplained mysteries or ambiguous characters left for the reader to wonder about after the last chapter. Life puzzles and mystifies enough; that is not the task of art. Nothing in the shape or the matter of the work should be extraneous; he agrees with Poe that every word and phrase must contribute to a common effect or purpose; otherwise, the story would do better without it. Conclusions must be appropriate and consistent with the whole. If they can be inevitable in the Aristotelian sense, well and good, but they must never be shocking or morbid if the plot presents any alternative:

> It is the blot on *Richard Feverel*, for instance, that it begins to end well; and then tricks you and ends ill ... the ill ending does not inherently issue from the plot ... It might have so happened; it needed not; and unless needs must, we have no right to pain our readers. (*Letters*, IV, 144)

A work of art is neat and finite because it is fully comprehensible in its sum. The novelist may deal, if he likes, with unclear subtleties of psychology, with the vagaries of philosophy, and the complexities of human conflict, but if he is wise he will sharpen his focus somewhere before the end. He will clarify distinctions, and give his creation a simplicity life does not have. The novel, Stevenson asserts, "is not a transcript of life, to be judged by its exactitude; but a simplification of some side or point of life, to stand or fall by its significant simplicity" (XIII, 357).

Thirdly, art should be "self-contained." In Stevenson's opinion, narrative fiction has an advantage over drama because in drama "the action is developed in great measure by means of things that remain outside of the art," that is, by real people as actors, properties, costumes, heard voices, and actual movements and gestures. If the best art is that which depends as little as possible upon the world outside itself, then the novelist can make up his own rules of logic and morality, or, if he likes, dispense with them altogether. Stevenson is fairly adept, especially in his early fiction, at sidestepping moral questions. As for logic, he had a properly Romantic contempt for it in a formal sense. "The heart," he wrote, "is trustier than any syllogism"; and he praised the novel of adventure for making its appeal "to certain almost sensual and quite illogical tendencies in man."

When he goes on to call art "rational," then, he does not mean it in a strictly philosophical sense. Nor does he so much refer to reason as it operates in daily life—sorting out existing possibilities and selecting real alternatives—but rather as it might operate in a fanciful world beginning with unlikely, even preposterous, assumptions, and moving from them to other more or less unlikely positions in an orderly and systematic way. In saying that art is rational, Stevenson is also reminding us that its realm is the mind. It is not only conceived and created in the mind of the artist, but its appeal, however simple or sensational, is through the senses to the intelligence:

> We admire splendid views and great pictures; and yet what is truly admirable is the mind within us, that gathers together these scattered details for its delight, and makes ... that intelligible whole. (XIII, 88)

The next adjective Stevenson uses to define art is "flowing," a word with which Hazlitt liked to describe the "warm, moving mass" of a painting or the vitality of a poem. In a way, Stevenson means much the same thing. What is wanted in fiction is coherence and movement, not only a reasonable connection between episodes and an observable relationship among characters, but motion, which for a writer of romance invariably means physical action on the part of the characters and its imaginative counterpart in the reaction of the reader:

> In anything fit to be called by the name of reading, the process itself should be absorbing and voluptuous; we should gloat over a book, be rapt clean out of ourselves ... This, then, is the plastic part of literature: to embody character, thought, or emotion in some act or attitude that shall be remarkably striking to the mind's eye. (XIII, 327–333)

For Stevenson, then, although he recognizes that he lives in an age in which "it is thought clever to write a novel with no story at all," one of the cardinal sins the novelist can commit is to arrest the flow of action, to allow his story to fall into a "kind of monotonous fitness,"—in other words, from his point of view, to be static and dull. This interpretation of "flow" veers from Hazlitt in much the same way Stevenson's aesthetic differs from that of Coleridge and James—that is, with regard to art as an imitation of life. When Hazlitt says that poetry "describes the flowing, not the fixed," he introduces that statement by asserting art's essential commitment to vitality. "Poetry," he says, "puts a spirit of life and motion into the universe."[15] Stevenson accepts the principle and necessity of motion in art, but to an extreme which seems deliberately to avoid the "spirit of life."

It is true that life is in a state of continuous flux, but the modes of change are various, uneven, and at times almost imperceptible. What is physiologically necessary in human nature is dramatically essential in narrative art: that periods of near-stasis precede and follow moments of extreme agitation. As an invalid Stevenson knew the corporeal validity of this better than most men, and perhaps it is as an invalid that he rejected it as a principle of fiction. "Seriously, do you like repose?" he asked Cosmo Monkhouse in a letter written in 1884. "Ye Gods, I hate it. I never rest with any acceptation ... Shall we never shed blood? This prospect is too grey" (*Letters*, II, 204–205). If life must now and then slow down almost to a stop, give in to inertia and to the tedium of rest and impotent anticipation, art need not succumb to the same limitation. The novel, particularly the romance, can spin out an endless series of hectic and exhausting episodes with rarely a pause between. When Stevenson wrote this kind of book, he achieved more or less what he wanted. The result is not very much like life; it is an invention of perpetual motion which, because of its relentlessly consistent rate, resembles the mechanical much more than it does the organic.

It is partly the realization of this lack of what Hazlitt calls "the living principle" in art which brings Stevenson to his final and most telling adjective, "emasculate." True, art has neither organic life nor gender; it cannot generate itself and it cannot die. But considering the chasteness of Stevenson's early experiments in adventure fiction, the choice of this strong metaphor evokes, deliberately or not, literal substantive connotations as well as figurative and formal ones. It has often been noted that, except in a few isolated instances, mostly found in the work of his later years, he avoided sex in his fiction. He did not simply avoid realistic treatment of physical sexuality (which is true of most Victorian novelists), but he shunned dealing with any but the most superficial relationships between the sexes, and often excluded women from his fictional world altogether. "This is a poison bad world for the romancer, this Anglo-Saxon world; I usually get out of it by not having any women in it at all" (*Letters*, IV, 12).

He sounds here as though he is lamenting the prudish morality of the age which prevented artists from dealing honestly with sex, and since this letter was written in 1892 (by which time he had begun bringing women more often into his fiction), the complaint is probably in earnest. But long before this, Stevenson, without the trace of a complaint, regularly avoided romantic love, even of that delicate, sentimental, and social variety permitted, indeed encouraged, by his age. As his definition suggests, sexlessness, in theory if not always in practice, is essential to his early concept of fiction.

It can be argued that Stevenson's prejudice is not strictly directed against women, but that he discriminates against matured masculinity as well. Not only are many of his heroes young boys and adolescents, but even his grown men lack potency and aggressiveness in their relations with other characters in the story and in the impression they leave upon the reader. His adult heroes, including Harry Hartley, Robert Herrick, Loudon Dodd, Henry Durie, and St. Ives, think of themselves as children not quite at home in the adult world. Neither their personality nor their gender has been fully developed. And this is precisely as Stevenson would have it. He wants no hero of his to be so carefully and elaborately described that his personality or his sex comes between the reader and narrative incident. "When the reader consciously plays at being the hero, the scene is a good scene" (XII, 339). Therefore, the disposition of every protagonist must be generalized and vaguely enough realized so that, at the appropriate moment of crisis, the reader can ignore him and "enter" the plot himself.

Hopkins, once again, provides a sympathetic and cogent interpretation of Stevenson's intention: "The persons illustrate the incident or strain of incidents, the plot, *the* story, not the story and incidents the persons."[16] Until later in his life Stevenson was so committed to this idea of characterization that he wrote a letter to Henry James in 1884 making a request which strikes the modern reader—and must have struck James—as curious indeed: "Could you not, in one novel, to oblige a sincere admirer ... cast your characters in a mould a little more abstract and academic ... and pitch the incidents, I do not say in any stronger, but in a slightly more emphatic key—as it were an episode from one of the old (so-called) novels of adventure? I fear you will not" (*Letters*, II, 256).

We hear again and again in Stevenson's remarks on the form and function of art, echoes of earlier critics and anticipatory murmurings of those who followed him. There is nothing noteworthy about that; it happens in criticism all the time. It is the peculiar, almost cavalier, combination of familiar critical concepts which constantly surprises us, and makes us pause before attaching a simple label to Stevenson.[17] He will chastise Fielding for writing novels in the spirit of the playwright, for being ignorant of the "capabilities which the novel possesses over the drama," and at the same time plead for necessary causation of incident, the ascendancy of action over character, and the inevitability of conclusion, all of which bear striking resemblance to Aristotle's first principles of drama.

He can agree with Coleridge on the futility and artlessness of attempting to reproduce life by means of an "exact" copy, and even borrow his words in praising Hugo for achieving "unity out of multitude" in his romances. But if we expect him to agree with Coleridge on the organic principle of art, the *forma informans*, we are disappointed. While Coleridge speaks of works of art in terms of natural metaphor, as "the loveliest plants," "of living power as contrasted with lifeless mechanism,"[18] Stevenson makes a comparison which abruptly and unexpectedly abbreviates the association with Romanticism, and casts out new lines of speculation toward the early twentieth-century formalism of T. E. Hulme: "A proposition of geometry does not compete with life," asserts Stevenson; "and a proposition of geometry is a fair and luminous parallel for a work of art" (XIII, 350).

In an essay entitled "Victor Hugo's Romances" he writes that one of the greatest advantages narrative fiction has over drama is the tremendous expanse it provides for the writer to cram with details of local color and historical background. "Continuous narration is the flat board on to which the novelist throws everything ... He can now subordinate one thing to another in importance, and introduce all manner of very subtle detail, to a degree that was before impossible" (XIV, 21). He goes on in the same vein to comment on what to him is the inexplicable absence of historical particulars in the novels of Fielding: "... It is curious ... to think that *Tom Jones* is laid in the year forty-five, and that the only use he makes of the rebellion is to throw a troop of soldiers into his hero's way" (XIV, 22). In this mood of attachment to historical incident and picturesque detail Stevenson sounds like the kind of Romantic that has prompted the familiar comparisons with Scott. Yet only eight years later, in "A Humble Remonstrance," he strikes a remarkably neoclassical, in fact Johnsonian, note while arguing in favor of generalized treatment of subject matter: "Our art is occupied, and bound to be occupied, not so much in making stories true as in making them typical; not so much in capturing the lineaments of each fact, as in marshalling all of them towards a common end" (XIII, 349).

It would seem, on the basis of these scattered quotations, that

Stevenson could not make up his mind about art, that he was slowly undergoing a change, or that some of these apparently inconsistent critical opinions are not in fact as contradictory as they at first appear. Each explanation has some truth in it. Stevenson, for example, did try his hand at the more expansive novel. Most notably in *Kidnapped* and *The Wrecker* there is a proliferation of detail, a reliance on digression, a looseness of structure, which, like the romantic works of Dumas and Scott, make some concessions to the untidiness of life. But his dominant tendency—from *Treasure Island* to *The Ebb Tide* and *Weir of Hermiston*—was to subordinate incidental detail to more general considerations of thematic pattern and narrative economy.

Stevenson had his own troubles with structural integrity, but his better judgment usually told him that he was not the kind of writer who could cope successfully with massive quantities of fact. Though he may have looked with admiration—and occasional envy—upon the sprawling works of some of his Romantic predecessors, his restless temperament usually had little patience with art when it became too heavily encumbered with the minuteness of life. Stevenson was in accord with Lang's approval of Hawthorne for not choosing to "compete with life," that is, for not making "the effort—the proverbially tedious effort—to say everything."[19]

It should be remembered that Stevenson's ventures into aesthetic theory, looked at in the context of his whole career, were exploratory rather than definitive. Even when he sounds most doctrinaire, one discovers a tendency, not uncommon among artist-critics, to state with special emphasis ideas still very much in the formative stage. Perhaps what is most remarkable is that in spite of the occasional and diffuse quality of his critical statements between 1874 and 1887, there emerges a surprisingly coherent rationale for his profession in the art of adventure.

4

In Stevenson's eyes a physically active and exciting existence bears to everyday life, especially the everyday life of a semi-invalid, something of the same relationship art bears to nature. Participation in a hazardous enterprise—climbing a mountain, fighting a duel, exploring an island—is a way of simplifying reality and therefore a way of pretending. Intense physical activity can induce an uncomplicated state of mind or an absence of mind; it is capable temporarily of abstracting a man from his ego. Stevenson employs curiously ornate and static diction throughout *An Inland Voyage* to describe a moderately rugged canoe trip he took down the Oise River in France during a period of good health. He reserves the vocabulary of adventure, not for rapids or storms or mysterious innkeepers, but for the serene mental state induced by the bodily fatigue which is the result of coping with these "hazards." "This frame of mind was the great exploit of our voyage ... the farthest piece of travel" (XII, 114).

But though it may provide unexpected moments of harmony, adventure, like art, is doomed to fail in its attempt to achieve a permanent ideal goal. Insofar as adventure is the active search for a state of perfect happiness, supposedly achieved through the attainment of limitless treasure, the discovery of utopian kingdoms, or union with a flawless woman, it is fated, as is art in its reaching out after ideal beauty, to fall short of its ultimate aim. The pleasure and value of both may more often than not be found in the process rather than in a clear perception of the end. In "Providence and the Guitar," first published in 1878, the strolling player's wife says of her husband and his friend the painter: "They are people with a mission—which they cannot carry out" (I, 384). And in "Precy and the Marionettes," from *An Inland Voyage*, Stevenson says that even the poorest actor has the stature and the dignity of an artist because "he has gone upon a pilgrimage that will last him his life long, because there is no end to it short of perfection." And a few sentences later: "Although the moon should have nothing to say to Endymion ... do you not think he would move with a better grace and cherish higher thoughts to the end?" (XII, 127)

It is the venture itself—the "mission," the "pilgrimage," the graceful movement—which is stressed in these statements and throughout so much of Stevenson's work, with little thought and less hope of achieving the distant ideal that draws the artist and adventurer on. One inevitable result of this attitude is that process becomes its own goal. Particular moral aims, political causes, and social crusades are swept under by the timeless and overwhelming wave of human energy. Because it cuts across the limitations of historical period and regional custom, gathering strength and momentum by virtue of the sheer sameness of its manifestations, bold physical exertion addresses man with a simple immensity which can make it appear glorious for its own sake. Like those of his contemporaries who found art to be its own justification, Stevenson defends the appeal of adventure as immutable and universal, transcending the historical accidents which make the manners and morals of one century or of one country different from those of another. "Thus novels begin to touch not the fine dilettanti but the gross mass of mankind, when they leave off to speak of parlours ... and begin to deal with fighting, sailoring, adventure, death or child-birth ... These aged things have on them the dew of man's morning; they lie near, not so much to us, the semi-artificial flowerets, as to the trunk and aboriginal taproot of the race"

(XIII, 238). Adventure, for Stevenson, like art for the aesthetes, has a kind of sacred purity about it which ought not to be tainted with moral or psychological convention: "... To start the hare of moral or intellectual interest while we are running the fox of material interest, is not to enrich but to stultify your tale. The stupid reader will only be offended, and the clever reader lose the scent" (XIII, 352). We would seem to be leading to the inevitable conclusion that Stevenson, like most "action" novelists, regards fiction, and therefore adventure, which is the material of his fiction, as an escape—an escape from the self and from time, a rejection of the present, of mortality, and of the responsibility of making moral judgments. There is an undeniable truth in this, and no one could assert it more clearly than Stevenson himself in a letter written to John Meiklejohn in February of 1880:

> When I suffer in mind, stories are my refuge; I take them like opium; and I consider one who writes them as a sort of doctor of the mind. And frankly, Meiklejohn, it is not Shakespeare we take to, when we are in a hot corner; nor, certainly, George Eliot—no, nor even Balzac. It is Charles Reade, or old Dumas, or the Arabian Nights, or the best of Walter Scott; it is stories we want, not the high poetic function which represents the world ... We want incident, interest, action: to the devil with your philosophy. When we are well again, and have an easy mind, we shall peruse your important work; but what we want now is a drug. (*Letters*, I, 322)

There is a tone in this statement that brings one of the various moods of Keats to mind, and perhaps it is a good thing that it does. Because, although we have already learned that we cannot always depend upon Stevenson to fulfill his Romantic promises, there should be a warning to us in the parallel, not to make the mistake so many critics once made with Keats—to take a few references to hemlock, Asian poppy, and poetry as a "friend to man," and with them to conclude that Keats is a poet of escape, and that is all that needs to be said about him.

If, in periods of mental suffering, Stevenson escapes by reading tales of adventure, it is safe to assume that much of his writing is done either in that state of mind or in anticipation of its advent in himself or in his readers. But the word "escape" is not finally very helpful in the description of a literary form. All art, inasmuch as it is selective and exclusive, is an escape from something whether it means to be or not. It is only fair, before we label a writer an "escape artist," as though that were a kind of

charlatanism not worthy of serious literature, to determine first what he
selects and what he excludes, what he is escaping from and what he is
escaping to. Otherwise we risk falling into Zola's misconception that the
novelistic school of realism, as opposed to the school of romance,
necessarily comes closer to the whole truth and complexity of life. In some
ways it obviously does, but it is salutary to remind ourselves that both are
bound to the limits of *fiction*.

Much more typical than his references to art as doctor, drug, or
medicine, are Stevenson's descriptions of it in terms of physical exercise and
endless exploration, a bracing and healthful activity, stimulating to the body
and purifying for the mind:

> O the height and depth of novelty and worth in any art! and O
> that I am privileged to swim and shoulder through such oceans!
> Could one get out of sight of land—all in the blue! Alas not,
> being anchored here in flesh, and the bonds of logic being still
> about us. But what a great space and a great air there is in these
> small shallows where alone we venture!   (II, 146)

This too may be regarded as a kind of escapist view of art, especially for
a semi-invalid, but it is not an absolute avoidance of life so much as it is a
simplification, a trimming down to what is clean, fresh, and controllable.
There is much of the latter-day classicist about Stevenson, particularly in his
reverence for the general, the categorical, and the formal. His first impulse
may be Romantic, but his second thought is almost always classical. We find
him again and again in his criticism beginning with Coleridge, concluding
with Aristotle; promising Hazlitt, delivering Johnson. The same tendency is
visible in much of his fiction as well. How often his novels and short stories
open in Romantic suggestiveness with inviting scenes of rustic nature or in
dark corners of Gothic kirk-yards, with hints of vague mysteries or
unspeakable passions, only to develop the clear outlines, in his early career,
of a child's game and later on, of moral fable.

5

Where Stevenson differs most notably from the Romantics, especially
Keats, is in his almost total inability to exist in uncertainty. This may seem a
peculiar conclusion to draw about a man who spent most of his professional
life experimenting in literary form and substance, theologically a skeptic, a
supporter of liberal and often unpopular political and social causes. And yet

limitation, boundary, explanation, is what he repeatedly seeks in his early and middle fiction as well as in his moral and aesthetic theory. His letters have been compared with Keats's and it is true that in his correspondence he may begin like Keats, probing the possibilities of the creative imagination, but he does not end like him, in uncertainty.

The metaphorical terms Stevenson uses to convey his idea of the poetic provide an interesting contrast with earlier Romantic images and reveal his tendency to circumscribe. In "A Chapter on Dreams," published in January 1888, he describes the unconscious activity of the imagination during sleep as accomplished by "Little People": "... what shall I say they are but just my Brownies, God bless them! who do one-half my work for me while I am fast asleep" (XV, 262).

In "The Lantern-Bearers," February 1888, he compares the inner poetic faculty of every man to a child's oil lantern hidden under a cloak: "... and all the while, deep down in the privacy of your fool's heart, to know you had a bull's-eye [lantern] at your belt, and to exult and sing over the knowledge" (XV, 241).

In the same essay Stevenson introduces the familiar symbol of a singing bird as a sign of the poetic essence of romance:

> There is one fable ... of the monk who passed into the woods, heard a bird break into song, hearkened for a trill or two, and found himself on his return a stranger at his convent gates; for he had been absent fifty years ... It is not only in the woods that this enchanter carols ... He sings in the most doleful places. The miser hears him and chuckles, and the days are moments. With no more apparatus than an ill-smelling lantern I have evoked him on the naked links ... A remembrance of those fortunate hours in which the bird has sung to us ... fills us with ... wonder when we turn the pages of the realist. There, to be sure, we find a picture of life in so far as it consists of mud and of old iron, cheap desires and cheap fears ... but of the note of that time-devouring nightingale we hear no news. (XV, 243–244)

Dream, flame, and a singing bird, have been used not only by the Romantics (though they were particularly common among them) but by writers of all periods as means to suggest the poetic, either at its creative source or in its ideal state of perfection. But Stevenson's treatment of these familiar images is unique. There is the obvious diminution of dream into the work of "Little People" and of the poetic flame into a flicker inside a boy's tin lantern, but there are other modifications and peculiarities as well.

The attempt, for example, to determine who the "Little People" are and how they go about their work is half-playful, but Stevenson is serious enough about establishing the relationship between dream and conscious artistry to conclude the essay with a fairly precise account of contributions from his world of sleep to his world of written fiction: "I can but give you an instance or so of what part is done sleeping and what part awake"; and then he goes on to explain how he dreamt part of *Dr. Jekyll and Mr. Hyde*. "All the rest was made awake, and consciously, although I think I can trace in much of it the manner of my Brownies. The meaning of the tale is therefore mine ... indeed I do most of the morality.... Mine, too, is the setting, mine the characters. All that was given me was the matter of three scenes, and the central idea of a voluntary change becoming involuntary."

Stevenson is careful to show exactly how much dream has gone into his story, to describe its quality, and to distinguish between it and the moral and stylistic additions of his conscious mind. The tendency, however whimsical, is not like that of Coleridge in *Kubla Khan* or Keats in *Sleep and Poetry*, to enlarge the concept of the imagination by associating it with the dark realm of dream, but rather to clarify and confine it by dutifully acknowledging which elements in his stories come from the unconscious rand which do not. Even in his most playful mood, he cannot ask with Keats, "Surely, I dreamt today, or did I see?" Stevenson insists upon noticing the difference between waking and dreaming. Even symbolically, Keats's question seems to have no relevance for him. Dream is not a challenge to his rational life or a symbol of the infinite possibilities of art; it is a contributor to his fiction—diminutive, quaint, and controllable, "some Brownie, some Familiar, some unseen collaborator, whom I keep locked in a back garret."

That Stevenson's image of the poetic flame should be confined within the narrow tin walls of a child's lantern is by itself characteristic. But he goes even further in his reaching out after certainty by assigning specific qualities and functions to his fire. He speaks of simple men without external signs of virtue or talent, "but heaven knows in what they pride themselves! heaven knows where they have set their treasure!" Interpreted cynically, this sounds like a justification for delusions of grandeur; taken sentimentally, we find in it some of the pathos of Gray's *Elegy Written in a Country Churchyard*; but, reduced to essentials, it seems a fairly reasonable description of the psychology of self-respect.

The poetic flame becomes associated with each man's ability to retain the youthful conviction that his ego is the center of the universe. Since this comforting assumption is neatly caged, there is no chance that it might prove a serious threat to the rational mind by coming into disenchanting contact with the "outside" world and growing uncontrollably from the pleasant into the painful. At the first signs that it might, Stevenson clangs shut the lantern gate or the garret door, and arrests his imagination with an excess of rhetoric and rationalization.

Perhaps the most interesting of the three images which Stevenson associates with the poetic is the bird. Here the metaphor itself does not undergo the external changes of the tampering toymaker, but remains a respectable Keatsian nightingale singing in the trees. It is the nature of the song and its effect on the listener that has changed. Stevenson recalls "those fortunate hours in which the bird has sung to us," tells how the "miser hears him and chuckles," and names him the "delight of each" who has fallen under his spell. The sense of coming momentarily in contact with death and eternity, which is so strongly sensed throughout Keats's ode, has vanished. The bird is no longer an obscured symbol, now seductive, now threatening, a perfect sign of immortal life or a cold reminder of death. Stevenson wants to say exactly what his nightingale is. It is an entertainer. It cheers and amuses. It does not draw us out of life, but takes us more quickly through it than a clock or a calendar.

Insofar as Stevenson's symbol, like Keats's, promises a release from the tedium and oppressiveness of daily life, it, too, is an emblem of escape. But whereas Keats pursues his restless search for ideal beauty to the edge of death and immortality, Stevenson pursues instead the more immediate pleasure of "love, and the fields, and the bright face of danger." While Keats's "escapism" sometimes seems the longing for eternity of a poet already "half in love with easeful Death," Stevenson's "escapism" is more often the life-wish of a man who thought himself only half-acquainted with the world of the living.

Throughout much of his adulthood, Stevenson was sickly and melancholy and subject to long periods of morbid depression. In the correspondence of over twenty-five years he refers continually to death; sometimes with irritation, as after recovering from a serious fever and wishing "a thousandfold" that he had "died and been done with the whole damned show forever" (*Letters*, I, 231); sometimes with whimsical resignation, as when he compared his body to a badly made jar, "and to make every allowance for the potter (I beg pardon; Potter with a capital P.) on his ill-success, [I] rather wish he would reduce [me] as soon as possible to potsherds" (*Letters*, I, 242); but most often, Stevenson's attitude toward death is one of pathetic fatigue and boredom: "For fourteen years I have not had a day's real health," he wrote in 1893. "I have wakened sick and gone to bed weary ... I was made for a contest, and the Powers have so willed that my battlefield should be this dingy, inglorious one of the bed and the physic bottle ... I would have preferred a place of trumpetings and the open air over my head" (*Letters*, IV, 243).

In 1894, less than three months before he died, he wrote to Charles Baxter: "I have been so long waiting for death, I have unwrapped my thoughts from about life so long, that I have not a filament left to hold by" (*Letters*, IV, 351).

Stevenson frequently contemplated death fondly as a comfort and a release from suffering, but he hesitated to reject life without ever having been physically strong enough to live it like other human beings. A healthy body was in its own way as much of a lure for him as easeful death. And though he broods over mortality in his letters and essays, he does not let it enter his fiction in a serious way until quite late in his career. His art, as he willingly admits, is to be an antidote to his life, not an image of it. Still, as Stevenson himself gradually came to realize, the peculiar nature of a medicine has its own way of reflecting and defining the disease for which it is prescribed.

Nonetheless, with the exception of an occasional poem or tale, Stevenson's artistic treatment of death in his early years has very little in common with that of the Romantic poets. The idea of death attracted and repelled Keats as dangerous and cold, but perfect and unchanging, like an exquisite urn or an unseen bird. Contemplation of it led him out of himself; it was his lure, and to put it in terms of the romancer rather than the Romantic, it was his intrigue and his adventure. For Stevenson, in the great bulk of his early fiction, what was mysterious, unknown, enchanting, was the idea of life. And he did not at first intend it in a very complicated or elevated sense. Just walking about with a good appetite, normal digestion, a strong leg and a clear head—that was what was wanted. In the years of young manhood when his health was particularly poor, he wrote yearningly of the simple pleasures of physical well-being:

> O for the good fleshly stupidity of the woods, the body conscious of itself all over and the mind forgotten, the clean air nestling next your skin ... the eye filled and content, the whole MAN HAPPY! Whereas here it takes a pull to hold yourself together; it needs both hands and a book of stoical maxims, and a sort of bitterness at the heart by way of armour. (*Letters*, I, 213)

To be able to stay out in the rain without catching a fever or to work hard enough at manual labor to get blisters—these things take on positively exotic overtones for Stevenson. And it is at this point that he takes leave of the Romantics and joins hands with Fielding and Defoe. Shamelessly he will steal from the Romantics their exuberance and exaltation (which do show signs of wear in Stevenson); he will snatch Shelley's flame and Keats's nightingale, but only on his own terms. At the first signs of morbidity, he is off to play with Robinson Crusoe and Joseph Andrews. As already mentioned, his early adventures contain the same curious combination of Romantic suggestiveness with neoclassical formalism that his critical essays do. The emotional quality of natural settings has importance even in Stevenson's earliest fiction; yet peopling his mysterious and incompletely perceived world are robust heroes with good and simple hearts, and dark-complexioned villains who have no particular motive for villainy other than that they happen to be "ornery."

6

As Stevenson's career progresses, we find works in which the walls of separation are weakened, and the weird and beautiful powers of nature encroach on the sturdy and mechanical characters, seeping into their blood, weakening their "type" and complicating their singularity. It would make life simpler for critics if novelists would change their creative habits more smoothly and consecutively than they do, but that is rare. In Stevenson's fiction, for example, we discover tentative signs of the integration of character, incident, and locale, as early as 1878, 1881, and 1882, which are the respective publication dates of "Will o' the Mill," "Thrawn Janet," and "The Merry Men." But it is not until 1888 and the publication of *The Master of Ballantrae* that Stevenson is able to sustain "unity out of multitude" at any length.

Without constructing a series of artificial stages through which he never passed in a systematic way, we might usefully select that year as the most significant turning point in his literary career. Aside from *The Master of Ballantrae*, it is the year of publication of several of his finest essays, including "Pulvis et Umbra," as well as the time when his health improved sufficiently for him to embark on the expedition to the South Seas from which he never returned. The justification of art and idea of adventure as described and interpreted thus far have come almost exclusively from letters, essays, and fiction written in the decade between 1878 and 1888. It is the period of *An Inland Voyage* and *Travels with a Donkey*; of *Virginibus Puerisque, Memories and Portraits*, and *Familiar Studies*; of *Treasure Island, New Arabian Nights, Prince Otto, The Merry Men, Dr. Jekyll and Mr. Hyde*, and *Kidnapped*. It is, in fact, the period of Stevenson's most popular juvenile works, and still the ones the modern reader is most likely to remember.

During this decade the elaborate style of the essays and the simplified accumulation of unlikely dangers in the fiction had become Stevenson's way of fending off the ordinary and the ugly. The language of the expository pieces is rich with metaphor, inversion, hyperbole, balanced phrases, and interior rhyme. Words become above all the media of a gorgeously decorative abstract art, like the figures in a Persian carpet, meaningful primarily as design, and appealing in their almost unearthly ability *not* to suggest nature. Simultaneously, the hazardous incidents of the early fiction are presented in terms so direct and simple as to suggest the comfortable monotony of ritual, the limited intensity of a child's game, and the lifeless validity of a mathematical proposition. The theory and the practice of this period are full of optimism and bravado, of carefree self-confidence, and perhaps a slightly excessive and artificial *élan*, which seems particularly strained when in reading the letters we realize it comes from a man with such slight reserves of physical and nervous energy.

The tone of Stevenson's work does gradually change and deepen, however, until in "Pulvis et Umbra," first published in April of 1888, it becomes evident upon close reading that he has admitted much to his judgments of life and art that we have not found earlier. The trouble is that he constructed the childish image of himself so well that people continue to read the Stevenson of 1888 as they read the Stevenson of 1881, in the same patronizing albeit affectionate way they would listen to a child of ten, extracting "cute" phrases and optimistic tidbits, and ignoring the rest. One can find reasons even in "Pulvis et Umbra" for Stevenson's admirers to regard him as an infant phenomenon rather than as a full-fledged adult professional. He does have a way of sounding like one schoolboy exclaiming to another, even when his subject is human misery:

> Ah! if I could show you this! if I could show you these men and women, all the world over, in every stage of history, under every abuse of error, under every circumstance of failure, without hope, without help, without thanks, still obscurely fighting the lost fight of virtue, still clinging, in the brothel or on the scaffold, to some rag of honour, the poor jewel of their souls! (XV, 295–296)

It is this almost frenzied expression of felicity in the face of disaster that has endeared Stevenson, and especially "Pulvis et Umbra," to generations of schoolmarms and their victims. But if we read the essay without a mind for extracting moral slogans to live by, if we read it as a whole piece without predetermination, it becomes evident that it is anything but one salvo of addle-brained optimism after another. (I do not mean to imply that it is unintelligent to be optimistic, but rather that one's reasons for being optimistic and the expression of those reasons can very easily be foolish. These charming follies unfortunately have been what Stevensonians have too often singled out of Stevenson.)

But one becomes aware on a careful reading of "Pulvis et Umbra" that the good cheer comes precariously close to hysteria; that the gay celebration of life in the midst of catastrophe, which has become a Stevenson stereotype, is mingled with an unfamiliar admission of ugliness and disenchantment. His description of the origins of life on earth might have pleased even Zola:

> This stuff, when not purified by the lustration of fire, rots uncleanly into something we call life; seized through all its atoms with a pediculous malady; swelling in tumours that become independent, sometimes even (by an abhorrent prodigy) locomotory; one splitting into millions, millions cohering into one, as the malady proceeds through varying stages. The vital putrescence of the dust, used as we are to it, yet strikes us with occasional disgust, and the profusion of worms in a piece of ancient turf, or the air of a marsh darkened with insects, will sometimes check our breathing so that we aspire for cleaner places. But none is clean: the moving sand is infected with lice; the pure spring ... is a mere issue of worms; even in the hard rock the crystal is forming. (XV, 291–292)

Certain parts of Stevenson's surprisingly repulsive description of organic life suggest that he, like the poet laureate, was forcing himself to come to terms with Darwin:

> All these prey upon each other, lives tearing other lives in pieces, cramming them inside themselves, and by that summary process, growing fat: the vegetarian, the whale, perhaps the tree, not less than the lion of the desert; for the vegetarian is only the eater of the dumb. Meanwhile our rotatory island loaded with predatory life, and more drenched with blood, both animal and vegetable, than ever mutinied ship, scuds through space with unimaginable speed. (XV, 292–293)

But Stevenson reserves his keenest disgust for man himself, and presses his point with a Swiftian energy unprecedented in his earlier works:

> What a monstrous spectre is this man, the disease of the agglutinated dust, lifting alternate feet or lying drugged with slumber; killing, feeding, growing, bringing forth small copies of himself; grown upon with hair like grass, fitted with eyes that move and glitter in his face; a thing to set children screaming;— and yet looked at nearlier, known as his fellows know him, how surprising are his attributes! (XV, 293)

Of course, the final sentence turns off Swift and brings back the undespairing and familiar Stevenson. But the words of revulsion have been uttered, and with a force which cannot adequately be halted by a dash, an optimistic cry, and an exclamation mark. Stevenson's distaste for physical life extends not only to what we ordinarily think of as the immediate causes of bodily suffering—sickness, hunger, decay—but to all the creative life processes, including reproduction, nourishment, and growth. In its combination of disgust and fascination, it is a response comparable to that of an adolescent to the first signs of his own puberty. Even the terminology of the essay suggests this in its references to simple organisms "swelling in tumours that become independent"; to reproduction "with its imperious desires and staggering consequences"; to man "grown upon with hair like grass"; and to the general notion that life in its most advanced stages is so filthy "that we aspire for cleaner places."

It is significant that Stevenson treats this "dying into life" much more clinically and grotesquely than his Romantic predecessors did. It suggests not simply a different and perhaps less powerful imagination, but, more importantly, it indicates a diminished faith in the power of the mature imagination to transcend the burden of natural life, a skepticism as well as a view of nature which Stevenson shared with his age. He is describing, and in a sense enacting in nineteenth century post—Romantic terms, the perennial fall from the childhood state of angelic innocence—golden, sexless, clean, and beautiful—to the mature state of manhood—unexpectedly brutish and knowing.

Stevenson explains in an early essay on "Child's Play" that what most distinguishes the child from the adult is his ability to exist in a tidy, make-believe world which has almost no reference to concrete reality:

> Children are content to forego what we call the realities, and prefer the shadow to the substance ... Whatever we are to expect

at the hands of children, it should not be any peddling exactitude about matters of fact. They walk in vain show, and among mists and rainbows; they are passionate after dreams and unconcerned about realities. (XIII, 144–147)

As many have been quick to point out, Stevenson's descriptions of children invariably serve equally well as descriptions of himself—at least of that part of him that was most in evidence before 1888. But what has not so often been noted is that the child's talent for disregarding or simplifying "matters of fact" had been, according to Stevenson's earliest aesthetic theory, an essential trait for all artists. Without Wordsworth's and Keats's faith in the powers of the mature imagination, Stevenson thought his choice was either to grow up (and therefore *out* of art) or to remain a child, deliberately, stubbornly, and as he half-suspected all along, unsuccessfully. One of the obvious difficulties is that the refusal to age, especially for a man past twenty-five, is a pure act of will which can be realized only in the imagination.

We are accustomed to a great many nineteenth-century authors— including Dickens, Mark Twain, Kipling, and J. M. Barrie—who, like Stevenson, created child-heroes with whom, in one way or another, they identified themselves. The enormous popularity of J. D. Salinger's *The Catcher in the Rye* and William Golding's *Lord of the Flies* suggests that modern sympathies may extend more readily to the older child undergoing disenchantment—that is, to the adolescent in crisis. Whereas Stevenson's Jim Hawkins can effectively don and shed exotic roles at will, Holden Caulfield's insecurities are only heightened by his comic-pathetic impersonations. The boys on Golding's island may be successful at assuming new roles by smearing their faces and rearranging their clothes, but then most of them are unable to change out of their disguises again. Going in search of buried treasure, Jim Hawkins becomes engaged in an invigorating and harmless adventure, but Salinger's adolescent hero finds the "great wide world," like his own efforts at changing personality, "phoney." And Golding's English schoolboys discover not pieces-of-eight but the devil on their island paradise. For the contemporary adolescent hero the treasure chest is either empty or harboring a serpent.

But Stevenson would have it otherwise. He fought like one struggling for life to keep evil, confusion, sorrow, and mutability out of his art. He built a literary theory like a fortress, constructed plots which he himself called "machines," and sharpened his style like a weapon on the masters of English prose. But by reading only his early works we have tended too readily to assume that his defenses were impregnable. On the contrary, there is a time

when, even for Stevenson, the child has to let in the man. He writes of it
sadly as late as the fall of 1894:

> As I go on in life, day by day, I become more of a bewildered child;
> I cannot get used to this world, to procreation, to heredity, to sight,
> to hearing; the commonest things are a burthen. (*Letters*, IV, 353)

The key word here is "bewildered," because, as Stevenson realized from the
beginning, the moment the child is sufficiently intruded upon by the world to
become bewildered by it, he has begun to yield up his innocence and his youth.

The history of Stevenson's gradual and painful maturing as an artist is
a narrative of conflicting tendencies—practice rebelling against theory, the
increasing encroachment of the "monstrous, infinite, illogical, abrupt, and
poignant" upon the "neat, finite, self-contained, rational, flowing, and
emasculate." It is not until the novel fragment, *Weir of Hermiston*, interrupted
by his death in 1894, that we have a work which for complexity, integrity, and
range, for narrative interest and sheer lyrical beauty, may be called a mature
masterpiece. And still the old love of adventure remains—deepened and
enlarged—but recognizable nonetheless. It is not, as some critics have
implied, this imaginative devotion to the active life which is the source of his
immaturity, but rather his prolonged failure to find an artistic harmony
between the externals of action and the intangible truths of human morality
and psychology. The early stories like *Markheim* and *Dr. Jekyll and Mr. Hyde*
which do make moral and psychological claims are as schizophrenic as their
protagonists. The "meaning" does not inhere to the action. It is introduced
ab extra and, as a result, is not only detachable but disposable.

The child in Stevenson—that quality of mind which allowed him to
close "the dazzle and confusion of reality" out of his art—was a long time
dying. But it did die. And Stevenson was never so unaware of himself as to
doubt seriously that it would:

> So in youth, like Moses from the mountain, we have sights of
> that House Beautiful of art which we shall never enter. They are
> dreams and insubstantial; visions of style that repose upon no
> base of human meaning; the last heart-throbs of that excited
> amateur who has to die in all of us before the artist can be born
> ... But ... though these dreams of youth fall by their own
> baselessness, others succeed, graver and more substantial; the
> symptoms change, the amiable malady endures. (XV, 184–185)

To understand the nature and increase of that "malady" we must begin where it does, in the "dreams of youth."

NOTES

1. Janet Adam Smith, *Henry James and Robert Louis Stevenson, A Record of Friendship and Criticism* (London, 1948), p. 277.

2. *Ibid.*, pp. 130–132.

3. G. K. Chesterton, *Robert Louis Stevenson* (New York, 1928), pp. 190–191.

4. George Saintsbury, *A History of Nineteenth Century Literature* (London, 1896), p. 337.

5. Émile Zola, *The Experimental Novel and Other Essays*, trans. Belle M. Sherman (New York, 1893), p. 43. The essays in this volume originally appeared in Russian and French reviews between 1875 and 1880. They were collected and published in a single volume for the first time in France in 1880, and it is in this form that they were probably available to Stevenson. For a further discussion of the chronology and influence of Zola's critical works, see Fernand Doucet, *L'Esthètique d'Émile Zola et son application à la critique* (The Hague, 1923), pp. 231–243.

6. *Adventures Among Books*, pp. 279–280. For a more complete exposition of Lang's part in "the battle between the crocodile of Realism and the catawampus of Romance," see his "Realism and Romance," *The Contemporary Review*, November 1887; "Romance and the Reverse," *St. James's Gazette*, November 1888; and Roger Lancelyn Green's *Andrew Lang, A Critical Biography* (Leicester, 1946), pp. 109–123.

7. Zola, *The Experimental Novel*, pp. 25–26.

8. *Ibid.*, pp. 54, 209.

9. *The Correspondence of Gerard Manley Hopkins and Richard Watson Dixon*, ed. Claude Colleer Abbott (Oxford, 1935), p. 114.

10. "A Note on Realism," *The Works of Robert Louis Stevenson*, 25 vols. (London, 1912), XVI, 236.

11. As quoted in Gérard Jean-Aubry, *The Sea Dreamer: A Definitive Biography of Joseph Conrad* (New York, 1957), p. 273.

12. "A Note on Realism," Swanston Edition, XVI, 239–240.

13. "The Art of Fiction," *Henry James and Robert Louis Stevenson*, ed. Smith, p. 75.

14. Samuel Taylor Coleridge, "On Poesy or Art," *Literary Remains*, ed. H. N. Coleridge, 4 vols. (London, 1836), I, 220.

15. William Hazlitt, "On Poetry in General," *The Complete Works of William Hazlitt*, ed. P. P. Howe, 21 vols. (London, 1934), V, 1–18.

16. *Hopkins and Dixon*, p. 114.

17. In a great number of the books written about Stevenson during the twenty-year period following his death, it was generally assumed that, on the basis of his interest in childhood and nature, he was clearly and indisputably a Romantic. A characteristic example of this opinion may be found in L. Cope Cornford's *Robert Louis Stevenson* (Edinburgh, 1899), chap. vi.

18. Coleridge, "Shakespeare's Judgment Equal to His Genius," *Literary Remains*, II, 66–67.

19. Lang, *Adventures Among Books*, p. 213.

DOUGLAS GIFFORD

Stevenson and Scottish Fiction:
The Importance of The Master of Ballantrae

This essay argues the case for three main propositions. These propositions are interconnected; and if tenable, I think that their combined meanings allow *The Master of Ballantrae* to emerge as a fine and neglected Romantic and symbolic novel in the tradition of *Wuthering Heights* and *Moby Dick*; and the finest expression of Scottish fiction's deepest concerns in the nineteenth century.

My first proposition is that there existed from 1814 till 1914 a school of Scottish fiction with its own recurrent themes, and its own distinguishable symbolism. My second is that nearly all of Stevenson's Scottish fiction (and much of his total output of fiction) is mainly unsuccessful exploration of the almost obsessional material of his relations with his family and with Edinburgh bourgeois society and Scotland. *The Master of Ballantrae*, I suggest, is the clearest and most symbolic expression of his deepest tensions in these areas and thus of major importance in his output. The rest of the Scottish fiction is to be considered as 'trial runs' for it. Consequently I propose a reconsideration of the novel, defending its structure and contrasting and varied settings against previous attack, and emphasising the crucial and highly subtle use of the 'unreliable narrator', the prejudiced family retainer Mackellar. If, for example, we compare his function with that of Nellie Dean in *Wuthering Heights*, we can see that Stevenson's creation has

From *Stevenson and Victorian Scotland*, ed. Jenni Calder. © 1981 by Edinburgh University Press and Douglas Gifford.

the more complex and profound role. As a result, the novel can be seen as sharing in what amounts to a tendency in the Presbyterian and 'Puritan' novel towards mutually exclusive interpretations and sharp ambivalence. *The Master of Ballantrae* bears comparison with *The Scarlet Letter* or *Moby Dick* or *The Private Memoirs and Confessions of a Justified Sinner* in this respect.

The first area of discussion concerns that school of Scottish fiction of 1814–1914. I choose these dates, those of Scott's *Waverley* and John Macdougall Hay's *Gillespie* respectively, because these novels seem to me to enclose both the comparatively unbroken century of continuity in Scottish social and cultural life (a continuity to be shattered by the effects of the First World War) and the major Scottish novels which satirise what they see as the destructive and divisive social stereotypes that the century of continuity brings about, especially in nineteenth-century Scottish attitudes to self and family.

But within the century 1814–1914 there existed not just one but at least three schools of Scottish fiction, with the possibility of a fourth. There were two schools of 'escape' from the dreary realities which were transforming Scotland from a broadly rural and peasant nation to one of the most industrialised in the world; and it is worth recalling that hardly any novelist worthy of the name till Grassic Gibbon (in *Grey Granite* in 1934) thought fit to take as a subject the effects of massive industrial urbanisation on people from such very different previous backgrounds. Edwin Muir called our first school of Scottish fiction 'escape to Scotland'. This describes what we all recognise as a kind of fiction which survives even now. We need only work back from Nigel Tranter and Dorothy Dunnett, through Neil Munro and the more robust action novels of S. R. Crockett, past the work of James Grant and William Black and—to his discredit let it be said—the Stevenson of *The Black Arrow* and *St. Ives*—to the more mechanical moving about of historical furniture of Walter Scott in *The Antiquary, Guy Mannering, Ivanhoe* and *The Talisman*, to realise the strength of a Scottish fiction which prefers to dress up what E. M. Forster called the 'And then... And then' type of narrative in historical guise.[1] The aim of such 'historical' fiction is in fact the opposite of historical, in that its central characters are familiar, ideal, and attractive to the modern reader, with the purpose of entertaining rather than illuminating the forces of real social change and their effect on society.

Our second kind of fiction of the period is often referred to as the Kailyard School of Scottish fiction. Here one enters more controversial ground—not as to what the school comprises, since most would accept that it has its hey-day in the work of J. M. Barrie, S. R. Crockett, Ian Maclaren and the like at the end of the nineteenth and beginning of the twentieth century. Controversy arises concerning two points: where the school begins and its final worth. Does the Kailyard originate with impulses to simplification and cliché which ante-date the novel, especially in poetry like that of Burns's 'Cottar's Saturday Night' and Hogg's 'Kilmeny'? Has Henry Mackenzie's *The Man of Feeling* (1771) a hand in the shaping of such surrogate mythology? Has even Jeannie Deans, that 'cow-feeder's daughter' of indubitable virtue, some charge to answer here? These are scurrilous charges to many Scots; and they may find me even more scurrilous when I suggest that the Stevenson of *Weir of Hermiston*, in correspondence with S. R. Crockett as he wrote the novel, was already tainted with the Kailyard tendency to excessive sentimentality and distortion of the psychologically true. Had I time enough I would enjoy trying to prove that *Weir* is a novel marred beyond redemption by the maudlin scenes of young Archie and Kirstie, a poor pair of children, 'playing the old game of falling in love'. 'Will I have met my fate?' wonders a Kirstie who seems to belong more to Crockett's *The Lilac Sunbonnet* than here, swallowing her sugar bool sweeties in church, and throughout chapter six making so many pretty little *People's Friend* changes of mood that shepherd-poet Dandie is driven to remark that 'at denner you were all sunshine and flowers and laughter, and now you're like the star of evening on a lake'![2] *Weir* has magnificent things in it, especially in the depiction of its demonic hanging judge jesting as he destroys the rags of self-respect of miserable Duncan Jopp. But it was becoming a Kailyard novel, and was besides far too mechanical in its laboured and anachronistic symbolism of the four black brothers who represent the hidden fire of Scottish peasantry, religion, poetry, and mechanical genius. Again, the Kailyard novel—and Stevenson's contribution to it, here and in novels like the nauseating piece of father-worship *The Misadventures of John Nicholson* or the indulgent pieces set in France like *The Treasure of Franchard* or *The Story of a Lie*—need not detain us long. Again, what we must acknowledge in leaving is that no less a critic than Francis Hart in his *The Scottish Novel* would take issue with all I have said, on the score that Scots are the last critics able to understand the true Edenic vision lying behind such redemptive fictions.[3] I accept the difference of opinion and pass on to our third, and most important, school of Scottish fiction.

We are left with two kinds of Scottish fiction to engage our serious critical attention. They are respectively a negative and satiric tradition of Romantic fiction and an affirmative, regenerative type which is only occasionally attempted by the major novelists—within our period, namely Scott, Stevenson and, less coherently, George Macdonald. And since, within our period, the attempts by these writers to portray in fiction the transcendence of Scottish limitations to social and personal development are less successful than their stronger and clearer satiric pictures of stagnating Scotland, we shall discuss their partial failure now, before considering the most significant recurrent type of Scottish fiction.

If I am granted for the moment what I have just suggested—that the strongest tradition is negative and satiric—then the fourth kind of Scottish fiction is the occasional attempt to create within such a framework a symbolic situation and eponymous hero within this situation representing Scotland regenerative. Scott tried this outstandingly in *Old Mortality* and *The Heart of Midlothian*, when in each case he created a situation where the sick forces of Scottish history in each novel were confronted by protagonists who drew their symbolic force from the fact that they represented 'nature's voice', and spoke for instinctive goodness of the heart such as Francis Hutcheson had argued for when he made the first utterances of the sentimental school of Scottish philosophy. My own liking and respect for Scott's work indeed relates to the extent to which he conscientiously tried from *Waverley* to *The Heart of Midlothian* to find the ideal figure to represent his case for liberal compromise and historical tolerance. Flora MacIvor, Henry Morton, and outstandingly, Jeannie Deans the cowfeeder's daughter, are the results in chronological and ascending order of that quest; and the fact that Flora fails because she is the reasonable woman identified with the unreasonable cause, that Morton fails because he cannot challenge the fact that it is not his idealism that wins the day but rather the Hanoverian and pragmatic settlement of 1689, and that Jeannie fails because her symbolic meaning as Heart of Midlothian and *Pilgrim's Progress* Mercy outweighs her naturalistic credibility, should not allow us to belittle Scott's genuine attempt to create a symbolic 'Condition of Scotland' novel. One admits his failure, as I think one must admit, for very different reasons, that of George Macdonald—and more important for our purposes, the failure in this respect of Stevenson.

And where does Stevenson ever attempt a novel of extended social comment on Scotland, with such a symbolic protagonist? I contend that this is to be found, broken-backed and inconclusive, but recognisable as such a transcendental attempt, in *Kidnapped* (1886) and *Catriona* (1893). The continuation of the adventures of David Balfour has long puzzled me. Indeed sustained length of treatment was always a problem for Stevenson—witness his *penchant* for the short tale, the series of related adventures, the novelette, and the number of unfinished tales. Sustained control of a large symbolic structure is not found often in his work, so it is all the more surprising that he should have felt, even after some time, that there was something unfinished, demanding resolution, in the matter of David Balfour. The questions this poses to us are three. First, what was there about David, of all his adolescent victim-heroes from the inept bourgeoisie of *The New Arabian Nights* and *The Dynamiter* to Jim Hawkins and Gordon Darnaway and John Nicholson, that made his actions different and worthy of further examination? Secondly, why suddenly decide to be ambitious of the long form when all previous work shows him happiest in the short story and novelette? And thirdly, what is there in *Catriona* which carries on, and relates to, the business of *Kidnapped*? It is true that David at the outset of *Kidnapped* seems to be another of those adolescents whose lives are to be ravaged by Chance, a recurrent and significant theme of the Stevenson who must frequently have felt that Chance was indeed the only factor which could liberate him from the suffocating restrictions of parental love and disapproval. Chance saves David's life at the top of the stairs of the House of Shaws; Chance steers Alan Breck, his *alter ego*, into his life. But—as we know from the letters—Stevenson's problems with David grew, and the character deepened and changed. Indeed, David and Alan Breck moved towards the positions of Henry and James Ballantrae, as they evolved towards a juxtaposition of dour Calvinist-derived commonsense and rigid moral earnestness and extrovert romantic-Celtic waywardness of imagination and emotion. But more important than this shadowy anticipation of the oppositions of *Ballantrae* and *Weir of Hermiston* is the fact that David is *not* to be contained within adolescent guidelines or within limits as foil to Alan Breck. He rapidly becomes *the* moral agent of the book, haunted by the tears of James of the Glen's wife, perceptive to the good (in a manner reminiscent of Jeannie Deans) even in his captors Hoseason and the ship's doctor. I suggest that in David, Stevenson makes the change from protagonist as adolescent victim of Chance adventure to protagonist as moral agent and witness in the manner of Henry Morton and Jeannie Deans. Why then continue his adventures into *Catriona*, especially when the major business of *Kidnapped* seems to be settled? His inheritance is assured, Alan Breck has escaped. What remains unsettled is an issue raised half-way through *Kidnapped*, an issue which I suggest is the first to engage David's new moral awareness, and an issue which—quite apart from Catriona herself—will form the major part of the novel *Catriona*. David witnessed the murder of the Red Fox, Campbell of Glenure. The second part of *Kidnapped* and the first part of *Catriona* are Stevenson's attempts to create a *Heart of Midlothian* novel of Scottish social regeneration. The fact that he fails should not blind us to the epic scale of his attempt. David, like Jeannie or Morton, is 'nature's voice', the suffering conscience of a 'grass roots' Scotland who, like them, sees about him in Prestongrange, in the corrupt legal system, in the ubiquitous expediency and social hypocrisy, a debased modern Scotland. Against this, like them, he pits his honesty, courage, instinctive sense of right. Alan refers to him as the queerest and most unique creature in Scotland; and, in a manner significantly close to that of Jeannie Deans, his journeys have symbolic force. (It is also significant that *Catriona* makes mention of the Porteous affair of *The Heart*, as well as the Wildfire Rocks and a strangely un-Stevensonian and prophetic hag who foresees the gallows beneath blackening bodies.) Like Jeannie, David comes from the country and humble background of Scotland. His journey, from Leith to the Orkneys to the West, *surrounds* Scotland, sampling Highland and Lowland culture, winning, like Jeannie, strange allies from whom he elicits reluctant goodness. Unlike Jeannie, he fails. His Bass Rock captivity represents the difference between Scott and Stevenson. James of the Glens is hung, and the first part of *Catriona* ends with what I read as a crucial abdication on Stevenson's part from involvement in 'the condition of Scotland'.

> So there was the final upshot of my politics! Innocent men have perished before James, and are like to keep on perishing (in spite of all our wisdom) till the end of time. And till the end of time young folk (who are not yet used with the duplicity of life or men) will struggle as I did, and make heroical resolves, and take long risks; and the course of events will push them upon the one side and go on like a marching army. James was hanged; and here was I dwelling in the house of Prestongrange, and grateful to him for his fatherly attention ... and the villains of that plot were decent, kind, respectable fathers of families, who went to kirk and took the sacrament!
>
> But I had had my view of that detestable business they call politics—I had seen it from behind, when it is all bones and blackness; and I was cured for life ... A plain, quiet path, was that which I was ambitious to walk in, when I might keep my head out of the way of dangers and my conscience out of the road of temptation. For, upon a retrospect, it appeared I had not done so grandly, after all; but with the greatest possible amount of big speech and preparation, had accomplished nothing.[4]

The quote is long, because it is so important. Once again I discover, in part two, in the overdone and often maudlin relations of the shy lovers David and Catriona in Holland, that unfortunate later tendency of Stevenson towards Crockett and Barrie and the Kailyard which I suggest would have spoiled even *Weir of Hermiston*. The quote above marks his typical unwillingness to confront and his inability to defeat the bourgeois values of father (that 'fatherly attention' of Prestongrange is so revealing!) and respectable Edinburgh. It's significant that his most bitter remarks on 'decent, kind, respectable ... families' has to be distanced and disguised in this and other fiction like *Weir* or *Dr Jekyll and Mr Hyde*.

Stevenson avoided the full task of evaluating his Scottish background. Does it then follow that we must position his work beneath that of Hogg or Scott, or in the present, Gunn or Gibbon? I think not. There still existed one tradition of Scottish fiction which could help him to genuine and full creativity—that of Scott's *Waverley* or *Redgauntlet*, of Galt's *The Entail*, and, to a lesser extent, of Hogg's *The Justified Sinner*. In *The Master of Ballantrae* Stevenson was to take this tradition and create its archetype.

What is this tradition and how is it recognisably different from, say, that of *Wuthering Heights*, or, at the end of the century, *The Mayor of Casterbridge*, both of which, in respect of use of landscape, or demonic local tyrants, resemble the Scottish novels?

Francis Hart in *The Scottish Novel* prefers other types of classification, which have their own validity but seem to me to avoid the outstanding tradition, which one critic, writing of George Douglas Brown's *The House with the Green Shutters*, described in poetry as having as its object the desire to

> Paint village hell where sadist monster mutters
> Till Scotland's one mad House with the Green Shutters
> Depict the lust that lurks in hall and hovel
> And build thereon a Scottish national novel.[5]

But the emphasis here on a kind of crude realism, endorsed by Angus McDonald when he quoted the poem, should not blind us to the fact that the tradition is essentially Romantic and symbolic. David Daiches went some way in identifying the polarities and their significance in his pioneer essay on 'Scott's achievement as a novelist', when he stressed that Scott's typical pattern of opposition placed Past against Present, Order against Disorder, and—very broadly—a cause of the Heart against a cause of the Head. Scott nearly always in his Scottish fiction chooses a period of civil disruption which presents such a possible pattern; but I would allege that the pattern of Scott is the base pattern for the serious and satiric Scottish novelist of the next century following *Waverley* in 1814.

The recurrent themes of nineteenth-century Scottish fiction of this kind are those of the divided self; the divided family which contains the broken self; the divided nation behind the fragmented family. Morbid states of psychology as frequent focal points of the fiction were recognised as early as 1933 by Kitchin;[6] and the converse of this, the use of a 'transitional devil simile', as Coleman Parsons calls it,[7] which is related to but not at all identical with the demonic and Byronic element in the work of the Brontës, becomes something of a *sine qua non* of the tradition. And here I would go further than Daiches or Kitchin and tentatively suggest that, taking the conclusions of Muir in his study *Scott and Scotland* (of the first part) one can derive a meaning from the recurrent pattern which is in its intensity and kind unique to the Scottish novel. Muir argued his 'dissociation of sensibility' theory in the first part of that study.[8] He suggested that the organic and whole culture of pre-1560 and the Reformation suffered separation into mutually exclusive parts; that emotion, as linked with the older Scottish language, was separated from thought, and consequently, when emotion and thought were thus separated, emotion became irresponsible and thought became arid; and if one felt in Scots and thought in English, one's feelings and expression of feeling in Scots would be likely to be self-indulgent and one's thoughts and expression of them somewhat arid.

I find it poignant and regrettable that Muir failed to apply the implications of this theory to the matter of his study, to Scott. Possibly dissociated by this time from Scotland himself, Muir failed to see that Scott did not always suffer a failure of creative and critical awareness. He further failed to see that Hogg, Galt, Stevenson, Brown and MacDougall Hay—to leave out Muir's contemporaries, Gibbon, Gunn and MacColla—did not fall victim to the divisive and degenerative forces of Scottish Materialism, Grundyism, and sentimental Romanticisation, but rather used them as materials for satire and exposure, albeit in apparently anachronistic guise. Thus *Waverley* satirises a central mentality which suffers 'tartan fever'; its central motif is that of the delusive dream, its reductive image of the highlands the 'bra' Highlander tat's painted on the board afore the change-house they ca 'Lucky Middlemass's'. Waverley is caught between irresponsible and yet obsessively greedy Highlanders, disorderly and deluded, and excessively mechanistic, depressingly orderly bourgeois systems represented by the merchants of Dundee and the unimaginative disciplines of the Hanoverian army, which Waverley finds impossibly stifling. The pattern is that of *Rob Roy*; and Rob Roy, cause of the Past, representative of the Scottish Outlaw Myth, Jacobite sympathiser, is blood cousin to Baillie Nicol Jarvie, canny merchant who welcomes the road 'West awa' yonder' to sugar, tea and tobacco from the American colonies, basis of Glasgow's flourishing. Scott tells us that Scotland has become the battlefield of the Heart and the Head. We may dislike his compromise solutions, but his satiric vision outstrips his rational suggestion for regeneration, just as his wonderful picture of the sick heart of Midlothian outstrips his naive pictures of Jeannie Deans making all well on the island (sic!) of Roseneath.

Hogg's *Sinner* does not fit so easily into this pattern, although related. Hogg's opposition there is of older, healthier, tougher Scotland as represented by the laird of Dalcastle against a sick modern evangelical religious consciousness. The Shepherd of Ettrick mourned in all his fiction a simpler Scottish transition, that of rural community with oral tradition of ballad and story giving way to a Scotland sick either through religion or social snobbery. But his Robert Wringhim looks forward to Henry Jekyll and, above all, Ephraim Mackellar, who destroys his firstborn son in pursuit of his materialist dream, anticipates Weir and more especially the brutal merchant figures John Gourlay and Gillespie Strang. John Speirs noted that Douglas Brown had put 'the nineteenth century in allegory' in *Green Shutters*.[9] Again, I'd go further, and suggest that the novel, like its relatives, is symbolic; that Gourlay represents Scottish greed, Scottish elimination of the gentler virtues and arts from its educational and social systems, that his devilish nature and stature represent the degeneration of wholeness and goodness in Scottish life. And the pattern is borne out in the placing, in all these novels, of a son (usually of the very same name as the father, in order to suggest that they are the parts of what should be a whole) who has, possibly to excess, the gentler virtues. Archie Weir's 'shivering delicacy' and 'splurging' are close to young John Gourlay's 'splurging' and hypersensitivity; Eochan Strang is their descendent and stands in exactly the same relation to his brutal father Gillespie.

Indeed, father–son opposition became the standard opposition of symbolic forces in the Scottish novel, with Gibbon and Gunn and even A. J. Cronin in *Hatter's Castle* using it occasionally as stereotype. What is fascinating is that Muir did not see that a novel such as *The Green Shutters* perfectly substantiated his theory of dissociation. If this be doubted, read the crucial central episode of the novel, when young John Gourlay tries for the Raeburn essay prize at Edinburgh University. Gaspy little sentences, vivid fragments of sense-impressions of an Arctic Night, are all he can manage. His professor makes extensive comment on both the talent, which captures the feeling of the thing, and its dangers. With *thought*, he says, and hard work, such a talent for pure feeling may become higher and consecrative— but without thought, dissociated from it, it would simply be a curse. Gourlay ignores the advice, and the House of Gourlay is destroyed. In *Latitudes* Muir discussed the novel—and failed to remember and to apply to it the very theory which lay at the heart of *Scott and Scotland*.[10] And if a critic like Muir could miss the deeper meanings of Brown's novel, it is not surprising that he and critics of Stevenson should miss the deeper meanings of *The Master of Ballantrae*.

I come now to my second proposition, that nearly all of Stevenson's Scottish fiction is mainly unsuccessful exploration of his personal relations with family, Edinburgh, and Scotland. No-one now would dispute that Stevenson's relations with his family, especially his father, produced deep tensions and guilts throughout his life. But it is not the finer points of biographical truth that matter too much. We need not explore too far the extent to which Stevenson took his youthful rebellions. This is less important than the evidence of the range of the stories that, out of this area of confused values, 'sad little mutinies', love and hate, came equally confused statements of ever-changing moral stance.

Simplifying Edwin Eigner's more ambitious and far more subtle groupings of Stevenson's stories,[11] it seems to me that the most useful starting point for an understanding of most of Stevenson's fiction is that of his moral ambivalence. Nearly all his stories, with the exception of the more straightforward tales of supernatural tradition such as 'The Bodysnatcher' or 'Tod Lapraik' move between two opposite poles of morality. Up till David Balfour nearly all his protagonists are adolescents confused about moral value. Although the earliest of these, the rather helpless middle class youths of *The New Arabian Nights* and *The Dynamiter* (1885) seem to move in the singularly amoral world of the exotic Prince Florizel (Mr T. Godall), that device of escape to adventure land is quickly ended. The later adolescents, from François Villon in 'A Lodging for the Night', to 'Will o' the Mill' to Denis de Boileau in 'The Sire de Malatroit's Door' live in a confused but singularly moral world. They have choices to make, values to declare. And what is outstanding is that they all choose differently. Stevenson can make none of them speak authoritatively and confidently for a fixed moral vision. Villon is the demonic adolescent who spares the kindly father figure; Denis is the innocent adolescent who is coerced into marriage by the devilish aristocrat Malatroit. Two youngsters, two father-figures; and their crossover of positions represents what happens in all Stevenson's fiction. In *The Misadventures of John Nicholson* a relationship between son and father repeats, with variation, the polarisation of 'A Lodging for the Night', with the settled middle-class father this time accepting (with nauseating Goodness) the capitulation of his prodigal son. One juxtaposes this with the transposed situation of *Weir of Hermiston*, where the student freethinking of Archie leads to a real compassion for his fellow humans which is revolted by the demonic and jesting insensitivity of his respectable Edinburgh father.

But, as Eigner noticed, Stevenson didn't often use an actual father–son confrontation.[12] Instead that confrontation is expressed in dualisms and pairings of contrasted characters. Frequently there is an adolescent witness to this, as with Jim Hawkins and his positioning between the world of the Liveseys and Trelawneys, Doctor and Squire, and the world of Long John Silver. The earlier part of *Kidnapped* shows this situation. Or, moving on to the point of respectable maturity as starting point, Dr Jekyll is shown as deliberately separating and indulging those parts of his nature which he regards as evil, in a personality akin to Villon or Silver. I do not say that Stevenson always rings such changes. Sometimes both kinds of protagonists—and the element of demonism—are rigidly controlled, as in 'Will o' the Mill', where Will is neither son or father, but evader of all struggle—and the Devil is thus watered down to a kindly Death Figure, who peacefully takes the aging but unaged Will (literally an uncommitted Will?) from a strangely unreal Neverland. Alternatively, Stevenson presents a story within a traditional type, such as the Gothic-Christian 'Markheim', or as in the Scottish traditional supernatural tales like 'Thrawn Janet' or 'The Merry Men'. The latter owes something too to Melville in its use of Puritan ambivalence and sea symbolism. But even in these stories one can detect a developing trait of Stevenson's work which *The Master of Ballantrae* will bring to fruition; namely that ambiguity which had, admittedly, been the hallmark of the traditional Burns-Hogg-Scott supernatural tale—but which was in Stevenson's hands to become a metaphor for something much deeper.

Thus, by the time he came to write *The Master of Ballantrae*, Stevenson had exhibited throughout his fiction two traits which were closely connected to his tortuous relations with his father and family background. The first trait led him to create perpetually in pairings or opposites—Prince Florizel and his dependant simple young men, Villon and his fatherly burgher, Frank Cassilis and his dour friend Northmour in *A Pavilion on the Links*, Jekyll and Hyde, Balfour and Breck. The second trait led him increasingly to deal with these or his other worlds with ambivalence, allowing neither of the groups, their values, or even the worlds of rationalism or the supernatural to have a final indubitable value.

Tentatively I suggest that two dominating concepts for Stevenson in the years around his father's death (1887) emerged in the ideas of 'Providence' and 'Chance'. 'Chance' had always played a significant role in his creations, dropping his inexperienced young men into worlds completely different from the settled, traditionally structured worlds of their parental background, amongst mad bombers, suicide clubs, exiled Bohemian princes of supernatural capabilities, treasure islands, lonely Hebridean bays with sunken galleons, and marriages with the beautiful daughters of devilish French aristocrats. Understandably it attracted Stevenson as an amoral 'way out' of his own dilemma of values, and thus became a fictional device for releasing himself and his protagonists from the weight of moral choice. But I feel that to the maturing Stevenson 'Chance' as a concept became something deeper, truer to the life of the later nineteenth century. By the time of *The Master of Ballantrae* it had become the sign of a way of life opposite to that represented by 'Providence', the force behind the world of Thomas Stevenson and Presbyterian Edinburgh. More clearly than ever before, Stevenson bases one Master of Ballantrae, Henry, in a world of 'Providence'; and the other Master of Ballantrae, James, in a secular, and, as one critic has called it, 'ur-existential', world of 'Chance' where his making of decisions on the basis of coin-tossing reflects his 'belief' in a random universe—and his disbelief in conventional morality or Mackellar's 'Providence'.[13]

It is crucial to my reconsideration of *The Master of Ballantrae* that we consider and continue to accept what most readers would initially agree is a fair reading of the novel. Such a reading would accept that in Mackellar we have a reliable witness to the fortunes of the house of Durrisdeer. He may be a somewhat pernickety, spinsterish Presbyterian of the old school, but in many ways such dry traits supply that very credibility which the reader so instinctively seeks in tracing the rights and wrongs of the various Durrisdeers. It is part of Stevenson's great skill that Mackellar supplies, effortlessly, this reader's need—in something resembling the way Nellie Dean answers a need in *Wuthering Heights*. Incredible and unnatural events are made palatable in both by being anchored to acceptable and reassuring figures of social certainty.

In this reading Henry becomes victim of history and James. Time has placed him in an inferior role; fate has given him less obvious gifts than James, less attractive to the neighbourhood and to Alison and his father. And what more likely than that the quieter brother to a charismatic and subtle extrovert should retreat somewhat within himself, repressing and denying through mingled stubbornness and jealousy the qualities which might rival those of his brother? Read like this, Henry's story is a painful tracing of misunderstanding and deliberate misdirection by James, whereby Alison's, their father's, and the world's view of Henry is belittled by Henry's reticence, bad luck, and James's guileful Art. In this reading the kinship of Henry to David Balfour stands out clearly, their mutual reserve actually adding to our liking for them, the underdogs of a world which prefers the superficial charm of a Breck or James Ballantrae.

Clearly, too, in this interpretation, James's is a study of evil. Black is his colour in dress and in image or association, from that 'very black mark' against him in the opening pages to the night settings that surround his most mysterious episodes. The transition from this motif of blackness to the imputation of demonic traits is effortless, from his childhood exploits when he masquerades against Wullie White the Wabster as Auld Hornie, or his father cries 'I think you are a devil of a son to me', to when he takes command of pirate Teach's ship 'little Hell', or later, when he appears as Satan in Milton's epic, a fallen angel. (We recall that Stevenson's 'editor' in his Preface remembered that a Durrisdeer 'had some strange passages with the devil'.) Most important is James's artfulness; one recalls that the Devil himself was Father of Lies, and James is in this respect very much a disciple, since he is utter master of the lie unstated, the contrived situation where he will affect a person or company with a gesture, an argument, or a song, theatrically and consummately presented. 'I never yet failed to charm a person when I wanted', he says to Mackellar at the end of the voyage on the *Nonesuch*, when even Mackellar admitted that James and he had come to live together on excellent terms. Taken this way, James is the *incubus*, the descendant of Hogg's Gilmartin, who haunts his brother as George Dalcastle was haunted in *The Justified Sinner*.

And taken this way the novel is a tragedy, whereby Henry, having been all but destroyed by this malevolent quasi-devil, completes his own and his family's destruction by descending to the dark levels of his brother; so much so that the running devil-motif comes in the closing stages to apply to Henry, and Henry's dealings become every bit as immoral and with even nastier people than James's or his 'colleagues'.

But I can never remember being happy with this reading. Even as youthful reader I could never understand how James, that supernaturally quick athlete of catlike reflexes and endless experience in the world's wildest scenes of action, could ever have lost the duel with his brother. For all the argument of 'contained and glowing fury', for all I had sympathy for Henry and anger against James for what he had done to him, it seemed even then too 'Boy's Own' a solution to suggest that sheer right welled up in depressed, cheated, deprived Henry at just the necessary moment. And, as I came to later Stevenson criticism, these feelings grew more acute. The narrators of the action, Mackellar and Chevalier Burke, changed too awkwardly, with little point; the locations changed too arbitrarily, too wildly from rain-gloomy Scotland to swamp-dank Albany or strange sea-voyages; poetic justice had been lost by reducing Henry's goodness to something so inconsequential that he was allowed to share the same grave as his devil-brother. Most damning consideration of all was that Stevenson committed the final artistic sin of changing his vision in mid-stream, having Henry reborn after the duel as a malevolent adult-child, crippled by guilt and warped into a new shape which increasingly rivalled the degradation of James.

I now argue that Stevenson wished only to allow this reading to exist *as a possibility*. With the example of Hogg's *Sinner* before him of 'reversible interpretation', with indeed the tendency of the Presbyterian and Puritan traditions in poetry and fiction towards alternative meanings familiar to him from examples as diverse as Burns's 'Tam o' Shanter' to Hawthorne's 'Young Goodman Brown' and *The Scarlet Letter*, Melville's *Moby-Dick*, and even his friend James's *The Portrait of a Lady* published some eight years earlier, there were many attractions towards a fiction of mutually exclusive interpretations. And the greatest of these attractions, I submit, would lie in the fact that such ambiguity would release Stevenson from all his previous need to struggle confusedly with emblems of a shifting moral consciousness. *The Master of Ballantrae* derives its greatness from the fact that it is the only novel of Stevenson's successfully to resolve—even although it is by sidestep and sleight of creative hand—the dilemma of values so manifest in the other fiction. This is not all. In solving his own problem of values by creating a novel which in effect has no definitive value structure at all, Stevenson created the classic version of the Scottish 'dissociation of sensibility' novel.

This, however, is to beg the question of Stevenson's other meaning for the novel. There are, after all, two Masters of Ballantrae. The very title poses a question similar to that of James in *The Portrait of a Lady*. It warns us, since it does not name the identity of the Master, of a struggle of brothers and opposed 'moralities'. And in this struggle, sensitive reading will show that from the very beginning Henry is not that symbol of undoubted worth that the first reading presupposes. From that first unnecessary 'You know very well that you are the favourite' when quarrelling with James, there is revealed something petulant and small in his personality. He is 'strangely obstinate' in silence when his true nature is misunderstood, and early we are told that he's 'neither very bad nor very able, but an honest, solid sort of lad'. Whatever else, he is certainly a dogged stay-at-home, emotionally—at least to the observer—a rather arid fellow, willing in the end to marry for the pity of the lady who loves his brother, 'by nature inclining to the parsimonious'. 'The weakness of my ground', he tells Mackellar, 'lies in myself, that I am not one who engages love'. When he is ill his instinctive preference for business emerges, 'mortifying' even Mackellar with 'affairs, cyphering figures, and holding disputation with the tenantry'.

But Stevenson is far too subtle to underdraw Henry to the point of symbolic simplicity. One of the most moving glimpses of the novel is of Henry, early on, doing the accounts of Durrisdeer with Mackellar, and falling into a deep muse, staring straight west into the sun over the long sands, where the freetraders, with a great force of men and horses, were scouring on the beach. Mackellar marvels that Henry is not blinded; Henry frowns, rubs his brow, smiles and says: 'You would not guess what I was thinking ... I was thinking I would be a happier man if I could ride and run the danger of my life, with these lawless companions.' Like James? Henry's tragedy is deepened by the fact that he knows his own malformation, and he knows that he cannot be what he is not. His trade is far from free, he recognises, as he tells Mackellar 'and with that we may get back to our accounts'.

The episode has however made us early aware of depths of rebellious feeling in Henry. Foreshortened emotions have their revenges, and Stevenson most effectively will show Henry's emerging in catastrophic fashion at the duel, and then, since guilt will refashion the man anew, emerging in yet more poisoned manner. After the duel, 'something of the child he exhibited; a cheerfulness quite foreign to his previous character'. This good humour is false, based as it is on brain-damaged forgetfulness, implying that Henry cannot face the reality of his actions. He beats the groom, which is 'out of all his former practice'; has 'a singular furtive smile'; and utters his black curse on James—'I wish he was in hell', in front of his son—which reveals how far the disease has gone in de-Christianising him. Out of dissociation of personality comes what looks very like evil, as he poisons his son's mind, and insists on his title as Master—'the which he was punctilious in exacting'. Need I follow his further deterioration? His psychosomatic degradation, as his body grows slack, stooping, walking with a running motion? By the end, in his employment of the dregs of Albany cutthroats to do away with James, he has paralleled if not outdone James's most suspect deeds.

If further evidence is needed that Stevenson early warns us to be on our guard against too facile moral appraisal of the brothers, consider how subtly he arranges their background and support. At first only Mackellar supports Henry, with one crucial exception. In chapter one, beyond the family, 'there was never a good word for Mr Henry', except for Macconochie, 'an old, ill-spoken, swearing, ranting, drunken dog'. On James's side, John Paul, 'a little, bald, solemn, stomachy man, a great professor of piety ...'; and, says Mackellar, 'I have often thought it an odd circumstance in human nature that these two serving men should each have been the champion of his contrary, and made light of their own virtues when they beheld them in a master'. Here is dissociation with a vengeance! Here is warning that strange compensations must be paid when whole critical and emotional awareness is lost. For beyond this lies a pattern of similar waywardness. The country opinion is never reliable. James becomes a false hero after the presumption of his death in the Rebellion, Jessie Broun unnaturally swinging against her former helper, Henry, and crying up her betrayer James as a saint. Can we then trust the picture when, in mirror image, James is isolated with Secundra Dass against a hostile Albany?

We come to the question at the heart of my discussion. And it is a question of *pattern*. Were we to give visual expression to the shape of our novel, it would resemble that of *Vanity Fair*, in that the fortunes of the principal pair of characters would complete two opposed rising and falling movements. Like the opposed nadirs and zeniths of Becky and Amelia, those of Henry and James would appear so

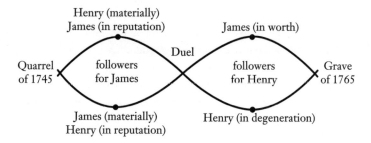

The comparison with Thackeray breaks down on closer inspection, however. The first movement, up to the duel, has as its theme (in this interpretation) the temporary triumph of Henry's appearance over his reality, while the second movement is not in fact a reversal of this so much as the restatement of a further riddle. And the answer to this riddle is dependant on the fulcrum of the entire novel, and the most brilliant device Stevenson ever employed. The answer to this novel's meaning lies with the character of Mackellar, who has influenced his changing pattern, at times decisively, as when he translates Alison from James's camp to Henry's with his carefully prepared dossier of letters which tell against James.

Why, virtually alone amongst his adolescent raconteurs, did Mackellar emerge as Stevenson's 'mouthpiece' now? Why did he decide to tell the tale through such an 'unrelated' persona? Was it simply to give him the credibility of Utterson the lawyer or Dr Lanyon of *Jekyll*, the reliability of

Rankeillor in *Kidnapped*? If this is the reason, why then include so many examples of Mackellar's own prejudices and defects of character? Not only is he 'squaretoes' to the exuberant free-traders, he is an 'old maid' to Alison, who accuses him of never ceasing to meddle in the House affairs. He is a 'devil of a soldier in the steward's room at Durrisdeer', by the tenants' report, and he, like Henry, has never attracted love—far less risked marriage. He actively dislikes women.[14]

I suggest that Stevenson was working in the tradition of the dramatic monologue; and this is a genre with a very strong set of Scottish roots which would be known to Stevenson. From Alan Ramsay's 'Last Words of Lucky Spence' to Burns's 'Holy Willie's Prayer'; from Hogg's 'Sinner's Account' in *The Justified Sinner* to Galt's fictional monologues of minister, provost, and Covenanting Avenger (in *Ringan Gilhaize*), the Scottish tradition of self-revealing, unintentionally self-satiric monologue is as strong as any Stevenson could find, say, in contemporary work like Browning's 'My Last Duchess'. Indeed, Mackellar springs into vivid black-and-white relief if one envisages him as a later Holy Willie or Robert Wringhim.

As basis then for my second interpretation, let us examine Mackellar in a little depth. And, as he is always insisting on chapter and verse, 'like a witness in a court' (a favourite device of Mackellar's, this presentation of apparently inconfutable detail, *as though* he is presenting a meticulous case) let us insist on examining his evidence as though it were being submitted to strict lawyerly scrutiny. For example, just what exactly is that 'very black mark' against James's name which Mackellar brings up in the opening pages? Mackellar, after mentioning the accusation, as we decide our basic loyalties, goes on, 'but the matter was hushed up at the time, and so defaced by legends before I came into these parts, that I scruple to set it down. If it was true, it was a horrid fact in one so young; and if false, it was a horrid calumny'.[15] Indeed, Mackellar lists as one of the Master's crimes that of his treatment of Jessie Broun. Are we to hear Stevenson endorsing this? Would more liberal questioning establish a picture of wild oats and stuffy disapproval? And as to the opening wilfulness of James's insistence on going out in the Rebellion—does not the blame finally rest with the weak father, the Master of Ballantrae of the time, who failed to act with authority? Mackellar displays his prejudice at every turn. One remembers his disapproval of James's reading matter (and his lace); 'Caesar's "Commentaries", ... Hobbes ... Voltaire, a book upon the Indies, one on the mathematics, far beyond where I have studied.'

But once suspected, examples of Mackellar's unreliability abound. I want to focus on four issues as crucial to the development of our acceptance or not of his word. They are the matters of the duel, of the dossier of spy papers concocted for Alison, the *Nonesuch* Voyage, and James's reception at Albany.

I have already indicated my unease concerning the outcome of the duel. We must remember that the most serious allegations of cowardly treachery are about to be made concerning James. All we have to go on is Mackellar's account. But if this is so, must we not take the account in all its parts? Including the preparations for the duel, when Mackellar told the brothers that he would prevent it?

> And now here is a blot upon my life. At these words of mine the Master turned his blade against my bosom; I saw the light run along the steel; and I threw up my arms and fell to my knees before him on the floor. 'No, no,' I cried, like a baby.
>
> 'We shall have no more trouble with him,' said the Master. 'It is a good thing to have a coward in the house.'[16]

Mackellar's reliability would seem at the very least to be impaired by his emotional instability. And now we have the duel itself.

> I am no judge of the play; my head, besides, was gone with cold and fear and horror; but it seems that Mr Henry took and kept the upper hand from the engagement, crowding in upon his foe with a contained and glowing fury. Nearer and nearer he crept upon the man, till of a sudden the Master leaped back with a little sobbing oath; and I believe the movement brought the light once more against his eyes. To it they went again on the fresh ground; but now methought closer, Mr Henry pressing more outrageously, the Master beyond doubt with shaken confidence. For it is beyond doubt he now recognised himself for lost, and had some taste of the cold agony of fear; or he had never attempted the foul stroke. I cannot say I followed it, my untrained eye was never quick enough to seize details, but it appears he caught his brother's blade ....[17]

I submit this long quote as a superb example of Stevenson's crafty duplicity of intention. Notice especially the arrangement of 'I am no judge', 'I believe', 'it seems', 'methought' and the like in contrast to the more typical Mackellar factual terseness, 'for it is beyond doubt' (twice), 'certainly Mr Henry only saved himself by leaping'. Would not any defence lawyer for James demolish the credibility of this account in very little time, on the basis that it argued first for essential limitations of subjectivity, and then proceeded to assert the validity of these subjective (and prejudiced) impressions?

Moving to the later business of the spy dossier we are yet again presented by Stevenson with crafty duplicity of purpose. On the face of it the four types of letter submitted to Alison in 1757 appear a fair and damning 'schedule', as Mackellar imposingly calls them, especially in the fourth type, the letters between James and the British Under-Secretary of State, which most effectively show James to have run with the hare and the hounds. There are two qualifying factors, however. The first is Mackellar's unholy glee at his find in raiding the Master's papers—'I rubbed my hands, I sang aloud in my glee. Day found me at the pleasing task'. One realises, too, that Alison, affected as she is by the dossier's toppling of James from his romantic pedestal, perceives what Mackellar does not, that the dossier is 'a sword of paper' against him. 'Papers or no papers, the door of this house stands open for him; he is the rightful heir.' Even more important is the question of James's guilt and treachery. I would now re-emphasize that the entire novel is based on a piece of duplicity; namely, the fact that the house of Ballantrae (like many others of the day) chose to solve the delicate problem of sending one son out with the Jacobites and keeping another at home as loyal to the established Crown. All were privy to this; Mackellar censures it not. Now recall the date of the submission of the dossier: 1757. The 'spy' letters ran from three years previously; that is, from 1754, almost ten years after the collapse of Charles's cause. By 1754, and with Charles increasingly the hopeless toper of Europe, are we to blame James for doing what his family had in 1745 condoned? It surely is a bit premature to ostracise James because Mackellar tells us he wrote to the 'English Secretary' (elsewhere *Under-secretary*) concerning what we are not in a position to know.

I must at this point, before being accused of overprotest concerning Mackellar, remind the reader that I also completely allow that James is a spy, that—according to another interpretation—Mackellar is utterly reliable. But, whatever his reliability in that interpretation, there is no question that, given greater exposure to James, his entire tone and relationship with James changes. Can this not be read as showing that, when the conditions for prejudice are changed, Mackellar also changes his judgements? Once again his credibility is in doubt, and nothing so damages his case as the *Nonesuch* voyage.

Warnings reminiscent of those surrounding Melville's *Pequod* abound; the ship is as rotten as a cheese, she is on what should be her last voyage. As these accumulate, we become aware that the ship is correlative to Mackellar's own strange guilty feelings. He suffers from 'a blackness of spirit'; he is poisoned as never before in soul and body, although he freely confesses that the master shows him a fair example of forbearance. Mackellar again denounces the Master's taste and style in reading (Richardson's *Clarissa*); and excels himself when he prays during the storm for the foundering and loss of the ship and all her crew, as long as the Master should thus be destroyed. Again the language indicates the disease within Mackellar. 'The thought of the man's death... took possession of my mind. I hugged it, I found it sweet in my belly', he tells us in a tone exactly like Robert Wringhim's. Ironically, the captain thanks him for saving the ship through prayer! Then follows his murder attempt on the Master, who (with that uncanny reflex swiftness that was his at all points but that of the duel) both escapes and pardons, in the fullest fashion, his would-be assassin. We must return briefly to the *Nonesuch* in a moment. Let me round off my four issues concerning Mackellar by pointing out that when James does arrive in Albany, he is accused of murder. In fact James is in this case guilty of nothing more than trying to cure his 'victim', young Chew. Mackellar will later learn of his innocence in this matter from the Chevalier Burke; but Mackellar refuses to correct the record, allowing yet another 'very black mark' to be stacked against his enemy. And in the closing sequences we see Mackellar condemning the fratricidal plans of Henry, but destroying his own moral validity by refusing to separate himself from Henry's cause.

We are left, in this interpretation, with a startling thought. Allowing that Secundra Dass, the mysterious Indian, is James's personal 'familiar', must we not begin to suspect that Henry is accompanied by his? One remembers that Mackellar is 'a devil of a steward'; he too dresses in black; and goes on board the *Nonesuch* 'as the devil would have it'. Once again our Devil metaphor makes a transition, and we look upon events in a different light.

After all, James, as Alison pointed out, is the rightful heir. What young man of spirit would not identify with the romantic cause of Prince Charles? Is it so improbable that a young man (James was not yet 24 in 1745) of imagination and passion should go the way in Paris of the aristocratic youth Burns describes in 'The Twa Dogs' as parading at operas and stews? That is, we admit that he was indeed a wild young man, but to deny that there was anything so devilish in his conduct? No-one doubts his courage or resourcefulness. And it is important to distinguish between James the younger and James on his return after the duel. James the younger was a spendthrift. The greatest amount of sympathy we can accord him then relates to the fact that when he returns he finds Mackellar and Henry organised against him, and that the woman who loves him is unavailable to him. But his second return is different. Even Mackellar admits this. In contrast to Henry, fattening and bitter,

The Master still bore himself erect ... perhaps with effort.... He had all the gravity and something of the splendour of Satan in the 'Paradise Lost'. I could not help but see the man with admiration, and was only surprised I saw him with so little fear.

But indeed ... it seemed as if his authority were quite vanished and his teeth all drawn. We had known him a magician that controlled the elements; and here he was, transformed into an ordinary gentleman, chatting like his neighbours at the breakfast board....[18]

James now wants enough of a reasonable settlement to go his own way, and it is now Henry who denies this and leaves him in the intolerable position of having to answer to Mackellar for bed and board. It is outstanding how James now adapts himself through a saving sardonicism to his demeaning role. He almost—and deliberately—parodies himself in his relation with Mackellar, as he draws himself up in anger in the halls of his ancestors when Mackellar tells him that he has only to keep in with him for his needs to be supplied, then deliberately deflates the situation by wryly commenting that this is a pleasing return to the principles of childhood. *He*, not Mackellar, creates that peculiarly intimate love–hate tolerance between them, and he tries on the *Nonesuch* to explain in metaphor to Mackellar what the difference is between their values and what may be the reality of Henry's attitude towards him. Just as Hogg's *Justified Sinner* summed itself up in the Auchtermuchty folk tale, so James crystallises his case in the tale of the Count and the Baron. Briefly and allegorically the tale told of long-standing enmity between the two. The ground does not matter, says James; but in the most subtle way possible the Count brings about the Baron's destruction, without blame attaching to himself in any way. This story goes to the heart of the novel. Reading it for the moment in the light of an interpretation sympathetic to James, we are reminded that throughout the novel James has continuously made use of the bible story of Jacob and Esau, with Henry always cast in the role of deceiving Jacob. Is he now trying to tell Mackellar that Henry is far more devious than Mackellar could ever realise? That he, James, has suffered from a subtlety beyond his own? I submit that the very lack of identification of either Henry or James with Count or Baron allows this possibility; and further, that the sequel, Mackellar's murder attempt and James's responses to it, take us as close as we are allowed to the essence of James. James tries to explain himself to Mackellar.

> 'Life is a singular thing.... You suppose yourself to love my
> brother. I assure you, it is merely custom.... Had you instead
> fallen in with me, you would today be as strong upon my side.'

Mackellar has no time for this attempt, and typically casts his description of
it in reductive and prejudicial terms.

> But he was now fairly started in his new course of justification,
> with which he wearied me throughout the remainder of the
> passage.... 'But now that I know you are a human being,' he
> would say, 'I can take the trouble to explain myself. For I assure
> you I am human too, and have my virtues, like my neighbours.'[19]

And James realises that Mackellar will once more return to his former
prejudices when he is again with Henry.

In all their exchanges, there gradually develops a sense that we are
observing diametrically opposed human types; types that are related to
Stevenson's ideas of 'Providence' and 'Chance'. I suggest that Mackellar,
however black or white we read him, speaks for Stevenson of that world of
conventional and revealed religious orthodoxy. He becomes Stevenson's
most subtle expression of his mingled feelings for pious respectability, family
solidarity, Bible-based moral values; and conversely, that James, however we
decide on his lack or possession of residual morality, represents a move by
Stevenson towards a modern world of disillusion, scepticism, lack of faith in
benevolent determinism. Thus James relies on Chance to decide his destiny,
and thus he is compelled to be the outsider, the stoic rebel, the causeless
hero. Their plight, that of traditional Scottish Conservatism locked in
misunderstanding with rootless Disbelief, is summed up in a telling exchange
as they leave Durrisdeer.

> 'Ah, Mackellar,' said he, 'do you think I have never a regret?'
> 'I do not think you could be so bad a man,' said I, 'if you had
> not all the machinery to be a good one.'
> 'No, not all,' says he: 'not all. You are there in error. The
> malady of not wanting, my evangelist.'[20]

I now leave my two interpretations; or rather, back off from them to
look at the significance of their sitting beside one another in uneasy relation.

My final claim for this novel is that it is the finest expression of what
Stevenson, like Hogg, Scott, Douglas Brown, MacDougall Hay, and even

later writers like Gibbon, exemplified in their own crises of identity, and what they successfully managed to objectify into fictional vision. The Durrisdeer family and estate represents the estate of Scotland, like Gibbon's Kinraddie in *Sunset Song* or Brown's Barbie. Their history, going back to Thomas of Ercildoune's prophecy that there would be an ill day for them when one tied and one rode (Henry tied and James rode), back to the Reformation, and back to the wise old Lord that we meet as existing Master, can be taken as eponymous, and symbolic of deleterious change in the nature of Scotland. The fragmenting effect of the Jacobite Rebellion ruins the integrity of the wise Master; and, leaving as he does such opposite and dissociated types as Henry and James, mirror images of each other and inheritors each of only a part of his wholeness, he himself becomes both literally and figuratively an anachronism in the novel, destroyed by the family division into Head and Heart. Henry and Mackellar are of course those forces of sober and arid Head; account-watching, love-repelling, feeling-repressing. James and Burke are their polar twins: romantic, self-indulgent, adept in the manipulation of feeling to the point of irresponsibility. 'Gnatique, patrisque, alma, precor, miserere', says the old Lord on his death bed; and he is weeping for the two sons, the hostile children of a divided country, who have as their badge the stained glass window bearing the family crest which Mackellar notices has an empty, clear lozenge of glass at its heart where their quarrel took the heart out of their identity, when the coin was flung through the window.

What makes this novel superior to others that have employed the same symbolic opposition is the way it rises above taking sides. Neither of these forces, brothers, opposing sets of qualities, have Right as their monopoly. The devil metaphor here, as opposed to Scott's usage, is flexible and destructive of either claim to rightness. The brothers thus rightly and symbolically share the same grave, having symbolically exiled themselves from their native and interior land.

Thus, briefly, but I hope effectively, I now justify the changing narrators, and the changing locations. If the meaning of the novel is in polarisation of values and human qualities, then the telling and location of the novel echoes that polarisation. Mackellar tells us much in his dry, domestic manner; but the manner of Burke, his chevalier style, reminds us that Mackellar too has his opposite, in its excessively flowery, self-indulgent *apologia* for the *picaresque*. Similarly, and echoing the theme of the brotherly opposition, there are domestic scenes and exotically placed foreign scenes. There is Henry's landscape of grey buildings and rain, and there is James's landscape of pirate deck and swamp. What is important is the final movement to a frozen wilderness, which worried Stevenson but does not at all worry the reader who has seen his instinctive skill in displacing both brothers from their humdrum or exotic backgrounds. If the results of history upon Scottish psyche were not just polarisation, but repression within each polarised part of its opposite, then the parts destroy each other with an unrealised and sterile longing for each other. This was Hogg's 'love–hate' relationship of Sinner and Devil; but for Stevenson the psychological fragmentation was even more complex, and more thoroughly tragic. Thus his brothers share the same grave, with balanced inscriptions which reflect the no-man's-land between them.

Stevenson thus rose above his own personal divisions on this one occasion, transforming what, on the whole, was a confused and immature vision into a remarkably modern and widely applicable comment on the difficulty of arriving in a Godless age at moral conclusion. He thus objectifies his own troubled mind, his relations with family and Scotland, the relations of any creative and troubled mind with Scotland as a whole, and a kind of spiritual fragmentation which is universal. There is Mackellar and James in many of us, Scots or not; and their goodness or otherwise is almost impossible to ascertain. I am left always, after reading the *Master*, with one of Stevenson's exotic descriptions of a physically arresting situation which symbolically says so much more; in this case, the scene where, on the *Nonesuch*, Mackellar, fascinated as a bird by a snake, watches the Master change position, endlessly.

> It was here we were sitting: our feet hanging down, the Master betwixt me and the side, and I holding on with both hands to the grating of the cabin skylight; for it struck me it was a dangerous position, the more so as I had before my eyes a measure of our evolutions in the person of the Master, which stood out in the break of the bulwarks against the sun. Now his head would be in the zenith and his shadow fall quite beyond the *Nonesuch* on the further side; and now he would swing down till he was underneath my feet, and the line of the sea leaped high above him like the ceiling of a room.[21]

If Mackellar had thought, he would have realised that he too was changing perspective for the Master, albeit his head was not in sunlight. I suppose, in the end, that what makes James more attractive, if not morally superior, to Mackellar or Henry, is that he has perspectives which Stevenson managed finally to give him, which we share, and which are denied to the Ephraim Mackellars or Henry Ballantraes.

Notes

1. E.M. Forster, *Aspects of the Novel* (London 1962: Pelican Edition) 45.

2. R.L. Stevenson, *Weir of Hermiston* (Chatto and Windus 1922) 112.

3. Francis Hart, *The Scottish Novel: a Critical Survey* (London 1978) 114–30.

4. R.L. Stevenson, *Kidnapped* and *Catriona* (Collins) 411–12.

5. Angus Macdonald, 'Modern Scots Novelists,' in *Edinburgh Essays on Scots Literature* (Edinburgh 1933).

6. George Kitchin, 'John Galt,' ibid., 113.

7. Coleman O. Parsons, *Witchcraft and Demonology in Scott's Fiction* (Edinburgh and London 1964) 296.

8. Edwin Muir, *Scott and Scotland; the Predicament of the Scottish Writer* (London 1936) *passim* and p.115.

9. John Speirs, *The Scots Literary Tradition* (London 1962) 142–51.

10. Edwin Muir, *Latitudes* (London, n.d.) 31–47.

11. Edwin Eigner, *Robert Louis Stevenson and Romantic Tradition* (Princeton 1966).

12. ibid., 212–13.

13. Alastair Fowler, 'Parables of Adventure: the debateable novels of Robert Louis Stevenson' in *Nineteenth-Century Scottish Fiction*, ed. Ian Campbell (Manchester 1979) 105.

14. Robert Louis Stevenson, *The Master of Ballantrae* and *Weir of Hermiston* (Everyman, 55) '... but I have never had much toleration for the female sex, possibly not much understanding; and ... I have even shunned their company. Not only do I see no cause to regret this diffidence in myself, but have invariably remarked that most unhappy consequences follow those who were less wise.'

15. ibid., 2.

16. ibid., 78.

17. ibid., 79.

18. ibid., 117.

19. ibid., 140–1.

20. ibid., 129.

21. ibid., 135.

K . G . S I M P S O N

Author and Narrator in
Weir of Hermiston

From all its chapters, from all its pages, from all its sentences, the
well-written novel echoes and re-echoes its one creative and
controlling thought; to this must every incident and character
contribute; the style must have been pitched in unison with this; and
if there is anywhere a word that looks another way, the book would
be stronger, clearer, and (I had almost said) fuller without it.[1]

T his is one of several important statements on the practice of fiction
made by Stevenson in the course of his debate with Henry James. It is
characteristic of the concern with technical and stylistic expertise which so
engaged Stevenson.

In *Weir of Hermiston* the 'one creative and controlling thought' is the
concept of judgement. Judgement, and the cognate concerns of duty,
conscience, and authority, are thematically central to the father–son conflict.
While it is recognized that Archie is the principal exemplar of these themes,
the point of this essay is to argue that Stevenson attempts to distance himself
from his narrator; and in deliberately raising the question of the reliability of
his narrator, he offers yet another instance of the limitations of individual
human judgement.

Stevenson's concern with judgement in *Weir* may be considered in
three respects: in relation to the writer's own personality and values; in

From *Robert Louis Stevenson*, ed. Andrew Noble. © 1983 by Vision Press, Ltd.

relation to Stevenson as a representative of identifiably Scottish values; and in the context of the movement in the practice of fiction away from authoritative statement on the part of the author-narrator (as in George Eliot, Thackeray, and Trollope) towards the twentieth-century novel's reflection, in its form, of the breakdown of absolute values, and the concomitant decline in the status and conviction of the narrator (the process sometimes referred to as 'Exit author/narrator').

According to Edwin Muir, 'had it been finished *Weir of Hermiston* would have been something unique in fiction, a modern saga, a novel combining two elements which are almost always disjoined: a modern sensibility and a heroic spirit'.[2] The point at issue is the degree of success achieved in uniting modern sensibility and heroic spirit. This leads one to a consideration which repays effort in much greater measure than hypothesis about the conclusion of *Weir* ever could: on the evidence available, what is the relationship between values and technique in *Weir* and, in particular, what consonance is there between the nature of the material and the technique of narration? Does *Weir* exemplify its author's contention that in prose 'idea and stylistic pattern proceed hand in hand'?[3] Does *Weir* substantiate James's claim that with Stevenson 'the form, the envelope, is there ... headforemost, as the idea'?[4]

Any attempt at an answer to this must first take account of the weight placed by Stevenson, in his theoretical writing, on narrative technique. 'A Humble Remonstrance' offers the fullest and clearest statement of Stevenson's views on this. In response to James's claims in 'The Art of Fiction', Stevenson wrote:

> What then is the object, what the method, of an art, and what the source of its power? The whole secret is that no art does 'compete with life'. Man's one method, whether he reasons or creates, is to half-shut his eyes against the dazzle and confusion of reality.[5]

Stevenson proceeds to the following pronouncement, which has the utmost significance for his fiction:

> So far as [literature] imitates at all, it imitates not life but speech: not the facts of human destiny, but the emphasis and the suppressions with which the human actor tells of them. The real art that dealt with life directly was that of the first men who told their stories round the savage camp-fire. Our art is occupied, and bound to be occupied, not so much in making stories true as in

making them typical; not so much in capturing the lineaments of each fact, as in marshalling all of them towards a common end.... The novel, which is a work of art, exists, not by its resemblances to life, which are forced and material, as a shoe must still consist of leather, but by its immeasurable difference from life, which is designed and significant, and is both the method and the meaning of the work.

Several aspects of this are noteworthy: the timely warning against excessive reliance on James's 'illusion of reality'; the primitivist nostalgia, that hankering after an earlier age when life and art were one, which has affected many modern writers but which may be related in Scotland to the post-Union insecurity, precisely the crisis of values and subsequent nostalgia out of which Macpherson's Ossian poems were born;, the emphasis on 'marshalling [facts] towards a common end', which, in *Weir*, is the author's concern with destiny and judgement (compare Stevenson's definition of the novel as 'not a transcript of life, to be judged by its exactitude, but a simplification of some side or point of life, to stand or fall by its significant simplicity',[6] about which there is more than a tinge of a characteristically Scottish reductionism); the recognition of the interinvolvement of 'method' and 'meaning'; and, above all, the importance of narrative voice as the basis of the version of 'human destiny'.

On another occasion Stevenson described the process whereby the writer selects and shapes the material of his fiction as 'the sentiment assimilating the facts of natural congruity'.[7] For Stevenson, the artist 'must suppress much and omit more'.[8] His annoyance with the readiness of the public to regard fiction as 'slice of life' is reflected in his protest to James: 'They think that striking situations, or good dialogue, are got by studying life; they will not rise to understand that they are prepared by deliberate artifice and set off by painful suppressions.'[9] For Stevenson this capacity for modulation and subordination is one of the particular strengths of fiction: one of the advantages of continuous narration over drama is that the writer 'can now subordinate one thing to another in importance, and introduce all manner of very subtle detail, to a degree that was before impossible'.[10]

Hugo is praised by Stevenson for setting before himself 'the task of realizing, in the language of romance, much of the involution of our complicated lives', and, in contrast with the 'unity, the unwavering creative purpose' of some of Hawthorne's romances, Hugo achieves 'unity out of multitude'; and 'it is the wonderful power of subordination and synthesis thus displayed that gives us the measure of his talent.' Stevenson distinguishes between Hugo's romances and 'the novel with a purpose', in that 'the moral significance, with Hugo, is of the essence of the romance; it is the organizing principle.'[11]

One side of Stevenson was striving for precisely this, but he was never to achieve it entirely satisfactorily. The imaginative expression of such moral purpose was perhaps incompatible with the Calvinist emphasis on predetermination. Underlying this judgement on Hugo is a compound of feelings: Hugo 'learned to subordinate his story to an idea, to make his art speak'. The aim of the artist is, for Stevenson, configuration; the writer is the source of a pattern, an alternative to the pattern of life which is the provision of Fate. 'The motive and end of any art whatever is to make a pattern', wrote Stevenson. Hence,

> That style is therefore the most perfect, not, as fools say, which is the most natural, for the most natural is the disjointed babble of the chronicler; but which attains the highest degree of elegant and pregnant implication unobtrusively; or, if obtrusively, then with the greatest gain to sense and vigour.[12]

Assessment of the degree of implication accomplished by Stevenson in *Weir* involves examination of the narrative technique employed in the novel. It is essential to consider not only the attitude of the narrator to his subject but also the attitude of the novelist to his narrator. Why did Stevenson choose the particular narrative mode employed in *Weir*, and why did he choose this particular narrator? How reliable is the narrator of *Weir*? Can it be that he is the object of authorial irony?

In *Weir* Stevenson uses first-person narration, as he did in many of his books. Percy Lubbock, noting that Stevenson may not have seen how logically his preference for first-person narration followed from the subjects that most attracted him, observed that Stevenson never had any occasion to use the first-person for enhancement of plain narrative as his subjects were 'strongly romantic, vividly dramatic'.[13] Hence the value of the use of Mackellar in *The Master of Ballantrae*: the fantasy of much of the material is contained within the form of Mackellar's doggedly realist account.

In *Weir* the narrator is similarly personalized by his style (though it is not that of Mackellar), but he is not identified specifically. This fact has given rise to some divergence of opinion as to the identity of the narrator. For instance, Leslie Fiedler goes so far as to comment on the deleterious effects of the choice of third-person narration, adding,

> Stevenson's instinctive bent was for first-person narrative; and
> when ... he attempts to speak from outside *about* his fiction, his
> style betrays him to self-pity (we *know* Archie is really the author,
> and the third-person singular affects us like a transparent hoax),
> sentimentality and the sort of 'fine' writing he had avoided since
> *Prince Otto*.[14]

The answer to this must be that though Stevenson has not identified his
narrator he has personalized him quite distinctly, and that instances of 'fine'
writing have to be attributed to him and not to Stevenson. Thus such
passages are further exemplification of human limitation, and in particular
limitation of judgement; and as such they are entirely consonant with the
central thematic concern of the book.

   In *Weir* the narrator is soon present in the first chapter as a source of
opinion and judgement. He states that 'chance cast [Jean Rutherford] in the
path of Adam Weir'; volunteers the view that 'it seems profane to call [the
acquaintance] a courtship'; and recounts that 'on the very eve of their
engagement, it was related that one had drawn near to the tender couple, and
had overheard the lady cry out, with the tones of one who talked for the sake
of talking, "Keep me, Mr. Weir, and what became of him?" and the profound
accents of the suitor reply, "Haangit, mem, haangit"' (195).[15] Fairly rapidly
the narratorial omniscience is personalized, though not identified, with the
narrator appearing thus in his own voice: 'The heresy about foolish women
is always punished, I have said, and Lord Hermiston began to pay the penalty
at once' (196). Such comment inevitably leads the reader to ponder the
identity of the narrative voice; and the tension between apparent
omniscience and personalization creates problems for Stevenson the further
the narrative advances.

   Stevenson's recognition of the importance of narrative voice leads to
the elevation of the narrator of *Weir* to the status of sophisticated and
conscious artist. The skill with which material of the narrative is
structured betokens a refined intelligence, and this might be held to
strengthen the case for identifying the narrator with the author.
Juxtaposition is used to considerable effect: witness the juxtaposing of the
exchange between Hermiston and Kirstie on the death of his wife, and the
ensuing account by the narrator entitled 'Father and Son' (204); the report
of the conversation between Archie and Dr. Gregory and the effect thereof
on Archie's feelings for his father reveals a fine sense of ironic ordering (215);
Archie's impassioned plea (with which Chapter Four ends) is deliberately
juxtaposed with the reductive account of Hermiston parish which follows it

(227); Archie's restraint and 'Roman sense of duty' are contrasted with the ensuing depiction of the restraint which life has imposed upon Kirstie's innately passionate nature (230–31); and, perhaps most tellingly, Chapter Six ends with Christina's romantic dreams while Chapter Seven, 'Enter Mephistopheles', begins with the arrival which is to prove their undoing. All of this suggests a fairly high level of conscious artistry. So, too, do the manifest ability to render character by means of distinctive style, and the capacity to use language in a way that reveals awareness of the symbolic or mythical dimension of the events of the novel. For instance, the exchange between Archie and Frank after Archie's denunciation of the hanging of Duncan Jopp occasions the following comment:

> And the one young man carried his tortured spirit forth of the city and all the day long, by one road and another, in an endless pilgrimage of misery; while the other hastened smilingly to spread the news of Weir's access of insanity, and to drum up for that night a full attendance at the Speculative, where further eccentric developments might certainly be looked for. (212)

The narrator is aware of the action on one level as *peregrinatio* threatened by Satanic temptation, while at the same time, with characteristic Scottish reductionism, he presents the devil-figure as basely and pettily human.

Frequently, too, the tone and the demeanour of the narrator are such as to encourage identification of narrator with author. Early in the first chapter the narrator offers himself as a source of authoritative comment, not just on the behaviour of the characters but on the extent to which it is typical of various classes or categories of human beings. He wishes to appear as someone who knows the ways of the world and the responses of men and women. At the same time he knows the Weirs and those with whom they come in contact. Of Archie's refusal, after the conversation with Glenalmond, to express further his feelings for his father, the narrator comments:

> With the infinitely delicate sense of youth, Archie avoided the subject from that hour. It was perhaps a pity. Had he but talked— talked freely—let himself gush out in words (the way youth loves to do and should), there might have been no tale to write upon the Weirs of Hermiston. But the shadow of a threat of ridicule sufficed; in the slight tartness of these words he read a prohibition; and it is likely that Glenalmond meant it so. (207)

The narrator is sufficiently confident to account for Archie's solitariness as follows: '... something that was in part the delicacy of his mother, in part the austerity of his father, held him aloof from all'; and to direct thus the reader's response to Hermiston: 'Sympathy is not due to these steadfast iron natures. If he failed to gain his son's friendship, or even his son's toleration, on he went up the great, bare stair-case of his duty, uncheered and undepressed.' And consideration of Archie's situation leads him to this generalization: 'Parsimony of pain, glut of pleasure, these are the two alternating ends of youth; and Archie was of the parsimonious.' The narrator never loses this readiness to relate the particular behaviour of his subjects to general human patterns. Of the final encounter between Archie and Christine the narrator observes that 'the schoolmaster that there is in all men, to the despair of all girls and most women, was now completely in possession of Archie' (283).

In such comment it is difficult not to hear the voice of Stevenson himself, and the same may be said of those passages where the narrator widens the range of his authority, discoursing on the distinctive attitude of the Scot to the past (233), or observing: 'not even the most acute political heads are guided through the steps of life with unerring directness. That would require a gift of prophecy which has been denied to man' (264–65). Noteworthy too is the narrator's readiness to formulate or interpret the response or behaviour of his characters. Of Hermiston's atmosphere of industry the narrator remarks that 'it was still present, unobserved like the ticking of a clock, an arid ideal, a tasteless stimulant in the boy's life' (206). In the following description of the attempts at converse between Archie and his father the choice of analogy is, quite deliberately, not to Archie's advantage:

> The father, with a grand simplicity, either spoke of what interested himself, or maintained an unaffected silence. The son turned in his head for some topic that should be quite safe, that would spare him fresh evidences either of my lord's inherent grossness or of the innocence of his inhumanity; treading gingerly the ways of intercourse, like a lady gathering up her skirts in a by-path. (209)

This fondness for analogy persists throughout *Weir*. Early in the final chapter comes this account of Christina's appearing before Archie: 'His first sight of her was thus excruciatingly sad, like a glimpse of a world from which all light, comfort, and society were on the point of vanishing' (283).

It is significant that, in his essay on Burns, Stevenson noted the importance of style to Burns, and claimed that 'it was by his style, and not by his matter, that he affected Wordsworth and the world.'[16] Almost immediately, however, he recognized another major quality in the poet, exclaiming 'What a gust of sympathy there is in him sometimes.' Precisely this combination of qualities is exemplified in Stevenson himself. James was to see the union of the sympathetic and the ironical in Stevenson as an essentially Scottish characteristic, finding in the Scottish background 'a certain process of detachment, of extreme secularization', and claiming: 'Mr. Stevenson is ... a Scotchman of the world. None other ... could have drawn with such a mixture of sympathetic and ironical observation the character of the canny young Lowlander, David Balfour.' James wrote of Stevenson's 'talent for seeing the familiar in the heroic, and reducing the extravagant to plausible detail', and the character, Alan Breck, he found 'a genuine study, and nothing can be more charming than the way Mr. Stevenson both sees through and admires it'. Parts of *The Silverado Squatters* James referred to as 'this half-humorous, half-tragical recital'.[17]

Such ambivalence of attitude, such 'compassionate irony' (the term is Furnas's),[18] is frequently the response of the narrator of *Weir*. This is exemplified in the account of the marriage of Jean Rutherford and Hermiston, and in that of the relationship between mother and son in such comments as 'The sight of the little man at her skirt intoxicated her with the sense of power, and froze her with the consciousness of her responsibility' (198). The union of sympathy and irony informs the description of the trial of Duncan Jopp. Here a meticulous realism of presentation is accompanied, without strain, by a compassion that is reminiscent of Dickens. But, in a way that Dickens was not always able to do, Stevenson has his narrator relate thus the particular to general human traits:

> There was pinned about his throat a piece of dingy flannel; and this it was perhaps that turned the scale in Archie's mind between disgust and pity. The creature stood in a vanishing point; yet a little while, and he was still a man, and had eyes and apprehension; yet a little longer, and with a last sordid piece of pageantry, he would cease to be. And here, in the meantime, with a trait of human nature that caught at the beholder's breath, he was tending a sore throat. (209)

It is essential to note here that the compassionate irony encompasses the account of Archie's response to the trial.

In Chapter Six, 'A Leaf from Christina's Psalm-Book', the same applies: common to the description of the Hermiston congregation and Archie's response to it is the same compassionate irony. This is precisely the attitude that is evinced towards the whole episode of the romantic involvement of Archie and Christina. Here is the description of Christina's awaiting Archie near the Weaver's Stone on the Sunday evening:

> By the time the sun was down and all the easterly braes lay plunged in clear shadow, she was aware of another figure coming up the path at a most unequal rate of approach, now half running, now pausing and seeming to hesitate. She watched him at first with a total suspension of thought. She held her thought as a person holds his breathing. Then she consented to recognise him. 'He'll no be coming here, he canna be; it's no possible.' And there began to grow upon her a subdued choking response. (259)

It is not only Christina's attitude that is in flux here: the narrator's own attitude is a composite one, as the fluctuation between amusement and sympathy indicates. The treatment of the romance between Archie and Christina is not Kailyard. Stevenson's narrator does not suppress the 'sugar bool' incident: he *chooses* to present it (when he could have omitted it) because it enables him to demonstrate his amused sympathy. And, to a large extent, *Weir* is about the narrator's attitude to his subject.

For all the apparent omniscience of the narrator, for all his readiness to pronounce with what seems to be authority, Stevenson is able to demonstrate that his narrator is far from being infallible; indeed he represents further exemplification of the central thematic concern of *Weir*—the limitation of human judgement. Despite the appearance of conviction, the word, 'perhaps', recurs with remarkable frequency in the narrative, as, for instance, in this comment on Archie and his father: 'there were not, perhaps, in Christendom two men more radically strangers' (208). A characteristic of the narrator is to embark upon an authoritative judgement, only to have to retreat into tentativeness. Of Archie's disinclination to socialize in the country the narrator writes: 'The habit of solitude tends to perpetuate itself, and an austerity of which he was quite unconscious, and a pride which seemed arrogance, and perhaps was chiefly shyness, discouraged and offended his new companions' (229). The narrator has, too, a tendency to beg the crucial question (Archie, who had just defied—was it God or Satan?—would not listen (212)); and he is, at times, made to say things which are simply silly. He remarks, for instance, of Archie's setting fines at the Speculative: 'He little thought, as he did so, how he resembled his father, but his friends remarked upon it, chuckling' (213); to which the reader is entitled to ask if it is likely that he would think such a thing. Similarly, the narrator says of Archie: 'He hated to be inhospitable, but in one thing he was his father's son. He had a strong sense that his house was his own and no man else's' (272). If the narrator has failed to observe the various other points of resemblance between father and son, then his vision is truly blinkered.

It should be noted too that on several occasions the narrator acknowledges his own inadequacy of judgement. In the course of the exchange between father and son his narrator remarks of Archie that 'he had a strong impression, besides, of the essential valour of the old gentleman before him, how conveyed it would be hard to say' (219). The narrator interrupts Kirstie's account of the death of Gilbert Elliott with a joke at both his expense and that of his source, Kirstie, 'whom I but haltingly follow, for she told this tale like one inspired' (236). The most telling admission, and subsequent demonstration of the circumscription of the narrator's judgement occurs in the midst of the account of young Kirstie's romanticizing. The narrator comments:

> Had a doctor of medicine come into that loft, he would have diagnosed a healthy, well-developed, eminently vivacious lass lying on her face in a fit of the sulks; not one who had just contracted, or was just contracting a mortal sickness of the mind which should yet carry her towards death and despair. Had it been a doctor of psychology, he might have been pardoned for divining in the girl a passion of childish vanity, self-love *in excelsis*, and no more. It is to be understood that I have been painting chaos and describing the inarticulate. Every lineament that appears is too precise, almost every word too strong. Take a finger-post in the mountains on a day of rolling mists; I have but copied the names that appear on the pointers, the names of definite and famous cities far distant, and now perhaps basking in sunshine; but Christina remained all these hours, as it were, at the foot of the post itself, not moving and enveloped in mutable and blinding wreaths of haze. (255–56)

Here the narrator is the target of a strong authorial irony. What is meant by 'a mortal sickness of the mind which should yet carry her towards death and despair'? Is the narrator ignorant of subsequent events and the nature of the revised ending? And, after the admission that 'every word is too strong', the narrative lapses into the stylistic excesses to which it is prone. Such 'fine writing' as appears in *Weir* is to be attributed to the narrator and further exemplifies his subjection to the ironic overview of the author. Likewise, sentimental excess in the writing (e.g. the description of Kirstie (281)) should be regarded as the response of the narrator.

Stevenson allows his narrator to reveal—and at times acknowledge—his fallibility. 'I have said she was no hypocrite', he writes of young Kirstie, 'but here I am at fault ... the steps of love in the young, and especially in girls, are instinctive and unconscious' (259). The account, which follows soon after, of the lovers' tentative approaches to one another ('He was sounding her ... a thrill of emotion' (261)) is self-consciously weighty and florid. From such obvious excesses Stevenson has taken care to distance himself. The following, also, has to be read as the comment of the narrator, from which the author has distanced himself:

> *Tantaene irae*? Has the reader perceived the reason? Since Frank's coming there were no more hours of gossip over the supper tray! All his blandishments were in vain; he started handicapped on the race for Mrs. Elliott's favour. (267)

When the narrator strikes this note he is being set up quite deliberately by the author. Adopting his authoritative 'public' voice, for instance, the narrator expounds upon the futility of condescension towards the Scots peasantry (269). All unwittingly he is made to sound more than a little patronizing himself.

The narrator both recognizes his own limitation of understanding and draws attention to the limited effectiveness of language in rendering experience when he offers the following account of Frank's discovery of the romance between Archie and young Kirstie:

> Here was Archie's secret, here was the woman, and more than that—though I have need here of every manageable attenuation of language—with the first look, he had already entered himself as a rival. It was a good deal in pique, it was a little in revenge, it was much in genuine admiration: the devil may decide the proportions! I cannot, and it is very likely that Frank could not. (274)

The manner in which this chapter ends is significant. The triumph of Frank's discovery leads to the comment that 'there was nothing vindictive in his nature; but, if revenge came in his way, it might as well be good, and the thought of Archie's pillow reflections that night was indescribably sweet to him' (276). It is difficult to reconcile the claim that 'there was nothing vindictive in his nature' with the evidence that the narrator has presented or, for that matter, with his entitling Frank's appearance 'Enter Mephistopheles'. How is the judgement of the narrator to be viewed? Is this simply one of his blind spots? Or is he, in the manner adopted intermittently by Fielding's narrator in *Tom Jones*, feigning fallibility? This latter possibility makes *Weir* into an even more complex work of irony, and at the same time it exacerbates the problem of comprehension for the reader: when is the narrator genuinely fallible, and when is he, as participant in Stevenson's ironic *schema*, obliged to simulate fallibility? On the occasion under consideration, after the apparent proof of his fallibility, the narrator—ironically—attempts to reassert his authority by resuming his omniscient Olympian manner as follows:

> Poor cork upon a torrent, he tasted that night the sweets of omnipotence, and brooded like a deity over the strands of that intrigue which was to shatter him before the summer waned. (277)

The effect of such 'fine writing' and flaunting of narratorial authority is counter-productive: it merely re-emphasizes the limitations of the narrator. Thus, one of the most potent ironies in *Weir* is that often when the narrator believes he has accomplished a particular effect, he has in fact achieved something quite different. Generally when he speaks with his authoritative voice the true omniscience is not his but Stevenson's. Not only his attitude to the characters, but also his attitude to himself and his narrative function, is in constant flux. The irony is that the narrator does not share in the author's and readers' awareness of this.

All of this would combine to suggest that *Weir* is a masterpiece of irony; that Stevenson, sublimely detached, leaves his narrator to over-reach and so demonstrate his limitations. This view of the novel is tempting, but there are major objections to it and it requires some qualification. Paradoxically, the difficulties arise principally from precisely that narrative energy and flux already identified, and in particular from Stevenson's use in *Weir* of the technique that has come to be known as Free Indirect Speech.[19] Intermittent rendering of the character's thought-processes by means of F.I.S. permits of identification and evaluation. As Spitzer pointed out, mimicry implies a mimic as well as a person mimicked.[20] With F.I.S., where mimicry is at the heart of the technique, this applies equally; and it should be added that mimicry implies not just the presence of a mimic but the presence of a mimic with an attitude towards his subject. Here once again irony may be critical or sympathetic (or a compound of these constituents in varying proportions), and irony again functions as a means of directing response. Perhaps the least complex instance of this in *Weir* is the occasion when the narrator adopts the voice of genteel society in order to subject it to irony. The response to Frank's tales about Archie is presented thus:

> He had done something disgraceful, my dear. What, was not precisely known, and that good kind young man, Mr. Innes, did his best to make light of it. But there it was. And Mr. Innes was very anxious about him now; he was really uneasy, my dear; he was positively wrecking his own prospects because he dared not leave him alone. (271)

As a passage of ironic writing, that could stand comparison with Jane Austen. The irony is compounded by the fact that the voice of genteel society relays the view of things—a totally inaccurate one—which Frank has been circulating.

Roy Pascal has noted that F.I.S. both evokes a particular character and places him in a context of judgement by the narrator.[21] This is true of each of the principals in *Weir*. In the early stages the use of F.I.S. is concise and economical. Here, for a moment, the narrator enters the mind of Mrs. Weir, both rendering her terms and evoking an attitude of compassionate irony:

> It was only with the child that she had conceived and managed to pursue a scheme of conduct. Archie was to be a great man and a good; a minister if possible, a.saint for ccrtain. (198)

There is comparable access to her mind and her terms in the ensuing account of her philosophy of tenderness and in her defence of Hermiston to Archie. In the case of Hermiston sympathy is rather less a constituent of the attitude evinced, but there is the same concision in the use of F.I.S., as here, for instance:

> There might have been more pleasure in his relations with Archie, so much he may have recognised at moments; but pleasure was a by-product of the singular chemistry of life, which only fools expected. (208)

Where there is more extensive use of F.I.S. it is in the case of Frank that it is most readily identified and consistently understood, possibly because the narrator's attitude to Frank is in the main unequivocal. Here is Frank's version of his enforced departure from Edinburgh society:

> Any port in a storm! He was manfully turning his back on the Parliament House and its gay babble, on port and oysters, the racecourse and the ring; and manfully prepared, until these clouds should have blown by, to share a living grave with Archie Weir at Hermiston. (265)

Such masterly ironic self-revelation is reminiscent of Jane Austen and, in the Scottish tradition, of Burns and Galt; and there is a potential for it in *St. Ives* which Stevenson chose not to exploit. It is sustained through Chapter Seven of *Weir*. The narrator presents thus Frank's reaction to his desertion by Archie:

> Innes groaned under these desertions; it required all his philosophy to sit down to a solitary breakfast with composure, and all his unaffected good-nature to be able to greet Archie with friendliness on the more rare occasions when he came home late for dinner. (266)

And this is his response to the Hermiston household: 'For the others, they were beyond hope and beyond endurance. Never had a young Apollo been cast among such rustic barbarians' (268). The mastery of this mode here is accomplished not because Frank is a shallow fool who lends himself readily to this sort of treatment; rather, it is because the narrator's attitude to Frank does not fluctuate.

With some of the characters, and Archie most conspicuously, the narrator's attitude does fluctuate, and it is here that Stevenson encounters some difficulties. For instance, the account of Archie's reactions during the trial of Duncan Jopp has passages of F.I.S., such as

> He thought of flight, and where was he to flee to? of other lives, but was there any life worth living in this den of savage and jeering animals? .... It seemed to him, from the top of his nineteen years' experience, as if he were marked at birth to be the perpetrator of some signal action, to set back fallen Mercy, to overthrow the usurping devil that sat, horned and hoofed, on her throne.... He saw the fleering rabble, the flinching wretch produced. He looked on for a while at a certain parody of

devotion, which seemed to strip the wretch of his last claim to manhood. (211)

Part of the difficulty in differentiating Archie's thoughts, rendered in F.I.S., from those of the narrator derives from the frequent similarity between their respective styles. This may be at least in part a result of the origin, as Lorck pointed out, of some instances of F.I.S. in the intense imaginative identification of narrator with character.[22]

In the lengthy sixth chapter, 'From Christina's Psalm-Book', there is sustained interplaying of external narration and F.I.S. Here F.I.S. is used to reflect character and to convey narratorial irony, while at the same time it participates in expressing the flux of the narrator's own response. In the account of Archie's reaction to the Hermiston congregation the use of Archie's own terms, the mimicking of his way of seeing, is used to reflect less than entirely favourably on him. In this, for instance, Archie appears as civilized urban man in whom the natural origins are concealed beneath a veneer of patronizing sophistication:

> The rest of the congregation, like so many sheep, oppressed him with a sense of hob-nailed routine, day following day—of physical labour in the open air, oatmeal porridge, peas bannock, the somnolent fireside in the evening, and the night-long nasal slumbers in a box-bed. Yet he knew many of them to be shrewd and humorous, men of character, notable women, making a bustle in the world and radiating an influence from their low-browed doors. He knew besides they were like other men; below the crust of custom, rapture found a way; he had heard them beat the timbrel before Bacchus—had heard them shout and carouse over their whisky-toddy; and not the most Dutch-bottomed and severe faces among them all, not even the solemn elders themselves, but were capable of singular gambols at the voice of love. (246)

Again the use of the individual's (inflated) terms against him is redolent of Jane Austen.

Especially in the scenes at Hermiston the appearance of inflated language often indicates the return of the narrative to Archie's viewpoint, Archie being thus represented as the urbane or unnatural in an otherwise predominantly natural world. Here Archie's strong but unfocused romantic mood is conveyed through its own terms, only to be undermined by reductive detail:

Vagrant scents of the earth arrested Archie by the way with
moments of ethereal intoxication. The grey, Quakerish dale was
still only awakened in places and patches from the sobriety of its
winter colouring; and he wondered at its beauty; an essential
beauty of the old earth it seemed to him, not resident in
particulars but breathing to him from the whole. He surprised
himself by a sudden impulse to write poetry—he did so
sometimes, loose, galloping octosyllabics in the vein of Scott—
and when he had taken his place on a boulder, near some fairy
falls and shaded by a whip of a tree that was already radiant with
new leaves, it still more surprised him that he should find nothing
to write. (246–67)

The echoes of Edward Waverley in the Highlands are more than accidental.
The irony is further compounded by the narrator's immediate uncertainty:
'His heart *perhaps* beat in time to some vast indwelling rhythm of the
universe.'

Throughout the record of the romance between Archie and young
Kirstie the narrator's attitude is a composite one, alternating between
amused observation and sympathetic identification. Here fluctuation of
narrative perspective, a feature throughout *Weir*, reaches its most
pronounced. The narrator offers this skilful mimicry of Archie's highly
romantic view of things:

Brightness of azure, clouds of fragrance, a tinkle of falling water
and singing birds, rose like exhalations from some deeper,
aboriginal memory, that was not his, but belonged to the flesh on
his bones. His body remembered; and it seemed to him that his
body was in no way gross, but ethereal and perishable like a strain
of music; and he felt for it an exquisite tenderness as for a child,
an innocent, full of instincts and destined to an early death. And
he felt for old Torrance—of the many supplications, of the few
days—a pity that was near to tears. (247)

The centre of interest then shifts to young Kirstie, and in the representation
of her response F.I.S. is used intermittently (e.g. 'If he spared a glance in her
direction, he should know she was a well-behaved young lady who had been
to Glasgow.... Even then, she was far too well-bred to gratify her curiosity
with any impatience' (248)). Equally, the narrator adopts from time to time
the persona of the detached and amused observer of the enduring social

comedy ('Presently he leaned nonchalantly back; and that deadly instrument, the maiden, was suddenly unmasked in profile' (249)). In the same tone the particular is related to the general ('According to the pretty fashion in which our grandmothers did not hesitate to appear, and our great-aunts went forth armed for the pursuit and capture of our great-uncles, the dress was drawn up so as to mould the contours of both breasts, and in the nook between, a cairngorm brooch maintained it' (250)).

There follows this quite remarkable passage in which narrator's observation and F.I.S. are so fused that it is difficult to differentiate them:

> Archie was attracted by the bright thing like a child. He looked at her again and yet again, and their looks crossed. The lip was lifted from her little teeth. He saw the red blood work vividly under her tawny skin. Her eye, which was great as a stag's, struck and held his gaze. He knew who she must be—Kirstie, she of the harsh diminutive, his housekeeper's niece, the sister of the rustic prophet, Gib—and he found in her the answer to his wishes. (250)

The preposterous nature of these analogies leads one to wonder if they are Archie's or the narrator's. Similarly, in the ensuing comment it is not easy for the reader to ascertain whether the narrator is distancing himself by means of irony from young Kirstie's romantic illusions or is, to an extent, identifying with them ('Christina felt the shock of their encountering glances, and seemed to rise, clothed in smiles, into a region of the vague and bright').

From Kirstie's viewpoint the narrative perspective moves on into this sequence where it fluctuates markedly:

> She took to reading in the metrical psalms, and then remembered it was sermon-time. Last she put a sugarbool in her mouth, and the next moment repented of the step. It was such a homely-like thing! Mr. Archie would never be eating sweeties in kirk; and, with a palpable effort, she swallowed it whole, and her colour flamed high. At this signal of distress Archie awoke to a sense of his ill-behaviour. What had he been doing? He had been exquisitely rude in church to the niece of his housekeeper; he had stared like a lackey and a libertine at a beautiful and modest girl. It was possible, it was even likely, he would be presented to her after service in the kirk-yard, and then how was he to look? And

there was no excuse. He had marked the tokens of her shame, of her increasing indignation, and he was such a fool that he had not understood them. Shame bowed him down, and he looked resolutely at Mr. Torrance; who little supposed, good worthy man, as he continued to expound justification by faith, what was his true business: to play the part of derivative to a pair of children at the old game of falling in love. (251)

Here the narrative has moved from F.I.S. rendering of Kirstie's viewpoint, through a comparable rendering of Archie's, to a characteristic narratorial interpretation of Torrance's feelings. The section that follows shows a fluctuation between narratorial comment and recurrent F.I.S. such as 'All would have been right if she had not blushed, a silly fool! There was nothing to blush at, if she *had* taken a sugarbool. Mrs. MacTaggart, the elder's wife in St. Enoch's, took them often. And if he had looked at her, what was more natural than that a young gentleman should look at the best-dressed girl in church' (F.I.S.). 'And at the same time, she knew far otherwise, she knew there was nothing casual or ordinary in the look, and valued herself on its memory like a decoration' (Narrator). 'Well, it was a blessing he had found something else to look at!' (F.I.S.). Thereafter there are passages of F.I.S. ('Here was a piece of nicety for that upland parish, where the matrons marched with their coats kilted in the rain, and the lasses walked barefoot to kirk through the dust of summer, and went bravely down by the burn-side, and sat on stones to make a public toilet before entering!') which are succeeded by narratorial interpretation ('It was perhaps an air wafted from Glasgow; or perhaps it marked a stage of that dizziness of gratified vanity, in which the instinctive act passed unperceived'). The brief return to F.I.S. ('He was looking after!') gives way in turn to the narrator's comment ('She unloaded herself of a prodigious sigh that was all pleasure, and betook herself to a run' (253)).

Throughout this chapter irony informs the flux of the individual vision. When Archie climbs the hill and enters the hollow of the Deil's Hag, he sees before him 'like an answer to his wishes, the little womanly figure in the grey dress and the pink kerchief sitting little, and low, and lost, and acutely solitary, in these desolate surroundings and on the weather-beaten stone of the dead weaver' (259–60). These terms, this way of seeing, are his. The narrative takes account of the flux of his response in that soon his thoughts are shown to have become quite different: 'This was a grown woman he was approaching, endowed with her mysterious potencies and attractions, the treasury of the continued race, and he was neither better nor worse than the average of his sex and age' (260). Within one sentence here F.I.S. has merged into narratorial judgement. While, in all of this, the views of the characters are demonstrably in flux, this is equally true of the view of the narrator.

In *Weir* Stevenson often fails to achieve F.I.S. in its purest form. At times the nature of the language used to reflect the activities of the mind is at odds with the nature of that mind as it is revealed through dialogue. Because of the narrator's readiness to interpret, F.I.S. is rarely sustained for long, and there is often a stylistic fusion between the rendering of the character's thought-processes and the narrator's subsequent commentary. Roy Pascal has noted that 'Lerch maintained that in S.I.L. (*style indirect libre*) passages the narrator disappears from the scene to be replaced by the character, whose self-expression borrows the narratorial form only in order to assume the full authoritativeness of narratorial statements.'[23] The situation in *Weir* is an unusual one: narratorial authority is shown to be suspect, but, paradoxically, the narrator is reluctant to absent himself for long from the process of narration. Here, for instance, the narrator comes close to rendering Archie's response from Archie's own viewpoint, but he is unwilling or unable to suppress his own attitude:

> He hated to seem harsh. But that was Frank's look-out. If Frank had been commonly discreet, he would have been decently courteous. And there was another consideration. The secret he was protecting was not his own merely; it was hers: it belonged to that inexpressible she who was fast taking possession of his soul, and whom he would soon have defended at the cost of burning cities. (273)

The following exemplifics thc constant shifting of the narrative perspective:

> He met Archie at dinner without resentment, almost with cordiality. You must take your friends as you find them, he would have said. Archie couldn't help being his father's son, or his grandfather's, the hypothetical weaver's grandson. The son of a hunks, he was still a hunks at heart, incapable of true generosity and consideration; but he had other qualities with which Frank could divert himself in the meanwhile, and to enjoy which it was necessary that Frank should keep his temper. (273)

Of this, the first two sentences are the narrator's; the third would be F.I.S. but for the term, 'hypothetical'; of the last sentence, the first part is F.I.S., and 'but he had other qualities … ff.' is the narrator's view.

Such flux of the narrative perspective in *Weir* reflects the complexity of, and indeed the deep divisions within, Stevenson's own values. Stevenson's own restlessness, for instance, finds expression in the constant shifting of narratorial stance. With justification Edwin M. Eigner has noted the extent of the opposition between activism and scepticism in Stevenson himself, suggesting that the problem of *The Great North Road* is that of *Hamlet* in the nineteenth century.[24]

In part, the fluctuation of the narrative in *Weir* can be seen as a manifestation of Stevenson's dramatic capacity: through his narrator he becomes, momentarily, the particular character. Thus the narrative of *Weir* fuses static and fluid, fixed points of reference and the flow of the mind, reality and version of reality. Rightly Kurt Wittig noted that 'in his determination to enter into his characters, Stevenson seizes on, and recreates, the sensuous impressions which they receive, together with the images, metaphors and comparisons which the impressions themselves evoke in their minds'; hence, 'as it exists only in the mind, it is not a static picture, but one that changes with the character's prevailing mood.'[25] To this one has to add that in *Weir* the effect is compounded by the fact that the picture changes too with the changing attitude of the narrator.

This practice is very much in line with Stevenson's theoretical writing on the subject of narration. He wrote of Balzac: 'I wish I had his fist—for I have already a better method—the kinetic—whereas he continually allowed himself to be led into the static.'[26] And he drew the following contrast between his theory and practice of fiction and those of James:

> [James] spoke of the finished picture and its worth when done; I,
> of the brushes, the palette, and the north light. He uttered his
> views in the tone and for the ear of good society; I, with the
> emphasis and the technicalities of the obtrusive student.[27]

In various weightings of emphasis, however, there was a characteristic degree of conflict or contradiction. Stevenson could exclaim: 'Vital—that's what I am at; first, wholly vital, with a buoyancy of life. The lyrical, if it may be, and picturesque, always with an epic value of scenes, so that the figures remain in the mind's eye forever.' But this claim has to be set alongside the following: 'Unconscious thought, there is the only method ... the will is only to be brought in the field for study and again for revision. The essential part of the work is not an act, it is a state.'[28]

Such complexities and contradictions are reflected in *Weir* in the fluctuating attitude of the narrator to his subject, and in the fluctuating relationship between Stevenson and his narrator. And the source is in the personality and values of the author. His letters record the flux of Stevenson's moods and feelings while he was at work on *Weir*. On 27 December 1893 he wrote: 'I am worked out and can no more at all', while the following day found him rejoicing: 'I have got unexpectedly to work again and feel quite dandy.'[29] The rootlessness and restlessness cannot be explained simply in terms of a reaction against a life of ill-health. They originate in the deeper psychological recesses of Stevenson the man and Stevenson the Scot. Muir noted that the expression on photographs of Stevenson is 'continually on the point of changing ... flying away perhaps to some place so absurdly childish or romantic that even its owner is not quite prepared to countenance it'.[30] Various factors account for this: the expressive energy innate within the older Scottish literary tradition endured but found itself allied uneasily to a rootlessness which the Union fostered; and the need to escape to a fluid world of the imagination is a reaction against the Calvinist legacy. In this context one can appreciate James's comments on Stevenson's 'sort of ironic, desperate gallantry, burning away, with a finer and finer fire', and the 'beautiful golden thread [which] he spins ... in alternate doubt and elation'.[31]

If Stevenson is something of a paradox, it is not just the case, as G. Gregory Smith suggested, that 'his is the paradox of the Scot'[32]: his is the paradox of the Scot as imaginative writer. Scotland, by virtue of both the cultural disorientation which followed the Union and the effects of the Calvinist influence, failed to experience Romantic idealism (or at least Scottish literature failed to reflect any such experience). From the eighteenth century onwards Scottish writers have known and expressed that alienation and that rootlessness which have emerged in European literatures only after the phenomenon of Romantic individualism's turning inward in the face of the pressures of mass society. It is in this respect that Stevenson is an embryo twentieth-century writer.

In a curious way the deleterious effect of Scottish values on Scottish literature (which Muir noted)[33] anticipates, in a specific cultural context, the general crisis of the novel in recent times, wherein the order, configuration, and authority inseparable from the traditional novel are regarded as suspect, since they are so much at variance with the chaotic flux of life. In this light the following comment of Furnas becomes acutely relevant: 'The more that miniature politics apparently distracted [Stevenson], the less sure he grew that art is the supreme human activity, the better he wrote, the more skilfully he sought such compassionate irony as *Hermiston* shows.'[34] As well as being the exponent of such irony, Stevenson is also, unwittingly, its subject.

If, as is often claimed, there is much of Stevenson in Archie, so there is much of him in the narrator of *Weir*. But as Archie is not Stevenson, so the narrator is not Stevenson. The use of the narrative persona in *Weir* represents Stevenson's attempt at self-confrontation and self-objectification. Was it inevitable that it would be less than entirely successful? It would seem so, in that the personalized narrator that Stevenson creates cannot credibly be omniscient; equally the choice of narrative method serves to restrict the role of the author-substitute to that of fallible observer. In *Weir* Stevenson encounters the difficulties which result from the combination of intermittent F.I.S. with personalized narration. F.I.S. is scarcely appropriate to personalized narration: the capacity to use F.I.S. implies considerable authority, if not omniscience, whereas personalization implies the individual view with all its natural limitations. In *Weir* the shifting of focus, the fluctuation between personal impression and authoritative statement, may occasion doubts as to the degree of control exercised by the author over both the intricate and often-ironic shifts of perspective and the concomitant direction of the reader's response.

The problem is largely explicable in terms of the incompatibility of the Calvinist legacy and art (which finds expression in the father–son conflict). In the writing of *Weir* Stevenson seems at last to have purged himself of his need to objectify himself as a limited being (this in itself is a manifestation of the Calvinist influence, and it is reflected in the almost-obsessive need for self-denunciation). Thus the use of F.I.S. in *Weir* reveals, ambivalently, a potential capacity for empathy and a highly reductive view of human limitation. The example of *Weir* shows that Stevenson could not permit the author-substitute to surrender completely the authorial right to authority.

That Stevenson found it impossible to relinquish narratorial authority and delegate it to his characters is more than accidental in the light of the author's own personality, values, and nationality, and the way in which these find expression in *Weir* in a concern with authority and judgement. Roy Pascal has commented that the 'hidden, omniscient narrator is the aesthetic counterpart of a now discredited providential God'.[35] This illuminates very clearly the central problem of Stevenson: Stevenson longed to discredit such a God but found it impossible so to do. Of his works, *Weir* in particular reflects the resultant tension between the impulse towards technical and narratorial experimentation and the awe of authority with which Calvinism endowed him. If *Weir* is an ironic study of human limitation, exemplified by both characters and narrator, perhaps the final irony is that it also demonstrates the extent to which Stevenson's own judgement succumbed (perhaps had to succumb) to racial and cultural pressures.

NOTES

1. 'A Humble Remonstrance', *Memories and Portraits* (London, 1924), Tusitala Edition, Vol. XXIX, p. 136.

2. 'Robert Louis Stevenson', *Edwin Muir: Uncollected Scottish Criticism*, edited and introduced by Andrew Noble (London and Totowa, NJ., 1982), p. 235.

3. 'On Some Technical Elements of Style in Literature', *The Works of Robert Louis Stevenson* (London, 1912), XVI, p. 247.

4. *Henry James and Robert Louis Stevenson: A Record of Friendship and Criticism*, edited with an introduction by Janet Adam Smith (London, 1948), p. 267.

5. *Memories and Portraits*, p. 135.

6. Ibid., p. 142.

7. Cited G. Gregory Smith, *Scottish Literature: Character and Influence* (London, 1919), p. 18.

8. 'A Note on Realism', *Works*, XVI, p. 238.

9. *The Letters of Robert Louis Stevenson*, edited by Sidney Colvin (New York, 1969), II, pp. 216–17.

10. 'Victor Hugo's Romances', *Familiar Studies of Men and Books* (London, 1924), p. 30.

11. Ibid., pp. 35, 48.

12. 'On Some Technical Elements of Style in Literature', *Works*, XVI, p. 245.

13. Percy Lubbock, *The Craft of Fiction* (London, 1921), p. 218.

14. Leslie Fiedler, 'RLS Revisited', *No! In Thunder* (London, 1963), p. 88. J. C. Furnas, *Voyage to Windward: The Life of Robert Louis Stevenson* (New York, 1951), p. 427, also praises the use of 'third-person narration' in *Heathercat and Weir*. In contrast, Kurt Wittig, *The Scottish Tradition in Literature* (Edinburgh, 1978), p. 263, notes that 'though the word "I" occurs rarely, it is told in the first-person singular'.

15. References are to the Everyman edition of *The Master of Ballantrae* and *Weir of Hermiston* (London and New York, 1925), with an introduction by M. R. Ridley.

16. *Familiar Studies*, p. 85.

17. *The House of Fiction: Essays on the Novel by Henry James* edited with an introduction by Leon Edel (London, 1957), pp. 125, 137, 130.

18. Op. cit., p. 429.

19. Hereafter referred to as F.I.S. See Roy Pascal, *The Dual Voice* (Manchester, 1977) for an excellent account of the characteristics and the development of the technique.

20. Cited Pascal, p. 18.

21. Ibid., pp. 79–5.

22. Ibid., p. 22.

23. Ibid., p. 22.

24. Edwin M. Eigner, *Robert Louis Stevenson and Romantic Tradition* (Princeton, 1966), pp. 52, 64.

25. Op. cit., p. 259.

26. Cited Janet Adam Smith, p. 267.

27. 'A Humble Remonstrance', *Memories and Portraits*, p. 141.

28. Cited Janet Adam Smith, pp. 41, 42.

29. Cited Furnas, p. 425.

30. Op. cit., p. 236.

31. Cited Janet Adam Smith, pp. 268, 269.

32. Op. cit., p. 288.

33. Op. cit., p. 229.
34. Op. cit., p. 429.
35. Op. cit., p. 139.

WILLIAM VEEDER

Children of the Night:
Stevenson and Patriarchy

So I sidled up to the old gentleman, got into conversation with him and so with the damsel; and thereupon, having used the patriarch as a ladder, I kicked him down behind me.

—Stevenson

I wonder why my stories are

—Stevenson

The psychoanalytic critic is a literary historian.

—William Kerrigan

My study of *Jekyll and Hyde* began as an attempt to answer two questions. Why are there, for all practical purposes, no women in Stevenson's novella? And why are the major characters, Jekyll, Utterson, and Lanyon, all professional men as well as celibates? These specific questions lead me toward the larger concerns, the enduring power, of *Jekyll and Hyde*. Since defining this power has become my project—in which answering the two questions about gender and profession plays a part—I should begin with what I take to be the overall concern of the novella. *Jekyll and Hyde* dramatizes the inherent weakness of late-Victorian social organization, a weakness that derives from unresolved pre-oedipal and oedipal emotions and that threatens the very possibility of community. Since these emotions

From *Dr. Jekyll and Mr. Hyde: After One Hundred Years*, eds. William Veeder and Gordon Hirsch. © 1988 by the University of Chicago.

appear in Stevenson's life, as well as in his novella and his culture, I will examine all three nodes in my study of the power of *Jekyll and Hyde*.

I will first set forth the social, psychological, and critical elements deployed in this study.

> It seems to me that the story of Jekyll and Hyde, which is presumably presented as happening in London, is all the time very unmistakably happening in Edinburgh. [Chesterton 51]

> The most important focus in the story, as we might expect, will be on Jekyll's attitude toward his double. [Eigner 145]

What these two sensible observations do not account for is what I want to explore. The site of *Jekyll and Hyde* is, I feel, not simply London or Edinburgh but the larger milieu of late-Victorian patriarchy; the focus of the story is less on Jekyll's attitude toward Hyde than on the way that the Jekyll/Hyde relationship is replicated throughout Jekyll's circle. Lanyon, Enfield, and Utterson participate so thoroughly in Jekyll/Hyde that they constitute an emblematic community, a relational network, which reflects— and thus allows us readers a perspective on—the network of male bonds in late-Victorian Britain.[1] This network marks a psychological condition as a cultural phenomenon. The cultural and psychological come together in Stevenson's famous statement of theme: that damned old business of the war in the members" (L2, 323). Because members of the psyche are at war, other members must be—family members, members of society, genital members. The resulting casualty is not simply Jekyll/Hyde but culture itself.

Focusing on society might seem to ally me with the many critics who interpret *Jekyll and Hyde* as an indictment of Victorian repressiveness, a tale of decorum and desire. "[Jekyll's] society ... refuses to recognize or accept the place of pleasure in identity" (Day 92).[2] Repression is indeed important in *Jekyll and Hyde*, but what is being repressed is not *pleasure*. Victorian culture *fosters* as well as represses pleasure in *Jekyll and Hyde*. To call Stevenson's men "joyless" (Miyoshi 471) is to overstate. "All intelligent, respectable men, and all judges of good wine" (43), Utterson and his peers are capable of genuine friendship (the word "friend" appears at least thirty-three times)[3] that expresses itself in "pleasant dinners" (43), particularly those hosted by Henry Jekyll, who entertains "five or six old cronies" early in the story (43), celebrates his return from reclusion by becoming "once more their familiar guest and entertainer" (56), and sees Utterson for the last time at "the doctor's ... small party" on January 8 (56). The pleasure of these gatherings is enhanced by their domestic nature. Rather than entertaining at clubs, old friends invite one another home. Again Jekyll is the model. His entrance hall is called by Utterson "the pleasantest room in London" (41).

Especially considering how much of Robert Louis Stevenson is invested in these companionable pleasures—his love of wine and boon fellowship—why does he include such pleasures in what I will argue is an ultimately damning presentation of Jekyll's circle? He could easily have satirized this group as he did other bourgeois males who "had at first a human air / In coats and flannel underwear. / They rose and walked upon their feet / And filled their bellies full of meat. / They wiped their lips when they had done, / But they were Ogres every one" (Calder 152). Stevenson foregoes so complete an indictment because society is not completely odious, pleasure not entirely interdicted. Of course, Stevenson wishes in his life and in *Jekyll and Hyde* that society were less hypocritical about pleasures natural and healthy, and even pleasures unnatural and unhealthy. But the companionable pleasures in *Jekyll and Hyde* function less by implicit contrast with outré desires than as emblems of promise tragically unfulfilled. Though boon fellowship should combine with public service to constitute the rewards of a professional life, the combination in fact constitutes a threat to society itself.

This threat cannot be explained by an interpretation that locates the novella's paramount tension between decorum and desire. Jekyll himself points to such a tension, and surely it is an awkward one: men who officially embody and articulate orthodoxy incline to violate it. This awkwardness is, however, not sufficient to account for Jekyll's anguish or Stevenson's novella. Established men have long since discovered how to mediate between decorum and desire. The old boys cover for one another. Lanyon will get Jekyll the chemicals regardless of what the night and secrecy may be hiding; Enfield will handle Hyde's trampling of the child without calling in the police. If, however, the repression of *pleasure* is not the principal dilemma in *Jekyll and Hyde*, another sort of repression is at work. Males use traditionally sanctioned social "forms"—friendship and professionalism—to screen subversive drives directed at *one another*. The dual roles of friend and attorney allow Utterson to express his own private anxiety about Jekyll's will; Lanyon uses his professional "services" to excuse his curiosity about Edward Hyde. "Under the seal of our profession" (80) rage what I will argue are the regressive emotions of oedipal sons and sibling rivals.

At stake in *Jekyll and Hyde* is nothing less than patriarchy itself, the social organization whose ideals and customs, transmissions of property and title, and locations of power privilege the male. Understanding the Fathers in *Jekyll and Hyde* is helped by seeing patriarchy both traditionally and locally: first in terms of its age-old obligations, then in terms of its immediate configuration in late-Victorian Britain. Traditionally the obligations of patriarchs are three: to maintain the distinctions (master–servant, proper–improper) that ground patriarchy; to sustain the male ties (father–son, brother–brother) that constitute it; and to enter the wedlock (foregoing homosexuality) that perpetuates it.[4] Exclusion and inclusion are the operative principles. Men must distinguish the patriarchal self from enemies, pretenders, competitors, corruptors; and they must affiliate through proper bonds at appropriate times. What Stevenson devastatingly demonstrates is that patriarchy behaves exactly counter to its obligations. Distinctions that should be maintained are elided, so that bonds occur where divisions should obtain; and affiliations that should be sustained are sundered, so that males war with one another and refuse to wed.[5]

As his love of boon fellowship indicates, Robert Louis Stevenson respects the bonds traditional with patriarchy even as he rages against the failures of patriarchs. He faults established men not only for being Fathers (dictatorial, repressed, hypocritical) but also for *not* being Fathers (rigorous, supportive, procreative). The author who within seven years of *Jekyll and Hyde* ensconced himself firmly, if wryly, as the patriarch of Vailima, who put the Athenaeum on his calling cards and was called by Gosse "the most clubbable of men" (Furnas 99), who quipped sincerely, "Let us hope I shall never be such a cad any more as to be ashamed of being a gentleman" (L2, 131), and who was increasingly moved by Thomas Carlyle ("the old man's style is stronger on me than it ever was" [L2, 28]), this author is finally closer in social vision to Carlyle than to, say, J. S. Mill. Despite fashionable nods to socialism, Stevenson inclines not to a Mill-like reorganization of society but to a Carlylean nostalgia for earlier probities.[6] Stevenson hates for the Fathers to be overbearing, but he hates still more for the Fathers to be weak. He criticizes his own father's presidential address to the Royal Society of Edinburgh for being "so modest as to suggest a whine"; he calls Thomas Stevenson's gloominess "plaguey peevishness"; and he adds, "My Dear Father,—Allow me to say, in a strictly Pickwickian sense, that you are a silly fellow" (L2, 243, 244).

Breakdowns in the three traditional obligations of patriarchy are so important to *Jekyll and Hyde* that I will structure my analysis of the novella in terms of them. But before undertaking that analysis, I must set forth the equally important role of patriarchy as an immediate presence in late-Victorian Britain. In the household of Thomas Stevenson, the patriarchal was inseparable from the professional. Engineering and medicine were, like law, "eminently respectable and had contributed much to Edinburgh's wealth and status" (Calder 2). The emergence of the professions as one of the major forces in social organization had occurred in Stevenson's own century. "Before the Industrial revolution," Larson establishes,

> even the profession of law ... had not yet developed the stable and intimate connection with training and examination that came to be associated with the professional model in the nineteenth century.... Professions are, therefore, relatively recent social products.... In England, of the thirteen contemporary professions ... ten acquired an association of national scope between 1825 and 1880.[7]

Upper-middle-class professional men are for Robert Louis Stevenson the principal expression of the patriarchal tradition in the Victorian period, despite the lingering presence of a landed, titled aristocracy and Stevenson's nostalgia for the gentry Balfours of his mother's line. Patriarchy, as Stevenson considers it, is essentially bourgeois. These men are not the products of ancient families and land tenure. Their bonds are formed through the educational process ("old mates both at school and college" [36]), which prepares men not for the aristocratic pleasures of leisure and sport but for the middle-class ideals of hard work and public service. "Name" is important because it constitutes not continuity of title but hard-earned respect.

As a third-generation professional, Robert Louis Stevenson has a rare perspective on patriarchy. In addition to the Fathers' egregious hypocrisies—leading citizens who go wenching on Saturday night and show up at church hungover provoke Stevenson to rage—there are subtler, finally more threatening disparities between roles and realities. Professions can function as empty forms that Fathers deploy to make sons conform to paternal wills and dreams. Stevenson feels particularly threatened because he is in part recoiling from the impact of professionalism upon his own father who wanted so intensely to place him in engineering or law. Thomas himself was coerced by *his* father into a profession for which he had no special aptitude. He admitted that he never mastered the formulae basic to structural engineering. Despite his dedicated scrutiny of nature, Thomas's mind proceeded by intuitive leaps; his true gifts were, like Louis's, literary and existential. He was a gifted storyteller, a sincere lover of reading, and a man graced with a tremendous if inhibited capacity for sensuous experience. In indicting the professions, Louis is thus doing more than striking back against paternal domination. He is trying to save himself from his father's fate.

The professions have additional moment for Robert Louis Stevenson because they relate to father in a second way. To explain this, I must posit what I will argue for in detail in section 2: Stevenson is, as Kanzer and Fiedler have maintained, a man torn by oedipal emotions. Although such emotions may seem a long way from Stevenson's concern with the professions in late-Victorian Britain, the two relate directly. Freud argues that desire, which is directed toward mother initially and is interdicted at the oedipal moment, can reappear under the pressures of adolescence—in its initial triangular configuration. Mother is again the object of desire, and father again the rival. Now, however, desire can be managed outside strictly domestic confines, in the realm of public action and career choice. (Work is the one outlet of human energy that Freud ranks along with sex.) Father–son quarrels over careers are thus often restagings of childhood antagonisms. Even a biographer as wary of Freudianism as Furnas attests that Louis's famous battles with Thomas over profession (and religion) are inseparable from the men's fierce possessiveness toward Margaret. In turn, a resolution of oedipal antagonisms through professional achievement becomes possible. The very fact that the Fathers' professional inadequacies are so present to Stevenson means that he is characterized by an adult awareness denied to patriarchs hypocritical or complacent. If Louis can go on to express this awareness in fiction, if he can indict fathers as Fathers by revealing the inadequacy of their professionalism, he will write the book that constitutes him professionally. By revealing in the fathers an unresolved oedipal rage that he himself is resolving in the revelation, Stevenson will extend the old war among the members from the domestic to the professional front and will thus have a chance for victory. But things, alas, are not this simple.

For one thing, awareness of patriarchal failure threatens the son. If he cannot respect the father's masculinity and achievement, the son cannot negotiate either the pre- or the post-latency stages of oedipal conflict; he cannot effect that bonding with the father that will confirm his own sense of sexual adequacy and will encourage him to contribute to society's welfare. Worse still, Stevenson knows that most of his indictment of patriarchal inadequacy can be turned back on himself. Not only is he too racked by unresolved oedipal rages, but he has not achieved by 1885 what he respects professionally—the writing of great books, which alone, despite the puffs of his friends, constitutes true professionalism in letters. Even hypocrisy can also be charged against Stevenson, too. His terrible quarrels with Thomas do not prevent him from continuing to accept his father's money.

Another problem for Louis is that fighting on two fronts—the professional as well as the domestic—has not shaped his art up through the middle of 1885. He has tended to configure himself as only, as still, a son. Besides the *Garden of Verses*, there is "Markheim," where the "war in the members" ends with the son surrendering to the (bad) father. *Jekyll and Hyde* was apparently conceived in the same spirit, but, quite astonishingly, Stevenson effects—between the Notebook Draft and the Printer's Copy—a change that enables him to fight both the domestic and the professional wars in his life. Discussing the novella's genesis, Stevenson lists first among the incorporated dream episodes "the scene at the window" ("A Chapter on Dreams"). Killing, in other words. Who is killing whom? In the Notebook Draft, Hyde's victim is "Lemsome." Lemsome incorporates Stevenson's worst fears about himself as a weak, grown-up son. "A youngish man of about twenty-eight, with a fine forehead and good features; anoemically pale; shielding a pair of suffering eyes under blue spectacles," Lemsome is called "an incurable cad" by the young author whom we have seen promise never to be "a cad any more." In killing Lemsome/Stevenson, Hyde/Stevenson is only visiting once more upon himself the anger that psychic health and maturity require him to direct outward at the fathers. By belaboring himself as failed son, Louis remains a failure; by not waiting for confrontation with the father, he precludes a therapeutic working through of oedipal emotions; by not directing anger at a patriarch, he prevents his feelings about professionalism from becoming central.

Stevenson escapes sonship by changing the character of Hyde's victim. Lemsome, the paradigm failed son of the Notebook Draft, becomes in the Printer's Copy the paradigm patriarch, Sir Danvers Carew. Carew, the only "Sir" in a novel filled with "sir"s, is essentially bourgeois: he is affiliated with the House of Commons, not the House of Lords; he lives in a London square, not a country house. Killing Carew means that Stevenson's self-hate is turned outward in an act of violence therapeutic both domestically and professionally. Carew is both a father surrogate and a Father. Since Carew as "an aged beautiful gentleman with white hair" (46) can stand in for the aging but still strikingly handsome Thomas Stevenson, Louis can deploy literary patricide to murder his "father" rather than himself. He can, moreover, enlist Carew in the other war in his life—the professional. Carew points Stevenson's rage toward the Fathers as well as toward father. Lemsome, whose suit "implied both a lack of means and a defect of taste," is "a bad fellow" of the lower middle class, whereas Carew is a distinguished man who contributes the professional initials "M.P." (53) to the long list set forth with Jekyll: "M.D., D.C.L., LL.D., F.R.S., &c." (35). Carew focuses Stevenson's rage at the patriarchs as professionals.

Stevenson's capacity to see what the fathers overlook and to announce what they hide does not, of course, result in any overnight change in him psychologically. But *Jekyll and Hyde* does constitute a milestone. The novella brings professional presence to Stevenson for the first time. The fame and the revenue that he needs so desperately begin to flow in, and they remain with him until death. He can, in turn, especially after the death of his father ("I almost begin to feel as if I should care to live; I would, by God! and so I begin to believe I shall" [Furnas 263]), take a less hostile stance against the patriarchy, a stance more in keeping with his essentially conservative nature. What happens is not that Stevenson comes to countenance all that he had once indicted in contemporary professionalism. Rather, with the passing years and increasing successes, Stevenson, like Carlyle, exercises a nostalgic return to an earlier, more feudal type of patriarchy that, in Louis's case, can mediate between the rigorous professionalism of the Stevensons and his historical fascination with the Balfours. I agree with Harvie that "we must see *Weir of Hermiston* ... as a conservative parable of law and duty.... Weir towers over every other character in the book.... Climbing 'the great staircase of his duty' he, in a social context, is a figure ... powerfully and sympathetically symbolic" (122, 123). Harvie is equally persuasive when he finds in Stevenson's own life a comparable move to nostalgic patriarchy. "Ultimately Stevenson's political creed is authoritarian but—unlike Kipling's—feudal and familial rather than technocratic. *Weir* is an image of the power of the legal system which underlay the Scots enlightenment, yet which was drawn from a pre-existent social state not unlike that which Stevenson himself tried to recreate in Samoa: a charismatic authority now being sapped by imperialist bureaucrats as much as by socialistic bureaucrats at home" (124).

Stevenson's involvement in *Jekyll and Hyde* means that the very psyche I am examining is not easy to define. On the one hand, the childhood into which the patriarchs of the novella regress can be seen as ultimately Stevenson's own. The "brown" fog that enwraps Utterson's world (48) is the farthest emanation of Louis's terrors, which emerged first as a childhood nightmare about the color brown, then reemerged as a boyhood nightmare about a brown dog, and eventually shaped itself into the Brownies who personified for him the unconscious processes themselves.[8] Likewise, the nighttime in which every violent event of *Jekyll and Hyde* occurs is a protraction of the long nights of fear that Louis endured as a sickly boy. "All night long in the dark and wet, / A man goes riding by. / Late in the night when the fires are out, / Why does he gallop and gallop about?" ("Windy Nights," 3–6).

On the other hand, my title for this essay is *children* of the night, not *child*, because *Jekyll and Hyde* cannot be reduced to the life of Robert Louis

Stevenson. He transforms biographical materials and emotions into a critical portrait of his times. He does so not by attempting a "realistic" fiction but by representing male anxiety itself. "Characters" are the *occasion* of this revelation. They act out patterns rather than express personal histories. They cannot be psychoanalyzed, but their actions can. My approach to the psyches of Stevenson's characters is basically through the insights of Stevenson's contemporary, Sigmund Freud.

Not only are Freud and Stevenson both products of late-nineteenth-century European culture; they share the more particular fact of personal concern with and anxiety about professionalism, fathers, and Fathers. Still more important, they envision the psyche, experience, and art as each multileveled and occlusive. "After all, what one wants to know is not what people did, but why they did it—or rather, why they *thought* they did it." This fascination with the workings of the psyche is eminently characteristic of Freud, but the words here are Stevenson's (L1, 35). Equally Freudian is Stevenson's insistence that "everything is true; only the opposite is true too: you *must believe both equally or be damned*" (Furnas 412). This recognition of experience as self-contradictory attunes Stevenson to the self-deceptive workings of the psyche in others and in himself.

> You [Henley] were not quite sincere with yourself; you were seeking arguments to make me devote myself to plays, unbeknown, of course, to yourself. [L1, 304]

> [I am a person who is] a hater, indeed, of rudeness in others, but too often rude in all unconsciousness himself.... we [he and Fanny] had a dreadful over-hauling of my conduct as a son the other night; and my wife stripped me of my illusions and made me admit I had been a detestable bad one. [L2, 275, 295

Stevenson sees art itself deriving from the same hidden sources of meaning and motive. *Jekyll and Hyde* "came out of a deep mine" (L2, 309). Stevenson's definition of art constitutes a Freudian challenge. "There is but one art—to omit" (L1, 173).

Jekyll and Hyde represents psychological experiences multilayered and repressed, and I will read it accordingly. As Dr. Jekyll hides beneath his distinguished professionalism the murderous Mr. Hyde, so the name "Jekyll" hides—as several critics have noted—the homicidal "je kyll."[9] Other names in the story work the same way. Dr. Lanyon, who dies because his professional judgment succumbs to his precipitate curiosity, is named

"Hastie"; Utterson, despite his years of dour legalism, is the utter son in several senses, as I will show later. Names, in turn, are emblematic of the multilayered workings of virtually every feature of *Jekyll and Hyde*. In terms of plot: as we wonder what Hyde is doing on his late-night excursions, we wonder why Carew is mailing a letter (47) late at night in what may be an unsavory neighborhood down by the river (46). In terms of characterization: as we are unsatisfied by Jekyll's rationalization of his desire for the potion, we question whether Utterson's concern for Jekyll's safety accounts adequately for his obsession with Edward Hyde. In terms of setting: as we experience the horrific last hour of Jekyll/Hyde, we ask why the laboratory is presented as so benignly domestic. And, emblem of all these emblems, why is Jekyll's chemist named, "Maw"?

In attempting to answer these and many other questions about the overdetermined narrative of *Jekyll and Hyde*, I make no claim that Robert Louis Stevenson is conscious of all their significances. Obviously he is not. What I do claim is that diverse elements coherently support Stevenson's thoroughly conscious indictment of late-Victorian patriarchy. The overdetermined nature of this indictment requires a comparable intricacy of response from readers. I see male emotions ranging from friendship to rivalry to homoerotic desire to homicidal rage; individual characters enact various roles, with Jekyll, for example; functioning as model bourgeois and oedipal son and oedipal father and sibling rival and homosexual lover; scenes are shaped by diverse forces, from the biographical, to the contexts of Western patriarchy and its late-Victorian manifestations, to patterns of consciousness based on Freudian models which help illuminate both the traditional and the immediate dilemmas of patriarchal culture.

My historical interest is where I want to end this introduction, because such an interest helps emphasize a fact about *Jekyll and Hyde* that has remained largely unrecognized by critics. Stevenson's novella expresses the malaise of late-Victorian Britain. Stevenson shares the belief of his apparently more representative colleagues—Gissing, Moore, James, Hardy—that Mrs. Grundy and Mr. Mudie must be extirpated and that British fiction must become an adult representation of adult realities. (This revulsion at hypocrisy is part of what Stevenson's biographers have repeatedly pointed to—his participation in his generation's disaffiliation from organized religion and enthusiasm for Darwin and other secular thinkers.) What makes *Jekyll and Hyde* particularly late-Victorian becomes clear in light of the novella's most relevant High Victorian predecessors, the paradigm novels of oedipal conflict—*David Copperfield*, *Great Expectations*, and *The Ordeal of Richard Feverel*. Dickens and Meredith here focus on the son and present the professional characters as largely incidental. By focusing on patriarchy and professionalism, Stevenson is reflecting the widely recognized "autumnal" quality of late-Victorian life, the sense that something was the matter not simply at home but in society itself. Oedipal antagonism functions in Stevenson not as the private drama of Pip and Richard Feverel but as the latent cause of cultural decline.

I. PROPER DISTINCTIONS AND ILLICIT ELISIONS

My analysis of Stevenson's patriarchs is structured in terms of their traditional obligations. Studying "proper" distinctions and male ties will bring me to wedlock, and thus to the causes and the consequences of woman's exclusion from *Jekyll and Hyde*. Making distinctions presupposes recognizing similarities. "I see you feel as I do," Enfield's words to Utterson after Hyde's first outrage (32), echo Enfield's earlier empathy with the doctor at the scene of the outrage. "He was like the rest of us.... I knew what was in his mind" (31). Utterson is comparably bound to Poole during Hyde's subsequent atrocities. "I felt something of what you describe" (68), the lawyer admits, after the two men have turned "both pale ... [with] an answering horror in their eyes" (61) and before "the two men looked at each other with a scare" (71). Such ideal solidarity between patriarchs and servants and among patriarchs is the context for distinctions that damn outsiders. The chief object of exclusion is of course Edward Hyde, whose absolute disjunction is insisted on by terms drawn from religion ("Satan ... devilish ... child of Hell ... Evil" [32, 36, 94, 68]), from zoology ("like a monkey ... ape-like" [69, 101]), and from mythology ("Juggernaut ... fiend ... troglodytic" [31, 36, 40]). These exclusionary terms express the patriarchy's need to confirm Hyde as a usurper. Utterson's fear that Hyde would "step into the said Henry Jekyll's shoes" (35) seems allayed by Lanyon's description of Hyde's "laughable" appearance. "His clothes ... although they were of rich and sober fabric, were enormously too large for him in every measurement" (77–78). Here is a patent pretender to a position that he literally cannot treasure up to.

Or so the patriarchs want to believe. To establish that traditional distinctions are breaking down in late-Victorian society, *Jekyll and Hyde* dramatizes the thorough implication of patriarchy in Edward Hyde. A wonderful pun bonds Lanyon with Hyde when the doctor is called "hide-hound ... hide-hound" (43). The cane that Hyde uses to kill Carew belongs ultimately to Utterson; the name that replaces Hyde's in the will of Jekyll is Utterson's own; and the expression that seems to confirm Hyde's alterity—

"the other" (40)—is soon applied to Utterson (41). Enfield shares Hyde's propensity for night stalking and for bringing along a cane (in the context of Cain [29, 30]). Hyde's caning of Carew has no counterpart in Enfield's conduct, of course,[10] but in his role as narrator, Enfield reveals a complicity in Hyde's first act of night violence that colors the scene significantly and thus warrants our close attention.

Take, for example, the epithets which Enfield applies to the child trampler. "My gentleman ... my gentleman ... my prisoner ... gentleman ... my man" (31, 32, 33). Even allowing both for the slightly more formal British usage of "my" in such expressions and for a touch of irony in Enfield's tone, these phrases certainly involve him more personally with Hyde than judgmental phrases like "this monster ... this demon ... this blackguard ... this beast" would have. Especially cued by "gentleman," we recognize in the outcome of the confrontation something closer to gentlemanly fellowship than we would expect. "So we all set off, the doctor and the child's father, and our friend and myself, and passed the rest of the night in my chambers; and next day, when we had breakfasted, went in a body to the bank" (32). How odd the interpolated—and thus ostensibly unnecessary—clause "when we had breakfasted." There is a civility, an instinct for form, that seems out of place if Hyde is really a fiend or troglodyte or ape. That "we all set off" is, moreover, inaccurate. All the women who partook so vigorously in the confrontation with Hyde are left behind. Of course, ladies could not enter a bachelor's flat at 4:00 A.M., but propriety is not the chief issue. Exclusion from Enfield's sentence and from the narrative's subsequent events occurs because "we" simply cannot mean "all." In Enfield's world, "we all" are all male. The old boys "in a body" exclude anybody else. Notice that the "all" includes the physician. Someone on this night was so ill that a doctor had to be called at 3:00 A.M., yet that doctor leaves the scene without ever seeing his patient. For the first of many times in *Jekyll and Hyde*, professionalism functions as a screen. The physician's night journey toward the patient has led to a very different goal—the presence of Hyde and the chambers of Enfield. "Chamber," which has already meant legal chambers in the novella (29), has its more private connotation here because the patriarchs will resolve this awkward matter privately. Even the law is an outsider when it does not foster the more absolute force of patriarchal will.

Exculpation of Hyde has marked Enfield's narration from the start. Though he expresses sincere outrage at Hyde behaving "like some damned Juggernaut" (31), Enfield makes our crucial first experience of Hyde quite benign. "I saw two figures; one a little man who was stumping along eastward at a good walk, and the other a girl of maybe eight or ten who was running as hard as she was able" (31). Note that "the other" here is not Hyde. "Little ... stumping along ... good walk" present him quite innocuously, whereas the other is the violent one running hard. We are then told that the two collided "naturally enough" (31). Why "naturally"? Since the streets have been established as absolutely quiet at 3:00 A.M., why didn't Hyde hear the furiously clattering feet of the girl and avoid her? Our suspicion is soon confirmed. "The rumour of the approach of any passenger preceded him by a longtime .... the footfalls of a single person, while he is still a great way off, suddenly spring out distinct from the vast hunt and clatter of the city" (38). Hyde's collision with the child is not inevitable, so why does an inveterate nightwalker like Enfield call it natural? At best, Hyde is socially insouciant if he is too preoccupied to hear the child's ringing footfall. At worst, Hyde did hear her coming, and collided with her intentionally. Either possibility is glossed over by Enfield's word "naturally."

Even with the aftermath of Hyde's outrage, Enfield reacts less wholeheartedly than his most indignant statements would warrant. He seems initially to respond like St. George when his fox-hunting expression "I gave a view hallow" (31) suggests he will run the malefactor to earth. Though he does indeed catch and collar Hyde, Enfield describes the pursuit with the idiom "I ... took to my heels" (31). He says, in other words, that he fled from, not after, Hyde. (The meaning "to flee from" is confirmed not only by the OED[11] but by Hyde himself, who apologizes to Lanyon with the words "my impatience has shown its heels to my politeness" [78]). An unconscious inclination to free Hyde, as well as the conscious determination to capture him, marks the patriarchy's uncomfortable implication in what it officially condemns. Enfield may call Hyde "a fellow that nobody would have to do with" (33), but he himself has already called Hyde "our friend" (32). The ironical edge to this expression in this context does not mitigate entirely the patriarchy's investment in the expression. Rather than nobody having anything to do with Hyde, everybody who counts has already had breakfast with him.

Hyde's stalking the London streets at 3:00 A.M. shows him up to no good, but Enfield is out at the same hour. What has *he* been doing? As a "well-known man about town" (29), Enfield explains himself with the glib "I was coming home from some place at the end of the world" (31). The name En(d)-field suggests that the patriarch is as much an extremist as the juggernaut. I even find myself wondering about that other nightwalker whom Hyde encounters, Sir Danvers Carew. What is he doing out? The official version is that he was "only inquiring his way.... he had been probably carrying [a letter] to the post" (46, 47). But I wonder. How could Carew not know his way to the mailbox if he were simply stepping out of his house to post a letter? Moreover, are we sure that Carew lives in this neighborhood? "Not far from the river" (46) could be a respectable place like Pimlico or Chelsea, but it could also be the rundown and dangerous docksides of Dickens, especially since a servant maid can apparently rent a whole house here (46).[12] And why does Carew carry no identification? Established men who leave their wallets behind but take their money and wander riverfront areas and engage young men in conversation—such men are recognizable types, particularly in light both of the prostitute who approaches Hyde at about the same hour (94) and of the verb "accosted" ("the old man bowed and accosted the other" [46]), which can mean "to solicit for immoral purposes." My point is not that Carew is such a man, but that Stevenson need not have set the situation up this way if he did not want to suggest the possibility of Carew's implication in Hyde. Stevenson need only establish unambiguously that Carew was mailing a letter at a postbox in his own square, that the servant maid was looking from her attic room in her master's own house, and that Hyde was trespassing into the neighborhood removed safely from Soho. The sheep would be distinct from the wolves. Instead, "man about town" is a term appropriate to Hyde and to Enfield and Carew. What all these men are "about" is unclear.

Distinctions blur so thoroughly that even an admirable servant of the patriarchy like Poole is implicated in Hyde. Poole speaks to Utterson "hoarsely" in a "broken" voice (62, 63), just as Hyde has addressed Utterson "hoarsely .... with a somewhat broken voice" (39, 40). What we take to be a sign of venality in Hyde—that he "did not look the lawyer in the face" (39) during their meeting in the bystreet—recurs with Poole who "had not once looked the lawyer in the face" (62) during their meeting in Utterson's home. Hyde's gesture of "stamping with his foot" (47) before Carew's murder is repeated by Poole who "stamped on the flags" (70) after Hyde's death. These associations of Poole with Hyde do not call seriously into question the servant's probity (context distinguishes each of his actions from Hyde's), but they do suggest that any male associated with patriarchy harbors a capacity for otherness.

Poole in this regard is aptly named. Watery depths belie the apparently taut surface of patriarchy. That Jekyll "is in deep waters" is recognized by Utterson (41), but the lawyer cannot see that the rest of the patriarchy is swamped, too. "The drowned city" of London (53) is their foggy common ground. Utterson and Poole entering "the deep well" of Jekyll's courtyard as "the scud had banked over the moon" (68) are in over their heads. They feel safer when they reach "the shelter of the theatre," but they cannot escape the depths simply by exchanging inside for outside. "Even in the houses the fog had begun to lie thickly" (51). Distinctions dissolve. Beneath the theater's "foggy cupola" (33), Utterson is particularly at risk because this realm that seems so ostensibly other is in fact close to home. The theater is called "gaunt" (51), the lawyer lives on "Gaunt Street" (39). Thus his home, which seemed safely apart from the scientific theater, is in fact associated with it. The reassuring distinctions and resolute differentiations essential to Utterson's repression of otherness are dissolved by the elision of inner and outer. All the world becomes a stage, as the drama of the unconscious is enacted in the "anatomical theatre" (88). Utterson, "though he enjoyed the theatre, had not crossed the doors of one for twenty years" (29). Nor does he realize that he has done so when he visits the anatomical theater for "the first time" (51). What Utterson has done is to bring together aspects of his life and personality carefully segregated and repressed. He has moved back through time, not only to his theater days but, since the anatomical theater is in effect a classroom, to his school days. What he will learn about now is body, the gross anatomy precluded by his celibate life. What he will be subjected to, what he will have an opportunity to learn (at last) about, is the animal in Jekyll and in all patriarchs, the Hyde in the doctor's laboratory. Whether Utterson—and Lanyon, who is "theatrical" (36)—will indeed learn from the opportunity is a question that cannot be answered until the end of Stevenson's novella.

What can be established now is that the blurring of distinctions extends outward to involve professionalism itself. Medicine and pharmacology, which seem so oriented to the cerebral and rational, are in fact a springboard into humanity's common pool of the unconscious. "Watery green" (79) is the ultimate color of Jekyll's potion because a sea change rife and strange has occurred within him. The watery potion is his "sea of liberty" (86). When he enters this realm, "a current of disordered sensual images running like a millrace" in his fancy carries Jekyll to "freedom of the soul" (83). The resulting "solution of the bonds of obligation" (83) indicates how the unconscious threatens all distinctions. "Solution," especially in the rationalist context of lawyers and doctors, suggests conscious cerebration with its chains of logical thinking; but in the watery pool of the unconscious, "solution" means the opposite. It means dissolution, and indicates the dissolute.

The underwater realm beneath the theater's cupola is in effect this watery green potion of Jekyll. Everyone swims in the same fantasy, because everyone shares the same unconscious. Merging or dissolving of oppositions characterizes all of befogged London, where "nine in the morning" can resemble "twilight" (48), where "this mournful reinvasion of darkness" inverts our most basic categories so that daytime London becomes "some city in a nightmare." The dissolution of distinctions in the solution of the unconscious finds its ultimate emblem in the home of Henry Jekyll. Critics have noted how the very different faces of the house—patrician entrance hall and ratty back door—reflect Jekyll's two roles of patriarch and nightstalker. As these are the two roles of one man, however, Stevenson cannot allow even an architectural dichotomy to remain intact. Front and back, which seem so different, are also alike. The entrance hall and the laboratory each features oak presses (41, 70); the presses in the hall are called by the name applied to the lab, "cabinet" (41); and the flooring at both ends of the house is flagstone (41, 71).

The impossibility of keeping the laboratory's antisocial experiments distinct from the foyer's hospitable welcome is emphasized by another feature of Jekyll's house. The "anatomical theatre" (88) is also known as "old Dr. Denman's surgical theatre" (76). Denman is the primal father, the absent origin.[13] Henry Jekyll may not seem to derive from him, Jekyll's "tastes being rather chemical than anatomical" (51). But the very word that jekyll applies to his laboratory, "cabinet," can mean "a den of a beast" (Jefford 69). That Jekyll's chemical tastes liberate Hyde's animality (beast as ape, den man as troglodyte) is revelatory not only of the doctor and the patriarchy but of late-Victorian society as well. In this period arise the sciences of anthropology and psychology. Darwin's tracing of human anatomy back to animal origins is complemented by anthropological and psychological attributions of social practices and emotional states to comparably archaic sources. The den is the origin of society.

Not only does patriarchal man derive from the den man, but patriarchy in its late-Victorian manifestation derives expressly from Denman. Dr. Jekyll inhabits the older doctor's house. Patrilineal succession—in keeping with Stevenson's view of the essentially bourgeois character of patriarchy in the nineteenth century—is not hereditary. It is professional. Jekyll effects succession through purchase rather than primogeniture, establishing a continuity of disciplines rather than of blood. As the professional son of Denman, Jekyll is the immediate heir to the primal den. Denman's "theatre" is also called "the dissecting rooms" (51) because what Stevenson dissects is the archaic nature of the life transferred from every father to every child, our residual savagery. The patricidal and fraternal rage that I will argue for in *Jekyll and Hyde* find their origin here. Freud posited the origin of civilization in the sons' slaughter of the father and their subsequent slaughter of themselves. Only then was the father exhumed as law and incorporated as conscience. And only *then* was patriarchy possible. Stevenson might subscribe to some such myth about the origins of society, but he would stress how inadequate conscience, patriarchal laws, and professional etiquette are in controlling the deepest antagonisms still raging in all us children of the night.

II. MALE TIES AND MEMBERS' WARS

The men of *Jekyll and Hyde* do not recognize the blurring of distinctions that implicates them in the other and that constitutes the general context of their lives. We readers are thus in a position of relative superiority to Jekyll's circle. What we see in particular is that the patriarchy's unconscious participation in Hyde threatens society itself because rage is directed not outward—through, say, imperialistic ventures—but back into communal life. In turn, communal safeguards, especially professionalism and friendship, function not to channel and contain but to screen and foster these destructive emotions. Males who should bond with fathers and brothers participate unconsciously in the oedipal anger and the sibling rivalry enacted by Edward Hyde. It is in light of the failure of male bonds that I will interpret the patriarchs' failure to marry—and thus the absence of women—in section 3.

Oedipal conflict and sibling rivalry are not obvious on the plot level of *Jekyll and Hyde*, where no fathers or brothers appear. Nor have scholars tended to see the novella in these terms.[14] Focusing first on the oedipal, I will begin with two passages that seem to me central to Stevenson's view of parent–child relations.

> Today in Glasgow my father went off on some business, and my mother and I wandered about for two hours. We had lunch together, and were very merry over what people at the restaurant would think of us—mother and son they could not have supposed us to be. [L1, 76]

> [Aboard a steamer] mine eye lighted on two girls, one of whom was sweet and pretty, talking to an old gentleman.... So I sidled up to the old gentleman, got into conversation with him and so with the damsel; and thereupon, having used the patriarch as a ladder, I kicked him down behind me. [L1, 30]

Louis is thus capable of seeing mother as object of desire, and of imagining himself dispatching a rival "patriarch." Desire proclaims itself in the Dedication to *A Child's Garden of Verses*, where Louis's beloved nurse,

Cummy, is called "my second mother, my first wife." Rivalry with older men appears also in print, as Stevenson recounts (in the third person) his dream

> of the son of a very rich and wicked man, the owner of broad acres and the most damnable temper. The dreamer (and that was the son) had lived much abroad, on purpose to avoid his parent; and when at length he returned to England, it was to find him married again to a young wife, who was supposed to have suffered cruelly and to loathe her yoke.... Meet they [father and son] did accordingly.... they quarrelled, and the son, stung by some intolerable insult, struck down the father dead. No suspicion was aroused; the dead man was found and buried, and the dreamer succeeding to the broad estates, and found himself installed under the same roof with the father's widow, for whom no provision had been made. ("A Chapter on Dreams")

Homicidal antagonism cannot be contained within the dream world or the essay's pages. Louis and Thomas Stevenson depict hostility in shockingly lethal terms. Thomas, who informs Louis that "you have rendered my whole life a failure.... I would ten times sooner see you lying in your grave than that you should be shaking the faith of other young men" (Furnas 66; Calder 69), goes on to lament to Margaret, "I see nothing but destruction to himself— as well as to us .... Is it fair that we should be half murdered by his conduct?" (Calder 134). Louis reciprocates. "I say, my dear friend [Fanny Sitwell], I am killing my father—he told me tonight (by the way) that I have alienated utterly my mother" (L1, 80). The last half of this sentence is as important as the first. Killing the father is counterproductive because the more the son fights for mother, the more she sides against him. Louis recognizes both the inevitability of father–son conflict ("a first child is a rival," he tells Gosse [L1, 277]) and the inevitable defeat of children of happy marriages. "The children of lovers are orphans," he says sadly enough (Calder 21).

What seems to me most telling about Louis's recognition of his inevitable defeat is that the recognition makes no difference—and that he knows this. Louis persists in the damned old war among the family members regardless of its outcome. Compulsion, the repeatedly repressed but inexorable recurrence of desire, is what oedipal conflict teaches him about the human psyche. Guilt and shame and resignation and love for the father whose love for him Louis never seriously doubted: all these forces cannot keep back an antagonism that surfaces in ways as diverse as the surfacings of oedipal rage in *Jekyll and Hyde*. For example, unable to appropriate Thomas's woman, Louis shifts to the professional level and takes what he can get. Editing his father's presidential address to the Royal Society of Edinburgh leaves Louis "feeling quite proud of the paper, as if it had been mine" (L2, 263). At other times, Louis uses the profession of writer to appropriate the father figure himself, turning the patriarch into the son whom Louis can then dominate. "When I have beaten Burns, I am driven at once, by my parental feelings, to console him with a sugar plum" (L1, 274).

To assume professionally the role of adult is more difficult for Stevenson in his fiction and poetry before *Jekyll and Hyde*. The patricidal protagonist of "Markheim" cannot escape sonship. And in the *Garden of Verses*, desire and antagonism are expressed through a persona perennially filial.

> We built a ship upon the stairs
> All made of back-bedroom chairs,
> And filled it full of sofa pillows
> To go a-sailing on the billows.
> ....
> We sailed along for days and days,
> And had the very best of plays;
>
> But Tom fell out and hurt his knee,
> So there was no one left but me.
> ["A Good Play" 1–4, 11–14]¹⁵

The poet with the father named Tom can throw his rival out, but he knows that isolation, not mother, is the reward. Is she in the *front* bedroom, the master('s) bedroom, where the real father sails real billows on softer pillows?

> And my papa's a banker and as rich as he can be;
> But I, when I am stronger and can choose what I'm to do,
> O Leerie, I'll go round at night and light lamps with you!
> ["The Lamplighter" 6–8]

> For though father denies it, I'm sure it [a stone] is gold.

> But of all my treasures the last is the king.
> There's very few children possess such a thing;
> And that is a chisel, both handle and blade,
> Which a man who is really a carpenter made.
> ["My Treasures" 12–16]

Wealth, the ultimate source of power in bourgeois patriarchy, is what the father as banker possesses and what the father as debunker of the stone denies to his son. In both cases the son rebels not by taking wealth directly from the father (such an emasculation would be too daunting) but by discovering alternative, superior values. "When I am stronger" means on the manifest level "stronger than I am now," but it suggests "stronger than father." Meanwhile, the son must be satisfied with Family Romance. Father is replaced by "real" men who do things rather than simply possess or debunk. The lamplighter illuminates for the boy the night where the father has hitherto held sway; the carpenter provides for the boy the tool to penetrate what has hitherto been barred. Reversed here is the usual pattern of the Family Romance where the child fantasizes moving up the social scale (my real parents are the King and Queen). Stevenson as upper-middle-class son envisions a move down to proletarian surrogates who (like D. H. Lawrence's gamekeepers) are capable of genuine puissance. The profession of the father is associated with impotence by the son who aspires to but obviously has not yet achieved professional status himself.

In both poems, the poet who is speaking through the boy has a wry distance that he shares with the adult reader. We know that the stone is not gold, that the boy will not become a lamplighter. This adult perspective could lead to what I defined in my introduction as essential to professional maturation for Stevenson: a comparable realization of the persistence and consequences of unresolved oedipal emotions in adult life. Wryness does not function this way in the *Garden*, however. Distancing effects proximity. As the verses are less about childhood than about an adult musing on childhood, so wryness acts to reinforce the fiction of our superiority to "childish" perceptions. Stevenson and we can then reexperience "childhood" realities. By indulging both in the desire/rage of oedipal emotions and in the guilt consequent on them, Stevenson allows himself and his readers to remain in thrall to the immaturity that we do not really want to escape.

Such regressiveness is not entirely harmful for Stevenson, however. His very sense that his regressive inclinations are shared by his adult readers means he has a critical perspective on adulthood as well as on childhood. He has defined the basic fact upon which Freud founded psychoanalysis—that adult difficulties derive from childhood traumas. Stevenson told William Archer: "The house [of life] is, indeed, a great thing, and should be rearranged on sanitary principles; but my heart and all my interest are with the dweller, that ancient of days and day-old infant man" (L2, 294). To dwell on this dweller is what Stevenson must do after the *Garden* and "Markheim." He must avoid self-defeating self-indulgence and must present the regressive desires of adulthood in terms of their deleterious consequences for society and self.

Oedipal rage seethes beneath the professional surface of *Jekyll and Hyde*. I will first discuss Henry Jekyll and the way Hyde expresses his pre- and postlatency rage against two "father"s—Carew and Lanyon. I will then show how Jekyll's anger is replicated throughout patriarchy, in the persons of Richard Enfield and Gabriel John Utterson.

When Henry Jekyll says of his first drinking of the potion, "that night I had come to the fatal crossroads" (85), he is saying more than that he had crossed the Rubicon. Readers who hear echoes of Oedipus's famous crossroads here can find confirmation throughout *Jekyll and Hyde*. "Hence the apelike tricks he [Hyde] would play on me ... burning the letters and destroying the portrait of my father" (96). Like so many statements by patriarchs in the novella, this one implies a strong disjunction—*he* ruined *my* father's portrait. In fact, Hyde is expressing Jekyll. As a "child of Hell" (94), Hyde is not only hellish but childish.

> I was the first that could plod in the public eye with a load of genial respectability, and in a moment, like a schoolboy, strip off these lendings and spring headlong into the sea of liberty. [86]

Jekyll intends his metaphor to express liberation into a freer future, but "like a schoolboy" confirms the regressive nature of his transformation into Hyde. Hyde's physical littleness ("little" is the first adjective applied to him [30]) serves in part to indicate immaturity. His "little room in Soho" (87) suggests a nursery, especially in contrast with the "tall proportions" of Jekyll's "[bed]room in the square" (87). Hyde's ludicrous appearance in Jekyll's too-large suit suggests a little boy dressing up in daddy's clothes. And so, when we read that "Jekyll had more than a father's interest; Hyde had more than a son's indifference" (89), we can interpret the "more"s as Jekyll cannot. Hyde has more than a son's indifference because he has a son's rage; Jekyll has more than a father's interest because he has a son's interest. As oedipal conflict appears first in childhood and then reappears after latency, Jekyll's oedipal conflicts are dramatized in two successive events separated by an interval of quiescence. Regressive rage erupts when Hyde "in no more reasonable spirit than that in which a sick child may break a plaything" (90) kills Sir Danvers Carew; this rage, recathected in postlatency terms of professionalism and friendship, then strikes down Dr. Lanyon.

Carew is, as we have seen, a model patriarch who radiates "an innocent and old-world kindness of disposition" (46). What fiend could kill so exemplary a gentleman? "There is of course no motive," Jefford maintains (70–71). Since every act is motivated, the apparent absence of provocation by Carew and the patent excessiveness of Hyde's reaction encourage us to look to the unconscious. What we see is a dramatization of the son's psyche, a playing out of oedipal, patricidal fantasy. Though "madman" and "ape-like" are applied to Hyde (47), these conventional explanations mask the true nature of a rage articulated initially by "stamping with his foot" (47). This is a gesture of petulant immaturity. In this context, Carew's exemplary nature marks him as the enemy whose slightest provocation will set Hyde off. And provocations do appear amid Carew's politenesses. Compare Stevenson's presentation of the men meeting—"the older man bowed and accosted the other" (46)—and an alternative version. "The older man bowed and greeted the small gentleman [this is Stevenson's epithet from the previous sentence]." My version is consistently benign. Stevenson's verb "accosted," which can mean to assault as well as to greet and to proposition, introduces the possibility of some aggressiveness from Sir Danvers. Stevenson's noun, "the other," suggests the alienation that would make Hyde hypersensitive to such aggressiveness. Or to condescension. "Something high too, as of a well-founded self content" (46) characterizes this man of "high position" (46) who towers above the "very small" Hyde (46). Does Carew seem high-handed to the embattled other?

> The older man bowed and' accosted the other .... from his pointing, it sometimes appeared as if he were only inquiring his way; but the moon shone on his face as he spoke, and the girl was pleased to watch it. [46]

In his commentary on this scene, Jekyll exclaims, "I declare, at least, before God, no man morally sane could have been guilty of that crime ..." So far, Jekyll seems singlemindedly orthodox, but his sentence is not over. "... guilty of that crime upon so pitiful a provocation" (90). For all his abhorrence of Hyde, Jekyll will not indict him unilaterally, will not absolve the fathers completely. "So pitiful a provocation" establishes that there was some provocation. The maid's narrative, with its "sometimes," "only," and "but," suggests that something more than "inquiring his way" must have occurred. For help in understanding what this is, we can look to the maid herself.

Why is the viewpoint in the murder scene female? Why is she positioned in the setting as she is? Why does she act (and not act) as she does? Answers in terms of mimesis do not account for the specifics of the scene as effectively as a reading in terms of fantasy projection. The viewpoint is female in part to assure the reader's sympathy for Carew through our empathetic response to her sympathy for him, but the maid's sympathy is complicated. Since woman's traditional association with sensitivity and pity would warrant her (and our) deeply emotional response to homicidal horrors, why does Stevenson go on and make this particular maid "romantic"? In addition to the answer that Peter K. Garrett has offered, another is suggested by the maid's positioning in the scene. With the woman up at the second floor window, the two men approach from opposite ends of the street and stop "within speech (just under the maid's eyes)" (46). The three figures form a triangle. The woman at the apex, the contending males squared off along the base: it is the classic oedipal configuration. Set in the place of the mother, the maid belongs to a patriarch, "her master" (46), and yet she is available to filial fantasy since she lives "alone" (46). Thus, although she is "romantically given" (46), she is not given to the patriarchy in any expressly sexual way that would preclude appropriation by the son. Positioning her "upon her box" (46) at the open window emphasizes her sexuality and availability.

Her actions and nonactions are, in turn, appropriate to her fantasy role. Why does she not cry out for help for Sir Danvers, and why does she faint for nearly *three hours* (47)? If she were positioned where Hyde could hurt her for crying out, fear would explain her silence and preclude any explanation in terms of oedipal fantasy. But situated safely above, the maid cannot be attacked by Hyde. We can therefore view her conduct in terms of the son's wish fulfillment. Silence implies consent. Mother does not cry out because she is captivated by the son's puissant attack on the weak father. Her fainting then functions as the next stage of the fantasy. Like the "little death" of orgasm, fainting attests to the son's adequacy as replacement for the father. Fainting also constitutes maternal complicity in the son's subversive assertion of himself, since she cannot call the police until Hyde has safely vanished from both the neighborhood and his Soho flat.

Since any situation of Hyde reflects an unconscious emotion of Jekyll's, we can suspect in the doctor an obsession with mother, too. With Jekyll, this link between the patricidal and the oedipal is more obliquely placed for several reasons, one of which is that he has on the conscious level repressed mother so completely that no female counterpart to the maid is possible. There is neither a picture of mother nor saved letters from her, as with father. There are, however, textual details that evoke questions. Why does Stevenson choose for Jekyll's chemist the bizarre name "Maw" (65)? Orality is stressed throughout the novel in the patriarchs' consumption of wine and in Jekyll's drinking of the potion. Orality enters the murder scene at the moment of death. "Tasting delight in every blow," Jekyll/Hyde "mauled the unresisting body" (90). Especially in light of "mauled," "Maw," which literally means mouth, suggests the ultimate source of oral satisfaction, Ma. The basically regressive nature of Jekyll's orality is expressed agonizingly in his cry, "find me some of the old" (66). Jekyll yearns to return to the old source of oral satisfaction. But he cannot. His biological mother is apparently dead, and, worse still, Jekyll is not dealing with *her* at Maw's. Men are in charge of Maw's, the "Messrs. Maw." Moreover, "the man at Maw's was main angry" (66). Why?

Jekyll has accused him of impurity. Jekyll's assumption that the new salt is "impure" (65) prompts him to demand "some of the old," purer substance. Later he realizes that it was the old which was tainted by some "unknown impurity" (96). This problem with the salt is of course essential to the eventual failure of Jekyll's pharmacological "experiment" as a scientific endeavor, but the psychological forces that impel him to experiment in the first place are also illuminated by the salt. On this level we have what Freud defines as characteristic of the son's response to parental sexuality (particularly primal scene fantasies).[16] Mother's possession by father is seen as violent and unclean. In *Jekyll and Hyde* what is presented in narrative terms—the man at Maws is very angry because he will not admit to impurity in his products—can be read in psychoanalytic terms as the father denying the son's interpretation of marital relations as impure. The angry father wants the son to both remove his interrupting presence and restrain his rival passion. The son must banish mother as an object of desire. Jekyll does this so absolutely that mother appears nowhere in the novella. Desire for her lingers, however, and reappears in Jekyll's initial desire for pure chemicals from the old times. "A return to the *old* days before I had made my discovery" is how Jekyll describes his reaction to his first public transformation into Hyde (92; my italics). Finally, however, Jekyll must accept the fact that desire is impure from the first. Does this acceptance, which every boy undergoes, lead in Jekyll's case to a sense that all subsequent relations with women are impure? Certainly the man who mentions no mother marries no wife.

Another death follows Sir Danvers's. To what extent is Lanyon a victim of murder? Critics have recognized an increasing violence in Hyde—ten years without incident, then the trampling of the girl, then the murder of Carew. Does Hyde's post-Carew career extend this trajectory of violence? Carew as a legislator, a lawmaker, can be seen as representing the Law to the son in the familial context. Like the Lacanian Absent Father, Carew represents interdiction to the son whose immaturity is manifest in the petulant rage with which he kills the father. Hyde takes the cane out with him on the night of father killing, as he did not on the night of the girl's trampling, because only now—with the Father—is the Phallus at stake. Lanyon, on the other hand, is not a legislator, but a professional peer. His association with the law comes through his role as articulator of the ethical standards appropriate to a profession in late-Victorian Britain. Hyde must, in turn, articulate antagonism in this postlatency situation in terms other than childish rage. To understand how murder is effected here, we should pause at the latency period between the two deaths.

Jekyll after Carew's death does not simply resume his former existence. He expressly returns to clinical medicine as opposed to the pharmacological "research" that has marked his career over the last dozen years and that has—crucially—alienated him from his friend Dr. Lanyon. As a clinician once more, Jekyll "laboured to relieve suffering ... much was done for others" (92). Others are also served by Jekyll's return to his friends as "once more their familiar guest and entertainer" (56). We are told explicitly that at Jekyll's January 8 dinner "Lanyon had been there" along with Utterson and that "the face of the host had looked from one to the other as in the old days when the trio had been inseparable friends" (56). Returning to friendship and to clinical medicine constitutes a patching up of Jekyll's dual rupture with Lanyon. "The great Dr. Lanyon" is exclusively a clinician who "received his crowding patients" in his house on "Cavendish Square, that citadel of medicine" (36). Thus Lanyon—despite the fact that he is Jekyll's peer in age and distinction—stands forth as the patriarch when he speaks for medical orthodoxy in denouncing Jekyll's deviation into pharmacological experimentation.

> ... it's been more than ten years since Henry Jekyll became too fanciful for me. He began to go wrong, wrong in mind.... I have seen devilish little of the man. Such unscientific balderdash," added the doctor, flushing suddenly purple, "would have estranged Damon and Pythias." [36]

Jekyll's angry response to Lanyon's oft-expressed strictures can, in turn, be seen in terms of the professional disagreements which shaped the development of Robert Louis Stevenson and of all too many sons.

> "I never saw a man so distressed as you [Utterson] were about my will; unless it was that hide-bound pedant, Lanyon, at what he

called my scientific heresies. O, I know he's a good fellow—you needn't frown—an excellent fellow, and I always mean to see more of him; but a hide-bound pedant for all that; an ignorant, blatant pedant. I was never more disappointed in any man than Lanyon." [43]

Jekyll's patching up of both his personal estrangement from Lanyon and his professional disengagement from orthodox medicine fares like most patch jobs. Pressure builds to the point of explosion.

"Lanyon, you remember your vows: what follows is under the seal of our profession. And now, you who have so long been bound to the most narrow and material views, you who have denied the virtue of transcendental medicine, you who have derided your superiors—behold!" [80]

That the speaker here is not Jekyll but Hyde establishes powerfully the nonmimetic, fantasy quality of the scene. Hyde, we are told, "was indifferent to Jekyll" (89); Hyde is, moreover, not a doctor. Thus in terms of mimesis there is no "our" profession that binds Hyde with Lanyon, as there is no reason for Hyde to care about either Lanyon's "material views" or Jekyll's "transcendental medicine." The scene of Lanyon's death makes sense as fantasy, however. Hyde expresses that professional rebellion against repressive authority that is no more resolved within patriarchy than the earlier physical rage was. The "you who have derided your superiors" is the patriarch who in the son's eyes pretends to a professional adequacy he patently lacks. At issue is again, still, mastery. Hyde murders Lanyon, as he did Carew, by preying on the victim's weakness. As Carew had no defense against Hyde's cane, Lanyon is helpless before verbal assault.

"And now," said he, "to settle what remains. Will you be wise? will you be guided? ... Think before you answer, for it shall be done as you decide .... if you shall prefer to choose, a new province of knowledge and new avenues of fame and power shall be laid open to you ... and your sight will be blasted by a prodigy to stagger the unbelief of Satan." [79]

In this rhetorical masterpiece, Hyde makes diverse appeals—to professional advancement ("new avenues to fame and power"), wonder ("a prodigy to stagger the unbelief of Satan"), free will ("if you prefer to choose")—which

Lanyon cannot possibly resist. "I have gone too far in the way of inexplicable services to pause before I see the end" (80). By getting Lanyon to—in effect—commit suicide, to die in response to stimuli embraced rather than thrust on him, Jekyll/Hyde gets patriarchal professionalism to confirm its own inadequacy. Lanyon, so the son's logic goes, deserves to die because his own weakness is what does him in. "Your superiors" are thus both Jekyll as transcendental scientist and Jekyll as rhetorical son. More violent than the killing of Carew insofar as it exploits human weakness more fiendishly, the oedipal murder of Lanyon is linked directly with Carew by Lanyon's last words—"the murder of Carew" (80).

Mother for the postlatency Jekyll/Hyde is represented by Hyde's housekeeper. Her materialization after the Carew killing indicates how desire for mother is recathected and played out in the ongoing fantasy, the accelerating trajectory of violence. That the housekeeper functions primarily on the level of fantasy is emphasized by her relative superfluity on the level of narrative, where she does only two things—admit Utterson and Newcomen to Hyde's flat and announce Hyde's doings on the previous night. Utterson/Newcomen as the law could readily have gotten a search warrant to enter the flat; and its ransacked state testifies eloquently to Hyde's previous doings there. Moreover, nothing about either the housekeeper's actions in the narrative or her more general domestic chores requires the text's stress on her age as "old ... old" (49). Seen in light of her first incarnation in the oedipal fantasy as the maid, mother as housekeeper has aged dramatically. Why? Mother's principal role in the postlatency son's fantasy is no longer expressly erotic. She must now believe in his adult adequacy in the face of patriarchal disapproval. Margaret Stevenson wounded Louis deeply by siding consistently with Thomas in the battles over profession and religion. As Louis put it, "you were persuaded [that I] was born to disgrace you" (L2, 193). Hyde's housekeeper has a similar conviction of filial failure.

> A flash of odious joy appeared on the woman's face. "All!" said she, "he is in trouble. What has he done?"
>
> Mr. Utterson and the inspector exchanged glances. "He don't seem a very popular character," observed the latter. "And now my good woman, just let me and this gentleman have a look about us." [49]

The housekeeper who initially presented "an evil face" (49) is now "my good woman" because she shows that her allegiance is ultimately with the law, with patriarchy. However intensely the son fantasizes his appropriation of mother and her approval of himself, he knows deep down that her heart belongs to daddy. The housekeeper's "smoothed" face (49) recalls the "smooth-faced man of fifty" who is the idol of patriarchy, Henry Jekyll (43); her "silvery hair" (49) resembles the "white hair" of both Lanyon and Carew (36, 46); and her "manners" are "excellent" (49) in accord with patriarchal practice and preference. As Jekyll's smooth professional surface is betrayed by "something of a slyish cast perhaps" (43), the housekeeper's face is smoothed "by hypocrisy" (49). Hypocritical mother has never really, the son knows, been part of his patricidal project, any more than that project can effect true emancipation from oedipal anxiety. Not only does patricide preclude the son's transition from mother to father, but anger at mother taints his continued tie to her. Misogyny, celibacy, and homosexuality are tangled in this tie to mother, as we will soon see. First, however, I must establish that the oedipal dilemma itself is endemic to all of patriarchy, that Stevenson's indictment of oedipal regressiveness has full cultural force because Hyde enacts the anger and desire of not only Henry Jekyll but all men in Victorian society.

With Richard Enfield, oedipal antagonism surfaces suddenly in a sentence that begins innocuously enough. "I feel very strongly about putting questions; it partakes too much of the style of the day of judgment. You start a question and it's like ..." (33). So far, Enfield has simply stated his dislike of prying. His point is clear, and sufficiently orthodox that nothing more need be said. When more is said, therefore, it speaks to another issue altogether.

> "... it's like starting a stone. You sit quietly on the top of a hill; and away the stone goes, starting others; and presently some bland old bird (the last you would have thought of) is knocked on the head in his own back garden and the family have to change their name. No sir ..."

This eruption is as peculiar as the unconscious itself. Striking down the father here presages the Carew killing. Since there is no essential, inevitable link between prying and killing, Enfield's apparently irrelevant simile must be powerfully relevant to him. As Jekyll is safe from prosecution after the Carew murder because his dirty work against the old man is done by his other, so the agent in Enfield's simile is safely removed ("you sit quietly") from an act that destroys an "old bird" and that is done by "others." Enfield's simile thus achieves the same result as Jekyll's potion. "No sir." Father is extirpated.

Moreover, "the family have to change their name." Why? Preserving one's good name is an obsession in *Jekyll and Hyde*, but the only real threat to one's name is perpetration of or complicity in disgraceful acts. Since the family in Enfield's metaphor is patently victimized by a freak accident, why would their name be endangered? Where is their complicity? Enfield obliterates the family—renders it nameless and therefore nonexistent as a family—at the moment of the father's extirpation because the extinction of genealogy itself is the ultimate aim of oedipal rage. The universality of this antidomestic anger is established by the "you." Enfield's interlocutor, his immediate "you," is Utterson, whose patricidal anger we will soon study, but the generalizing force of Enfield's simile extends "you" out to all of us complicitous children. The victimized father is "the last you would have thought of" because you cannot examine the simile closely enough to recognize whom you are in fact thinking of killing off. "You" is Enfield too, of course, any son as metaphor maker. "The day of judgment" is indeed at hand, and the son "on the top of a hill" is looking down like God the Father on the doomed father. The son is doubly safe—because he now is "high" and because the whole thing has been only a metaphor, a mere figure of speech.

The oedipal antagonism of Jekyll's fellow patriarchs is announced through Richard Enfield, but the ultimately maternal orientation of patriarchy requires for its presentation the ampler occasion of Gabriel John Utterson. He, unlike Enfield, is implicated directly—as opposed to metaphorically—in patricidal rage. Hyde, having killed Carew with the lawyer's stick (48), behaves bizarrely afterward in ways that confirm his link with Utterson. Why does Hyde not dispose of the obviously incriminating "other half" of the murder weapon, and why does he leave it specifically "behind the door" (49)? "The other," the phrase common to Hyde, Jekyll, and Utterson, appears here because Hyde as other has expressed the patricidal desire of the other owners of the cane, Jekyll *and* Utterson. The stick is not disposed of, is waiting for Utterson to find it, because it is (still) his stick, his weapon, the expression of his unconscious desires. The stick left "behind the door," rather than, say, flung into the fireplace with the checkbook, emphasizes Utterson's parallel with Jekyll who changes into Hyde—thus achieving the transformation that Utterson can only partake in projectively—behind the door of his laboratory.

Also like the regressive Jekyll, Utterson is characterized by orality. On the first page of the novel, we learn that Utterson is sociable "when the wine was to his taste" and that he drinks gin when "alone, to mortify his taste for vintages." Since Utterson does not drink to excess, why does mortification occur to him at all? His dour religiosity is an obvious answer, but I think there is a deeper reason, a tension reflected in Utterson's name. As the utter son, the devoted heir of patriarchy, he utters the truths of the fathers (as solicitor and as editor-narrator); but as udder son he remains regressively oriented to the breast.[17] His orality is a trait that Nabokov has stressed ("everything is very appetizingly put. Gabriel John Utterson mouths his words most roundly" [180]). Jefford rightly finds wine associated in the novel with domesticity and warmth, but whereas Jefford concludes that wine represents Stevenson's social ideal (52–54), I find this ideal undercut by the compensatory aspect of Utterson's drinking. For example, the Printer's Copy of *Jekyll and Hyde* offers the following revelatory moment:

> He [Utterson watching Jekyll's back door] made long stages on the pavement opposite, studying the bills of fare stuck on the sweating windows of the cookshop, reading the labels on various lotions or watching the bust of the proud lady swing stonily round upon him on her velvet pedestal at the perfumers; but all the time still with one eye over his shoulder, spying at the door.

Utterson's unconscious is imaged forth here. That a son is barred from mother—thus creating feelings of oral deprivation—is represented by the window glass that bars Utterson's way to oral gratification. The "sweating ... cookshop" associates warmth (and physicality) with food, while the "bill of fare" on the window indicates that Utterson cannot reach either. As a man literally out in the cold, he cannot get beyond the perceptual and verbal to the sensual and nutritious. "Bust," which of course means "statuette" on the manifest level, locates the maternal focus of Utterson's latent desires.

That preoedipal oral desire for mother coexists in the patriarchal psyche with oedipal anxieties about father is reflected in the two-directional nature of Utterson's gaze in the street scene. He is not only looking directly at the bust but also "spying" on Jekyll's door "with one eye over his shoulder." That Jekyll can be the oedipal father to Utterson as well as the oedipal son in his own fantasy life is facilitated by Stevenson's presentation of the doctor as the very embodiment of patriarchy—"M.D., D.C.L., LL.D., F.R.S., &c." (35). With professional degrees in law as well as medicine and with a loyal Society fellowship as well as a thriving practice, Jekyll as "a tall, fine build of a man" (66–67) stands forth impressively to speak for the fathers. "I was born ... to a large fortune, endowed besides with excellent parts, inclined by nature to industry, fond of the respect of the wise and good among my fellowmen" (81). Against so representative a patriarch Utterson directs the patricidal antagonism characteristic of the oedipal son. Though he can only spy furtively on the domestic door of Henry Jekyll the sleeping patriarch, Utterson can breach with impunity the professional door of Dr. Jekyll the errant scientist. What the breach reveals is what we have seen throughout *Jekyll and Hyde*—that the professional is a screen for the domestic.

> The candle was set upon the nearest table to light them [Utterson and Poole] to the attack; and they drew near with bated breath to where the patient foot was still going up and down, up and down in the quiet of the night.
>
> "Jekyll," cried Utterson, with a loud voice, "I demand to see you .... if not by fair means, then by foul—if not of your own consent, then by brute force!" .... The besiegers, appalled by their own riot and the stillness that had succeeded, stood back a little and peered in. There lay the cabinet before their eyes in the quiet lamplight, a good fire glowing and chattering on the hearth, the kettle singing its thin strain, a drawer or two open, pages neatly set forth on the business table, and nearer the fire, the things laid out for tea; the quietest room you would have said.... [69–70]

Of the many odd aspects of this scene, the one I want to begin with is its *domesticity*. Nothing about a professional laboratory requires the quiet lamp and good fire, the kettle and tea. What we have bodied forth here, as we did with the bust in the perfumer's window, is the subconscious of Gabriel John Utterson. For him, Jekyll/Hyde is father/mother in cozy domesticity. Only by seeing the break-in as a kind of parlor primal scene can I explain why Utterson is "appalled." The scene seems, morally speaking, a simple case of sheep versus goat; the forces of order bring into containment the force of disorder. Yet Stevenson reverses the polarities. Utterson is the "loud" one, Hyde the "patient." The echoed words "quiet ... quietest" link Jekyll/Hyde's domestic harmony with nature's evening. Since right is apparently on Utterson's side, why is *he* the one associated with "riot"? An answer lies in Utterson's cry, "let our name be vengeance" (68). Ostensibly Utterson is responding with righteous indignation. "I believe poor Harry is killed, and I believe his murderer ... is still lurking in his victim's room" (68). But the scene works more complicatedly than this. The very word "vengeance" in so allusive a novella evokes the biblical warning, "Vengeance is mine, saith the Lord" (Romans 12:15). Prohibitions against taking matters into one's own hands are, in this case, equally strong on the legal side. Utterson is justified in breaking down the door only if he is saving Jekyll's life. If poor Harry is dead already and Edward Hyde is still in the room, Utterson must call the police. Hyde cannot escape in the interim because the room's only windows are barred and its only doors are blocked by Poole, Utterson, Bradshaw, and the knifeboy. The riot that "appalled" Utterson is instigated by more than anger at Hyde killing Jekyll. Utterson through his surrogate Poole is directing against Jekyll the oedipal "vengeance" that Jekyll directed against Carew through Hyde. For Utterson, Jekyll is father at this moment.

> Poole swung the axe over his shoulder; the blow shook the building, and the red baize door leaped against the lock and hinges. A dismal screech, as of mere animal terror, rang from the cabinet. Up went the axe again, and again the panels crashed and the frame bounded; four times the blow fell; but the wood was tough and the fittings were of excellent workmanship; and it was not until the fifth, that the lock burst in sunder, and the wreck of the door fell inwards upon the carpet. [69]

This moment echoes the murder of Carew. As the murder weapon was of "tough and heavy wood" (47), the door's "wood was tough"; as Carew's beaten "body jumped upon the roadway" (47), the beaten "frame bounded"; as Carew's "bones were audibly shattered," the "panels crashed." Utterson is acting out that oedipal rage which Stevenson in "The House of Eld" figured so graphically in terms of wood and axes. "Old is the tree and the fruit good; / Very old and thick the wood. / Woodman, is your courage stout? / Beware! the root is wrapped about / Your mother's heart, your father's bones; / And like the mandrake comes with groans."

To understand a second way in which traditional male bonds are sundered, in which regressive violence is directed within the patriarchy, we should consider Utterson's antagonism toward Jekyll's other self, Edward Hyde. Fratricidal, not patricidal, rage is at work here, as another of the sacred ties of patriarchy is snapped. Stevenson, though an only child, knew sibling rivalry as well as oedipal rage. His sentence to Gosse from which I excerpted earlier reads in full: "A first son is a rival [of the father], a second is a rival of the first." Sibling rivalry is hard for Stevenson to avoid because, as his biographers have detailed, he cannot avoid falling in love with older married women who have children. What I want to stress is the consequence of this tendency to make the beloved into mother and thus the lover into son: other sons become rivals. Having told Fanny Sitwell expressly that "you have another son" in himself (Calder 74), Louis goes on to establish his sonship in and through the extirpation of Fanny's own son, Bertie. "And now I think of you reading it [my letter] in bed behind the little curtain, and no Bertie there, I do not know what longing comes over me to go to you for two hours" (Calder 74). With Fanny Stevenson, matters are much the same, as she realizes. "I love ... to see my two boys so happy" (Furnas 342). Louis and Lloyd were devoted to one another (even to the point of collaborating on fiction), but given Louis's insatiable demands for affection and attention, how could he not know moments of resentment at Fanny's devotion to the biological son who never ceased depending on her for financial as well as emotional support? "The war in the members" involves all family members.

Sibling rivalry characterizes patriarchal behavior in *Jekyll and Hyde* through what critics have never discussed—Stevenson's manifold allusions to Genesis. The biblical tales of Cain and Abel and of Esau and Jacob feature sons fighting for paternal approbation. Cain's desire to win the "respect" of God the Father (5:4) leads to the murder of Abel; Jacob's determination to win the "blessing" of Isaac (27:16) results in the disaffiliation of Esau. Alerted to fraternal rivalry on page 1 of Jekyll and Hyde when Utterson expresses approval of "Cain's heresy .... I let my brother go the devil in his own way," we soon encounter allusions to Esau and Jacob. (These rival brothers are expressly established by Stevenson as the prototypes of the sibling rivals, in *The Master of Ballantrae*.) Jacob's famous dichotomy—"my brother is a hairy man, and I am a smooth man" (27:11)—is replicated in Jekyll and Hyde. Like smooth Jacob, Jekyll is "smooth-faced" (43). Like Esau, whose "hands were hairy" (27:23), Hyde's hands are "thickly shaded with a swart growth of hair" (88). Esau from birth is Hyde-like, since he comes forth "hairy all over like a hair-cloak" or hide (25:25). As Jacob appropriates this cloak (in effect) by putting animal hides onto his hands and neck (27:16), Jekyll can "assume, like a thick cloak, that [body] of Edward Hyde" (86). Jekyll's "red" potion (79), which transforms him into Hyde, recalls the "red pottage" (25:30) that achieves a comparable effect for Jacob, who is in effect transformed into Esau—by being made heir—once the elder brother consumes the red substance.

The very fact that Esau is the *elder* brother, however, indicates that Stevenson has dealt complexly with his source. He has reversed the whole biblical situation, insofar as the relative ages of his characters should require the pairing of Jekyll with Esau and Hyde with Jacob. And there are ways in which Jekyll is Esau and Hyde Jacob. Jekyll is linked to the hirsute Esau by his nickname "Harry" (68). Like Esau's "good raiment" (27:15) which is appropriated by Jacob, Jekyll's "rich and sober" suit bedecks Hyde. Finally the elder, homicidal Cain of the biblical story is paired in Stevenson's story

not only with the younger Hyde who murders with a cane, but also with the
elder doctor who owns the cane and is named "je kyll."

Complicating the parallels between fictional characters and their
biblical counterparts enables *Jekyll and Hyde* to avoid the simple dichotomy
of the biblical parables. Genesis's message of "two separate nations"
(25:23)—Abel versus Cain, Jacob versus Esau—confirms that myth of the
chosen people and thus that exclusion of the other, which is the basic myth
of patriarchy. Stevenson insists that the other is the only nation. Patriarchs
in *Jekyll and Hyde* harbor toward one another the same fraternal rivalry that
we see in Genesis. Jekyll, for example, intends to express devotion to his
lifelong friend Lanyon by saying, "there never was a day when ... I would not
have sacrificed ... my left hand for you" (74). The idiom is "my right hand."
Jekyll's compliment is left-handed because patriarchs, despite their ostensible
unity, put self before brotherhood, make brother into other. Utterson is
sincerely shocked at Carew's death and sincerely concerned for Jekyll's
welfare, but on a deeper level his conduct reflects Cain's question, "Am I my
brother's keeper?" (4:9). Utterson considers "the death of Sir Danvers ...
more than paid for by the disappearance of Mr. Hyde" (56). Utterson enacts
Cain's heresy and lets his brother Carew go to the devil (or to St. Peter) in
his own way—provided that Hyde goes to hell, too.

Hyde, though considerably younger, is Utterson's sibling rival. As the
younger brother Jacob appropriated Esau's birthright, Hyde poses a
comparable threat to Utterson, who returns obsessively to the spectre of
Hyde as "heir to a quarter-million pounds sterling" (48). Like Cain, who
expresses his fear of disaffiliation in Hyde-like terms—"from Thy face shall
I be hid" (4:14)—Utterson fears that he will be hidden by the younger man
inheriting. ("Agents of obscure enterprises," as well as "shady lawyers" [40],
are taking over Jekyll's neighborhood.) Lawyer Utterson is thus not simply
being his brother's keeper (or attorney) when he admonishes Jekyll about the
will. Obsessed with the possibility that Hyde will inherit, Utterson uses
professional concerns to screen his refusal to participate in disinheriting
himself. The Printer's Copy indicates how friendship as well as
professionalism screens his obsession. "He made up his mind to even stretch
friendship in so good a cause." The Notebook Draft emphasizes how
emotional the discovery of the codicil is for the supposedly "cold, scanty"
(29) lawyer.

> On the desk of the business table [in Jekyll's laboratory], among
> a neat array of papers, a very large envelope was uppermost, and
> bore, in Dr. Jekyll's hand, the name of Mr. Utterson. The lawyer

tore it open and as his hands were shaking with emotion, the enclosures fell to the floor. The first was a will, …

That Utterson replaces Hyde in the codicil to the will (72) proves to be an expensive triumph. Jekyll, as well as Carew, must pay for the disappearance of Mr. Hyde.

III. MISOGYNY AND HOMOSEXUALITY

We have seen so far that patriarchs in *Jekyll and Hyde* fail to live up to their traditional obligations of maintaining proper distinctions and of effecting filial and fraternal bonds. Their third failure—to marry—involves a misogyny that derives, like the other patriarchal failures, from unresolved ambivalences toward mother. Here again Stevenson manages to transform materials from his own life into a critical portrait of his times.

Robert Louis Stevenson has been widely and quite properly acclaimed for his "chivalry" toward women—his tenderness to Cummy, his deference toward the fair sex generally and his defense of prostitutes in particular, his devotion to Fanny Sitwell as "Madonna," his concern for the reputation of the precariously poised Mrs. Fanny Vandegrift Osbourne. There are, however, darker emotions as well. Antagonism toward woman is particularly surprising in Stevenson when it strikes the much cooed over Cummy. Having assured her that "God will make good to you all the good you have done," Louis cannot end his sentence without adding, "and mercifully forgive you all the evil" (L1, 37). Resentment here, like oedipal rage, carries over into Stevenson's fiction. "*John Knox* goes on, and a horrible story of a nurse which I think almost too cruel to go on with: I wonder why my stories are always so nasty" (L1, 177). The two-pronged attack on the spiritual father of Scotland and the surrogate mother of Louis continues for more than a month. "I have been working hard at John Knox, and at the horrid story I have in hand, and walking in the rain. Do you know this story of mine is horrible; I only work at it by fits and starts, because I feel as if it were a sort of crime against humanity—it is so cruel" (L1, 178).

That the crime is not against "humanity" is probably what prompts Stevenson to eventually destroy the nurse story. Repression operates even more powerfully on anger at mother herself. When Thomas lashes Louis with having "utterly alienated" Margaret, the father is not only indicting the son for unnatural cruelty. He is also reconfirming his own conjugal bond with Margaret—and thus her "betrayal" of her son. Louis feels the pain of mother's preference no less than the power of father's possession.

My Dear Mother,—I give my father up. I give him a parable....
And he takes it backside foremost, and shakes his head, and is
gloomier than ever. Tell him that I give him up. I don't want such
a parent. This is not the man for my money.... Here I am on the
threshold of another year, when, according to all human
foresight, I should long ago have been. resolved into my
elements; here am 1, who you were persuaded was born to
disgrace you—and, I will do you the justice to add, on no
insufficient grounds—no very burning discredit when all is
done.... There is he [Thomas], at his not first youth, able to take
more exercise than I at thirty-three, and gaining a stone's weight,
a thing of which I am incapable. There are you: has the man no
gratitude? There is Smeoroch [the dog]: is he blind? Tell him for
me that all this is
NOT THE TRUE BLUE!   [L2, 193–94]

How symptomatic it is—Louis sincerely desiring to relieve paternal gloom,
and then capitalizing on his failure in order to attack Thomas. But more is
being expressed here than oedipal rage. Mother too is attacked. "You were
persuaded [I] was born to disgrace you." The alienating force of maternal
doubt (Margaret stuck by Thomas in all the battles with Louis) is
compounded by Mother's status as father's possession. "There are you: has the
man no gratitude? There is Smeoroch: is he blind?" Especially highlighted by
the syntactic parallelism, the equation of mother with dog reduces marriage
to a master–pet and even to an animal relationship. Biological maternity is
rejected outright when Louis tells his Madonna, Mrs. Sitwell, that "nobody
loves a mere mother as much as I love you" (Calder 76).

The virtual exclusion of woman from Stevenson's pre-1890s fiction is at
times explained away by him. *Treasure Island*, for example: "no women in the
story, Lloyd's orders; and who so blithe to obey? It's awful fun boy's stories; you
just indulge the pleasures of your heart, that's all" (L1, 61). This explanation
opens itself to some nice objections, but there is a more direct line to take.
When Lloyd Osbourne's peers are not the readership of a novel and yet the
novelist continues to exclude women, there is obviously a continuity between
the children's and the adult enterprises. The violence inherent in such exclusion
of woman bursts forth in 1886 when Edward Hyde is roaming the night streets.

Once a woman spoke to him, offering, I think, a box of lights. He
smote her in the face, and she fled. [94]

Since Jekyll remembers all the other particulars of his day as Hyde (the hotel was in Portland Street, the letters were sent registered, etc.), why is he unsure what the woman offered Hyde? A woman who walks the streets late at night asking men if they need a light is offering quite another type of box.[18] And Jekyll (and Stevenson's readers) know it. Jekyll does not want to admit that the violence of Hyde's response is directed against female sexuality, for such an admission would confirm misogyny too starkly.

Hyde's first act of violence partakes of misogyny, since Stevenson makes the trampled child female. Though we know she is on the streets because she is on an errand of mercy, Hyde's violence to her presages his treatment of the streetwalker. Patriarchy is implicated in the girl's injury because Enfield's response to her and to her female partisans emphasizes the complicity of his narration in Hyde's violence. "Then [after the collision] came the horrible part of the thing; for the man trampled calmly over the child's body and left her screaming on the ground" (31). Is any reader of this sentence prepared for Enfield's next remark? "It sounds nothing to hear." That Enfield goes on to add "but it was hellish to see" does not unring the bell. Enfield's first sentence has been *horrible* to hear. Although modesty at his storytelling prowess is probably Enfield's rationale for the disclaimer "it sounds nothing to hear," he nowhere else apologizes for narrative skills that are obviously first rate. "... her screaming on the ground. It sounds nothing to hear...." Enfield's sequence of words turns a deaf ear to the girl's screams. Downplaying her suffering mitigates Hyde's offense in the same way that Enfield did earlier when he presented the girl as the violent "other" and made Hyde the one proceeding "at a good walk."

Adult females fare still worse in Enfield's subsequent narration.

> We told the man we could and would make such a scandal out of this.... And all the time, as we were pitching it in red hot, we were keeping the women off him as best we could, for they were wild as harpies. I never saw a circle of such hateful faces. [32]

No wonder the women were not invited to breakfast. What we do wonder is whether the women are actually more violent than the men. "Harpies" suggests a different order of virulence from "pitching it in red hot." Is Hyde actually more endangered by the women than by the men? Or are the men "keeping the women off" him in order to keep him to themselves in Enfield's chamber? "They were as wild as harpies. I never saw such a circle of hateful faces." Enfield might defend himself from charges of misogyny by insisting that the "circle" here is a sweeping indictment of red-hot men as well as women harpies. But Enfield's syntax prompts a more exclusive reading. "They ... harpies ... hateful faces." Our equation of women with hateful is particularly likely once Stevenson deletes from the Printer's Copy the next clause of the sentence: "I declare we looked like fiends."

Comparable doubts about Utterson's attitude toward women surface when another night woman appears. "It was a wild, cold, seasonable night of March, with a pale moon lying on her back ..." (63). Sexual innuendo would be precluded if Stevenson did here what he does in his letters—keep gender out of the description altogether. "There was a half-moon lying over on its back ... a very inartistic moon that would have damned a picture" (L1, 194). Instead, the *Jekyll and Hyde* sentence emphasizes gender by associating "her" with clouds "of the most diaphanous and lawny texture" (63). The erotic evocation of diaphanous nightwear is complicated by the violence of describing clouds as a "flying wrack"—evoking the meaning of "wrack" as "wreck/destruction" and recalling the other violent night flights in the novella.

Whose description, whose perception, is all this? Since Utterson is the ostensible point of view in the chapter, is he the source of the bizarre image of the moon on her back? Certainly Utterson has already projected on reality a vision of commercialized sexuality.

> The inhabitants [of Jekyll's bystreet] were all doing well ... laying out the surplus of their gains in *coquetry*, so that the shop fronts stood along that thoroughfare with *an air of invitation*, like rows of smiling *saleswomen*. Even on Sunday, when it *veiled its more florid charms* ... the street shone out in contrast to its dingy neighbourhood, like a fire in a forest. [30; my italics]

This description ends with the conventional, Chamber of Commerce notion that "with its freshly painted shutters, well-polished brasses, and general cleanliness and gaiety of note [the street] instantly caught and pleased the eye of the passenger." Why, then, does Stevenson introduce language so unconventional with chamber of commerce descriptions, so redolent of female sexuality and so suggestive of prostitution and rampant passion? Since Enfield and Utterson are walking down the street, are we to assume that the description of it reflects the tendency of men professional and misogynistic to associate commerce with whoring? Since this street is the site in the Notebook Draft of "the bust of the proud lady ... at the perfumer's," does bust in the service of commerce show woman as whore? Lloyd Osbourne spoke for the patriarchy: no women.

That patriarchs in *Jekyll and Hyde* are too misogynistic to wed may explain why there are so few women in the novella, but it does not explain why patriarchs are misogynistic. To begin to answer this question, I must complicate things further. Men antagonistic to women are attracted to men. Jekyll and Hyde fit quite obviously into a long tradition of male doubles— from Caleb Williams and Falkland, Frankenstein and the Monster, and Robert Wringhim Cowan and Gil Martin, to Eugene Wrayburn and Bradley Headstone, and on to Dorian Gray and his picture. *Jekyll and Hyde* draws on this tradition for both structural and psychological components. Structurally, the interchange between a pair of men—as in the Cain/Abel and Damon/Pythias stories foreground by Stevenson—shapes the staging of or constitutes subject matter in every scene in the novella:

> Cain and Abel (29), Utterson and Enfield (29), Enfield and Hyde (31–32), Utterson and Lanyon (36), Damon and Pythias (36), Utterson and Hyde (37), Mr. Hyde and Mr. Seek (38), Utterson and Poole (41), Utterson and Jekyll (43), Hyde and Carew (46), Hyde and the servant Maid's master (46), Carew and Utterson (47), Utterson and Newcomen (49), Utterson and Jekyll (51), Utterson and Guest (53), Utterson and Enfield (60), Utterson and Poole (62–73), Utterson and Lanyon (74), Lanyon and Jekyll/Hyde (77–80).

In terms of psychology, the homoerotic element so prominent in the tradition of the male double recurs in *Jekyll and Hyde*. "There was something queer about that gentleman," Poole says of Hyde (68). Homosexual inclinations areas occluded as they are intense in *Jekyll and Hyde*, because patriarchs contribute to their culture's repressions of inversion, even as they incline toward it. "The more it looks like Queer Street, the less I ask," Enfield admits (33). But repression cannot thwart desire absolutely. What happens to language in Enfield's and Poole's sentences—the traditional Victorian connotation of "queer" as "odd" shading into its later connotation of "homoerotic"[19]—occurs also in the psyches of patriarchs and in the plot of the novella, as celibate men replace women with one another. Take, for example, the fact that Hyde is called Jekyll's "favorite" (48). Would Utterson be so worried about a blackmail threat to Jekyll, would the doctor be so vulnerable to disgrace, if his secret related only to women? Especially in light of other features—both the general context of public school friendships ("old *mates* at school and college") and the specific situation of Hyde entering Jekyll's domain from the rear, and from a "by-street"[20]—Nabokov's response to "favorite" is appropriate.

> Favorite ... sounds almost like *minion*. The all-male patterns that Gwynne has mentioned may suggest by a twist of thought that Jekyll's secret adventures were homosexual practices so common in London behind the Victorian veil. Utterson's first supposition is that Hyde blackmails the good doctor—and it is hard to imagine what special grounds for blackmailing would there have been in a bachelor's consorting with ladies of light morals. Or do Utterson and Enfield suspect that Hyde is Jekyll's illegitimate son? ... But the difference in age as implied by the difference in their appearance does not seem to be quite sufficient for Hyde to be Jekyll's son. Moreover, in his will Jekyll calls Hyde his "friend and benefactor," a curious choice of words perhaps bitterly ironic but hardly referring to a son. [194]

The point as I see it is not that patriarchs "really are" homosexual, as though this were one state, but that late-Victorian professional men feel emotions that they can neither express nor comprehend. An aura of homosexuality serves to signal both the homoerotic nature of many male bonds and the lethal consequences of them.

> He [Utterson] sat on one side of his own hearth, with Mr. Guest, his head clerk, upon the other, and midway between them, at a nicely calculated distance from the fire, a bottle of a particular old wine .... the room was gay with firelight. In the bottom the acids were long ago resolved; the imperial dye had softened with time, as the colour grows richer in stained windows; and the glow of hot autumn afternoons on hillside vineyards was ready to be set free and to disperse the fogs of London. Insensibly the lawyer melted. [53–54]

Granted that on one level a tender human friendship exists between these men: friendship cannot account for all the details, the agents of affect, that appear in the scene. Why, for example, in a scene that ostensibly is pure plot contrivance—a handwriting expert is brought in to examine Hyde's script and, with supreme convenience, is presented with Jekyll's as well—are there so many layers of literary materials? "The melting mood" is one of Victorian fiction's conventional expressions for emotional surrender, but I have never seen the expression applied to a man. Utterson melts in a scene almost parodic of conventional seduction—the irresistible male guest, the cozy warmth of the evening privacy, the lubricating bottle of wine. Sensuousity in Utterson's scene is intensified by the infusion of Keats. As Utterson's bottle has "long dwelt unsunned in the foundations," Keats's wine in the "Ode to a Nightingale" "hath been / Cooled a long age in the deep-delved earth" (11–12). Wine that radiates "the glow of hot autumn afternoons on hillside vineyards" in Utterson's passage tastes, in Keats's, of "the country green, / ... and sunburnt myrth! / O for a beaker of the warm south" (13, 14–15). Keats wants to "drink, and leave the world unseen" (19) because a world so redolent of death makes mockery of the body's warm sensuality. Utterson too is "ready to be set free," but what shackles him is not mortality. "The room was gay." Homophobia is the shackle that his body's deep-buried sensuality seeks to slip.[21]

Mr. Guest is not Utterson's chief object of desire, however. "Familiar guest" is Utterson's term for Henry Jekyll (56). Utterson's scene with Guest has its counterpart with Jekyll "[who] now sat on the opposite side of the fire ... you could see by his looks that he cherished for Mr. Utterson a sincere and warm affection" (43). Genuine friendship obtains between these men, as it did between Utterson and Guest. But as the word "gay" in the first fireside scene is echoed by "gaily" in the second (43), so professional concerns mask personal obsessions in the second scene as they did in the first. Then the relation of lawyer to clerk screened Utterson's attraction to this house guest; now the relation of lawyer to (quasi)client allows Utterson to discuss Jekyll's choice of Edward Hyde as his heir. Utterson here is not only dealing with his sense of Cain—like exclusion from the will but also exploring the reason for his exclusion—Jekyll's mysterious "intimacy" with Hyde. Help in defining this intimacy is provided by another scene where professionalism acts as a screen in Utterson's relationship with Jekyll. "The hand of Henry Jekyll (as you [Utterson] have often remarked) was professional in shape and size; it was large, firm, white and comely" (87–88). To descant on the beauty of the beloved's hands is conventional enough for a lover, but what heterosexual man speaks, let alone often, about the hands of a man? The Notebook Draft version sentence reads, "The hand of Henry Jekyll, as we have often jocularly said, was eminently professional in shape and size; it was large, firm, white and comely, the hand of a lady's doctor in a word." The revisions of the sentence focus attention on Utterson. He rather than "we" discussed the hand; no jocularity is admitted; and deletion of the dig at lady's doctors precludes any heterosexual link of Jekyll and ladies. What we are left with is

Utterson's sensual and obsessive attention to Jekyll, and the "professional" as
a screen for the obsessional.

Jekyll's role in the psychology of the novella is thus as overdetermined
as desire itself. The oedipal father and the regressive son is also the male
lover.

> ... [Utterson] would see a room in a rich house, where his friend
> lay asleep, dreaming and smiling at his dreams; and then the door
> of that room would be opened, the curtains of the bed plucked
> apart, the sleeper recalled, and, lo? There would stand by his side
> a figure to whom power was given, and even at that dead hour, he
> must rise and do its bidding. [37]

This scene, we should note immediately, is not happening, it is being
imagined. We focus less upon the Jekyll–Hyde relationship than upon
Utterson's relation to it. Although Utterson insists that his friend's safety is
the issue, there is a deeper concern with his friend's bondage. The "power"
of Hyde, more than the danger to Jekyll, obsesses Utterson here. This
obsession has the force of duration. The will "had *long* been the lawyer's
eyesore.... out of the shifting, insubstantial mists, that had so *long* baffled his
eye, there leaped up the sudden, definite presentment of a fiend" (35–36; my
italics). In making his will, Jekyll has lost his will.

Utterson's long obsession with Hyde's power is brought into violent
focus on this particular night by the revelation of Hyde's key: "... whipped
out a key, went in ... 'You are sure he used a key?' ... drew a key from his
pocket like one approaching home ... blowing in the key ... 'Mr. Hyde has a
key.' ... 'he still had his key with him'" (32, 34, 39, 41, 67). Beyond the
obviously erotic aspects of whipping out and going in, there is the
possessiveness that these acts signify for Utterson. "His friend's strange
preference or bondage (call it what you please)" (38). We can call it what we
please because preference and bondage are interchangeable in light of Jekyll's
will, or rather Hyde's. Identities merge. "As he [Utterson] lay and tossed in
the gross darkness of the night and the curtained room" (37), he imagines
"the curtains of the bed plucked apart." The connection between "curtained"
and "curtains" links Utterson's bed with Jekyll's, and thus associates Utterson
with Jekyll's intimacy with Hyde. "The figure ... haunted the lawyer all night;
and if at any time he dozed over, it was but to see it glide more stealthily
through the sleeping houses" (37). The conversion of Jekyll's house into
houses signals that Utterson is unconsciously imagining Hyde's entry into
other night places. Is one of these the "gross darkness" of Utterson's own

repressed desire? His reference to Jekyll's "strange preference or bondage" occurs *after* we learn that the lawyer's own "imagination ... was engaged, or rather enslaved" (37).

Utterson is thus attracted to, as well as emulous of, Edward Hyde. Once Hyde gets Jekyll's will, he becomes that will. He becomes in effect what has always attracted Utterson to Jekyll. That Hyde can be seen as the penis of Jekyll was proposed years ago by Dr. Mark Kanzer. Though I believe Kanzer is close to the mark, his argument—that Hyde is small and deformed—seems weak. Kanzer describes as anatomical what is symbolic.[22] Hyde is Jekyll's phallus. Or rather, Hyde represents two contradictory perceptions of patriarchy: the patriarchal claim to phallic presence, to power, control, will; and (as we will see in section 4) the opposite, the patriarchal sense of itself as absent, the reality of impotence and dysfunction. Hyde is the phallus insofar as Utterson sees him as "the figure to whom power is given." Hyde's possession of the key to Jekyll's place (in every sense) puts into his hands the perquisites of patriarchy—ownership, access, ultimately the power to reify the nonself. Status as Jekyll's heir in the legal will assures the lawyer that Hyde can exercise his will over the future as well as the present. Utterson fosters this power, for he preserves the will in "the inmost private part of his safe" (35). This detail is so odd that it warrants explanation. Since Utterson did not draw up the will, since Jekyll's inheritance is in fact the responsibility of some other attorney, why does the novella emphasize Utterson's role in preserving the document? He must have a symbolic, psychological relationship with it. However repressive Utterson's act of shutting away the will is, and however the document assures his disinheritance from Jekyll, Utterson's "private" is the receptacle that keeps "safe" the will/phallus of the next patriarch. Utterson has no comparable will of his own.

Why are there no women in *Jekyll and Hyde*? Because patriarchs seek men. Why, then, is there the aura of homosexuality and not the fact of genital intercourse? Because what patriarchs seek in men is mirroring. Professionalism allows relations to seem "mature" and yet to remain at a postlatency "adolescent" stage, which in turn replicates the preoedipal stage of mother–child mirroring. Why patriarchs crave such mirroring, why they fear truly mature relationships with peer-aged women, becomes clear when we see what Jekyll sees in his mirror. Edward Hyde. Experiencing "new life ... the raging energies of life ... all his energy of life" (84, 95), Jekyll testifies that Hyde's "love of life is wonderful" (96). Jekyll makes evident the most elemental desires of patriarchy—to thwart death and to effect immortality.

"The bonds of obligation ... the dryness of a life of study ... plod[ding] in the public eye with a load of genial respectability ... the self-denying toils of my professional life" (83, 85, 86, 91). Jekyll is indisputably bored with conventional probity and intensely alive to outré pleasures, but he cannot be explained in terms of any vulgar hedonism. A finer explanation offers itself if we take another of Jekyll's self-characterizations—"the elderly and discontented doctor" (90)—and provide the explanatory causality that Jekyll's coordinate syntax cannot acknowledge. "Discontented" *because* "elderly," Jekyll once again uses professionalism to screen his emotional state. This time what he is repressing is not oedipal rage and regressive desire but the fear of death that lies behind them both. By saying that he is tired of being a dutiful doctor, Jekyll expresses his anxiety about tiring, aging.

Jekyll is waging war against time itself. This war involves patriarchy not only in its specifically late-Victorian, professional manifestation, but also in its traditional form. Patriarchy presupposes time, constitutes an accommodation with mortality. Patrilineal succession envisions the endurance not of an individual but of the tradition. A son gets to become a father because he accepts the next stage: the handing on of his status to a younger successor and the going on to death. Jekyll in effect goes back on the bargain: "... that what was dead, and had no shape, should usurp the offices of life ..." (95). Jekyll fears the inanimate taking over the animate, process being returned to stasis. "The restrictions of natural life" (91) are what obsess him. Since body allows for the fragmentation that leads to dissolution (as opposed to mere dissoluteness), what Jekyll seeks is wholeness. Hyde is the "idol in the glass" because he is the mirror reversal of life's very sequence, the integration sought by the "imperfect and divided" doctor (84). Thus "Hyde struggling after freedom" seeks the "liberty" (90) of timelessness.

That this "liberty" is called a "sea" links Jekyll's escape from mortality to the fluidity images that mark his transformation into Hyde—the "current of disordered sensual images" that runs "like a millrace" in his fancy (83)—and thus to his obsession with orality. The Jekyll who "swallowed the transforming draught" compared himself with a "drunkard" (90). In drink, as in "the sea of liberty," Jekyll seeks the ultimate oneness, amnoetic, maternal. To "spring headlong into the sea" (86) suggests reverse birth, as the "impenetrable mantle" of Hyde suggests the womb where Jekyll's "safety was complete." The "pangs of dissolution" (85) involve nothing less than the dissolution of identity itself as a way to dissolve time. In the mirror of mother is oneness.

Against the attraction of maternal security, woman as wife cannot prevail. Misogyny, Hyde's punching the face of the prostitute, is the inevitable response to peer-aged women whose desires draw the son on to adulthood and thus to death. The prostitute offers fire, and Jekyll seeks water. She offers light, and he desires darkness.

IV. Consequences and Conclusions

Immortality through regression is a doomed dream, and Jekyll knows it. Notice that he keeps saying "young*er*" (83, 84; my italics), not young. He speaks of Hyde's "comparative youth" (90) because he knows that you cannot unring a bell. "Lighter, happier in body .... more express and single ..." (83, 84). Jekyll senses the comparative nature of any change in nature. However restrictive "natural life" is, the struggle against those restrictions is unnatural. And doomed. The consequences of regression are manifest in *Jekyll and Hyde* both immediately (as impotence and dysfunction) and more generally (as solipsism and nonbeing).

First, impotence. The murder of Carew leaves Hyde "trembling ... and still hearkening in my wake for the steps of the avenger" (91). Any violent victory is chimerical. Killing Carew snaps "the stick ... in the middle under the stress" (47). One half of the stick ending up in "the neighbouring gutter" (47) suggests that the self-hate which caused the son to assault the father has only increased, since murder confirms the filial impotence that prompted the assault in the first place. "Neighbouring" reaffirms the social nature of all human actions. Hyde may disregard the bonds of patriarchy and strike out self-aggrandizingly, but he remains in a neighborhood. There are neighbors to witness his crime; there is within himself the abiding sense of community, which guiltily directs his broken stick to the appropriate gutter.

The association of guilt with impotence persists as the homicidal narrative proceeds. Hyde's apprehensive state soon after the murder of Carew—"still harkening in my wake for the steps of the avenger" (91)— reappears months later as he encounters his next victim. Lanyon "bid him enter, [but] he did not obey me without a searching backward glance into the darkness of the square. There was a policeman not far off, advancing with his bull's eye open" (77). Here, as with Utterson, the son's basic anxieties are projected onto experience. The association of "bull" with the authoritative male—and with the law he embodies and enforces—confirms the son's belief in the father's phallic superiority. Castration cannot harm the father because his superiority neither resides in a specific organ nor abides in a particular man. Superior by virtue of the son's perception of his superiority, the father bull returns still more puissant when filial inadequacy is compounded by filial guilt.

Emasculation, in turn, characterizes Hyde himself. He ultimately represents less the phallus than patriarchal pretensions to it. Despite all his "masculine" traits of preternatural strength and animal agility, Hyde is prey to what the late nineteenth century associated particularly with women. "Wrestling against the approaches of hysteria" (78), Hyde resembles Jekyll's "hysterical whimpering" housemaid (64), just as Jekyll himself (who calls his fears "unmanning" [58]) is repeatedly characterized by the conventional feminine trait that marked the maid at the window—"faintness ... half fainting ... faint ... faintness" (53, 80, 92). Hyde, the erstwhile phallic predator, is heard "weeping like a woman" (69). Effeminacy marks his "steps [that] fell lightly and oddly, with a certain swing ... different indeed from the heavy creaking tread of Henry Jekyll" in his patriarchal role (69). How reminiscent of the moon "lying on her back" is Hyde's corpse as Utterson "turned it on its back" (70).

The other half of the shattered cane goes to Utterson because his association with the subconscious rage expressed through Hyde requires his association, too, with the guilty impotence of filial failure. Utterson, like Hyde (and like all "honest" men, the lawyer attests), feels "terror of the law" when police are near (48). The broken stick that he shares with Hyde indicates their common guilt and prepares us for Utterson's version of Hyde's impotence–patriarchal dysfunction. Utterson and his peers fail to assume the leadership that is the responsibility and the glory of patriarchy. In Jekyll's absence, his servants are "like a flock of sheep" (63). That they are looking to the patriarch as Good Shepherd is confirmed when a grateful servant cried out, "Bless God! it's Mr. Utterson" (64). Can Utterson fulfill this role? Attestations to his decisiveness in the break-in scene ("'my shoulders are broad enough to bear the blame' ... [he] led the way" [68]) are undercut by moments almost comically indecisive. After announcing to Poole with a seriousness appropriate to his patriarchal station, "if you say that [Jekyll is murdered] ... I shall consider it my duty to break in that door," and after receiving from Poole the apparently appropriate response of, "Ah, Mr. Utterson, that's talking," the lawyer goes on.

> "And now comes the second question.... Who is going to do it?" ...
> "Why, you and me, sir," was the undaunted reply.
> "That's very well said," returned the lawyer. [67]

Who else would do the breaking in once Utterson announces it as his duty? "Undaunted" characterizes the servant rather than the lawyer because

Utterson is daunted and daunting. "That's talking" becomes ironical in light of the subsequent exchange; Utterson is all talk, whereas Poole's words are genuinely "well said" because they bespeak action. Two pages later, Utterson seems at last galvanized to action and utters the cry, "let our name be vengeance," but his very next sentence is, "Call Bradshaw" (68). That the lawyer actually has a task for Bradshaw does not prevent us from feeling an immediate drop in intensity here. Even the act of reading is beyond Utterson. "He caught up the next paper; it was a note in the doctor's hand and dated at the top. 'O Poole,' the lawyer cried, 'he was alive and here this very day. He ...'" (72). After listening to Utterson go on for seven more lines, Poole speaks for the reader when he intervenes. "Why don't you read it, sir?" Utterson's answer—"Because I fear"—is quite moving as an admission of what all human beings feel at times. But we cannot be overly impressed with Utterson here because we recognize that he does not fight back determinedly against the fear that, unacknowledged, undermines most of what typifies the patriarchy.

Gentlemanly manners, for instance. Ostensibly one of patriarchy's principal tools for handling experience, manners function like professional etiquette in *Jekyll and Hyde*, less as a mode of action than as a screen for fears and rages. In the break-in scene, Poole provides Utterson with the crucial letter to Maw's: "'This is a strange note,' said Mr. Utterson; and then sharply, 'How do you come to have it open?'" (66). At a moment of peril, the lawyer quibbles about etiquette—and with a servant of unimpeachable probity who subsequently answers Utterson's question resoundingly (the note was opened by the man at Maw's). What is not answered is why Utterson asked the question in the first place. He is afraid at every level, and uses manners and superior rank to turn aside from the crucial, threatening issues. Earlier in the scene when he confronted the servants huddled sheeplike,

> "Are you all here?" said the lawyer peevishly. "Very irregular, very
> unseemly: your master would be far from pleased."
>   "They're all afraid," said Poole. [64]

The servants share Utterson's "fear," but rather than admit the common plight of them all, the lawyer focuses on decorum as a way of venting anxiety while maintaining superiority. "Peevishly" contrasts with "master" to stress both how trivial manners are at so dire a moment and how far Utterson is from the mastery appropriate to patriarchy. A still more invidious contrast establishes the moral issue involved in manners. Utterson makes a bargain with Hyde:

> "How did you [Utterson] know me?" he [Hyde] asked.
> "On your side," said Mr. Utterson, "will you do me a favour?"
> "With pleasure," replied the other. "What shall it be?"
> "Will you let me see your face?" asked the lawyer. [39]

After Hyde masters his disinclination to comply, he insists on the other half
of the bargain.

> "And now," said the other, "how did you know me?"
> "By description," was the reply.
> "Whose description?"
> "We have common friends," said Mr. Utterson.
> "Common friends!" echoed Mr. Hyde, a little hoarsely. "Who
> are they?"
> "Jekyll, for instance," said the lawyer.
> "He never told you," cried Mr. Hyde, with a flush of anger. "I
> did not think you would have lied."
> "Come," said Mr. Utterson, "that is not fitting language."
> The other snarled aloud into a savage laugh. [39–40]

Hyde is three times called "the other" here, but the liar is Utterson. Hyde
does the gentlemanly thing and keeps his bargain; Utterson not only fails to
keep his part but resorts to manners when caught red-handed. "Fitting
language" is what the liar insists on. No wonder Hyde laughs.

Utterson with the lie, like Enfield with the breakfast, shows that
patriarchs will do whatever they wish, and then insist on a veneer of "proper"
conduct. That such self-indulgence is not only inherently weak and morally
wrong but potentially fatal is attested to by Lanyon during Hyde's midnight
visit. Besides giving Hyde a lesson in manners—"'You forget that I have not
yet the pleasure of your acquaintance. Be seated.' And I showed him an
example, and sat down in my customary seat" (78)—Lanyon seeks to control
the situation by other traditional guarantors of order. "As I followed him into
the bright light of the consulting room, I kept my hand ready on my weapon.
Here, at last, I had a chance of clearly seeing him. I had never set eyes on him
before" (77). Lanyon has never seen anything like Hyde, yet the doctor is
relying on traditional defenses. "The bright light of the consulting room"
represents the light of reason that this positivist clinician trusts in to
illuminate life's mysteries. And if reason should fail, there is always force.
Lanyon's weapon being "old" (77) suggests both that violence is an age-old
patriarchal solution to problems and that this solution is old-fashioned,

outmoded. "Self-defense" Lanyon indeed needs, but what he needs defense against is his self. Hyde is a threat only to the extent that Lanyon cannot resist his own curiosity. Though the doctor maintains his gentlemanly facade, "affecting coolness that I was far from truly possessing" (79), he has no more self-control than the rest of the patriarchs. "I have gone too far in the way of inexplicable services to pause before I see the end" (80). What he sees is Jekyll, and it ends him. Why?

Professionalism functions here to screen the same homoerotic attractions and ultimate impotence that characterize other patriarchs. "Under the seal of our profession" (80) occurs most unprofessional behavior because Lanyon's "curiosity" and "services" (80) go far beyond clinical medicine. As little Hyde grows into large Jekyll, Lanyon sees the transformation as expressly erectile: "there came, I thought, a change—he seemed to swell" (80). The aura of phallic presence here parodies the fact of patriarchal impotence. With his life "shaken to its roots" (80), Lanyon soon dies. Especially in light of Otto Rank's insight that the return of the double is the advent of death,[23] Lanyon seems doubly doomed because Jekyll and Hyde are both his doubles. Jekyll the patriarch/scientist is Lanyon's reflection in the cultural mirror, so that when Jekyll is also Hyde, Dr. Lanyon cannot accept his own alterity, cannot accept himself as Hyde too. When the man named "Hastie" (80) meets a man entering with "haste" (77), he is in effect confronting his mirror image. And it kills him. Hasty Lanyon is unable to resist the knowledge proffered by Hyde because that knowledge is already hidden in the doctor's unconscious. Characterized *before* the Hyde scene by "a shock of hair prematurely white" (36), Lanyon is already shocked by his unconscious sense of participation in Jekyll's other side (this is why Lanyon has inveighed so ferociously against Jekyll's transcendental medicine). But Lanyon has never advanced to the maturity of a self-control based on self-knowledge. Defended only by manners, bright lights, gun, and "the seal of our profession"—the old weapons of traditional responses—Lanyon, who has never had to face the Hyde hidden within us all, succumbs to the epiphany which is self-revelation.

Death does not eliminate all the patriarchs of Jekyll's circle, but the consequences of regressive desire do ultimately mark all of patriarchy with a kind of solipsistic nonbeing.

Next, in the course of their [Utterson's and Poole's] review of the chamber, the searchers came to the cheval glass, into whose depths they looked with an involuntary horror. But it was so

turned as to show them nothing but the rosy glow playing on the
roof, the fire sparkling in a hundred repetitions along the glazed
front of the presses, and their own pale and fearful countenances
stooping to look in.

"This glass has seen some strange things, sir," whispered
Poole.

"And surely none stranger than itself," echoed the lawyer, in
the same tone. [71]

Both the staging and the style of this scene are revelatory. Why is the mirror
turned up? How it might have become turned this way—Jekyll/Hyde hit it
as he fell—does not mean that it *must* be so turned. The odds are better that
a small man falling in a large room would not have hit the mirror. Once
again, setting functions to reveal psyche. The upturned mirror cannot reflect
the dead Hyde on the floor. Utterson and Poole are looking down, bent over
staring into the mirror, but they do not see into "depths." They see
upward—the "rosy" glow and "sparkling" light of domestic bliss. They are
too frightened, too "pale and fearful," for their "involuntary" glance to
recognize the reality they want to ignore. Patriarchs who have wanted to
overlook Hyde and death manage to overlook both at this moment of
supposed "depth" perception.

The consequences of rejecting the other are reflected stylistically in
Stevenson's passage. Compare

But it was so turned as to show them nothing but the rosy
glow ...

and

But it was so turned as to show them only the rosy glow ...

Syntax in Stevenson's sentence makes us make a mistake. Providing a direct
object to "show" completes a basic syntactic unit. We read: "it was so turned
as to show them nothing." The construction "nothing but" then carries us on
to the opposite meaning, to what the mirror does show, but the syntax of the
sentence's initial ten words has given no hint that the "nothing but"
construction will appear. What is the effect of the syntax making us assume
that the mirror showed nothing when in fact it shows to the patriarchs their
very faces?

The "strange things" that the mirror has seen are principally Jekyll and
Hyde, who are each direct reflections and mirrored reversals of one another
as doubles. The mirror is their solipsistic world. Utterson and his double, his

reflecting Poole, are in that world in every sense. Their faces appear in the mirror because their lives are inseparable from the lives of Jekyll and Hyde, from the plot of *Jekyll and Hyde*. Diction emphasizes the reflected and self-reflexive relation of Utterson and Poole when the lawyer "echoed" the servant "in the same tone." Utterson as the uttering son who replicates the values of the fathers mirrors in his upright life the professional probity of Jekyll, Lanyon, and Carew; Utterson as the repressed son who cannot find utterance for anger and oral deprivation is reflected in the rages of Hyde, who dies by drinking poison.

The conjunction of orality and the cheval glass marks the men of *Jekyll and Hyde* as caught in the Lacanian mirror stage. The failure to resolve oedipal tensions and to unite with peer-aged women leaves patriarchs in diadic relations (Damon–Pythias, Utterson–Enfield, Utterson–Poole), which screen the persistence of the mother–child bond. The "imaginary" nature of homosocial harmony is reflected in the other intimation of Stevenson's syntactically ambiguous sentence—that there is nothing in the mirror. Utterson demonstrates—and indeed constitutes—himself as "nothing" by his very denial of the mirror. When Poole says, "this glass has seen some strange things," and the lawyer replies, "and surely none stranger than itself," Utterson singles out the mirror itself as odd. What he is saying on the literal level—that a cheval glass is unusual in a laboratory—is an evasion on the psychological level. At this dire moment, many things are stranger than the mirror. By not in effect accepting his image in the glass, Utterson can deny his membership in the Jekyll–Hyde group of mirror gazers, the solipsistic, narcissistic men who see in other men the workings of their own desires. Utterson's very verb "echoed" confirms him, however, as a rearticulation of others. His rejection of the self as other is the ultimate solipsism, the absolute mirror. As the diadic mirroring with the mother constitutes a denial of everything outside the relationship, including death, so Utterson's denial of his relationship with the mirror as external object confirms his own imaginary status, his essential nonbeing.

This brings me to one last, epitomizing—because mirroring and irreflective—quotation from Henry Jekyll. "He, I say—I cannot say, I" (94). Identity is doubly isolating because Jekyll can think of himself as other when he should not, and cannot think of himself as other when he should. He is not Hyde, thus Hyde must be a "he" rather than an "I." But Jekyll is also not really I "the elderly and discontented doctor" (90). Because Jekyll cannot bring together his two selves, his conscious and unconscious, he is neither self. Thus "I cannot say, I" means more than Jekyll's inability to call himself Hyde. Jekyll cannot call himself anything. A patriarchal system that sets out to assure self-definition by excluding undesirables ends up by excluding itself, through the exclusion of half of every self. If you cannot call the other "I," you cannot name yourself.

Stevenson would thus agree with Lacan and others that identity is mirrored alienation, though he would insist that alienation can become community if we can accept the alienated and alienating other as the self. The novella's patriarchs cannot do this, however. Jekyll, who imagines that he can banish Hyde "like the stain of a breath upon a mirror" (86), proves as transitory as his mirror image whose death coincides with his own. The images of Utterson and Poole are comparable stains on the cheval glass. They lack depth and permanence because they do not know themselves as absence. They suffer—on the level of narrative—the fate of Jekyll, who thinks that the potion which can distinguish him from Hyde means that "my troubles will roll away like a story that is told" (75). In the end, Jekyll realizes that his life coincides with his story, that he will die not twitching on the floor but putting down his pen. "This is the true hour of my death" (96). Utterson and Enfield do not realize even this. Utterson reads the narratives of Lanyon and Jekyll in the assumption that meaning and thus being will result, but what happens is that Utterson fades from the narration, becoming only a character in Jekyll's narrative. Enfield is not even named here. He has been absorbed in the novel's last word, "end." What could be conventional—and thus reassuring and patriarchal—if it were "the end," becomes an unsettling reassertion of continuity as "an end." This end is both final and one of many. Patriarchy remains a fiction that is over and is still going on.

NOTES

I would like to express my gratitude to colleagues who, as they have done so generously in the past, gave time and ideas to my work: Richard D. Altick, Lawrence Buell, Frederick Crews, Paul J. Emmett, Jr., Robert A. Ferguson, Susan M. Griffin, Gordon D. Hirsch, Lawrence Rothfield, Ronald Thomas, Mark Turner; particularly Lauren Berlant, Lisa Ruddick, Jeffrey Stern, and Richard Strier. I would also like to thank the seminar on literature and psychoanalysis at the Chicago Institute for Psychoanalysis for the help with a draft of this essay; and the students in my Anglo-American Gothic classes and seminars, especially Timothy Child, Douglas Jones, and Karen Rosenthal.

1. Though critics have not given detailed attention to any of Jekyll's peers, they have at times mentioned ambiguities of characters on which I will focus. Eigner, who calls Enfield "a sturdy young business man" (188), also lists him among "the 'down-going men'" (146). Hennelly, recognizing that Enfield blackmails Hyde as Enfield supposes Hyde is doing to Jekyll, says, "even Enfield ... is symbolically returning from some Hyde-like, dark quest beyond civilization and consciousness" (13). See also Nabokov (189) and Saposnik (111). With Lanyon, the "hasty" aspect has been rioted by Egan (31), the "hide-bound" by Hennelly (11) and Fraustino (236). Fraustino goes on to attribute Lanyon's

dilemma to a "society [which] purposely cultivates self-deceit in obscuring from its Lanyons the truth about themselves" (236). Saposnik concentrates on Lanyon himself as one who "abandoned Jekyll because he was afraid of the temptation to which he finally succumbed" (111). Utterson has, expectably, generated the widest range of interpretation. Most complimentary are Block's crediting of Utterson with "the acquisition of knowledge through intense sympathy" (448), Saposnik's calling him "a partisan in the best sense of the term" (110), Hennelly's saying that "only Utterson seems to be finally 'free' within such a cultural straight-jacket [Victorian repressiveness].... Only he achieves, in the tale's idiom, the 'balanced' ideal" (10, 11), and Heath's listing Utterson along with Enfield as a man with a "shaken but healthy identity" (104). Most critical are Miyoshi's contention that "there is something furtive and suppressed about him .... [his tolerance] looks suspiciously like the result not of charity but of indifference" (471); Egan's, that Utterson "remains to the end only the bewildered onlooker" (31); and Fraustino's, that Utterson fails because he "attempts to articulate reality by means of language" (237).

2. Besides Day and Miyoshi, see Eigner, Fraustino, Hennelly, Saposnik, and Welsch.

3. "Friend" and its derivatives occur on pages 29 (three times), 30, 32 (twice), 35, 36 (four times), 37, 38, 39 (three times), 40, 41, 51, 52 (twice), 53, 56 (three times), 57, 58 (four times), 59 (twice), 66, 72, 74, 75, and 90.

4. Among numerous discussions of patriarchy recently, those particularly helpful to me have been: Veronica Beechey, "On Patriarchy," *Feminist Review* 1 (1979): 66–82; Christine Delphy, "Patriarchy, Feminism, and Their Intellectuals," *Close to Home*, tr. and ed. by Diana Leonard (Amherst: University of Massachusetts Press, 1984), 138–53; George B. Forgie, *Patricide in the House Divided* (New York: W. W. Norton and Co., 1979); Annette Kuhn, "Structures of Patriarchy and Capital in the Family," in *Feminism and Materialism*, ed. Annette Kuhn and Ann Marie Wolpe (London: Routledge and Kegan Paul, 1978), 42–67; Gerda Lerner, *The Creation of Patriarchy* (New York: Oxford University Press, 1986); Catharine A. MacKinnon, "Feminism, Marxism, Method, and the State: An Agenda for Theory," *Signs* 7(1982): 515–44; Roisin McDonough and Rachel Harrison, "Patriarchy and Relations of Production," in *Feminism and Materialism*, 11–41; Janice A. Radway, *Reading the Romance* (Chapel Hill: University of North Carolina Press, 1984); Michael Paul Rogin, *Subversive Genealogy* (Berkeley: University of California Press, 1983); Gayle Rubin, "The Traffic in Women: Notes on the 'Political Economy' of Sex," in *Toward an Anthropology of Women*, ed. Rayna R. Reiter (New York: Monthly Review Press, 1975), 157–210; and Eve Kosofsky Sedgwick, *Between Men* (New York: Columbia University Press, 1985).

5. Henry James a century ago noted the absence of women in Stevenson's work (Maixner 292). In 1939, Gwynn, calling Jekyll's circle "a community of monks" (130), concluded that "a sure instinct guided him [Stevenson]. Insistence on the sexual would have brought colours into the story alien to its pattern; what he desired was to convey the presence of evil wholly divorced from good" (131). Stevenson's "instinct" is defended by Saposnik with a different argument. "The Victorian era was male-centered; and a story so directed at the essence of its moral behavior is best seen from a male perspective.... [also] a peculiarly masculine breed of asceticism" pervades the tale (110). Even Nabokov says that "a certain amiable, jovial, and lighthearted strain running through the pleasures of a gayblade would then have been difficult to reconcile with the medieval rising as a black scarecrow against a livid sky in the guise of Hyde" (194). Day has much more usefully connected the "striking" absence of women with the sickness of Victorian relations as

Stevenson sees them. "In their search for pleasure, Henry Jekyll and Dorian Gray throw off the feminine world of respectability and thus their pursuit takes on a purely masculine, sadistic form, finally transformed into the masochism of suicide" (92). Recently Heath has included the absence of women in his extensive discussion of sexuality in *Jekyll and Hyde*.

6. Harvie makes an excellent case for Stevenson's fundamental conservatism. First locating Stevenson in the general swing to the right that characterized the 1870s and 1880s, Harvie then concentrates on the man himself. Though "Stevenson, fundamentally always a Tory, did his bit for journalistic Unionism when in 1887 he dreamed up a crazy scheme of moving his whole family to Ireland.... Stevenson is much more logically conservative than we generally credit him with being.... Stevenson was, by birth, a Scottish Tory" (112–13). This group, however establishment-oriented, shared Louis's "hatred of pharasaism and humbug" (113). Retaining from his early socialist days "his religious belief, and an imaginative sympathy—not so much with the poor *per se*, as with their attitude to the rich," Stevenson fairly quickly "became a solidly anti-Gladstonian Tory whose hostility to Liberalism while less rancid than, say, Rudyard Kipling's, far pre-dated the split of 1886" (115).

7. Magali Sarfatti Larson, *The Rise of Professionalism* (Berkeley: University of California Press, 1977), 4, 5.

8. Stevenson mentions these instances of "brown" in "A Chapter on Dreams"; Kanzer connects them in his interpretation of Stevenson's psychological life.

9. For critics who discuss "je kyll," see Egan (30), Miyoshi (473), Saposnik (note 11).

10. Violence also colors Enfield through his name. "Enfield" is both the Sussex site of the Royal Small Arms Factory founded in the eighteenth century and the weapons produced there. "Enfield riflemen" and "Enfield skirmishers" were important components of the British infantry. Stevenson's fascination with the military was lifelong and is well documented by his biographers (Furnas 22, 198, 201, 202, 208, 387; Calder 38, 41, 47, 120, 159). Ordnance, in particular, recurs often in Stevenson's correspondence up through 1886. "Grenades and torpedoes ... artillery range ... big short ... minute guns ... 'a red canon-ball' ... platoon firing ... fire a gun to leaward" (L1, 41, 227, 300; L2, 20, 28, 151). In addition, there is, of course, *Ben Gunn*. Enfield's genealogy is, therefore, long and violent; what is unique about him is his placement in the ostensibly genteel world of Victorian patriarchy.

11. From its first entry in 1547 to its most recent, the OED records as the meaning of "to take to one's heels" only "to run away."

12. The maid could be house-sitting for her master during his absence, but the month of October (46) seems too late for any seasonal vacation and the expression "living alone" seems inappropriate to house-sitting. The possibility of homosexual innuendo in the Carew/Hyde encounter is raised by Charyn in his "Afterword" to the Bantam edition of the novella (New York: 1981), 113.

13. For devolution in Stevenson, see Block and Lawler.

14. Kanzer and Fiedler examine oedipal features of Stevenson's personality and various works but do almost nothing with *Jekyll and Hyde*. Hennelly sees the link to Oedipus but discusses it only in terms of "self-actualizing choice.... [Jekyll] like Oedipus, chooses his own fate" (12). Calder is willing to recognize "oedipal jealousy" in Stevenson's "cry of exclusion 'my mother is my father's wife'" (75), but she resolutely denies Stevenson's "need for a mother figure" (70). Why? Because Stevenson desired Mrs. Sitwell sexually. Calder is unquestionably correct about the nature of Stevenson's desire for Fanny Sitwell, but

Calder does not allow for the fact that sexual desire can indicate precisely an attraction *to* mother, if the son has indeed found a woman who evokes his lingering oedipal and pre-oedipal desires. Calling Mrs. Sitwell "mother" can both be "part of his later rationalization" after Fanny declined any sexual liaison (70) and still reveal the reality of Louis's initial oedipal/sexual desire for her.

15. In *A Child's Garden of Verses*, illustrated by Charles Robinson (Boulder, Colo.: Shambhala Publications, 1979). Subsequent poems are cited from this edition, with line references included in the text.

16. Freud's fullest description of the primal scene is in his analysis of the wolfman (from the *History of an Infantile Neurosis*, in *The Standard Edition of the Complete Psychological Works of Sigmund Freud*, vol. 17, tr. James Strachey [London: Hogarth Press, 1964], particularly "The Dream and Primal Scene," 29–47). Among critics of Stevenson, Kanzer is by far the most perceptive about primal scene materials in Louis's life and work.

17. Critics who concentrate on the lawyer's first and second names draw understandably benign conclusions about his character. Hennelly discusses "Gabriel Utterson's prophetic narrative like that of his angel namesake" (12); Saposnik finds in him "a combination of justice and mercy (as his names Gabriel John suggest)" (10). In my reading of *Jekyll and Hyde*, the benign potential of Utterson's first names is undercut by the nature of his utterances. His story is prophetic in the ironic sense that his inability to see augers the decline of Victorian patriarchy; justice and mercy are just what he cannot articulate when the stakes are highest and the threats most immediate. No annunciation is voiced by this Gabriel who generates neither progeny nor ample insight; little light is divided from darkness by this John for whom the notion of "in the beginning was the word" signifies an ironic imprisonment of language.

18. In addition to the tradition that extends from Pandora's box to Portia's caskets, there is the slang association of "box" with the female genital, which Spears calls "widespread" by the 1900s.

19. "Queer" meaning "male homosexual" has entered "general slang" by the early 1900s, according to Spears; Partridge (8th edition) locates the same meaning "since ca. 1900."

20. "By-street" occurs repeatedly in the novella where "side street" or even "street" would have sufficed mimetically. The OED lists "bisexual" as early as 1824, when Coleridge uses it in *Aids to Reflection*.

21. Establishing that "no scholarly work has been done on the origins of 'gay' in the sense under discussion [meaning male homosexual, and an embarrassment of riches complicates its history," John Boswell locates "*gai*" meaning "a openly homosexual person" as early as fourteenth-century France (*Christianity, Social Tolerance, and Homosexuality* [Chicago: University of Chicago Press, 1983], 43). Stevenson's excellent knowledge of French and his presence in the artistic communities of Paris and Barbizon, make his knowledge of the French usage of *gai* probable. By "the early 20th century," Boswell adds, "'gay' was common in the English homosexual subculture." Stevenson's acceptance into Bohemia and into the literary inner circle of Britain, where Pater and Wilde moved with their followers, where the *Yellow Book* group and other London aesthetes would flourish by the early 1890s, and where close friends like Gosse revealed homosexual inclinations, means that Stevenson's hearing by 1886 a password common a few years later is highly likely. Eve Kosofsky Sedgwick makes a forceful case for the homoerotic connotations of the words "gay" and "queer" in Henry James's turn-of-the-century story "The Beast in the

Jungle" ("The Beast in the Closet: James and the Writing of Homosexual Panic" in *Sex, Politics, and Science*, Selected Papers for the English Institute, 1983–84, ed. Ruth Bernard Yeazell [Baltimore: Johns Hopkins University Press, 1984], 148–86). James was of course in close contact with *The Yellow Book* and Gosse, as well as with homosexual young men such as Jocelyn Perse. From my recent immersion in Anglo-American gothic fiction between 1885 and 1914, I have little doubt that the use of "gay" and "queer" in the homoerotic sense was widespread in the years before 1900.

Furnas establishes quite properly that Stevenson's "times allowed *friend* a significant warmth greater than ours now permit.... in the 1870's, particularly in intellectual-aesthetic circles, 'friends' were gloatingly added up and acknowledged claims not dissimilar to, though less formal than, those of blood-brothers in preliterate cultures" (39). Furnas then goes on, "let no fool try to read perversion into the above. It is difficult to comprehend Louis's relations with Bob Stevenson or Henley or Henry James without understanding precisely what was meant or not meant by his ability frankly to write, 'I love you, Henley, from my soul'" (39–40). Furnas's defensiveness here highlights the questions that his rhetoric wants to repress. Calder is less anxious: "It is noticeable again and again, in men who may well have had no hidden homosexual tendencies (and also in men who did—Edmund Gosse, for instance) that the male appreciation of Stevenson was often intensely physical" (65). For me the issue is not whether Stevenson's friends were latently or actively homosexual but whether his sensibility and his experience allowed for perception of the homoerotic bonds that characterize the men of *Jekyll and Hyde*. Compare, for example, Stevenson's response to seeing Henley and Jekyll's response to becoming Hyde: "the look of his face was like wine to me" (Furnas 106); "the thought ... delighted me like wine" (91). Henley's conflicts with Fanny quite obviously involve rivalry. "Henley was jealous of the love and time Louis gave to his wife. For it is clear that Henley was, in a sense, in love with him.... Henley's jealousy rivaled Fanny's.... like many others, Henley loved Louis" (Calder 95, 164). Among these others was Sidney Colvin. "(Fanny) believed Louis's love for Colvin to equal his love for her. Colvin himself was not above jealousy" (Calder 155). Triangles were complicated by Louis's penchant for role reversal. He often configured the maternal Fanny in startlingly masculine terms. Calling her "my dear fellow" and "My dearest little man," he sounds, as Furnas recognizes, an "unusual note ... his letters to her sound almost like Damon writing to Pythias" (256, 257). In turn, personalities as strong as Fanny's and Henley's draw out the feminine side of Louis, which Henley stressed in the early version of his famous poem on Stevenson. "With a subtle trace / Of feminine force.... a streak of Puck, / More Cleopatra, of Hamlet most of all." That Henley later changed these lines to "With trace on trace / Of passion, impudence, and energy.... a streak of Puck, / Much Antony ..." confirms in the very act of repression the "feminine" appeal that Louis exercised. Stevenson was conscious of this feminine component. He admits to giving Seraphina "a trait taken from myself" (L2, 338); he recognizes in Alexander's portrait of hire "a mixture of aztec idol, a lion, an Indian Rajah, and a woman" (L2, 342–43). Stevenson's capacity to envision various roles for himself and others and to evoke and reciprocate strong emotions in persons of both sexes are for me marks of his exceptional interest as a human being and sources of his psychological penetration as a writer.

22. Kanzer uses the word *phallus* but clearly he means penis ("Hyde is small and possessed of some nameless deformity" [Geduld 122]).

23. Otto Rank, *The Double*, tr. and ed. Harry Tucker, Jr. (Chapel Hill: University of North Carolina Press, 1971).

GEORGE DEKKER

James and Stevenson:
The Mixed Current of
Realism and Romance

In "The Art of Fiction" (1884), Henry James celebrates the novel's "immense and exquisite correspondence with life" (79).[1] He asserts the primary claims of observation, firsthand and adult; hence of contemporary experience and the example of the French realist novelists; of the "work" of art. In "A Humble Remonstrance" (1884), written in "genial rejoinder" (101) to Jones's essay, Robert Louis Stevenson protests that there is a radical disjuncture between art and life as we normally experience it. He argues for the priority of imagination and the child's perspective; for universal experience and the models provided by romancers of all times and places; for the "play" of art. If the pattern of oppositions sounds familiar, so it should. This debate of the 1880's clearly updates a controversy about the nature and merits of fictional realism and romance that "novelists" and "romancers" had been carrying on for nearly a century and a half.[2] In turn, James's contributions to the controversy have probably done more than anybody else's to make it seem worth continuing and to shape its terms for modern criticism. Although Stevenson's critical writings have not survived their occasions, the examples of his bravest romances and braver life challenged James to move beyond the realist canons of "The Art of Fiction" and work toward a synthesis that would incorporate the romance values of play, imaginative freedom, and what he was latex to call "the finest feelings."

From *Critical Reconstructions: The Relationship of Fiction and Life*, eds. Robert M. Polhemus and Roger B. Henkle. © 1994 by the Board of Trustees of the Leland Stanford Junior University.

To understand Stevenson's role in the development of James's fictional theory, we must try to see him as James saw him rather than as he appears from the diminishing perspective of the 1990's. Few interpreters of James's criticism appear to have made this imaginative effort or to have reflected much on the rich trove that survives from the James–Stevenson relationship.[3] Besides the two manifestoes of 1884, there are over forty letters written between 1884 and 1894, two long essays on Stevenson that James published in 1888 and 1900, and numerous allusions demonstrating that Stevenson's ideas and example haunted and influenced him to the end. My aim here is not to survey these materials in any detail but rather to explain more fully how James and Stevenson differ in "The Art of Fiction" and "A Humble Remonstrance"; to isolate from James's writings to and about Stevenson that special duality which, for James, made him so deeply appealing and significant—so "great" as a man and author; and to contend that the preface to *The American* (1907), James's most influential and controversial statement about the realism–romance polarity, is itself best read as a Romantic ode in prose, with distinct Stevensonian reverberations.

I

James replied to "A Humble Remonstrance" with a warm personal letter in which he expressed his appreciation of Stevenson's "suggestive and felicitous" remarks and his conviction that "we agree ... much more than we disagree." Disclaiming complex or covert aims, James assured Stevenson that "The Art of Fiction" was "simply a plea for liberty." While we may be sure that rather more was involved and that Stevenson was not taken in by this disarming encapsulation, the frequent appearance both of the words "liberty" and "freedom" and of their opposites ("proscription," "a priori," "prescription," "suppression," "dogma," etc.) suggests that James's plea for liberty is both important in itself and at the root of much else in the essay. Indeed, as Leo Bersani and others have argued, it is at the root of nearly everything James wrote.[4]

The first of the two major liberties James claims for the novelist is freedom from the restrictive and trivializing expectations of the Anglo-American reading public. Against the popular conception of the novel as a form of entertainment dedicated to supplying predictably cheerful endings and matter suitable for "young people," he argues that the novelist's high artistic "cause" is the same as that of the painter, while the novelist's commitment to finding and telling the truth about life is as uncompromising as the historian's or philosopher's (56). "Experiment," which links the novelist's with the scientist's investigations of life, is another key word. But the one that echoes through the essay almost as persistently as "freedom" and its cognates is "serious."

James probably intended this array of lofty analogies and verbal repetitions not so much to browbeat squeamish or philistine readers as to brace fellow novelists against their pressures—and also, of course, against those of compromising editors. He had often experienced these pressures himself, as in 1877 when *Atlantic Monthly* editor William Dean Howells protested against the unhappy ending of *The American*. James's response was very much in the spirit of "The Art of Fiction" and, as we shall see, the more interesting because he was later obliged to eat his brave words. If he had ended his novel with the marriage of Christopher Newman and Madame de Cintre, he wrote Howells, "I should have made a prettier ending, certainly; but I should have felt as if I were throwing a rather vulgar sop to readers who don't really know the world and who don't measure the merit of a novel by its correspondence to the same."[5]

Allusions to the once-powerful "Evangelical hostility" to fiction help us to place "The Art of Fiction" with other passionate (and rhetorically cunning) "defenses" of the seriousness and moral value of literature, such as Sidney's "An Apology for Poetry" or Shelley's "A Defense of Poetry." It belongs as well to another familiar nonfictional genre, the romantic manifesto, in the claims it makes for a second major liberty for the novelist: freedom from the restrictive artistic formulas devised by critics on the basis of past performances by other writers. As Ian Watt explains in *The Rise of the Novel*, romanticism and novelistic discourse were intimately related through their emphasis on individualism and originality, and their resistance to "those elements in classical critical theory which were inimical to formal realism."[6] The polemic of "The Art of Fiction" is squarely in this tradition.

The immediate occasion of James's essay was a public lecture, delivered earlier in 1884 and also entitled "The Art of Fiction," by the popular novelist Walter Besant. Although Besant expressed a suitably elevated sense of the greatness of the novel form, his lecture's approach to questions of "art," like that of other briskly professional progeny of Horace's *Ars Poetica*, was predominantly commonsensical and prescriptive: keep a notebook; young ladies brought up in quiet country villages should not write about garrison life; "If you have tried the half-dozen best publishers, and been refused by all, realize that the work *will not do.*'"[7] James's approach is so different that we may wonder why he recycled Besant's title. In his opening remarks, James displays some uneasiness about "so comprehensive a title" (53), but claims to find a "pretext for my temerity" in Besant's usage—a deferential gesture that is itself an ironic pretext. So far from a timid following of example, James's "copying" is a decisive act of appropriation that says, in effect, that the entire job must be done over again. It says, too, that the well-meaning Besant did not understand the meaning of the words—"Art" especially—that *he* had had the temerity to use.

For James, "Art" principally means that which cannot be reduced to practical tips or generic axioms to be passed on from the elder to the rising generation. Starting from the radically individualistic premise that the ways novels can be "interesting" (the only "general responsibility" to which they can be held) are "as various as the temperament of man, and ... successful in proportion as they reveal a particular mind, different from others," he defines the novel as "a personal impression of life" (62). This definition accords precisely with Ian Watt's dictum that the "primary criterion" of the novel is "truth to individual experience."[8] On this showing, traditional generic distinctions, such as that between the novel and romance, can have "little reality or interest" (71) or are positively misleading, since each novel must be a new beginning with its own laws of development. Lest this privileging of the unique personal impression seem less a liberation from the dead hand of the past than a crippling limitation for writers who have seen little of the world, James explains that the direct experience that both he and Besant call for includes, indeed is inseparable from, imaginative experience. "When the mind is imaginative—much more when it happens to be that of a man of genius—it takes to itself the faintest hints of life, it converts the very pulses of the air into revelations" (66). No less "Romantic" in thought and vocabulary is his corollary claim that the product of this imaginative extension of experience is "a living thing, all one and continuous, like every other organism, and in proportion as it lives will it be found, I think, that in each of its parts there is something of each of the other parts" (69). Thus understood, the novelistic work of art might well be said to "compete with life" (55, 68). James's plea for artistic liberty culminates in a celebration of the "splendid privilege" of the novelist to work with a form that has "so few restrictions" that "the other arts, in comparison, appear confined and hampered" (84). Such is the plenitude of novelistic fiction, open to all manner of seeing and rendering life, that "talents so dissimilar as those of Alexandre Dumas and Jane Austen, Charles Dickens and Gustave Flaubert, have worked in this field with equal glory."

Very much in the same pluralistic spirit is James's judgment earlier in the essay that *Treasure Island* is "delightful ... it appears to me to have succeeded wonderfully in what it attempts" (80). However, a thoughtful reader would be hard pressed to find firm ground in "The Art of Fiction" for judging Dumas or even Dickens or Austen equal to the author of *Madame Bovary*, or for taking the author of *Treasure Island* seriously. Despite James's paean to the imagination and the catholicity of taste he displays, his essay consists mainly of an eloquent restatement of the doctrines of contemporary French and American exponents of novelistic realism. It is out of their window in the House of Fiction that he is looking when he maintains that the measure of success for novelistic fiction is its "closeness of relation" (75) to life, its ability to let us "see life *without* rearrangement," and when he ventures that "the air of reality (solidity of specification) seems ... the supreme virtue of a novel" (67). Wishing to steer clear of the implication that the novelist is a mere transcriber or copier of life's surfaces, he allows that "Art is essentially selection" (75); but wary on the other hand lest selection be construed to legitimize censorship, he insists that "it is a selection whose main care is to be typical, to be inclusive." In sum, a work of fiction is most a novel, and better for being so, when it is a novel in the tradition of Balzac.

To this tradition *Treasure Island* obviously did not belong, but the novel with which James chose to compare it, Edmond de Goncourt's *Chérie* (1884), just as obviously did. *Chérie* invited the comparison inasmuch as it too featured a child protagonist, but it was written for an exclusively adult audience and in fact carried the documentary procedures of French realism to an unprecedented extreme. Conceiving his role as a novelist to be that of "a historian of those who have no history,"[9] Goncourt had announced in the preface to *La Faustin* (1882) that his next novel would be a study of a young girl's psychological and physiological development, and appealed to his female readers to become his collaborators by writing to him anonymously about their intimate experiences in growing up. Rightly seeing himself among "the bringers of the new,"[10] Goncourt claimed in the preface to *Chérie* that the result of this collaboration was a novel lacking in incidents, reversals, and intrigue, but abounding in interior drama and having its destined place in the evolution of the novel from the adventure romances of the early nineteenth century to what would eventually supersede the novel form itself, "a book of pure analysis."[11]

Although James saw the evolution of the novel somewhat differently and believed that *Chérie*, like other Goncourt experiments, was more interesting in theory than practice, he had assimilated much of that theory and, as Ezra Pound in his generation also would, wished to honor the elderly French novelist as a major spokesman for the Make-It-New approach to writing. In juxtaposing *Chérie* with *Treasure Island*, then, James was implicitly invoking a historical and critical schema that left scant room for Stevenson's "delightful" little novel. Explicitly, however, he only expressed the reservation that in the case of *Chérie* he could appeal to his own experience to say "Yes" or "No" (80). "I have been a child, but I have never been on a quest for a buried treasure, and it is a simple accident that with M. de Goncourt I should have for the most part to say No."

To which Stevenson promptly rejoined: "If he has never been on a quest for buried treasure, it can be demonstrated that he has never been a child. There never was a child (unless Master James) but has hunted gold, and been a pirate.... Elsewhere in his essay Mr. James has protested with excellent reason against too narrow a conception of experience; for the born artist, he contends, the 'faintest hints of life' are converted into revelations" (94). Both here in "A Humble Remonstrance" and in other essays Stevenson contends that the imaginative child, trailing clouds of glory, is a primitive literary artist ("the born artist" precisely) and therefore a proper touchstone for literary theorists.

This thesis is stated more vulnerably in "A Gossip on Romance," written before "A Humble Remonstrance" but published as its preliminary and companion piece in Stevenson's 1887 collection of essays, *Memories and Portraits*: "The dullest of clowns tells, or tries to tell, himself a story, as the feeblest of children uses invention in his play; and even as the imaginative grown person, joining in the game, at once enriches it with many delightful circumstances, the great creative writer shows us the realisation and the apotheosis of the day-dreams of common men. His stories may be nourished with the realities of life, but their true mark is to satisfy the nameless longings of the reader, and to obey the ideal laws of the day-dream."[12] Thus broadly and unqualifiedly formulated, Stevenson's theory of fiction is undeniably escapist. Nor can it help to explain why one writer, perhaps Stevenson himself, fits the category of "great creative writer" whereas another, say, a scriptwriter for *Dallas*, does not. However, our immediate concern is not with the adequacy of Stevenson's theory but simply with what it was and how it differed from James's. How are the fundamental relationships between writer, reader, narrative form, and "the realities of life" reconstituted when James's model of the novelist as a specialty imaginative adult observer is replaced by a daydreamer who combines a child's capacity for shared imaginative play with an adult's awareness of tine "realities of life"?

"Shared" may be the key word. James stresses a novelist's freedom to differ in his view of life and art not only from other novelists but from readers as well, conceding readers the same freedom to differ but not one iota more. Indeed, the readers posited in "The Art of Fiction" are mainly characterized as obtuse, sentimental, and interfering, more likely to be satisfied consumers of Besant's *All Sorts and Conditions of Men* than of *The Portrait of a Lady*. As might be expected of a writer who reached a far wider audience than either Besant or James, Stevenson's emphasis falls on the bond of experience that reader and author share as people who have learned to read and write, who have become aware of some of the realities of life, but who have not outgrown a basic human need to play roles and make up stories.

This bond being granted, the art of fiction becomes (at least at one level) very practically rhetorical. Counting upon the reader, like himself, to have "ardently desired and fondly imagined" a life of adventure in youthful daydreams, the "cunning and low-minded" author of *Treasure Island* "addressed himself throughout to the building up and circumstantiation of this boyish dream. Character to the boy is a sealed book; for him, a pirate is a beard in wide trousers and literally bristling with pistols. The author ... himself more or less grown up, admitted character, within certain limits, into his design; but only within certain limits" (94). To be more or less grown up" is, for Stevenson, to strike the right balance between survival of the child's expansive imaginative faculty and acquisition of the adult's understanding of limits and character. As James was later to emphasize, this balance is crucial to Stevenson's limited but distinguished achievement as a fictionalist. A mature moralist and literary technician, he was also one of the preeminent Victorian mythmakers, and had a profound intuitive understanding of the contending forces central to the Freudian scheme of human development. Like Mark Twain, he conducts his boy heroes, Jim Hawkins and David Balfour, on journeys of adventure such as they (and all children) might have vaguely imagined for themselves; but he is always aware, and always makes his adult readers aware, of ranges of experience beyond the boys' ken—of the drives, motives, and designs that lie behind a beard in wide trousers.

But the balance achieved in his practice depends in his theory on qualifiers grudgingly conceded or hastily tacked on. Shorn of these qualifiers, Stevenson's is a projective theory of fiction, a sort of nursery version of Northrop Frye's. For him, the great fictionalist is the writer who does the best job of reimagining and retelling what are, at bottom, the same old stories—in short, and in traditional terms, a "finder" rather than a "maker." This is the underlying reason why, at the outset of "A Humble Remonstrance," he (misleadingly) maintains that "what both Mr. James and Mr. Besant had in view" was not the art of fiction but rather "the art of narrative" (87). Since the stories being narrated anew in novels (as likewise in narrative poems or prose romances such as *Morte D'Arthur*) are known to everybody, James's individualistic definition of the novel as "a personal impression of life" (62) is far wide of the mark. In some ways far more old-fashioned than James, in others he strikes us as much more modern—even modernist. Thus he deals with James's mimeticism by allowing that "circumstantiation" (what Frye would call realistic displacement) is necessary, but he is scornful of James's contention that the novelist can or should try to "compete with life." Life, he rejoins, "is monstrous, infinite, illogical, abrupt, and poignant; a work of art, in comparison, is neat, finite, self-contained, rational, flowing, and emasculate" (92). At points where he implicitly concedes that novelistic fiction has a correspondence with the life we wakefully experience rather than the one we dream, his emphasis falls on the principles of rigorous selection, abstraction, and simplification—principles common to all the arts, and readily endorsed by James, but scarcely *the* hallmark of the novels James most admired or that he wrote himself.

Although pointedly eschewing any organic analogy, Stevenson agrees with James that after his own fashion the novelist can compete with life by creating a work of art with its own wholeness and unity: "For the welter of impressions, all forcible but discrete, which life presents, it substitutes a certain artificial series of impressions ... all aiming at the same effect, all eloquent of the same idea, all chiming together like consonant notes in music" (91). The analogy with music appears likewise in "A Gossip on Romance": "The right kind of thing should fall out in the right kind of place; the right kind of thing should follow; and not only the characters talk aptly and think naturally, but all the circumstances in a tale answer to one another like notes in music."[13] Stevenson was a poet as well as a prose writer, and had a wonderful ear for the variety and music of English. James, whose ear was more limited, took little pleasure in vocal or instrumental music but was deeply responsive to the visual arts. In Stevenson's fiction, characters are likely to overhear; in James's, they always see.

When, years later, James complained that *Catriona* "subjects my visual sense, my *seeing* imagination, to an almost painful underfeeding" (239), Stevenson responded:

> I *hear* people talking, and I *feel* them acting, and that seems to me to be fiction. My two aims may be described as—
> > 1st.   War to the adjective.
> > 2nd.   Death to the optic nerve.
> Admitted we live in an age of the optic nerve in literature. For how many centuries did literature get along without a sign of it? (241)

This pithy manifesto of 1893 seems to recall the advice to the novice fictionalist with which he concluded "A Humble Remonstrance": "In this age of the particular, let him remember the ages of the abstract, the great books of the past, the brave men that lived before Shakespeare and before Balzac" (100). Of course he was right that, in fiction, the nineteenth century was to an unprecedented degree the age of the particular and the optic nerve; the massing of visual details was essential to novelistic realism in the tradition of Balzac. His reasons for mistrusting this development were similar to Wordsworth's for deploring the "tyranny" of the eye, "most despotic of our senses."[14] The eye, riveted on a host of distinct external particulars, had the power to hold in thrall both the heart that bonded human to human and the imagination that unified both natural scenes and works of art. Stevenson had what James called the "*hearing* imagination" (239) and, for many conscious and unconscious reasons, he preferred to analogize fiction with music, of all arts the least directly mimetic and most dedicated to making the right things fall out in the right places and "answer to one another" like ideal writer to ideal reader and dream to dream.

How was it, then, that writers so opposed in background, temperament, theory, and fictional practice soon became fast friends and mutual admirers? Part of the answer has to be that, although they had less in common than James wished to acknowledge, they were probably further apart in their aims and methods when they wrote "The Art of Fiction" and "A Humble Remonstrance" than at any other point in their careers. Although we tend to think of the later Stevenson principally as the romantic rover of the South Seas, his tendency in fiction after *Kidnapped* (1885) was to move gradually in die direction of more realistic treatment and more adult subject matter—to become increasingly preoccupied with what lay behind "a beard in wide trousers."[15] Adult sexuality, although handled discreetly and sometimes even coyly in *The Master of Ballantrae* and *Catriona*, achieves a new importance in those novels and becomes central in *The Beach of Falesa* and the great fragment *Weir of Hermiston*. Whereas the author of *Treasure Island* had no need of James's "plea for liberty" and did not mention it once in "A Humble Remonstrance," he was forced to permit his candid treatment of relations between natives and white traders in *The Beach of Falesa* to be bowdlerized. Now he lamented: "This is a poison bad world for the romancer, this Anglo-Saxon world; I usually get out of it by not having any women in it at all" (266). As for James, neither before nor after 1883–86 was he nearly so committed to the precepts and procedures of post-Balzacian realism. Never after *The Bostonians* and *The Princess Casamassima* (both 1886) did he write a novel that smacked so strongly, if intermittently, of Daudet, the Goncourts, and even Zola.

James once declared that Stevenson was "the sole and single Anglo-

Saxon capable of perceiving ... how well [James's fiction was] written" (188). Although doubtless a sincere expression of the admiration they felt for each other as literary craftsmen, this praise probably says more about James's low opinion of contemporary critics than about his confidence in Stevenson's overall judgment of fiction. In letters to James, Stevenson expressed keen if usually vague appreciation for many of his works, but clearly preferred *Roderick Hudson* (1875) above the rest. In truth, greatly though he admired James's technical skills and moral insights, Stevenson sometimes found his fiction hard going, and succeeded in liking it only by misreading it. James must have been baffled by some of his friend's enthusiastic preferences. What did he make of Stevenson's "falling in love" with Olive Chancellor (*The Bostonians*) and Adela Chart ("The Marriages"), two of his most astringent studies of female psychology?[16] He was obviously distressed by Stevenson's impatient judgment that *The Portrait of a Lady*—so rich in visual detail, so subtle in its leisurely exposure of motive and relation—was "BELOW YOU to write and me to read" (166). This outburst was singular, however, in all senses of the word, and Stevenson was generally able to cope by recalling the romantic novels of James's youth, by misreading the later ones, or by transferring his disapproval to other targets.

A fascinating example of the transference strategy is the short section he added to the *Memories and Portraits* version of "A Humble Remonstrance." Shifting attention from James, Stevenson identifies Howells as "the bondslave, the zealot" of the "school" of realist fiction who "thinks of past things as radically dead" and also "thinks a form can be outlived." Summing up his objections to realist doctrine, he contends that "the danger is lest, in seeking to draw the normal, a lean should draw the null, and write the novel of society instead of the romance of man." Sadly, claims Stevenson, Howells was "of an originally strong romantic bent—a certain glow of romance still resides in many of his books, and lends them their distinction."[17]

Stevenson's remarks about Howells's unfortunate development away from romance partly repeat and partly reverse ones Howells himself had made in 1882 about James's development. In a major midcareer assessment of the James *oeuvre*, Howells commented that the early stories had

> a richness of poetic effect which he has since never equalled....
> Looking back to those early stories, where Mr. James stood at the
> dividing ways of the novel and the romance, I am sometimes
> sorry that he declared even superficially for the former. His best
> efforts seem to me those of romance; his best types have an ideal

development, like Claire Belgarde and Bessy Alden and poor Daisy and even Newman. But, doubtless, he has chosen wisely; perhaps the romance is an outworn form, and would not lend itself to the reproduction of even the ideality of modern life. I myself waver somewhat in my preference—if it is a preference.[18]

Regarded as literary criticism, Howells's performance here is comically indecisive and inept; and it is easy to see why James soon responded by firmly rejecting the distinction between novel and romance, and why Stevenson just as firmly redrew it as a distinction between the "romance of man" and the mere "novel of society." But Howells's images of dividing ways and wavering, besides suggestively recalling major tropes of Scott and Hawthorne, accurately register the tensions experienced by the many nineteenth-century readers and fictionalists who wanted, please, more of both—more of realism *and* more of romance—and got them, too.

Instructed as much by Stevenson's life as by anything he or Howells wrote, James began to think more deeply about the meaning and value of romance, in life, in fiction, than ever before. From Stevenson too he learned, or relearned, that play could be "serious" as well as "delightful" and was essential to creative work.

II

In his final delirium, after suffering two strokes, James supposed himself to be one of the favorite subjects of his recreational reading—Napoleon Bonaparte—and dictated letters concerning the decoration of imperial apartments in the Louvre and Tuileries. So far from being ravings, these letters are coherent, dignified, commanding: the assumption of the Emperor's persona is complete. We naturally wonder how far they disclose unconscious longings for power and status on the grandest possible scale, and also how they are linked with other, much less connected utterances recorded near the end:

Individual souls, great ... of [word lost] on which great perfections are If one does ... in the fulfillment with the neat and pure and perfect—to the success or as he or she moves through life, following admiration unfailing [word lost] in the highway—problems are very sordid.

One of the earliest of the consumers of the great globe in the interest of the attraction exercised by the great R.L.S. [Robert

Louis Stevenson] of those days, comes in, afterwards, a visitor at
Vailima and [word lost] there and pious antiquities to his
domestic annals.[19]

The fitful outcroppings of a broken mind can prove almost nothing and are
cited here only because the occasion and the seeming lack of connection
between Napoleon, Stevenson, and Henry Adams (the "visitor at Vailima")
make even more striking the connections they actually would have had for
James in his right mind. For him, Napoleon and Stevenson were alike
"great" inasmuch as each turned his life into a romance by making reality
conform to the requirements of his imagination. Adams and Stevenson, on
the other hand, typified temperamental opposites: *il penseroso* with a
debilitating streak of morbidity, who left James depressed and dispirited;
l'allegro with a strengthening admixture of sanity, who restored his sense of
fun and play and braced hum for living and working.

When Adams passed through London in 1891 after visiting Stevenson in
Samoa, James wrote to a mutual friend that "I like him, but suffer from his
monotonous disappointed pessimism."[20] His experience with Steven son was
as different as possible. Words he uses recurrently to characterize his friend are
"romantic," "charm," "boy," "fun," "happy," and "genial." In his first letter to
Stevenson, he writes: "The native *gaiety* of all that you write is delightful to me,
and when I reflect that it proceeds from a man whom life has laid much of the
time on his back ... I find you a genius indeed" (102). The conjunction of
"gaiety" and "genius" confirms our hunch that when James refers earlier in the
letter to Stevenson's "genial rejoinder," he is using "genial" as Coleridge and
Wordsworth did to suggest that the true spring of creative activity was "Joy"—
the "genial spirits" of "Tintern Abbey" and "Dejection: An Ode."

The other word he applies to Stevenson with consistently double
significance is "happy," meaning both cheerful and felicitous. In a passage
describing Stevenson's peculiar combination of "jauntiness" and care for
style, he comments that Stevenson's "sense of a happy turn [of phrase] is of
the subtlest" (131). Other examples are "his happiest [= best] work" (140) and
the "impression ... of deepening talent, of happier and richer expression"
(268). But surely the most moving and revealing usage occurs in the letter
James wrote to Edmund Gosse immediately after they learned of Stevenson's
death: "I'm not sure that it's not for *him* a great and happy fate; but for us the
loss of charm, of suspense, of 'fun' is unutterable."[21]

From "happy" and "fun" it is but a short hop back to "boy" and "play."
James was fond of children and their games, and made them the subject of
some of his finest later fiction. But throughout his career and, as we have

seen, especially during the 1880's, he reacted strongly to the trivializing forces of the literary marketplace and its audience of "young people" by insisting the writing and reading of fiction were or should be deeply serious adult activities. Therefore, however much he liked children or his friend Louis, he was never entirely at ease with the writings Stevenson addressed partly or mainly to children, much less with any suggestion that authors were all children at heart.

In his first full-length essay on Stevenson's writings, James emphasizes the balance Stevenson claimed for himself: "He describes credulity with all the resources of experience, and represents a crude stage with infinite ripeness.... Sometimes, as in *Kidnapped*, the art is so ripe that it lifts even the subject into the general air; the execution is so serious that the idea (the idea of a boy's romantic adventures) becomes a matter of universal relations" (132). This is all very handsome, but phrases such as "crude stage" and "lifts even the subject" suggest that although the "execution" is serious the "idea" or "subject" is not. Again, to say of *Treasure Island* that "it is all as perfect as a well-played boy's game" (154) and that it is "in its way a classic" may strike us as a very just summation and one with which Stevenson would have been well satisfied, but the qualifications implicit in his phrasing suggest that James continued to have doubts about the ultimate seriousness of an art so frankly and happily committed to the value of "make-believe."

Those doubts he retained to the end. Meanwhile, distinguishing between the art of fiction and the art of living, he rejoiced in Stevenson's refusal to accept the limiting "reality" of an invalid condition. In his long review essay on *Letters to His Family and Friends* (1899), James remarks that Stevenson "was so fond of the sense of youth and the idea of play that he saw whatever happened to him in images and figures, in the terms, almost, of the sports of childhood" and then quotes Stevenson on the subject of his near-encounters with death: "I keep returning, and now hand over fist, from the realms of Hades. I saw that gentleman between the eyes, and fear him less after each visit. Only Charon and his rough boatmanship I somewhat fear" (259). This is but one example of Stevenson's "imagination always at play, for drollery or philosophy, with his circumstances." In turn, Stevenson's "desperate larks" (184) in the remote South Seas inspired James to draw playful metaphors of his own out of the diverse realms of erotic play and the big top: "You are indeed ... the wandering Wanton of the Pacific. You swim into our ken with every provocation and prospect—and we have only time to open our arms to receive you when your immortal back is turned to us in the act of still more provoking flight" (187). In a later letter, James refers to his friend's "projects—and gyrations! Trapezist in the Pacific void!" (241).

In James's eyes, Stevenson's greatest game was to convert "that splendid life, that beautiful, bountiful thing ... into a fable as strange and romantic as one of his own" (248). From 1887 onwards James recurs again and again to the idea that, at great risk and against great odds, Stevenson "in a singular degree, got what he wanted, the life absolutely discockneyfied, the situation as romantically 'swagger' as if it had been an imagination made real" (269). As James well knew, Stevenson's actual "situation" was nearly as full of hardships, deprivations, and indignities as the one experienced by David Balfour in *Kidnapped*. And yet, like David's adventure in the Scottish Highlands, Stevenson's in Samoa *was* "romantically 'swagger,'" too. The crucial difference was that David neither imagined boldly nor sought his great adventure, whereas Stevenson did both, taking charge of his life in a way that compelled James's admiration. It is perhaps worth remarking that James's own "escape" to Europe had been similarly purposeful and productive—and, while outwardly deficient in "swagger," was also a romantic adventure.

Was it James's conclusion, then, that Stevenson lived a greater romance than any he ever wrote? Yes; but to say so is rather to affirm the greatness of the life as James saw it than to imply that he had major reservations about Stevenson's talent and achievement as a fictionalist. For while James was growing in appreciation of the function and value of Stevensonian play, Stevenson was maturing as a man and writer, until in *Weir of Hermiston*, left unfinished at his death, he became the sort of fictionalist James could unreservedly admire. *Weir*, so completely adult and "serious" and yet so inventive and "romantic," left nothing at odds between Stevenson the writer and James the reader, between play and work. "The Pacific," wrote James,

> made him, 'descriptively,' serious and even rather dry; with his own country ... he was ready infinitely to play.... In *Weir* especially, like an improvising pianist, he superabounds and revels, and his own sense, by a happy stroke, appeared likely never more fully and brightly to justify him; to have become even in some degree a new sense, with new chords and possibilities. It is the 'old game,' but it is the old game that he exquisitely understands. (274)

In this moment of enthusiasm for the "happy" way Stevenson plays "the old game," James seems ready even to reverse the valence of "serious."

Stevenson—or Stevenson much more than any other "influence"—

made James understand that to be *homo sapiens*, or even *homo faber* very successfully, a person had likewise to be *homo ludens*. As Johann Huizinga's classic study *Homo Ludens* explains, play enters constitutively into a range of central human activities—recreational, erotic, artistic, religious; enters, indeed, into the very creation of a human order. "First and foremost," says Huizinga, "all play is a voluntary activity.... By this quality of freedom alone, play marks itself off from the course of the natural process. It is something added thereto and spread out over it like a flowering, an ornament.... Play casts a spell over us, it is 'enchanting,' 'captivating.'"[22] These extracts distill the essence of Stevenson's significance for James and have an important bearing on his efforts after "The Art of Fiction" to reconsider the relationship between realism and romance. The "quality of freedom" in play and by extension in romance is also a quality essential to moral and artistic action. Perhaps the charge should not be that romance is escapist but that realism is defeatist?

James's first essay on Stevenson is a crucial document in the history of his rethinking the relationship between realism and romance. In it he restates the generic premise of "The Art of Fiction": "The breath of the novelist's being is his liberty; and the incomparable virtue of the form he uses is that it lends itself to views innumerable and diverse" (149). Although he doesn't say so, it is obvious that he would still resist any attempt to "separate" the novel from the modern prose romance. The novel form as he envisages it can subsume both the "novel of society" and the "romance of man"—and more. Now, however, James's plea for liberty works in favor of that elusive quality (as distinct from fictional genre), "romance": "The doctrine of M. Zola himself, so meagre if literally taken, is fruitful, inasmuch as in practice he romantically departs from it." James's point about Zola is the point that Stevenson had made earlier about Howells. Now James's emphasis falls on the leavening effect of romance rather than on the "truth of detail" and "solidity of specification" (67) likewise so abundantly present in Zola and so resoundingly endorsed as "the supreme virtue of a novel" in "The Art of Fiction." James is beginning to associate romance in fiction positively with imaginative freedom and play: here it is the genie in the Naturalist machine.

Stevenson, James dryly remarks, "does not need to depart" from a theory in order "to pursue the romantic." What he doesn't remark, but clearly means, is that Stevenson's theory is in its way just as meager as Zola's and equally fruitful when he departs *realistically* from it. On several occasions later in the essay James explains how Stevenson creates an "indescribable mixture of the prodigious and the human, of surprising coincidences and familiar feelings" (155). In *Kidnapped* especially we find "the author's talent for seeing the actual in the marvellous, and reducing the extravagant to plausible detail" (158). Over "the whole business," James says, is the "charm of the most romantic episode in the world—though perhaps it would be hard to say why it is the most romantic, when it was intermingled with so much stupidity." As for Stevenson's enthusiasm for romances of adventure in the tradition of Alexandre Dumas, James comments: "He makes us say, Let the tradition live, by all means, since it was delightful; but at the same time he is the cause of our perceiving afresh that a tradition is kept alive only by something being added to it. In this particular case—in *Doctor Jekyll* and *Kidnapped*—Mr. Stevenson has added psychology" (152). Since James's generosity to R.L.S. the novelist is at the expense of R.L.S the theorist, it is but fair to note that Stevenson himself had previously claimed that "true romantic art ... makes a romance of all things.... *Robinson Crusoe* is as realistic as it is romantic; both qualities are pushed to an extreme, and neither suffers."[23]

James offers a patch of ground for romance in realist fiction when he argues that the novelist "who leaves the extraordinary out of his account is liable to awkward confrontations" in an "age of newspapers," for the "next report of the next divorce case ... shall offer us a picture of astounding combinations of circumstance and behaviour." While Stevenson doubtless would have agreed with this argument, he patently had something more in mind when he contrasted the romance of man with the novel of society. For him, as James well knew, the "extraordinary" also meant things of rare value and importance. James explains: "even if he did not wave so gallantly the flag of the imaginary and contend that the improbable is what has most character, he would still insist that we ought to snake believe. He would say we ought to make believe that the extraordinary is the best part of life, even if it were not, and to do so because the finest feelings—suspense, daring, decision, passion, curiosity, gallantry, eloquence, friendship—are involved in it, and it is of infinite importance that the tradition of these precious things should not perish."[24]

This inward paraphrase of Stevenson's credo as a romancer also lists many of the personal qualities James associated with his friend. They were qualities, too, that he celebrated in his own bravest heroes and heroines, and the reference to precious things perishing inevitably makes us look ahead to the doomed heroine of *The Wings of the Dove* and back to the "finest" people in James's life who contributed to his conception of Milly Theale—preeminently Minny Temple but also Alice James and "the great R.L.S."

III

When he returned to *The American* in the course of revising and prefacing his fictions for the New York Edition, James also returned to ideas and motifs that belong especially to his dialogue with Stevenson. The rambling, elliptical, and yet wonderfully resourceful argument of the preface to *The American* is an extension of that dialogue. At first glance, these reminiscences are surprising, since *The American* antedates the friendship and apparently was not among the novels by James that Stevenson most appreciated. But it was reworking this novel, reflecting on the nature and origins of its chief strengths and weaknesses, that inspired James to rejoin the romance versus realism debate. Other fictionalists—notably Balzac, George Sand, and Hawthorne—contributed to his reflections on the subject, but it was Stevenson's life and writings that had most directly and movingly exemplified romance for him and prompted his own deepest thinking about it. So it was almost a matter of course that the principal negative and positive qualities associated with romance in his writings to and about Stevenson should reappear in this preface: the jejeune, escapist, and potentially dangerous nature of romantic make-believe; the creative freedom of play; the case for the extraordinary (or the "finest feelings"); the "fruitful" mingling of realism and romance.

But if the qualities James associates with romance remain essentially the same, the form he now employs to define and relate those qualities is quite different from that of a manifesto such as "The Art of Fiction" or a midcareer assessment such as his 1888 essay on Stevenson, All of the New York Edition prefaces combine personal reminiscence, theoretical pronouncement, and more particularized analysis of fable and treatment in the novel under discussion. However, they vary fairly widely in tone, length, and focus; as might be expected, analysis tends increasingly to displace reminiscence as James comes to deal with more recent works. The prefaces to the early novels—*Roderick Hudson*, *The American*, *The Portrait of a Lady*, and *The Princess Casamassima* are all romantically rich in nostalgic recollections of the settings and personal circumstances in which the novels were written. But the preface to *The American* is "Romantic" likewise in a more historically specific and revealing sense. Because of its fluid associative shifts between past and present and its complex, ambivalent weighing of the gains and losses involved in the transition from innocence to experience, it is, of all the prefaces, closest in structure and feeling to a Romantic ode such as Coleridge's "Dejection: An Ode," Wordsworth's "Ode: Intimations of Immortality" or "Tintern Abbey." Indeed, when

James refers to "Gray's beautiful Ode" (1057), that is, "Ode on a Distant Prospect of Eton College," he invokes the chief eighteenth-century prototype of such odes.[25]

James delighted in the poetry of his century; on Daniel Mark Fogel's reckoning, "by far the greatest number of explicit allusions in James are to the English Romantic poets."[26] Questions of direct influence aside, the main topic of the preface is a twofold "Wordsworthian" antithesis between the claims of realism and romance (particularly in *The American* but more generally, too) and between a remembered younger self who supposed he was practicing realism and an elder self who recognizes that it was romance all along. The second, then versus now, antithesis dominates the beginning of the preface as, in images reminiscent both of "Tintern Abbey" and "Resolution and Independence," James summons up scenes where the "story" came to him and the novel itself was written: "the long pole of memory stirs and rummages the bottom, and we fish up such fragments and relics of the submerged life and extinct consciousness as tempt us to piece them together" (1058). Portraying his 33-year-old self as an "artless" babe in the woods, he recalls "the habit of confidence that ... a special Providence ... despite the sad warning of Thackeray's "Denis Duval" and of Mrs. Gaskell's "Wives and Daughters" (that of Stevenson's "Weir of Hermiston" was yet to come) watches over anxious novelists condemned to the economy of serialisation.... And yet as the faded interest of the whole episode becomes again mildly vivid what I seem most to recover is, in its pale spectrality, a degree of joy, an eagerness on behalf of my recital" (1053).

Reminiscences at once nostalgic and ironic lead to a richly nuanced contrast between "the free play of ... unchallenged instinct" (1057) in his youthful "surrender to the ... projected fable" of *The American*, and the "free difficulty" which he now perceives to be inseparable from the "free selection—which is the beautiful, terrible *whole* of art" (1061). The idea that selection is the *whole* of art is distinctively Stevensonian, and, sure enough, James's meditation on it prompts recollection of Stevenson's dictum on a related topic: "Robert Louis Stevenson has, in an admirable passage and as in so many other connexions, said the right word: that the partaker of the 'life of art' who repines at the absence of the rewards ... might surely be better occupied." In the passage James apparently has in mind, Stevenson explains why "the lights seem a little turned down" in some of his later, less popular writings dealing with social injustices in America and the South Pacific: "What I wish to fight is best fought by a rather cheerless presentation of the truth. The world must return some day to the word duty, and be done with the word reward. There are no rewards, and plenty duties."[27]

The then-versus-now scheme of the preface can be reduced to the following key words and phrases:

THEN	NOW
bliss of ignorance	awakened critical sense
rewards	duties
free play	labor
bondage of ease	free difficulty
Providence/muse/surrender	free selection
romance	realism

Although this abstract seems overly schematic, it accords with James's dictum in the preface to *Roderick Hudson* (1907) apropos the antithetical heroines of that novel: "One is ridden by the law that antitheses, to be efficient, shall be direct and complete" (1052). Clearly, we are dealing with a Jamesean version of the Fortunate Fall in which the artist protagonist, graduating from a passive state of delusive ease and freedom, takes charge of his own destiny. He then experiences a fate resembling that of the heroes and heroines of many of James's own novels, including Christopher Newman—except in the crucial particular that at the end of the day they have their "duties" while he has his "rewards" in the form of the novels themselves and the power to write more of them. For him the fall is fortunate indeed, and it cannot matter much if there is an untrespassable chasm between his present and his former self. Or so we might suppose, reading James rhapsodize about the "constant nameless felicity" of the mature writer of fiction, "with the toil and trouble a mere sun-cast shadow that falls, shifts and vanishes" (1061). James's triumphant progress over the years from romance to realism is mainly a matter of growing up. Thus far, the Stevenson who figures positively in the preface to *The American* is the later, "grown-up" Stevenson, author of *Weir* and realistic critic of Anglo-American imperialism.

The famous definition of romance James gives in this preface is couched in the familiar terms of freedom and constraint:

> The only *general* attribute of ... romance that I can see ... is the fact of the kind of experience with which it deals—experience liberated, ... disengaged, disembroiled, disencumbered, exempt from the conditions that we usually know to attach to it and ... drag upon it, and operating in a medium which relieves it, in a particular interest, of the inconvenience of a *related*, a measurable state, a state subject to all our vulgar communities. (1064)

James's argument is developed by means of an extended metaphor whose vehicle is not fully revealed until, like a magician, he suddenly produces a toy:

> The balloon of experience is ... tied to the earth, and under that necessity we swing, thanks to a rope of remarkable length, in the more or less commodious car of the imagination; but it is by the rope we know where we are, and from the moment that cable is cut we are at large and unrelated: we only swing apart from the globe—though remaining as exhilarated, naturally, as we like, especially when all goes well. The art of the romancer is "for the fun of it," insidiously to cut the cable, to cut it without our detecting him. What I have recognized then in "The American" ... is that the experience here represented is the disconnected and uncontrolled experience—uncontrolled by our general sense of "the way things happen"—which romance ... palms off on us. (1064)

"Disconnected," "uncontrolled," and "palms off" make romance sound irresponsible, escapist, and deceitful. Small wonder that Michael Davitt Bell, commenting on the same passage, says that "for James, then, the essence of romance lies in its moral irresponsibility."[28]

Clearly, James still harbors some of the suspicions of romance that, with varying degrees of sophistication and intelligence, realists and moralists have always had. The irony here is that the novel whose unhappy ending he had defended against Howells as realistic now fails on precisely those grounds. Although he obviously exaggerates the extent of his ingenuousness at the time he wrote *The American*, it is true that his acquaintance with the European aristocracy was then comparatively superficial and that his picture of the haughty Bellgarde family disdaining rich Christopher Newman is largely a projection of democratic myth. From the later and more worldly perspective of the author of *The Golden Bowl*, the representation of the Bellegardes' behavior is so patently "uncontrolled by our general sense of 'the way things happen'" that it appears false and immature. If *The American* is the product of such guileless "surrender to ... the projected fable," and if it is also an example of romance, what adult interest can the book or the genre have?

Yet despite his misgivings about romance and about *The American* in particular, James in his old age found a place in the New York Edition canon for the novel and also a place in his scheme of good things for "fun" and "play" and, above all, "freedom." He obviously feels some nostalgic good will toward his prelapsarian self and finds he can experience "the joy of living over ... the particular intellectual adventure" of writing that romance. If this return to his former self is possible, perhaps travel in the opposite direction is, too. Perhaps, after all, the child is the father of the man.

Which brings us back to Stevenson. When James referred to the habit of confidence" that a serializing novelist persists in feeling "despite the sad warning" of Thackeray's, Gaskell's, and Stevenson's last works, he cannot have forgotten the questions Stevenson himself asked in "AEs Triplex": "Who, if he were wisely considerate of things at large, would ever embark upon any work much more considerable than a halfpenny post card? Who would project a serial novel, after Thackeray and Dickens had each fallen in mid-course?"[29] If Stevenson had been more "wisely considerate" than romantically aspiring, he would have achieved far less and would not have left the great fragment of *Weir*. So the Arcadian innocence of the "confident" young romancer who wrote *The American* may have been practical wisdom on at least one count.

Upon reexamination, many of the negative qualities James associates with childhood and romance can be seen to have a strong positive valence as well. The exhilarating balloon ride is a "genial" experience; the sense of "fun," expansion, and gravity overcome is psychologically refreshing and valuable. This ride through space may remind us of his earlier image of Stevenson's "gyrations" as the "Trapezist in the Pacific void!"—an image of soaring, of performance for sheer joy in the exercise of skill and energy and freedom. And of course James's playful metaphors are themselves supreme examples of such performance. No doubt about it, among the many things he is doing in this preface James is reaffirming the Stevensonian message that to be *homo sapiens* one must also be *homo ludens*.

And play has a moral as well as a recreational dimension. Huizinga explains that "play only becomes possible, thinkable and understandable when an influx of *mind* breaks down the absolute determinism of the cosmos. The very existence of play continually confirms the supra-logical nature of the human situation."[30] Stevenson was the player *extraordinaire* whose writings and life (for a time) defied all the determinisms of his age, including those of Henry Adams and "the School of Balzac." James, although a friend of Adams and one of the most persistent champions of the French realists, could never accept their pessimistic determinism.[31] Therefore, while heeding the threatening sound of "uncontrolled" and "disconnected," we do well to remember that "liberty," "liberated," and "freedom" usually have the most positive connotations in James's moral/aesthetic vocabulary. Moreover, as Peter Brooks has recently argued, *The American* is centrally and at many levels—generic as well as moral and psychological—about the quest for freedom.[32]

Positive connotations are surely present when James speaks of "experience liberated ... from the conditions that we usually know to ... drag upon it." Happily for the novelist, the "life of art," of the genial creative imagination, confers a power of "free selection" rarely available in ordinary life. To be sure, for the artist as for others freedom entails risks and labor and the paradoxical necessity of either using or forfeiting it. But without a larger measure of freedom than is usually present in life or represented in realistic fiction, there can be little scope for artistic creation *or* for moral action—or for what James calls "the finest feelings."

There is no clearer instance of such feelings being realized in fiction than the "last view" James gives us of the hero of *The American* turning from the perfidious Bellegardes and, despite his power to do them harm without danger to himself, acting with "practical, but quite unappreciated, magnanimity ... a strong man indifferent to his strength and too wrapped in fine, too wrapped above all in *other* and intenser reflexions for the assertion of his 'rights'" (1055). According to James, it was at the moment he imagined Newman's *unconstrained* magnanimity that his "conception unfurled ... the emblazoned flag of romance" (1057). It is impossible to say whether James at this point recalled his figure of Stevenson waving "so gallantly the flag of the imaginary," but his account of Newman's "extraordinary" behavior makes no apology for the experience represented being "uncontrolled" but seems rather to endorse Stevensonian romantic principle. What we recognize here is the moral, the supremely responsible face of romance.[33]

Perhaps it was, finally, as a moral rather than as an aesthetic exemplar that James prized Stevenson above all. When he names the novelists of "largest responding imagination before the human scene" (1062), he does not mention Stevenson, even though his ghost may be said to haunt this preface. His ghost is present not least when James explains that the interest of such a novelist is greatest "when he commits himself" in the directions both of romance and realism "by some need of performing his whole possible revolution, by the law of some rich passion in him for extremes ... of Scott, of Balzac, even of the coarse, comprehensive, prodigious Zola, we feel ... that the deflexion toward either quarter has never taken place.... His current remains therefore extraordinarily rich and mixed, washing us successively with the warm wave of the near and familiar and the tonic shock ... of the far and strange." Here James seems to be echoing and brilliantly elaborating Stevenson's contention that "true romantic art ... makes a romance of all things.... *Robinson Crusoe* is as realistic as it is romantic; both qualities are pushed to an extreme, and neither suffers." Although James himself had emphasized the admixture of realism in Stevenson's fictions, it is obvious that there was a marked "deflexion" toward romance in most of them and that, in James's eyes, this made Stevenson a lesser novelist than one whose current remained extraordinarily rich and mixed.

In life, however, the "deflexion" meant a career that exemplified "the finest feelings" and bravely repudiated the deterministic certainties of the age. Far better than most of their contemporaries, James was able to see beyond the surface glamor and "swagger" to the essential fineness and moral achievement of Stevenson's life. But because James was as much of as apart from his time, he was also able to join wholeheartedly in the general apotheosizing of a man who, in defiance of "that gentleman" Hades and of gravity itself, had raised, levitated, himself from his invalid's couch to shine as *the* romantic literary hero for the era. Stevenson himself anticipated this fate in his figure of the man who "reckons his life as a thing to be dashingly used and cheerfully hazarded ... keeps all his pulses going true and fast, and gathers impetus as he runs, until, if he be running towards anything better than wildfire, he may shoot up and become a constellation in the end."[34] "There he is—" wrote James in 1899, "he has passed ineffaceably into happy legend" (277).

Notes

1. For convenience and brevity of documentation, I draw as many quotations as possible from Janet Adam Smith's compilation of James's and Stevenson's writings to and about each other, *Henry James and Robert Louis Stevenson: A Record of Friendship and Criticism* (London: Rupert Hart-Davis, 1948), cited hereafter in these notes as Smith. Page references for quotations from Smith are given parenthetically in the text. When immediately succeeding quotations come from the same or adjacent pages in Smith, no page references are given.

2. For a recent concise account of the origins and progress of the novel-versus romance controversy, see George Dekker, *The American Historical Romance* (Cambridge, Eng., and New York: Cambridge University Press, 1987), pp. 14–28. The most influential modern reemployments of the novel/romance polarity are Richard Chase, *The American Novel and Its Tradition* (Garden City, N.Y.: Doubleday, 1957), and Northrop Frye, *Anatomy of Criticism: Four Essays* (Princeton: Princeton University Press, 1957). Chase's contention that the romance form of the novel dominates the American novel tradition has spawned a voluminous critical literature, a current summary of which is given in the end notes to Emily Miller Budick, "Sacvan Bercovitch, Stanley Cavell, and the Romance Theory of American Fiction," *PMLA 107* (1992): 78–91. A good account of James's relation to the romance tradition is Elsa Nettles, *James and Conrad* (Athens: University of Georgia Press, 1977), pp. 80–109.

3. All of James's and Stevenson's biographers pay some attention to what was, after all, a very famous literary friendship. The fullest and most thoughtful account of their

literary relations is in Smith, pp. 9–47. Especially pertinent to the issue of the James/Stevenson debate about realism and romance is Sarah B. Daugherty, *The Literary Criticism of Henry James* (Athens: Ohio University Press, 1981), pp. 121–22, 162–64.

4. Leo Bersani, *A Future for Astyanax* (Boston: Little, Brown, 1976), p. 132: "the recurrent Jamesian subject ... is freedom."

5. Letter to William Dean Howells, dated March 30, 1877, *Henry James Letters*. Vol. 2: 1875–1883, ed. Leon Edel (Cambridge, Mass.: Belknap Press of Harvard University Press, 1975), p. 105.

6. Ian Watt, *The Rise of the Novel: Studies in Defoe, Richardson, and Fielding* (1957; rpt., Harmondsworth: Penguin, 1963), p. 313.

7. Walter Besant, *The Art of Fiction: A Lecture Delivered at the Royal Institution* (London: Chatto and Windus, 1884.), p. 38.

8. Watt, *Rise*, p. 13.

9. Edmond de Goncourt, *Préfaces et manifestes littéraires* (Paris: G. Charpentier, 1888), p. 59.

10. Ibid., p. 67.

11. Ibid., p. 66.

12. Robert Louis Stevenson, "A Gossip on Romance," *Memories and Portraits* (New York: Charles Scribner's Sons, 1887), p. 255.

13. Ibid., pp. 255–56.

14. William Wordsworth, *The Prelude* (1850), XII: 88–207.

15. When Stevenson revised *"A Humble Remonstrance"* for inclusion in *Memoties and Portraits*, he changed "a pirate is a beard in wide trousers and literally bristling with pistols" to "a pirate is a beard, a pair of wide trousers and a liberal complement of pistols" (p. 289). The cleaned-up version is less vivid and suggestive, and also less open to objection.

16. For Stevenson's oddest judgments on James's fiction, see Smith, pp. 108, 165–66, and 207–8.

17. Stevenson, *"A Humble Remonstrance,"* pp. 298–99.

18. "Henry James, Jr.," rpt. in *Discovery of a Genius: William Dean Howells and Henry James*, ed. Albert Mordell (New York: Twayne, 1961), pp. 117–18.

19. *The Complete Notebooks of Henry James*, ed. Leon Edel and Lyall H. Powers (New York: Oxford University Press, 1987), p. 584.

20. *Letter to Sir John Clark dated December 13, 1891, Henry James Letters*, Vol. 3: 1883–1895, ed. Leon Edel (Cambridge, Mass.: Belknap Press of Harvard University Press, 1980), p. 367.

21. *Letter to Edmund Gosse, December 17, 1894., Henry James Letters*, vol. 3, p. 495.

22. Johann Huizinga, *Homo Ludens: A Study of the Play-Element in Culture* (Boston: Beacon Press, 1955 [1938]), pp. 7, 10. More recent theorists of play, such as Roger Caillois and Herbert Marcuse, offer insights pertinent to the argument of the present essay, but Huizinga's cultural perspective and vocabulary are closer to those of James and Stevenson.

23. Stevenson, *"A Gossip on Romance,"* p. 264.

24. When he revised "Robert Louis Stevenson" for publication in *Partial Portraits* (1888), James changed "imaginary" to "imaginative." See *Henry James: Lilerary Criticism*, ed. Leon Edel (The Library of America; Cambridge, Eng.: Cambridge University Press, 1989), p. 1249.

25. Preface to *The American* (1907), rpt. in *French Writers, Other European Writers, The Prefaces to the New York Edition*, ed. Leon Edel (The Library of America; Cambridge, Eng.:

Cambridge University Press, 1984.), p. 1057. Subsequent page references to this edition of the preface are given parenthetically in the text; they may be readily differentiated from Smith references because they have four digits. Wordsworth appended a note to "Tintern Abbey" explaining that, contrary to appearances, it had many of the leading features of an ode (e.g., rapid transitions and impassioned versification) and suggesting that a flexible approach to questions of generic identity might serve readers well by highlighting such features where they might not be expected.

26. Daniel Mark Fogel, *Henry James and the Structure of the Romantic Imagination* (Baton Rouge: Louisiana State University Press, 1981), p. 5.

27. *Vailima Letters: Correspondence Addressed to Sidney Colvin, November 1890 to October 1894.*, in *Letters and Miscellanies of Robert Louis Stevenson*, vol. 17 (New York: Charles Scribner's Sons, 1896), p. 96.

28. Michael Davitt Bell, *The Development of American Romance: The Sacrifice of Relation* (Chicago: University of Chicago Press, 1980), p. 8.

29. Stevenson, "AEs Triplex," *Virginibus Puerisque*, in *The Travels and Essays of Robert Louis Stevenson*, vol. 13 (New York: Charles Scribner's Sons, 1898), p. 104.

30. Huizinga, *Homo Ludens*, p. 3.

31. For James on the subject of social determinism in Zola and Balzac, see *"Honore de Balzac"* (1913), *French Writers*, p. 151.

32. Peter Brooks, "The Turn of American," in Martha Banta, ed., *New Essays on The American* (Cambridge, Eng.: Cambridge University Press, 1987), pp. 43–67. Besides offering a brilliant reading of the novel, Brooks provides an excellent brief account of its relation to the French realist tradition.

33. I am not alone in arguing for the positive "liberating" connotations of romance in James's fictional theory. Cf. Mark Seltzer, *Henry James and the Art of Power* (Ithaca, N.Y.: Cornell University Press, 1984.), p. 138: "Nor does the recourse to romance indicate merely a desire to escape the real.... His art, James declares, is an attempt to project the ideal alternative and 'antidote' to a limited and limiting social scene." Martha Banta, *Henry James and the Occult: The Great Extension* (Bloomington: Indiana University Press, 1972), pp. 54–61, explains how romance is the necessary vehicle for treating the "more things in heaven and earth than are dreamt of in the philosophy" of positivistic science and realistic fiction.

34. Stevenson, *"AEs Triplex,"* p. 103. James quotes this passage in his 1888 essay on Stevenson (Smith, p. 143).

STEPHEN ARATA

The Sedulous Ape: Atavism, Professionalism, and Stevenson's Jekyll and Hyde

In an early review of *The Strange Case of Dr. Jekyll and Mr. Hyde* (1886), Andrew Lang noted the most striking feature of Robert Louis Stevenson's tale. "His heroes (surely *this* is original) are all successful middle-aged professional men."[1] Indeed, one could hardly miss the novel's foregrounding of the stature enjoyed by "Henry Jekyll, M.D., D.C.L., LL.D., ER.S., etc."[2] In Lang's view this interest in professional men defined Stevenson's novel at least as much as its portrayal of the grotesque Edward Hyde. If *Jekyll and Hyde* articulates in Gothic fiction's exaggerated tones late-Victorian anxieties concerning degeneration, atavism, and what Cesare Lombroso called "criminal man," it invariably situates those concerns in relation to the practices and discourses of lawyers like Gabriel Utterson, doctors like Henry Jekyll and Hastie Lanyon, or even "well-known men about town" (29) like Richard Enfield. The novel in fact asks us to do more than simply register the all too apparent marks of Edward Hyde's "degeneracy." It compels us also to examine how those marks come to signify in the first place. As Stevenson understood, one thing professional men tend to be good at is close reading. Another is seeing to it that their interpretations have consequences in the real world. *Jekyll and Hyde* proves to be an uncannily self-conscious exploration of the relation between professional interpretation and the construction of criminal deviance. The novel is also a displaced meditation

From *Fictions of Loss in the Victorian Fin de Siecle*. © 1996 by Cambridge University Press.

on what Stevenson considered the decline of authorship itself into "professionalism."

In Edward Hyde, Stevenson's first readers could easily discern the lineaments of Lombroso's atavistic criminal. In one of degeneration theory's defining moments, Lombroso had "discovered" that criminals were throwbacks to humanity's savage past. While contemplating the skull of the notorious Italian bandit Vilella, Lombroso suddenly saw history open up before him, illumined as if by lightning.

> This was not merely an idea [he wrote many years later], but a revelation. At the sight of that skull, I seemed to see all of a sudden, lighted up as a vast plain under a flaming sky, the problem of the nature of the criminal—an atavistic being who reproduces in his person the ferocious instincts of primitive humanity and the inferior animals.[3]

"Thus were explained anatomically," Lombroso continues, such diverse attributes as the "enormous jaws, high cheek bones, prominent superciliary arches, solitary lines in the palms, extreme size of the orbits, [and] handle-shaped ears" of the criminal, as well as various moral deformities like the propensity for "excessive idleness, love of orgies, and the irresponsible craving of evil for its own sake." These features were all signs of a form of primitive existence which normal men and women had transcended but which the criminal was condemned to relive. In his physiognomy as in his psyche, the atavistic criminal bore the traces of humanity's history and development.[4]

From the first publication of Stevenson's novel, readers have noted the similarities between Lombroso's criminal and the atavistic Mr. Hyde.[5] Lombroso's descriptions of criminal deviance fit snugly with longstanding discourses of class in Great Britain. Lombroso's work first reached a wide audience in England thanks to Havelock-Ellis's *The Criminal* (1891); the combined influence of Ellis and Lombroso was in part due to the ease with which the new "scientific" categories mapped onto older, more familiar accounts of the urban poor from Mayhew onward. As we saw in Chapter 1, much of the "legitimacy" of degeneration theory derived from the way it reproduced the class ideologies of the bourgeoisie. Equating the criminal with atavism, and both with the lower classes, was a familiar gesture by the

1880s, as was the claim that deviance expressed itself most markedly through physical deformity.[6] Stevenson's middle-class readers would have had as little trouble deciphering the features of the "abnormal and misbegotten" Hyde, his "body an imprint of deformity and decay," as Stevenson's middle-class characters do (78, 84). "God bless me," exclaims Utterson, "the man seems hardly human. Something troglodytic, shall we say? ... or is it the mere radiance of a foul soul that thus transpires through, and transfigures, its clay continent?" (40). Utterson's remark, moreover, nicely demonstrates how old and new paradigms can overlap. He at once draws on familiar Christian imagery—Hyde's foul soul transfiguring its clay continent—and a Lombrosan vocabulary of atavism, with Hyde-as-troglodyte reproducing in his person the infancy of the human species.

In considering degenerationism as a class discourse, however, we need to look up as well as down. Both Lombroso and Nordau argue that degeneration was as endemic to a decadent aristocracy as to a troglodytic proletariat. And, indeed, Hyde can be read as a figure of leisured dissipation. While his impulsiveness and savagery, his violent temper, and his appearance all mark Hyde as lower class and atavistic, his vices are clearly those of a monied gentleman. This aspect of Hyde's portrayal has gone largely unnoticed, but for Stevenson's contemporaries the conflation of upper and lower classes into a single figure of degeneracy would not have seemed unusual. Lombroso's criminal may have been primitive in appearance, but his moral shortcomings—"excessive idleness, love of orgies, the irresponsible craving of evil"—make him a companion of Jean Floressas des Esseintes and Dorian Gray, not Vilella. Nordau took pains to insist that the degenerate population "consists chiefly of rich educated people" who, with too much time and means at their disposal, succumb to decadence and depravity.[7]

Lombroso and Nordau have in mind not only the titled aristocracy but also a stratum of cultured aesthetes considered dangerously subversive of conventional morality. That Stevenson meant us to place Hyde among their number is suggested by the description of his surprisingly well-appointed Soho rooms, "furnished with luxury and good taste" (49). Hyde's palate for wine is discriminating, his plate is of silver, his "napery elegant." Art adorns his walls, while carpets "of many plies and agreeable in colour" cover his floors. This is not a savage's den but the retreat of a cultivated gentleman. Utterson supposes that Jekyll bought the art for Hyde (49), but Stevenson in a letter went out of his way to say that the lawyer is mistaken. The purchases were Hyde's alone.[8]

In Edward Hyde, then, Stevenson created a figure who embodies a bourgeois readership's worst fears about both a marauding and immoral

underclass and a dissipated and immoral leisure class.⁹ Yet Stevenson also
shows how such figures are not so much "recognized" as created by middle-
class discourse. He does this by foregrounding the interpretive acts through
which his characters situate and define Hyde. Despite the confident
assertions of the novel's professional men that Hyde is "degenerate," his
"stigmata" turn out to be troublingly difficult to specify. In fact, no one can
accurately describe him. "He must be deformed somewhere," asserts Enfield.
"He gives a strong feeling of deformity, though I couldn't specify the point.
He's an extraordinary-looking man, and yet I really can name nothing out of
the way. No, sir ... I can't describe him" (34). Enfield's puzzled response finds
its counterparts in the nearly identical statements of Utterson (40), Poole
(68), and Lanyon (77–78). In Utterson's dream Hyde "had no face, or one
that baffled him and melted before his eyes" (36–37). "The few who could
describe him differed widely," agreeing only that some "unexpressed
deformity" lurked in his countenance (50). That last, nearly oxymoronic
formulation—"unexpressed deformity"—nicely captures the troubled
relation between the "text" of Hyde's body and the interpretive practices
used to decipher it. Hyde's stigmata are everywhere asserted and nowhere
named. The novel continually turns the question of Hyde back on his
interlocutors so that their interpretive procedures become the object of our
attention. "There is my explanation," Utterson claims. "It is plain and
natural, hangs well together and delivers us from all exorbitant alarms" (66).
It is also, we are immediately given to understand, wrong, though its
delusions differ only in degree from other "plain and natural" explanations
brought forward in the tale.¹⁰

Indeed, what makes *Jekyll and Hyde* compelling is the way it turns the
class discourses of atavism and criminality back on the bourgeoisie itself. As
Lang recognized, Stevenson's novel is finally more concerned with its
middle-class professional "heroes" than it is with the figure of Edward Hyde.
Among the story's first readers, F. W. H. Myers felt this aspect acutely, and it
prompted him to protest in a remarkable series of letters which suggest that
he interpreted Hyde as a figure not of degenerate depravity but of bourgeois
"virtue."¹¹

Shortly after its publication Myers wrote to Stevenson, whom he did
not know, enthusiastically praising *Jekyll and Hyde* but suggesting that certain
minor revisions would improve the novel. After noting some infelicities of
phrasing and gaps in plotting, Myers came to what he considered the story's
"weakest point," the murder of Sir Danvers Carew. Hyde's mauling of
Carew's "unresisting body" offended the decorous Myers ("no, not an elderly
MP's!"), but his primary objection was that such an act was untrue to Hyde's

nature. Because "Jekyll was thoroughly civilized ... his degeneration must needs take certain lines only." Hyde should be portrayed as "not a generalized but a specialized fiend," whose cruelty would never take the form Stevenson gave it. At most "Hyde would, I think, have brushed the baronet aside with a curse."

Stevenson's reply was polite, passing over the bulk of Myers's suggestions in silence. He did pause to correct him on one subject, though, that of a painting in Hyde's lodgings. Myers had questioned whether the doctor would have acquired artwork for his alter ego. Stevenson answered that Hyde purchased the painting, not Jekyll. Myers's response was disproportionately vehement. "Would Hyde have bought a picture? I think—and friends of weight support my view—that such an act would have been altogether unworthy of him." Unworthy? Myers and his weighty friends appear to feel that Hyde's character is being impugned, that his good name must be defended against some implied insult. Asking "what are the motives which would prompt a person in [Hyde's] situation" to buy artwork, Myers suggests three, none of which, he argues, applies to Hyde's case.

> 1. There are jaded voluptuaries who seek in a special class of art a substitute or reinforcement for the default of primary stimuli. Mr. Hyde's whole career forbids us to insult him by classing him with these men.
> 2. There are those who wish for elegant surroundings to allure or overawe the minds of certain persons unaccustomed to luxury or splendour. But does not all we know of Hyde teach us that he disdained those modes of adventitious attractions?...
> 3. There are those, again, who surround their more concentrated enjoyments with a halo of mixed estheticism ... Such, no doubt, was Dr. Jekyll; such, no doubt, he *expected* that Mr. Hyde would be. But was he not deceived? Was there not something unlooked for, something Napoleonic, in Hyde's way of pushing aside the aesthetic as well as the moral superfluities of life? ... We do not imagine the young Napoleon as going to concerts or taking a walk in a garden.... I cannot fancy Hyde looking in at picture shops. I cannot think he ever left his rooms, except on business. (17 March 1886)

This is a most unfamiliar Hyde! On the evidence of Myers's letter we would have to pronounce him an upstanding citizen. Myers clearly perceives how easily Stevenson's Hyde could be taken not for a brute but for a dandy. At no point is Myers worried that Hyde might be considered atavistic. Instead, he is concerned that Hyde's reputation not be smeared by association with "jaded voluptuaries" and aesthetes. In attempting to clear him of such charges, Myers presents Jekyll's alter ego as the very image of sobriety and industry, manfully disdainful of the shop window, the art gallery, the concert hall—of anything that might savor of the aesthetic or the frivolous. Myers praises Hyde's simplicity of dress: he is not a fop but a "man aiming only at simple convenience, direct sufficiency." Unconcerned with personal adornment, he is "not anxious to present himself as personally attractive, but [relies] frankly on the cash nexus, and on that decision of character that would startle" those less forceful than himself.

We might dismiss Myers's reading as eccentric, especially given the absence of any irony in his references to Hyde's "business," freedom from personal vanity, or reliance on the cash nexus (blackmail and prostitution appear to be the primary drags on his resources). Yet Myers's admittedly exaggerated response illuminates an important aspect of Stevenson's novel. Edward Hyde may not be an image of the *upright* bourgeois male, but he is decidedly an image of the bourgeois male. While Hyde can be read as the embodiment of the degenerate prole, the decadent aristocrat, or the dissipated aesthete, it is also the case that his violence is largely directed *at* those same classes. Of the three acts of violence we see Hyde commit, two— his trampling of the little girl and his striking of the prostitute—involve lower-class women. Hyde's third victim is the novel's only titled character, Sir Danvers Carew. That Hyde shares Myers's disdain for aesthetes is made plainer in Stevenson's manuscript draft of the novel. There, Hyde murders not Sir Danvers but a character who appears to be a caricature of the aesthetic stereotype, the "anoemically pale" Mr. Lemsome. Constantly "shielding a pair of suffering eyes under blue spectacles," Lemsome is considered by the respectable Utterson as both "a bad fellow" and "an incurable cad."[12] "The substitution of Carew for Lemsome suggests that the two characters were connected in Stevenson's mind, just as for Nordau aesthetes like Oscar Wilde are grouped with troubling aristocrats like Lord Byron as disruptive of middle-class mores.

Mr. Hyde thus acts not just as a magnet for middle-class fears of various "Others" but also as an agent of vengeance. He is the scourge of (a bourgeois) God, punishing those who threaten patriarchal code and custom. Indeed, the noun used most often in the story to describe Hyde is not "monster" or "villain" but—"gentleman." This novel portrays a world peopled almost exclusively by middle-class professional men, yet instead of attacking Hyde, these gentlemen more often close ranks around him.[13]

Enfield's "Story of the Door," though it begins with Hyde trampling a little girl until she is left "screaming on the ground" (31), concludes with Enfield, the doctor, and the girl's father breakfasting with Hyde in his chambers (32). Recognizing him as one of their own, the men literally encircle Hyde to protect him from harm. "And all the time ... we were keeping the women off him as best we could, for they were as wild as harpies. I never saw a circle of such hateful faces; and there was the man in the middle, ... frightened too, I could see that" (32). The homosocial bonding that occurs in this scene is only intensified by its overt misogyny. Though both he and the doctor profess to feel a profound loathing for Hyde, Enfield refers to him with the politeness due a social equal, consistently calling him "my gentleman" or "my man." Indeed, Enfield derives vicarious pleasure from watching Hyde maul the girl.[14] Though he could easily have prevented their collision, Enfield allows them to run into one another "naturally enough" (31). Neglecting to intervene until Hyde has finished his assault, Enfield describes the incident with some relish, nonchalantly admitting to Utterson that the beating "sounds nothing to hear" (31). (Though he goes on to say that it "was hellish to see," that does not unring the bell.) That Hyde acts out the aggressions of timid bourgeois gentlemen is emphasized once again in the beating of Sir Danvers. That gesture of "insensate cruelty" is performed with a cane "of some rare and very tough and heavy wood" (47), which was originally in the possession of Gabriel Utterson. The stick breaks in two, and Stevenson takes care to let us know that both halves make their way back into the lawyer's hands after the murder (47, 49).

It is Edward Hyde's covert affinities with professional men that prompted Myers to describe him as a kind of bourgeois Napoleon. Myers recognized that Stevenson had created a figure whose rage is the rage of a threatened patriarchy. It is only a seeming paradox to say that Hyde is most like himself when he behaves like a gentleman. Yet to leave matters here would do an injustice to the complexity of Stevenson's vision, an injustice Myers himself is guilty of. While *Jekyll and Hyde* is a compelling expression of middle-class anger directed at various forms of the Other, the novel also turns that anger back on the burgesses themselves, Stevenson included.

It does this in part by taking as one of its themes the education of a gentleman, in this case Mr. Hyde. Most critical accounts of the novel have with good reason focussed on the social and psychological pressures that led Jekyll to become Hyde. Yet Stevenson is also concerned with the reverse transformation. That is, the novel details the pressures which move Hyde closer to Jekyll.[15] It is one thing to say that Hyde acts out the aggressive fantasies of repressed Victorian men, another altogether to say that he comes eventually to embody the very repressions Jekyll struggles to throw off. Yet this is in fact a prime source of horror in the tale: not that. the professional man is transformed into an atavistic criminal, but that the atavist learns to pass as a gentleman. Hyde unquestionably develops over the course of the novel, which is to say he becomes more like the "respectable" Jekyll, which in turn is to say he "degenerates." Degeneration becomes a function not of lower-class depravity or aristocratic dissipation but of middle-class "virtue."

Needless to say, Mr. Hyde's education into gentlemanliness exacts a considerable cost. The Hyde who ends his life weeping and crying for mercy (69) is not the same man whose original "raging energies" and "love of life" Jekyll found "wonderful" (95–96). By the time he is confined to the doctor's laboratory, Hyde is no longer Jekyll's opposite but his mirror image. Where earlier the transitions between Jekyll and Hyde were clean and sharp (and painful), later the two personalities develop a mutual fluidity. By the end the doctor's body metamorphoses continually from Jekyll to Hyde and back again, as if to indicate that we need no longer distinguish between them.

How does one become a gentleman? If born into a good family, by imitating one's father. That Jekyll and Hyde stand in a father–son relationship is suggested by Jekyll himself (89) as well as by Utterson (37, 41–42), who suspects that Hyde is the doctor's illegitimate offspring. After "gentleman," the words used most often to describe Hyde are "little" and "young."[16] The idea that Hyde is being groomed, as Utterson says, "to step into the said Henry Jekyll's shoes" (35), is reinforced by the doctor's will naming him sole heir, as well as by the lawyer's description of this "small gentleman" (46) as Jekyll's "*protégé*" (37). Indeed, when Jekyll assures Utterson that "I do sincerely take a great, a very great interest in that young man" (4) he sounds like a mentor sheltering a promising disciple.

If Hyde is to assume his mentor-father's position, he must be indoctrinated in the codes of his class. As Jekyll repeatedly insists, Hyde indulges no vices that Jekyll himself did not enjoy. What differs is the manner in which they enjoy them: Hyde openly and vulgarly, Jekyll discretely and with an eye to maintaining his good name. As Hyde learns from his encounter with Enfield, gentlemen may sin so long as appearances are preserved. Having collared Hyde after his trampling of the little girl, Enfield and the doctor are "sick ... with the desire to kill him" (thus replicating Hyde's own homicidal rage), but "killing being out of the question" they do "the next best": they threaten to "make such a scandal... as should make his name stink" (31–32). They extort money as the price of their silence, in the process teaching Hyde the value of a good reputation. "No gentleman but wishes to avoid a scene," Hyde acknowledges. "Name your figure" (32). When Enfield winds up his narration of this incident by telling Utterson that "my man was a fellow that nobody could have to do with" (33) he seems to be describing not a violent criminal but a man who cannot be trusted to respect club rules.

A commitment to protecting the good names of oneself and one's colleagues binds professional men together. Utterson, remarkably unconcerned with the fates of Hyde's victims, directs all his energies toward shielding Jekyll from "the cancer of some concealed disgrace" (41). Sir Danvers' death awakens fears that the doctor's "good name ... [will] be sucked down in the eddy of the scandal" (53). After the murder Jekyll himself admits, "I was thinking of my own character, which this hateful business has rather exposed" (52). As Enfield's actions indicate, blackmail is an acceptable way to prevent such exposure. Utterson mistakenly believes that Hyde is blackmailing Jekyll, but rather than going to the police he hits on the happier and more gentlemanly idea of blackmailing Hyde in turn (42). By far the most potent weapon these men possess, however, is silence. Closing ranks, they protect their own by stifling the spread not of crime or sin but of indecorous talk.[17] In turn, the commitment to silence ultimately extends to self-censorship, a pledge not to know. Utterson's motto—"I let my brother go to the devil in his own way" (29)—finds its counterpart in Enfield's unvarying rule of thumb: "The more it looks like Queer Street, the less I ask" (33). ("A very good rule, too," Utterson agrees.) Enfield explicitly equates knowledge with scandal when he says that asking a question is like rolling a stone down a hill: "presently some bland old bird ... is knocked on the head ... and the family have to change their name" (33). Knowledge's harm is suffered most acutely by Dr. Lanyon, whose Christian name of Hastie nicely indicates his fatal character flaw. Warned by Hyde that it is always wiser not to know, Lanyon nevertheless succumbs to that "greed of curiosity" (79) which leads directly deathward.

By means of Mr. Hyde, Jekyll seeks of course to slough off these same burdens of respectability, reticence, decorum, self-censorship—of gentlemanliness—and "spring headlong into the sea of liberty" (86). In tracing the arc of Hyde's brief career, however, Stevenson shows how quickly he becomes simply one of the boys. Over the last half of the novel Stevenson links Hyde, through a series of verbal echoes and structural rhymes, to various bourgeois "virtues" and practices. Not only do we discover Hyde beginning to exercise remarkable self-control—that most middle-class of virtues and seemingly the furthest from his nature—but we hear him speaking confidently in Jekyll's tones to Lanyon concerning the benefits of science and the sanctity of "the seal of *our* profession" (80; my emphasis).[18]

The kind of structural rhyming I refer to is most noticeable during Hyde's death-scene, when Utterson and Poole, having violently burst in the door of the rooms above Jekyll's laboratory, are startled by what they find.

> The besiegers, appalled by their own riot and the stillness that had succeeded, stood back a little and peered in. There lay the cabinet before their eyes in the quiet lamplight, a good fire glowing and chattering on the hearth, the kettle singing its strain, a drawer or two open, papers neatly set forth on the business table, and nearer the fire, the things laid out for tea; the quietest room, you would have said, and except for the glazed presses full of chemicals, the most commonplace that night in London. (69–70)

We are apt to share their bewilderment at first, since this is the last tableau we might expect Stevenson to offer us at this juncture in the story.[19] Yet it has been carefully prepared for. The novel is full of similar domestic tableaux, invariably occupied by solitary gentlemen. When they are not walking or dining, it seems, these men sit at their hearths, usually alone. It is Utterson's "custom of a Sunday ... to sit close by the fire, a volume of some dry divinity on his reading-desk" (35). When the lawyer visits Lanyon, he finds the doctor sitting alone over his wine after dinner (36). Later he finds Jekyll in nearly the same position (51). Utterson shares a friendly fireside bottle of wine with Mr. Guest, though their conversation leaves him singularly unhappy (54–55). It is one of Stevenson's triumphs that he transforms the hearth—that too-familiar image of cozy Victorian domesticity—into a symbol of these men's isolation and repression. In turn, the most notable thing about the scene Utterson and Poole stumble upon is that it is empty of life. The lamplight soothes, the kettle sings, the chairs beckon—but no one is home. Recognizing this, we recognize too the subtle irony of calling it "the most commonplace" sight to be seen in London.

We next discover that the lifeless Hyde's "contorted and still twitching" body lay "right in the midst" of this scene (70). On the one hand, it is a fit setting for Hyde's last agony and suicide. The terrors suffered by Hyde during his final days arise in part from his surroundings: the very symbols of bourgeois respectability that he exists to repudiate do him in. On the other hand, he seems to feel bizarrely at home in these surroundings. If for instance we ask who set the table for tea on this final night, the answer has to be Hyde and not Jekyll, since Utterson and Poole, prior to breaking in the door, agree that they have heard only Hyde's voice and Hyde's "patient" footsteps from within the room that evening (69). (Poole insists that his master "was made away with eight days ago" [65].) Beside the tea things is "a copy of a pious work for which, Jekyll had ... expressed a great esteem, annotated, in his own hand, with startling blasphemies" (71). We may be tempted to think that Hyde is responsible for those annotations, but that is not what the sentence says.[20] These are not fussy or pedantic quibbles, but rather indicate how carefully Stevenson has blurred the boundary between the two identities. It is Jekyll who is now blasphemous and who violently berates the man at Maw's (66), Hyde who sets a quiet tea table and cries to heaven for mercy.[21] On adjacent tables Utterson and Poole discover two cups, one containing the white salt used in jekyll's potion, the other containing the white sugar used in Hyde's tea (71). Both are magic elixirs: the first transforms a gentleman into a savage while the second performs the reverse operation. Having found his place by the hearth, Mr. Hyde knows what posture to assume: "Thenceforward, he sat all day over the fire in the private room, gnawing his nails; there he dined, sitting alone with his fears" (94). If this sounds more like Utterson or Lanyon than the Hyde we first met, it is meant to. Bitter, lonely, frightened, nervous, chewing his nails (we recall that Utterson bites his finger when agitated [65]), and contemplating violence: Edward Hyde is now a gentleman.

THE SEDULOUS APE

The Strange Case of Dr. Jekyll and Mr. Hyde is an angry book, its venom directed against what Stevenson contemptuously referred to as that "fatuous rabble of burgesses called the public."[22] The novel turns the discourses centering on degeneration, atavism, and criminality back on the professional classes that produced them, linking gentlemanliness and bourgeois virtue to various forms of depravity. At the same time the novel plumbs deep pools of patriarchal anxiety about its continued viability. Indeed, *Jekyll and Hyde* can be read as a meditation on the pathology of late-Victorian masculinity. Jekyll's case is "strange," Stevenson suggests, only in the sense that it is so common among men of the doctor's standing and beliefs.

Yet if *Jekyll and Hyde* is a consummate critique of the professional men who formed the bulk of its readership, the novel was also self-consciously written to please, which it did. In no respect is Stevenson more of his age than in the tortuous acts of self-definition and self-positioning that allowed him at once to dismiss and to court the fatuous rabble.[23] Ironically, the publication of *Jekyll and Hyde* marked the emergence of Robert Louis Stevenson as a "professional" author in the narrow sense of being able, for the first time, to support himself solely by means of his trade. No longer a coterie writer relying on his father for financial help, Stevenson now enjoyed a popular acclaim that would last until his death. He professed to find such acclaim distressing, a mark of artistic failure and an indication that he had become, in his stepson's words, "the 'burgess' of his former jeers."[24] "I am now a salaried party," Stevenson wrote to William Archer after the success of *Jekyll and Hyde* led to a lucrative commission from an American magazine. "I am a *bourgeois* now; I am to write a weekly paper for *Scribners'*, at a scale of payment which makes my teeth ache for shame and diffidence ... I am like to be ... publicly hanged at the social revolution."[25] "There must be something wrong in me," he confided to Edmund Gosse, "or I would not be popular."[26]

Stevenson's critique of professional discourses in *Jekyll and Hyde* turns out also to be a displaced critique of his own profession. The 1880s and 90s, like the 1830s and 40s, constitute a key moment in the professionalization of authorship over the course of the nineteenth century. The founding of The Society of Authors, the revision of international copyright laws, the widespread adoption of the full royalty system, and the appearance of full-time professional literary agents like A. P. Watt and William Morris Colles were only the most visible among many signs of this process.[27] In the early stages of his career Stevenson took little interest in (and little care of) his finances. Like many writers, he usually sold his copyrights for a lump payment instead of negotiating for royalties. Moreover, as Peter Keating points out, even when Stevenson did not sell his books outright, as in the case of *Treasure Island*, he *thought* he had.[28]

After 1884, following the founding of The Society of Authors and the vigorous consciousness-raising campaign led by its first president, Walter Besant, such financial naiveté was no longer possible. Yet Stevenson still ambivalently resisted the idea that imaginative writing constituted a professional discourse. His resistance was based on two factors. First, he saw professionalism as inseparable from the middle classes, that fatuous rabble he preferred to jest at rather than join. Second, he associated professional writing with a functionalist "realism" which he in theory opposed. As we saw in Chapter 1, it was precisely this kind of realist prose that was invariably held up as the norm against which "deviant" writing was measured. Nordau linked traditional notions of mimesis—"every word ... connotes a concrete presentation or a concept"—both with "healthy" art and with his own critical writing. This linkage was made not just by pathologists but also by many of those who, like Besant, were most interested in professionalizing the author's trade. With realism designated as the language of professionals, Stevenson in opposition turned to what he (often vaguely) called "style" as the mark of the truly imaginative writer.

Thus, for Stevenson, to be professional was to be bourgeois, and to be bourgeois was to embrace the very blindnesses, evasions, and immoralities delineated in *Jekyll and Hyde*. Indeed, the salient biographical fact to recall here is that the novel was composed during Stevenson's three-year "imprisonment" at Skerryvore, the Bournemouth house purchased by Thomas Stevenson for his son and daughter-in-law.[29] This was a period of personal crisis and transition for the writer. Prior to it were years of self-styled bohemianism, fashionable dabblings in socialism, and occasionally self-indulgent nose-thumbings at "the fathers," his own included. Until he took possession of Skerryvore, Stevenson had never had a permanent address. In his letters he repeatedly refers to his occupancy of the house as a capitulation to bourgeois convention, a "revolt into respectability."[30] To Gosse he complained: "I am now a beastly householder," and when Archer came to visit he found his friend ensconced in the heart of "British Philistinism."[31] Stevenson's always-fragile health was never worse than during these years, nor were his always-difficult relations with Thomas ever pricklier. When Thomas died in mid-1887 Stevenson immediately fled house and country, not returning to England during the seven remaining years of his life.

The biographical context throws some light on the motivations underlying *Jekyll and Hyde*. Writing it was in part an expression of self-loathing for what Stevenson perceived as his betrayal of former ideals.[32] Yet, as his letters and essays indicate, Stevenson was also intensely engaged at this time with the question of what it meant to be a professional author. For him, the normative definition of professionalism came, as it did for most writers of the period, from Besant, whose lecture "The Art of Fiction," delivered in April 1884 to the Royal Institution, prompted lengthy replies first from Henry James and then from Stevenson. Besant, having recently helped organize The Society of Authors, was explicitly interested in redefining fiction-writing as a profession analogous to the law, medicine, certain sciences, and other of the arts. If the "fine arts" like painting or sculpture enjoy a status denied to writers, he contends in the lecture, that is because they are organized into culturally sanctioned professional institutions. Besant correctly perceived that the painter who was permitted to append "R.A." to his name was accorded a respect no novelist could win.[33]

Throughout the essay, however, Besant's implicit model for the fiction-writer is not the painter or sculptor but the professional scientist.[34] Wedded to the twin gods of positivism and empiricism, the Besantian novelist recognizes that fiction is "of this world, wholly of this world" and therefore seeks to reproduce the surfaces of life exactly as he finds them. Like the scientist too, the novelist reports his findings in a "transparent" prose, one that refuses to call attention to itself as writing. For Besant such transparency is the mark of professional writing in all disciplines. It at once vouches for the truth of the information conveyed while also ensuring that the professional's "products" will find the widest possible market. In the view of his detractors, however, Besant had succeeded primarily in degrading fiction-writing from a sacrament into a trade. He urges novelists to look after their self-interest by considering their products first as marketable commodities and only secondarily as art. For many writers Besant's position was scandalous, akin to the mercenary views confessed by Anthony Trollope in his recently published autobiography (1882).[35] James eloquently objected to Besant's rules for successful novel-writing, rules which Besant offered as analogs to the procedural protocols that governed professional activity in other disciplines but which James considered as forming a risible do-it-yourself manual.[36]

In their replies James and Stevenson self-consciously distance themselves from Besant's professional author. They reject his implicit claim that the novel's function is to reproduce middle-class ideology by means of a facile mimesis. Both men were uncomfortable with the idea that the interests of the professional author ought to be at one with what Stevenson refers to elsewhere as "that well-known character, the general reader."[37] Of the two men, Stevenson took the more radical position by embracing a non-functionalist "style" as a kind of anti-mimesis. He argues that literature has nothing to do with reproducing reality but "pursues instead an independent and creative aim." Fiction, "like arithmetic and geometry" (two sciences, significantly, whose practitioners were not considered professionals in the nineteenth century), looks away from "the gross, coloured, and mobile nature at our feet, and regard[s] instead a certain figmentary abstraction." The novel in particular lives "by its immeasurable difference from life.[38] That difference is achieved only through a painstaking attention to what Stevenson terms the "technical elements of style." According to him, this craft so long to learn, unlike Besant's easily mastered rules, is precisely what separates true writers from the general public, making the former unpopular with all but the blessed few who cultivate "the gift of reading."[39] Affirming that "the subject makes but a trifling part of any piece of literature" and that "the motive and end of any art whatever is to make a pattern" and not to reproduce "life," Stevenson situates himself in opposition to dominant notions of realism, and thus also in opposition to the model of professional authorship proposed by Besant.[40]

It can be argued that, in rejecting Besant, Stevenson simply embraces a different model of professionalism, one that would become increasingly familiar in the modernist period. Certainly, in his hauteur regarding the reading public, as well as in his commitment to the values of craft, of style, of culture and taste, Stevenson participates in that reshaping of authorial self-presentation that Jonathan Freedman has identified most notably in James, Pater, and Wilde. As Freedman suggests, rejecting the middle-class marketplace could be a highly marketable strategy, just as distancing oneself from both the Besantian professional and the general reader could be a way of asserting one's own more authentic professionalism.[41]

Yet while James, Pater, and Wilde—all consummate modernist professionals by Freedman's standards—have been assimilated into the modernist canon, Stevenson has not. "There are doubtless many reasons for this exclusion, but one has to do with Stevenson's conspicuously split allegiances, his dual commitment to aestheticism and "style" on the one hand and to what George Saintsbury called "the pure romance of adventure" on the other.[42] A feuilletonist who wrote pirate stories, Stevenson combined a Paterian attention to the intricacies of style and form with blood-and-thunder celebrations of male adventure. While aestheticism in turn became a key component of much Modernist writing, adventure did not. Stevenson's champions in the twentieth century have almost always been those who, like Proust and Nabokov, recognize in him a fellow dandy. Critical considerations of his adventure stories have, by contrast, tended to thrust him firmly back into the nineteenth century. I will take up the late-Victorian "male romance" more fully in Chapter 4; here I note only that the male romance was itself a rejection of both realism and professionalism. Unlike aestheticism, however, it rejected them in the name of a reimagined male bourgeois identity. It was thus a form of critique—occluded, self-interested, contradictory—arising from within the patriarchy itself. Stevenson's simultaneous embrace of aestheticism and adventure thus possesses a certain coherence, yet it was also the source of significant incoherences. Like Oscar Wilde, Stevenson cultivated a style both aesthetic and personal that carried within it an implicit critique of conventional middle-class mores. Yet like Andrew Lang, Rider Haggard, Arthur Conan Doyle, and other votaries of the male romance, Stevenson used the conventions of "adventure" (and again, those conventions could be said to structure both his work and, especially after the move to Vailima, his life) in an attempt to reshape his male middle-class readership and ultimately to affirm his ties to them.

That Stevenson felt this split in his allegiances with special acuteness while writing *Jekyll and Hyde* is suggested by his account of the story's genesis offered in "A Chapter on Dreams" (1892). In this essay Stevenson writes that

Jekyll and Hyde, like many of his tales, originated in a dream which he simply transcribed and elaborated. Indeed "I am sometimes tempted to suppose ... [that] the whole of my published fiction ... [is] the single-handed product of some Brownie, some Familiar, some unseen collaborator, whom I keep locked in aback garret" of the mind "while I get all the praise."[43] Stevenson's conscious self—"what I call I, my conscience ego, the denizen of the pineal gland"—is left merely to bring some order to the Brownies' ideas and then to "dress the whole in the best words and sentences that I can find and make" (XVI, 187). For post-Freudian readers this account of creativity's sources in the unconscious will sound familiar. Like Freud, Stevenson is deeply indebted to Romantic paradigms of the artist: "A Chapter on Dreams" in effect reimagines Shelley's Cave of Prometheus in proto-psychoanalytic language. Like Freud, too, Stevenson distinguishes between dream and waking world in terms of a series of productive contrasts: energy and order, licentiousness and morality ("my Brownies have not a rudiment of what we call a conscience" [XVI, 188]), spontaneity and craft, and so on. It seems especially appropriate that Edward Hyde should spring from a dream, since like the Brownies he is so easily identified with the raging energies of the id.

Yet Stevenson's unconscious is distinctly un-Freudian in one respect, for it has developed what can only be called a business sense. Over the years, Stevenson writes, he has come to dream only *marketable* stories, for the denizen of the pineal gland has no use for any other. Where once the Brownies told tales that, though powerful, were "almost formless" (XVI, 178), now "they have plainly learned ... to build the scheme of a considerate story and to arrange emotion in progressive order" (XVI, 186–87). They now "dream in sequence" and "tell ... a story piece by piece, like a serial" (XVI, 187). This new-found restraint arises not from any intrinsic love of aesthetic form but because the Brownies "have an eye to the bankbook" and "share in [Stevenson's] financial worries" (XVI, 186). "When the bank begins to send letters and the butcher to linger at the back gate ... at once the little people begin to stir themselves" (XVI, 183).[44]

Despite its comic tone, the essay's point is a radical one: in what Stevenson called "the days of professional literature"[45] even the ostensibly unbridled play of the unconscious has come to be determined by the exigencies of the pocketbook. Stevenson has become a professional author whether he would or no. In "A Chapter on Dreams" the creative unconscious is not, as it sometimes was for the Romantics or for Freud, a place elsewhere, freed from the disabling pressures of history. Instead it is decisively shaped by those pressures. To survive, an author must not only write to order but also dream to order. So well trained have the Brownies become, the essay ironically concludes, that they have begun to fantasize potentially marketable stories in styles entirely unlike Stevenson's own. "Who would have supposed that a Brownie of mine should invent a tale for Mr. Howells?" (XVI, 189). In learning to write like William Dean Howells, that champion of sturdy realist prose, the Brownies demonstrate that they know better than Stevenson himself what goes down best with the reading public. Increasingly dissevered from any individual ego, the Brownies place themselves in willing bondage to the demands of the marketplace. Stevenson, thought by the world to be the "author" of his tales, is only an amanuensis—"I hold the pen ... and I do the sitting at the table ... and when all is done, I make up the manuscript and pay for the registration" (XVI, 187–88)—transcribing tales he can claim no credit for, since they come not from some deep authentic self but from the culture itself. If Stevenson succeeds in giving his middle-class readers what they want, the essay concludes, that is because they have manufactured his stories for him.[46] "A Chapter on Dreams" is in essence an elegy for Romantic paradigms of creativity. The Romantic visionary genius has become the Besantian purveyor of goods, a kind of literary shopkeeper.

"A Chapter on Dreams" also gives further weight to the claim that *Jekyll and Hyde* traces the gradual taming of Edward Hyde into a parody of bourgeois respectability. Like Hyde, the Brownies find that lawlessness and, licentiousness simply do not pay, and that they must adjust accordingly. As in the novel, Stevenson concludes that there is no place elsewhere, no human activity not already saturated with ideology. The creative unconscious is shown to be wholly acculturated: not in opposition to bourgeois morality but unavoidably pledging fealty to it.[47] In a striking and bitter letter to Gosse, Stevenson called this servicing of the public: a form of prostitution. "We are whores," he wrote, "some of us pretty whores, some of us not: whores of the mind, selling to the public the amusements of our fire side as the whore sells the pleasures of her bed."[48] His further point is that under modern conditions whoredom is the writer's only option. In another letter he returned to this same metaphor: "like prostitutes" professional authors "live by a pleasure. We should be paid if we give the pleasure we pretend to give; but why should we be honoured?"[49]

What begins to emerge is a cluster of veiled equivalences, with threads linking Stevenson, his creative Brownies, Edward Hyde, and the prostitute-writer within a larger web comprising middle-class ideology, commerce, and the ethics of professionalism. *Jekyll and Hyde*, I would argue, is in part a symbolic working through of these linkages. We recall for instance that bourgeois commerce is implicitly associated with whoring in Stevenson's description of the "thriving" commercial street which Jekyll's house backs on to, its "florid charms," "freshly painted shutters," and "well polished brasses" giving luster to goods displayed "in coquetry; so that the shop fronts stood along that thoroughfare with an air of invitation" (30). The doctor's house fronts on to "a square of ancient, handsome houses, now for the most part decayed from their high estate" and given over to vaguely disreputable trades, "shady lawyers, and the agents of obscure enterprises": the once-fine homes are "let in flats and chambers to all sorts and conditions of men" (40). Readers who hear in this last passage a covert reference to Besant's popular 1882 novel, *All Sorts and Conditions of Men*, might speculate that Stevenson is indirectly including professional authorship among the shady and obscure trades of modern life. Even without the specific connection to Besant, we note that Jekyll's house is surrounded front and back by the trappings of bourgeois life, a life described in terms of the seedy, the disreputable, the garish, the decayed. Such linkages—commerce and prostitution, prostitution and authorship, authorship and professionalism, professionalism and bourgeois ideology, and so on—suggest that we might usefully approach *Jekyll and Hyde* as an indirect attempt by Stevenson to size up his situation as a professional writer at the close of the nineteenth century.

The novel in fact turns out to be obsessively concerned with writing of various kinds: wills, letters, chemical formulae, bank drafts, "full statements," and the like. Like "A Chapter on Dreams," *Jekyll and Hyde* worries over the question of authenticity. Just as in the essay Stevenson feared that his writing originated not in some genuine self but in a market-driven unconscious, so in the novel he continually links writing with forgery and other kinds of "inauthentic" production. Enfield first discovers Hyde's identity when he reads his name written on a cheque that Enfield "had every reason to believe ... was a forgery." That in fact "the cheque was genuine" only convinces Enfield that the deception runs deeper than he had imagined (32). Hyde was known even earlier to Utterson through Jekyll's will, which the lawyer considers an affront to "the sane and customary sides of life" (35) and whose irregularities he "never approved of" (43). Even before he makes his first appearance in the present of the novel, then, Hyde is associated with writing that is at once "professional"—bank drafts and legal testaments—and yet also somehow irregular and thus troubling. In both instances, moreover, Hyde stands to benefit financially, just as in "A Chapter on Dreams" Stevenson says his own "irregular" writings proved to be the most lucrative.

Jekyll too is implicated in the production of questionable writing. Utterson, after hearing Mr. Guest's analysis of Jekyll's letters, is driven to conclude that the doctor has begun to "forge for a murderer" (55). We also recall that, Jekyll's downfall results from the "impurity" of his original chemical formulae, and that it is precisely out of that impurity that Hyde originally springs (96).[50] We cannot finally separate Jekyll's writing from Hyde's, however, since a central conceit of the story is that they write identical hands. "Of my original character," the doctor notes, "one part remained to me: I could write my own hand" (93). Hyde can sign Jekyll's cheques and Jekyll can write Hyde's letters because their "characters" (in both senses of that word) are the same. Ever vigilant, F. W. H. Myers objected to this conceit, saying that it showed a "want of familiarity" on Stevenson's part "with recent psycho-physical discussions" concerning the individuality of handwriting.[51] Once again fingering a pressure point in the novel, Myers argued that no two hands could be identical, since each individual's unique and authentic character is reproduced via the characters on the page. In a parallel vein, both Rider Haggard and E. T. Cook took exception to Jekyll's will, claiming that the law would never recognize such a document because it could not be securely attributed to Jekyll himself.[52]

    Jekyll and Hyde of course takes as its explicit theme the possibility that the self is not unique and inviolable. Yet Myers, Haggard, and Cook seem relatively untroubled by the novel's "revelation" that two distinct subjectivities inhabit the same "self." All three men instead attest to the anxiety that arises from the suspicion that writing itself might be entangled in this same indeterminacy. As their appeals to science and the law further suggest, vast realms of social discourse operate on the assumption that writing and selfhood are interchangeable. Yet it is precisely this faith that both "A Chapter on Dreams" and *Jekyll and Hyde* undermine. In this context it is worth noting that Stevenson himself has often been criticized for not being sufficiently "present" in his own writings. In 1927, at the nadir of Stevenson's reputation, Leonard Woolf dismissed him as having "no style of his own." His writing is "false," Woolf contended; at best he was a mimic, "a good imitator."[53] The "no style" argument is common in Stevenson criticism, and interestingly finds its complement in the equally common claim that Stevenson is merely a stylist. During his lifetime both William Archer and George Moore criticized Stevenson for being all style and no substance.[54] What links these seemingly contradictory assessments is their shared suspicion that there may be no "self" visible in Stevenson's writing, no discernible subjectivity expressed there. Rather than style being the man, it seems that in Stevenson's case style—whether his own or borrowed—replaces the man. Stevenson occasionally critiqued himself along these same lines, claiming that as a writer he was merely "a sedulous ape" who did no more than mimic the styles of the writers who came before him.[55] This self-characterization links Stevenson back to Edward Hyde, himself a "sedulous ape" who learns to his great cost how to mimic his "betters."

Given this context, we can readily agree with Ronald Thomas's claim that *Jekyll and Hyde* enacts the modernist "disappearance of the author." Thomas notes, for instance, how often in the story writing is tied to vanishing.[56] "When this shall fall into your hands," Jekyll predicts in his last letter to Utterson, "I shall have disappeared" (72). Earlier, the lawyer's apprehensions concerning Jekyll's will centered on the provision that it come into effect upon the doctor's "disappearance or unexplained absence" (35). Hastie Lanyon likewise pens his narrative (also "not to be opened until the death or disappearance of Dr. Henry Jekyll" [58]) knowing that it will not be read until after his decease. It is thus only fitting that the novel concludes by foregrounding this link between the act of writing and the death of selfhood: "as I lay down my pen," reads the book's final sentence, "I bring the life of that unhappy Henry Jekyll to an end" (97).

That last sentence points the problem with particular sharpness, since it leaves unclear to whom "I" refers. Though the document is labelled "Henry Jekyll's Full Statement of the Case," within the statement the first person shifts referents with notorious frequency. The final few paragraphs contain sentences in which "I" means Jekyll, sentences in which "I" means Hyde, and sentences in which both Jekyll and Hyde are referred to in the third person, leaving an authorial "I" unattached to any self. The oft-cited confession of ontological anxiety—"He, I say—I cannot say, I" (84)—is in one sense misleading, since the "Full Statement" says "I" all the time. We merely do not always know who "I" is. Like the conscious self posited in "A Chapter on Dreams," the "I" of the "Full Statement" holds the pen and sits at the desk yet cannot unequivocally claim to be author of the document.

This dissociation of writing from selfhood is especially conspicuous in what is after all meant to be an autobiographical narrative. When Jekyll begins his confession in properly Victorian fashion ("I was born in the year 18— to a large fortune, endowed besides with excellent parts, inclined by nature to industry," and so on [81]), we might expect him to at last write himself into the kind of coherence ostensibly promised by the autobiographical form.[57] What he finds instead is a self increasingly fragmented and estranged from "his" own writing. "Think of it—I did not even exist!" (86).

Jekyll and Hyde covertly enacts, then, a crisis in realist writing alongside its more overt thematizing of a crisis in bourgeois subjectivity. That these crises find expression in a story "about" criminal degeneracy should not surprise us, since traditional humanist notions of both realism and identity were deeply embedded in the normative categories deployed by degenerationists. *Jekyll and Hyde* self-consciously dismantles those categories, though it does not offer any to replace them, since Stevenson too felt himself estranged both from his "professional" self and from his writing. It is easy to see his subsequent flight to Samoa as a finally futile attempt to reclaim the possibility of pure Romantic expression. The irony, of course, is that exile made him more popular than ever with the middle-class reading public in Britain.

NOTES

1. See *Robert Louis Stevenson: The Critical Heritage*, ed. Paul Maixner (London: Routledge & Kegan Paul, 1981), 200–01.

2. Robert Louis Stevenson, *The Strange Case of Dr. Jekyll and Mr. Hyde* (1886; rpt. Harmondsworth: Penguin, 1979), 35. Further page references to this novel are given parenthetically in the text.

3. *Criminal Man According to the Classification of Cesare Lombroso*, briefly summarized by his daughter Gina Lombroso Ferrero, with an introduction by Cesare Lombroso (New York and London: G. P. Putnam's Sons, 1911), xiv. The following quotations can be found on xiv–xv.

4. Daniel Pick usefully situates Lombroso's work both in the context of Italian class politics and in relation to opposing theories of criminality developed in mid-century Prance. See *Faces of Degeneration*, 109–52. On Lombroso's reception and influence in England, see 176–89, and William Greenslade, *Degeneration, Culture and the Novel*, 88–102.

5. John Addington Symonds for instance read the story as a parable of atavistic man. See his March 1886 letter to Stevenson, reprinted in *Critical Heritage*, ed. Maixner, 210–11. Recent critics who have studied the tale's indebtedness to theories of criminality, atavism, and devolution include Ed Block, Jr., "James Sully, Evolutionist Psychology, and Late Victorian Gothic Fiction," *Victorian Studies* 25 (Summer 1982), 443–67; Donald Lawler, "Refraining *Jekyll and Hyde*: Robert Louis Stevenson and the Strange Case of Gothic Science Fiction," in *Dr. Jekyll and Mr. Hyde After One Hundred Years*, ed. William Veeder and Gordon Hirsch (Chicago: University of Chicago Press, 1988), 247–61; Martin Tropp, "*Dr. Jekyll and Mr. Hyde*, Schopenhauer, and the Power of the Will," *The Midwest Quarterly* 32 (Winter 1991), 141–55; and Marie-Christine Lepps, *Apprehending the Criminal: The Production of Deviance in Nineteenth-Century Discourse* (Durham: Duke University Press, 1992), 205–20.

6. See Gertrude Himmelfarb, *The Idea of Poverty: England in the Early Industrial Age* (London: Faber and Faber, 1984), esp. 312–400, and Gareth Stedman-Jones, *Outcast London: A Study in the Relationship Between Classes in Victorian Society* (Oxford: Clarendon Press, 1971), esp. 127–51, 281–313. Judith Walkowitz shows how degeneration, atavism, criminality, and class came together in the social discourses of the 1880s in *City of Dreadful Delight: Narratives of Sexual Danger in Late-Victorian London* (Chicago: University of Chicago Press, 1992), ch. 7.

7. Nordau, *Degeneration*, 7.

8. See Stevenson's letter of 1 March 1886 to F. W. H. Myers in *The Letters of Robert Louis Stevenson*, ed. Sidney Colvin, 4 vols. (New York: Charles Scribner's Sons, 1911), III,

326: "About the picture, I rather meant that Hyde. had bought it himself, and Utterson's hypothesis of the gift an error."

9. Elaine Showalter emphasizes the class dimensions of Stevenson's tale, though she sees Hyde simply as a bourgeois fantasy of an eroticized proletariat. She argues that we should read the novel's class interests in terms of "the late-nineteenth-century upper-middle-class eroticization of working-class men as the ideal homosexual objects." Hyde's proletarian status makes him a figure both of fear and desire for Stevenson's professional gentlemen. See Showalter, *Sexual Anarchy: Gender and Culture at the Fin de Siècle* (Harmondsworth: Penguin, 1990), 111.

10. Referring to the proliferation of interpretations of Hyde within the novel, Veeder and Hirsch argue that "*Jekyll and Hyde* engages ineptly in self-analysis in order to call into question the very possibility of such analysis and to complicate comparable analytic moves by the reader." See "Introduction" to *Jekyll and Hyde After One Hundred Years*, ed. Veeder and Hirsch, xii. By arguing for such awareness, they usefully reverse a long-standing tradition of seeing Stevenson as the most innocent of writers, one whose value was separate from his intentions. The most powerful articulation of this latter position is still G. K. Chesterton's in his *Robert Louis Stevenson* (New York: Dodd, Mead, 1928): "I am by no means certain that the thing which he preached was the same as the thing which he taught. Or, to put it another way, the thing which he could teach was not quite so large as the thing which we could learn... [Stevenson] had the splendid and ringing sincerity to testify ... to a truth which he did not understand" (22–23). In other words, as the professional reader whose learning is needed to make sense of an unself-conscious text, Chesterton plays Jekyll to Stevenson's Hyde.

11. Myers wrote four letters to Stevenson on the subject of *Jekyll and Hyde* (21 February, 28 February, and 17 March 1886, and 17 April 1887), which are reprinted in *Critical Heritage*, ed. Maixner, 213–22.

12. See "Collated Fractions of the Manuscript Drafts of *Strange Case of Dr. Jekyll and Mr. Hyde*," in *Jekyll and Hyde After One Hundred Years*, ed. Veeder and Hirsch, 24. For a general discussion of Stevenson's alterations from manuscript to printer's copy to first edition, see William Veeder, "The Texts in Question," *ibid.*, 3–13.

13. My reading makes few distinctions among Enfield, Utterson, Lanyon, and Jekyll, whom I take as types of the bourgeois professional rather than as individuals, and thus largely interchangeable. For readings that do make such distinctions, see Block, "James Sully," 448; Mark M. Hennelly, Jr., "Stevenson's 'Silent Symbols' of the 'Fatal Cross Roads' in *Dr. Jekyll and Mr. Hyde*," *Gothic* 1 (1979), 10–16; Irving Saposnik, *Robert Louis Stevenson* (New York: Twayne, 1974), 10; and Stephen Heath, "Psychopathia Sexualis: Stevenson's *Strange Case*," *Critical Quarterly* 28 (1986), 104. Block, Hennelly, and Saposnik single out Utterson as the novel's only "healthy" character, while Heath nominates both Utterson and Enfield for that honor. Closer to the position I take is that of Masao Miyoshi, *The Divided Self: A Perspective, on the Literature of the Victorians* (New York: New York University Press, 1969), who also stresses the interchangeability of the primary male characters, noting that the "important men of the book ... are all unmarried, intellectually barren, emotionally joyless, stifling" (297).

14. In "Children of the Night: Stevenson and Patriarchy," William Veeder argues for Enfield's vicarious participation in this scene and notes that "exculpation of Hyde has marked Enfield's narrative from the start." In *Jekyll and Hyde After One Hundred Years*, ed. Veeder and Hirsch, 107–60, at 117–18.

15. I owe this idea to a suggestion made by William McKelvy in an unpublished essay (1993) on *Jekyll and Hyde*.

16. Veeder suggests that when Hyde appears at Lanyon's door ludicrously engulfed in Jekyll's oversized clothes we are likely to be reminded of a little boy dressing up as daddy; see "Children of the Night," 126.

17. "Here is another lesson to say nothing" (34). "Let us make a bargain never to refer to this again" (34). "This is a private matter, and I beg of you to let it sleep" (44). "I wouldn't speak of this" (55). "I cannot tell you" (57). "You can do but one thing ... and that is to respect my silence" (58). "I daren't say, sir" (63). "I would say nothing of this" (73). As Lepps points out regarding the opening conversation between Enfield and Utterson, "the novel begins with the silent recognition of an unsayable relation between an unnameable high personage and an indescribable creature" (*Apprehending the Criminal*, 210).

18. In recounting how Hyde negotiated for Lanyon's help to retrieve the chemical, Jekyll emphasizes how Hyde on this occasion "rose to the importance of the moment" and mastered himself "with a great effort of the will" (93–94). Regarding Hyde's subsequent conversation with Lanyon, both Veeder and Peter K. Garrett have noted that Hyde now speaks in the professional tones of Jekyll. See Veeder, "Children of the Night," 131, and Peter K. Garrett, "Cries and Voices: Reading *Jekyll and Hyde*," in *Jekyll and Hyde After One Hundred Years*, ed. Veeder and Hirsch, 59–72, at 66.

19. Among previous critics of the novel, only Veeder has discussed this scene, coming to conclusions quite different from mine. He reads the tableau as a projection of Utterson's unconscious, a "kind of parlor primal scene," with "Jekyll/Hyde as father/mother in cozy domesticity" ("Children of the Night," 136). Veeder's reading is richly suggestive, though it neglects what I take to be an important facet of Stevenson's description, namely that the tableau is an empty one: no one is alive to enjoy the cozy domesticity.

20. Later of course Jekyll accuses Hyde of "scrawling in my own hand blasphemies on the pages of my books" (96), though even this leaves room for doubt as to ultimate responsibility. Jekyll, had he wished to be conclusive, could have, said "scrawled in his own hand," since the two men share the same handwriting.

21. For readings that place Hyde's weeping in the context of late-Victorian discourses on femininity, see William Patrick Day, *In the Circles of Fire and Desire: A Study of Gothic Fantasy* (Chicago: University of Chicago Press, 1985), esp. 91–92; and Janice Doane and Devon Hodges, "Demonic Disturbances of Sexual Identity: The Strange Case of Dr. Jekyll and Mr/s Hyde," *Novel* 23 (Fall 1989), 63–74.

22. Letter to Edmund Gosse dated 2 January 1886; see *Letters*, II, 313.

23. For a reading of *Jekyll and Hyde* as "an unconscious 'allegory' about the commercialization of literature and the emergence of a mass consumer society in the late-Victorian period," see Patrick Brantlinger and Richard Boyle, "The Education of Edward Hyde: Stevenson's 'Gothic Gnome' and the Mass Readership of Late-Victorian England," in *Jekyll and Hyde After One Hundred Years*, ed. Veeder and Hirsch, 265–82.

24. Lloyd Osbourne, *An Intimate Portrait of R. L. S.* (New York: Charles Scribner's Sons, 1924), 59.

25. Letter to Archer dated October 1887; see *Letters*, III, 19.

26. Letter to Gosse dated 2 January 1886; see *Letters*, II, 313.

27. See Peter Keating, *The Haunted Study: A Social History of the English Novel 1875–1914* (London: Seeker & Warburg, 1989), 9–87; Nigel Cross, *The Common Writer:*

Life in Nineteenth-Century Grub Street (Cambridge: Cambridge University Press, 1985), 204–23; and N.N. Feltes, *Literary Capital and the Late Victorian Novel* (Madison: University of Wisconsin Press, 1993).

28. See Keating, *Haunted Study*, 16–17. W.E. Henley negotiated with Cassell's on Stevenson's behalf for the book publication of Treasure Island. Cassell's offered a £100 advance on royalties covering the first 4,000 copies plus £20 for each additional 1,000 copies. Stevenson thought he had sold his copyright for £100.

29. Thomas Stevenson bought the house as a wedding present for Fanny Stevenson. She and Louis lived there between January 1885 and August 1887. Thomas died in May 1887, and Louis almost immediately insisted on moving, though Fanny by all accounts was happy at Skerryvore. Ian Bell writes that "in Samoa, Stevenson never spoke of the place. It was as though he had expunged the memory of imprisonment, despite having written some of his most famous works while living—like a 'weevil in a biscuit'—at the house:" See Bell, *Robert Louis Stevenson: Dreams of Exile* (Edinburgh: Mainstream, 1992), 179.

30. Quoted in Frank McLynn, *Robert Louis Stevenson: A Biography* (London: Hutchinson, 1993), 240.

31. Letter to Gosse dated 12 March 1885; see *Letters*, II, 271. Archer is quoted in J. A. Hammerton, ed., *Stevensoniana: An Anecdotal Life and Appreciation of Robert Louis Stevenson* (Edinburgh: John Grant, 1907), 75. Jenni Calder quotes an unpublished letter of Fanny's: "The tramp days are over, and this poor boy is now, for the rest of his life, to be dressed like a gentleman." See Calder, *Robert Louis Stevenson: A Life Study* (New York: Oxford University Press, 1980), 152.

32. Stevenson was clearly uneasy at this time about his loss of faith in socialism. Joking to Gosse that "the social revolution will probably cast me back upon my dung heap" at Skerryvore, Stevenson said his political change of heart was sure to bring upon him the wrath of H.M. Hyndman, the socialist politician. "There is a person Hyndman whose eye is upon me; his step is beHynd me as I go." (Letter dated 12 March 1885; see *Letters*, II, 271.) Readers who feel Edward Hyde lurking in that "beHynd" (night also recall the emphasis given in the tale to Hyde's sinister footsteps and disconcerting gaze. Equating Hyde with Hyndman (and thus with socialism) gives additional weight to readings that focus on the class issues raised in the novel. For an opposing view, see Christopher Harvie's argument for Stevenson's lifelong, thoroughgoing Toryism in "The Politics of Stevenson," in *Stevenson and Victorian Scotland*, ed. Jenni Calder (Edinburgh: University of Edinburgh Press, 1981), 107–25.

33. See Walter Besant, *The Art of Fiction* (Boston: Cupples, Upham, 1884), p. 6.

34. Useful discussions of the Besant–James–Stevenson debate can he found in Feltes, *Literary Capital*, 65–102; John Goode, "The Art of Fiction: Walter Besant and Henry James," in *Tradition and Tolerance in Nineteenth-Century Fiction*, ed. D. Howard, J. Lucas, and J. Goode (London: Routledge and Kegan Paul, 1966); and Mark Spilka, "Henry James and Walter Besant: 'The Art of Fiction' Controversy," *Novel* 6 (Winter 1973).

35. See Keating, *Haunted Study*, 9–15, for the furor Trollope caused, particularly by his insistence that novelists were no different than shoemakers or tallow-chandlers.

36. See Henry James, "The Art of Fiction," in *Essays on Literature; American Writers; English Writers*, ed. Leon Edel and Mark Wilson (New York: Library of America, 1984), esp. 49–53. James had reason to be worried, since the late 1880s and the 90s saw a boom in "how-to" manuals for writers, many of which were written under the unofficial auspices of The Society of Authors. See Keating, *Haunted Study*, 71–73; and Cross, *Common Writer*, 211–12.

37. "On Some Technical Elements of Style in Literature" (1885), in *The Works of Robert Louis Stevenson*, ed. Sidney Colvin, 25 vols. (London: Chatto and Windus, 1911), XVI, 242.

38. "A Humble Remonstrance" (1885), *Works*, IX, 152–53.

39. "Books Which Have Influenced Me" (1887), *Works*, XVI, 274..

40. The first quotation is from "The Morality of the Profession of Letters" (1881), *Works*, XVI, 266, the second from "On Some "Technical Elements of Style in Literature," *Works*, XVI, 243.

41. Jonathan Freedman, *Professions of Taste: Henry James, British Aestheticism, and Commodity Culture* (Stanford: Stanford University Press, 1990).

42. George Saintsbury, "The Present State of the English Novel" (1888), in *The Collected Essays and Papers of George Saintsbury 1877–1920*, 4 vols. (London: Dent, 1923), III, 126. On Stevenson and adventure, see Edwin M. Eigner, *Robert Louis Stevenson and Romantic Tradition* (Princeton: Princeton University Press, 1966). On Stevenson as an aesthete and consummate stylist, see Vladimir Nabokov, *Lectures on Literature*, ed. Fredson Bowers (New York: HBJ, 1980), 179–205.

43. *Works*, XVI, 187. Further page references to this essay are given parenthetically in the text.

44. Stevenson wrote to Myers that *Jekyll and Hyde* was written to ward off "Bytes the Butcher." Letter to Myers dated 1 March 1886; see *Letters*, II, 325.

45. Letter to T. Watts-Dunton dated September 1886; see *Letters*, II, 348.

46. Stevenson's version of the novel's genesis agrees in outline with the stories told by Fanny Stevenson and Lloyd Osbourne while significantly altering the emotional and moral valences of their accounts. According to both Fanny and Lloyd, Fanny found Louis's first, dream-inspired draft of the novel unsuitable. Louis, she said, "had treated it simply as a story, whereas it was in reality an allegory." After a heated argument, Louis burned the manuscript and started over to produce a version more in keeping with Fanny's moral vision of the story. Both Fanny and Lloyd report that Louis agreed that his second, Fanny-inspired draft of the tale was more marketable. In "A Chapter on Dreams" the two stages are collapsed together: the Brownies both produce the original tale and simultaneously revise it into a marketable story. The censor, rather than being outside the author (in this case in the person of Fanny), is instead thoroughly internalized. For Lloyd's account of *Jekyll and Hyde*'s writing, see *Intimate Portrait*, 62–67; for Fanny's, see Nellie van de Grift Sanchez, *The Life of Mrs. Robert Louis Stevenson* (New York: Charles Scribner's Sons, 1920), 118–19.

47. It can of course be argued with some justice that "A Chapter on Dreams" simply rationalizes Stevenson's failure to be the subversive he sometimes claimed he was. As Veeder points out, the successive drafts of *Jekyll and Hyde* show him toning down and in some cases deleting potentially objectionable material. See "The Texts in Question," 11–12.

48. Unpublished letter quoted in Calder, *A Life Study*, 291. We might in turn connect the letter's invocation of the "amusements of the fireside" to *Jekyll and Hyde*'s portrayal of the hearth as the site of bourgeois isolation and solipsism.

49. Letter to Gosse dated 2 January 1886; see *Letters*, II, 313.

50. Ronald Thomas convincingly argues that Hyde is "the product of Jekyll's pen." See "The Strange Voices in the Strange Case: Dr. Jekyll, Mr. Hyde, and the Voices of Modern Fiction," in *Jekyll and Hyde After One Hundred Years*, ed. Veeder and Hirsch, 78.

51. *Critical Heritage*, ed. Maixner, 215.

52. The objections of Haggard and Cook are reprinted in *Critical Heritage*, ed. Maixner, 202–03.

53. Leonard Woolf, "The Fall of Stevenson," in *Essays on Literature, History, Politics, Etc.* (London: Hogarth, 1927), 41.

54. See William Archer, "Robert Louis Stevenson: His Style and Thought" (1885), rpt. in *Critical Heritage*, ed. Maixner, 160–69; and George Moore, *Confessions of a Young Man* (1886; rpt. Swan Sonnenschein, 1892), 284–87.

55. "A College Magazine," *Works*, IX, 37.

56. Thomas, "Strange Voices," 79.

57. Most recent studies of the novel have stressed what can be called the heteroglossia of the "Full Statement," its deployment of a multitude of conflicting voices and perspectives. A notable exception to this critical trend is Garrett, who argues for the formal and ideological conservatism of Jekyll's narrative while acknowledging the "factors that resist" the novel's drive toward monovocality. See Garrett, "Cries and Voices," 59–61.

ALAN SANDISON

Treasure Island:
The Parrot's Tale

'Were you never taught your catechism?' said the Captain. 'Don't you
know there's such a thing as an Author?'
— 'The Persons of the Tale'

'You could say that the parrot ... was Pure Word. If you were a French
academic, you might say that he was *un symbole du Logos*.'
— Julian Barnes, *Flaubert's Parrot*

In *Treasure Island* a parrot gets the last word, and turns out to be a two-
hundred-year-old deconstructionist. Moreover, these last verbal fragments
uttered by an uncomprehending fowl, while they effortlessly rupture
conventional relations between signifier and signified, are, firstly, the fine but
troublesome summation of a composition which signifies Jim Hawkins'
accession to authority via authorship, and, secondly, the surprising means of
galvanising Jim out of his sleep and having him sit up in bed in fear and
horror of that 'accursed island' on which, one might have thought, he had
enjoyed his finest hour.

So we have a problem. Jim tells us at the outset that he has taken up his
pen at the behest of his companions 'to write down the whole particulars' of
the treasure-island adventure. Can we now accept the narrative-composition
as proof of his having achieved the estate of Author—of independent, mature

From *Robert Louis Stevenson and the Appearance of Modernism: A Future Feeling*. © 1996 by Alan
Sandison.

authority—or do we find our expectations confounded by a raucous old parrot screeching the eviscerated words of a defunct pirate?

One way of reading *Treasure Island* is as carnivalesque masquerade where traditional authority, in a variety of categories, is gleefully subverted. Such an approach would foreground Long John Silver as chief 'masker'—appropriately enough for he is a master of (moral) disguise—but it would also have to include his cherished parrot which is also a dissembler, for 'Cap'n Flint', that cornucopia of naval history and bad language, is, in fact, a lady. General reversal is almost a standard component in Stevenson's fiction: we have only to think of the 'old maid' Mackellar, or of Colonel Geraldine in *New Arabian Nights*, or of David Balfour playing wife to Alan Breck's fiddler in their long and inconclusive march, or Ramsey in 'The Castaways of Soledad' who makes the immodest suggestion that he should become the official hostess to the oddly-named Captain Crystal, the better to entertain the crew.

Whatever caprice drove Stevenson to endow his parrot with the female gender, it is clearly more than a courtesy for her to be given the last word. Roosting securely in Jim Hawkins' dreams, with a life-tenure the equal of his, she declines to be written out of the story; so helping to secure the survival of her master, who has been. (The awful possibility has to be faced that the parrot's gender may have survived from her original and improbable incarnation *as a hen* in an earlier version of the tale; but Stevenson's characteristically assiduous re-writing would, I am sure, have removed all accidental vestiges of such an ignoble descent. The trio of females in *Treasure Island* are alike in embodying certain contradictions: Jim's mother is materialist rather than maternal, Silver's black wife is, despite the colour-coding, an accomplice and Cap'n Flint is a female masquerading as a male parrot.)

So is it Jim's word against the parrot's? In a hell devised by French theorists the parrot can be seen as undeconstructible: an ageless allusion (to a dead pirate), the language of its discourse can never be at variance with itself since it signifies nothing to its subject. Howbeit, she is, at the same time, well-nigh, indestructible: 'Now that bird', says Silver 'is, may be, two hundred years old, Hawkins—they lives forever mostly; ...' (63). Notwithstanding her great age and vast experience, Cap'n Flint appears no more than a 'babby'. Moreover, despite having been present at innumerable naval engagements and learning to speak the language of such events, she is still Long John's 'poor old innocent bird' protected from contamination by incomprehension. Is this meant to comfort us as perusers of Jim's book? Or is it meant to comfort Jim who may be similarly protected from his exposure to Long John Silver? Is he still an innocent after witnessing, and in truth participating in, innumerable gruesome killings and sundry other bad deeds? Or is he parroting the parrot, so to speak, who/which had learned to scream 'Pieces of eight!' on another treasure hunt which had turned up 'three hundred and fifty thousand of 'em'. Jim's scream is modified into a memoir but there may be a covert allusion to that first hoard when he dilates on the contrasting variety of coinage in Flint's treasure—and on the pleasure it gave him: 'It was a strange collection, like Billy Bones' hoard for the diversity of the coinage, but so much larger and so much more varied that I think I never had more pleasure than in sorting them' (215). At any rate, we can quite properly think of Jim as No. 2 parrot on the grounds that he is responsible for sustaining the memory—if not, indeed, the presence—of Silver by *his* words. Silver, we are told, 'can speak like a book when so minded' (62) and maybe that is just what he's doing through Jim, courtesy of 'Cap'n Flint'.

All the foregoing questions, probing various possibilities, could be rolled up into one general question: what kind of text is this? Is it, for example, a 'mere' adventure-story, or is it a *Bildungsroman* with Modernist anxieties about the problematics of language and textual authority? Should the carnivalesque option be pursued? That there are carnivalesque elements is, I believe, undeniable and these, it could be argued, have some responsibility for the ambiguity in the text towards authority. Thus while Jim's gradual acquisition of authority (or Authority, if we are thinking of Lacan's symbolic order) is a serious matter and, insofar as it reflects the dynamic which drives the adolescent adventurer to take the action he does, constitutes the tale's bed-rock, Long John Silver frequently comes near to burlesquing authority—at least in its excessively conventional embodiment on the *Hispaniola* in those three archetypes of social hierarchy, the Squire, the doctor and the ship's captain.

Nonetheless the carnivalesque does not seem to provide an adequate focus within which *all* the story's parts can be seen to come together, nor does it make sufficient allowance for the seriousness of Jim's quest. Before any attempt to establish one which does, an objection has to be anticipated. It has been said (by *Punch*) that to attempt a serious critique of P. G. Wodehouse is to take a spade to a soufflé. Alastair Fowler at the end of a penetrating analysis of *Treasure Island*, and perhaps mindful of *Punch*'s scorn (and of Alexander Pope), similarly cautions readers against breaking a butterfly on the wheel, or making it walk the plank. Yet Stevenson's attitude to his texts is a sophisticated one and part of his perfectly evident relish in writing derives from his gleeful participation in subverting his own text. What he is doing, however, goes well beyond mere mischievousness or self-indulgence.

Authority (or authorship) in all its variety is a constant preoccupation with him: he yearns for its legitimation in him—the blessing, in the biblical sense even though he knows that it will only come, if it comes at all, by an act of self-assertion, even usurpation, for which he, unlike Jacob, lacks resolve.

In the excellent essay already referred to, Alastair Fowler is surely right when he notes that what Jim finds particular pleasure in, in sorting the coinage, are the figures of authority which are imaged in these coins, for what he is appreciatively running through his fingers are 'the pictures of all the kings of Europe for the last hundred years'. Fowler also notes the Jungian 'treasure hard to attain' archetype—'selfhood, independence, identity'—and, in suggesting that this is more truly Jim's objective, describes the book as being for the most part not really about treasure or the search for it; rather, it 'recounts a series of contests for power'.[1]

In another excellent essay Wallace Robson, pondering the reasons for the treasure-hunt being somewhat marginalised, discreetly favours Freud over Jung and advances the argument that '[t]he avoidance of the 'treasure' theme ... may have something to do with Stevenson's personal stabilisation at that time'. He is thinking, of course, of Stevenson's recent marriage and the 'degree of resolution' he had achieved in the difficult relationship with his father.[2] It has, I believe, a great deal to do with this *and* with Jim's role in the 'contests for power' which together account for the serious theme of the book and explain why Jim should be frightened by a parrot.

All Stevenson's major fiction involves some form of tension or conflict between sons and 'figures of authority from the class of fathers'.[3] Many, if not indeed most, of these stories have to do with a young man unable to attain that level of maturity and independence necessary for him to meet the obligations imposed on him by the adult world. In the most serious cases, these young men are trapped in a limbo between adolescence and manhood. *Weir of Hermiston*, *Kidnapped*, *Prince Otto*, *The Ebb-Tide* all have central characters who are, in this sense, 'failures'.

Jim Hawkins, however, is not in this category. Here in *Treasure Island* we have one of the few cases where the adolescent *does* win through to transcend his condition; so much so that he is invested by his much older companions with responsibility for 'authoring' the text of their adventures, a charge of some significance from a writer on the threshold of Modernism. Jim's development is notable for being the first and very nearly the last such achievement by someone in his position in Stevenson's work. If there is the hint of a shadow lying across it in the closing sentences, it is nothing to the great question-mark which hangs over the comparable case of David Balfour in *Catriona* whose epiphany as a piece of hormone-deficient ivy wrapping himself round Catriona's knees is parasitic rather than priapic and carries little conviction that he has at long last proved himself capable of that individuation which will allow him to take his place in the adult world.

That Jim succeeds to man's estate is almost certainly a reflection of Stevenson's 'personal stabilisation' as Robson calls it. After the agonies of the 1870s where his hopeless infatuation with Mrs Sitwell was compounded by an apparently endless sequence of shattering rows with his father, Stevenson had finally married, though the effort to do so nearly cost him his life. *Treasure Island*—or the bulk of it—was composed in the bosom of his new family; Fanny and her son Lloyd Osborne were both there, and the composition enjoyed the benevolent participation of his father since both parents were also part of the holiday menage sojourning in the Scottish Highlands.

In conventional Freudian psychology, *Treasure Island* is easily seen to be a *locus classicus* in the representation of the adolescent confronted by the castrating father-figure who, however, already bears the marks of the son's desire to turn the tables on him by being himself maimed, that is symbolically emasculated. This extends even to the image of authority in the effigy of Admiral Benbow (a hero of Stevenson's incidentally), hanging as a sign in front of the inn which takes the sabre-cut Bill Bones aims at Black Dog, a cut so deep that '[y]ou may see the notch on the lower side of the frame to this day' (12).

Bones, like so many of Stevenson's father-substitutes, is a man of fine physique: he is 'a tall, strong, heavy, nut-brown man' with, however, the mark of a sabre-cut across one cheek, 'a dirty, livid white' (3). He exudes authority, 'looking as fierce as a commander' and is recognised by young Jim as a man 'accustomed to be obeyed or to strike'. Jim's response to him might be described as pleasurably fearful and a sort of intimacy is quickly established between them. That Bones lives in some dread of visiting seafarers is soon obvious to the inn-keeper and his family, and Jim becomes sufficiently partisan to describe himself as 'a sharer in his alarms' (5). Already, it would seem, there is a hint of fluidity in the boundaries between Jim's and the pirates' moral world.

Bones' domination of the 'Admiral Benbow's' patrons—he 'tyrannised' over them, we're told—is synchronised with the rapid decline in Jim's father's health. In fact, Jim believes his father's death to have been hastened by his fear of Billy who effectively displaces him as *patron*. As the natural father continues to fade, another substitute, Black Dog, appears. He is distinguished by a maimed left hand, having lost two 'talons', and he, too, exerts a menacing degree of authority over Jim. However, he alternates between threats and attempts at ingratiating himself: '"I have a son of my own", said he, "as like you as two blocks, and he's all the pride of my 'art. But the great thing for boys is discipline, sonny—discipline"' (11). Later, Jim is 'this dear child here, as I've took such a liking to' (12).

The next in this almost phantasmagoric sequence of threatening authority-figures or bad fathers is Blind Pew, a 'horrible, soft-spoken, eyeless creature' (20) who terrifies Jim much more than the other two. As a result of his visit, Billy Bones dies, his death occurring on the day after the funeral of Jim's father. Jim himself links the two events in a way which begs an interesting question:

> It is a curious thing to understand, for I had certainly never liked the man ... but as soon as I saw that he was dead, I burst into a flood of tears. It was the second death I had known, and the sorrow of the first was still fresh in my heart (21).

This contrasts sharply with the prosaic, almost off-hand account Jim gives of his father's death:

> But as things fell out, my poor father died quite suddenly that evening, which put all other matters on one side. Our natural distress, the visits of the neighbours, the arranging of the funeral, all the work of the inn to be carried on in the meanwhile, kept me so busy that I had scarcely time to think of the captain, far less to be afraid of him (18).

There is not much sign of mourning in this matter-of-fact description of his 'natural distress'; any outburst of grief seemingly, and indeed curiously, having to wait the expiry of Billy Bones. Yet his tears then are perhaps as much a sign of his growing maturity as their (apparent) absence at his father's death, for what Jim is learning is something about the unreliability of appearances and the ambiguities of the moral order—as reflected in himself as well as in others.

Billy Bones has unquestionably perpetrated atrocious acts of wickedness, but through him Jim makes a number of discoveries about himself—one being that 'he was far less afraid of the captain himself than anybody else who knew him' (5), and another that he could still feel some pity for this bloodthirsty old pirate who had so comprehensively offended against a Christian society's most cherished values. Jim is even mature enough already to recognise (unlike his father) that the captain's presence, notwithstanding his wickedness, did the inn no harm, that he might even help to energise the community and at the same time assist it in its self-definition:

> I really believe his presence did us good. People were frightened at the time, but on looking back they rather liked it; it was a fine excitement in a quiet country life; and there was even a party of the younger men who pretended to admire him ... (6).

Jim is sharply distinguishing his own from his father's over-anxious and imperceptive reaction, as he does again when he tells how his father 'never plucked up the heart' to ask the captain for the money due to him, and describes him as living in terror of his obstreperous guest (6).

The most notable and powerful of all the surrogate and maimed fathers does not, of course, make a physical appearance in this sequence. Much more tellingly, Long John Silver haunts Jim's dreams. A little later in the book Smollett sharply criticises Trelawney for telling the secret of their voyage to the parrot, meaning that everyone knows it. (The Squire thinks he's referring to Silver's parrot and Smollett has to explain that 'It's a way of speaking' [55].) Here in the account of his dream Jim broadcasts his own secret almost as promiscuously and with as little comprehension as the parrot—or so we are led to assume.

> How that personage haunted my dreams, I need scarcely tell you. On stormy nights, when the wind shook the four corners of the house and the surf pounded along the cove and up the cliffs, I would see him in a thousand forms, and with a thousand diabolical expressions. Now the leg would be cut off at the knee, now at the hip; now he was a monstrous kind of a creature who had never had but the one leg, and that in the middle of his body. To see him leap and run and pursue me over hedge and ditch was the worst of my nightmares (5).

There is more here than 'simply' the Oedipal castration of the father or the fear of personal castration: there is also the ambiguous fear on the part of the son that the potency of the father will be incestuously visited upon him.[4]

Set over against the collection of threatening 'fathers' found among the pirates, we get a trio of authority-figures in Smollett, Trelawney and Livesey. Initially, we might assume that Trelawney the Squire, as the social superior of the other two, would be the principal of the group and when Jim first visits him at the Hall this seems about to be confirmed:

> The servant led us down a matted passage, and showed us at the end into a great library, all lined with bookcases and busts upon the top of them, where the squire and Dr Livesey sat, pipe in hand, on either side of a bright fire (34).

Nothing, it appears, could be more conspicuously redolent of accepted hierarchical authority, literary, historical and social, than such a scene. Yet as the tale unfolds we come to realise (as does Jim) that things are not quite what they at first seem.

It becomes clear fairly quickly, for example, that Trelawney is sorely lacking in personal authority. He cannot keep his own or other people's counsel—'you cannot hold your tongue', Livesey tells him roundly—is highly irresponsible and gullible to a degree. He gets at odds with his captain almost immediately and, had it not been for Livesey's intervention, would have dismissed him. The contrast between Trelawney and Smollett could hardly be more marked. Smollett is uncommunicative, authoritarian in all matters under his command, forthright and decisive. In fact, of the three he is the only one who truly conforms to the stern, uncompromising, judgemental father whom we often find the young Stevenson hero pitting himself against—or perhaps, on occasion, even creating. It is of more than passing significance, then, that this father-figure is disabled by a wound in the middle of the adventure and thereafter poses no further threat to Jim's freedom of action. Eventually he is made subject (as all the others are) to Jim's pen—a highly effective form of subjugation whether we think of him as Alexander Smollett, captain of the *Hispaniola*, or Tobias Smollett, precursor-author.

When Smollett is wounded, the man who takes over the leadership of the Squire's party is not Trelawney himself but Dr Livesey. From the start of the book whether asserting himself over Billy Bones in the 'Admiral Benbow' or comfortably sharing in the privileged surroundings of the Squire's library, Livesey is a figure of quiet but confident authority. Drawn in sharp contrast to the unbending, unsympathetic Smollett, he exercises over Jim an influence grounded on benevolence and—significantly—a generous readiness to recognise Jim's deserts.

On several occasions Livesey is brought into conflict with other father-figures and shown to be their superior. When he refuses to be silenced by Billy Bones, obstreperously presiding over the 'Admiral Benbow's' parlour, the beached pirate draws a knife. Livesey orders him to put it away or he will see that he hangs: 'Then followed a battle of looks between them; but the captain soon knuckled under, put up his weapon, and resumed his seat, grumbling like a beaten dog' (8). The doctor's authority is further underlined by his disclosure in this episode that he is also a magistrate; which, incidentally, offers another instance of the imbrication of medicine, the father-figure and the law which is to be found elsewhere in Stevenson's fiction (in particular in *Jekyll and Hyde*).

Livesey is equally undaunted when he confronts the ruthless and treacherous Long John Silver. In everything the doctor is Silver's polar opposite: a man of the utmost integrity, hating deception, steadfast and loyal. He makes no bones about his abhorrence of all Silver stands for and cheerfully admits to his willingness to have seen him cut down by his enraged followers at the empty treasure-site had Jim Hawkins not been in the way. Again, the contrast between these two authority-figures is brought out when Livesey's innate compassion is contrasted with Silver's inhumanity. The doctor, hearing the sounds of (as he thinks) delirium coming from the camp of the few remaining pirates, tells Silver that he is half-inclined to go and treat the sufferers, and this exchange follows:

> '... if I were sure they were raving ... I should leave this camp, and, at whatever risk to my own carcase, take them the assistance of my skill'.
>
> 'Ask your pardon, sir, you would be very wrong,' quoth Silver. 'You would lose your own precious life, and you may lay to that ... these men down there, they couldn't keep their word ... and what's more, they couldn't believe as you could.'
>
> 'No,' said the doctor. 'You're the man to keep your word—we know that.' (216–17)

It is, of course, Livesey who brings about Silver's defeat.

If these confrontations between Livesey and the others might seem to suggest a contest between good and bad fathers and the kind of authority they assert, there may be another example in Smollett's attitude to Jim when he brusquely orders the latter to the galley with the words 'I'll have no favourites on my ship.' He, the quintessentially harsh and repressive father, addresses these words not to Jim but, almost as a challenge, to the doctor, who is possessed of a rival moral authority based not, perhaps, on showing favour, but at least on kindness and consideration. Just as he asserts himself over Bones and Silver, Livesey, in effect, repeats his success with Smollett by assuming the direction of the Squire's party when the captain is disabled. All the decisions are his and everything is managed with understated self-confidence: '... I did what I thought best ...' (212).

It could be argued that it is Smollett's resentment at Jim's success in finding in Livesey another 'father', an alternative moral authority which will nurture his (Jim's) own, which impels him to make his rather gnomic remark to Jim at the end: 'You're a good boy in your line, Jim; but I don't think you and me'll go to sea again. You're too much of the born favourite for me' (214). To look with favour on any 'son' is more than this autocratic 'father' can bring himself to do since it is a step towards his own disempowerment. Significantly, having dismissed Jim, he immediately turns his attention to Silver, to whom he reacts quite neutrally: '"What brings you here, man?" "Come back to do my dooty, sir," returned Silver. "Ah!" said the captain, and that was all he said.' The difference in his attitude to Silver is drawn to our attention by these last few words. Smollett, having cast off or disinherited the intrepid Jim for being too much of the born favourite, now extends favour to the reprobate pirate and accepts his return to 'dooty' without demur. There is clearly a sense in which these two surrogate fathers are on the same side.

Livesey's behaviour suggests a very different paternal model. Even in the face of Jim's desertion of their party in the stockade, the doctor conspicuously refuses to condemn his action out of hand. His criticism is muted yet very much to the point:

> 'Heaven knows I cannot find it in my heart to blame you; but this much I will say, be it kind or unkind: when Captain Smollett was well, you dared not have gone off; and when he was ill, and couldn't help it, by George, it was downright cowardly!' (193)

Pinpointing Jim's lack of scruple as this does, highlights the authenticity of Stevenson's portrayal of the adolescent negotiating his rite of passage. In seeing his opportunity to circumvent the 'father's' authority and taking it, Jim, *does* display selfishness; yet his act is a necessary one if he is eventually to learn to take responsibility for his own decisions and his own life. Throughout the story Jim's acceptance of Livesey's authority is instinctive if tacit, but at the reproof administered here (not angrily but 'sadly'), Jim becomes a boy again—and a repentant one at that—and bursts into tears.

This telling exchange invites comparison with another between a 'real' father and son: that of Adam Weir and Archie in *Weir of Hermiston*. Livesey's assertion of authority is of a kind diametrically opposed to *Weir's* but is extremely close kin to Lord Glenalmond's. These two men exercise great influence with tact, restraint and affection over a young man growing up. Each views the young man's aspirations to an independent position for himself sympathetically and in doing so is contrasted with a father-figure who does not.

In Livesey's case the figure in question is primarily Silver (who, in the last section of the book, literally ties Jim to himself with a length of rope), but, as has been implied, shadowed-in behind him is Captain Smollett who also has a good deal in common with Adam Weir. While Livesey admires the Captain (as Glenalmond does Weir) he does not share his idea of authority based on rigorous demarcations uncompromisingly enforced. Smollett, first described as 'a sharp-looking man, who seemed angry with everything on board', delivers an ultimatum to the Squire's party before they leave Bristol requiring that things be done on the *Hispaniola* exactly according to his wishes or he will resign his command. His attitude is not an unreasonable one in his position but it puts him at the extreme of the range and makes him not just an uncompromising enforcer of the law but something of a martinet. It is notable that it is only by Livesey's quietly but effectively interposing his own kind of authority between Smollett and Trelawney that Smollett is reconciled to his post.

Dr Livesey is, in fact, a father-figure of a kind we encounter throughout Stevenson's fiction. As such he can easily be seen as a son's apology for the antagonistic portrayal of the father as harsh, uncaring and judgemental: for characters like Attwater in *The Ebb-Tide*, Ebenezer in *Kidnapped*, Weir in *Weir of Hermiston*. It is something of a commonplace of Freudian analysis to see the representation of the father in these terms as a sort of parricide for which the 'oedipal regressive' must do penance:

> An Oedipus, to atone for his crime, must put out the eyes that have gazed on the mother he has wed and the father he has slain. An author has other means of propitiation and penance. He can perform the comforting miracle of restoring his father to life in the most exalted form; he can re-create the father in the image that he (the son) loved best; he can call into existence a father-ideal toward whom no 'son' could have the slightest objection.[5]

Dr Livesey is just such an ideal father whom no son could object to, as are in varying degrees, Alan Breck in *Kidnapped*, Davis in *The Ebb-Tide* and Glenalmond in *Weir of Hermiston*. The latter is of particular significance (as we shall see in a later chapter) for in this book Stevenson exposes quite clearly the son's role in *creating* such an accommodating surrogate. Livesey has in full measure what all of these men have to some extent: a protective, affectionate concern for the 'son', a willingness to recognise his merits and no inclination whatsoever to put obstacles in the way of his development. 'Every step, it's you that saves our lives', he says to Jim, acknowledging the effect of the latter's initiatives and so of his progress towards equality of participation in the responsibilities of adulthood. All that said, a caveat still needs to be entered when we are marshalling good and bad father-figures: in *Treasure Island* there is no clear-cut division allocating the 'bad' father-figures to the pirates and the 'good' to the Squire's party. Jim expresses more grief at the death of the murderous Billy Bones than he does at that of his own father, while Smollett's hostility towards him remains to the end implacable. Silver's, as we shall see, is a highly complex case.

Finally, one might note that even Livesey may have a mote in his compassionate eye for he prides himself on having served with the Duke of Cumberland at Fontenoy. The year was 1745: in the next year this able general acquired his notorious sobriquet 'Butcher' Cumberland for what were seen as his brutal tactics in the battle of Culloden which ensured the decimation of the Jacobite forces and the disfavour of romantic nationalists like Stevenson. And one truly last point for Freudians: nearly all the ideal fathers (including Livesey) are bachelors, for which reason alone they are less challenging to 'penitent' sons.

I have said that in *Treasure Island* we have almost the only example of a young Stevensonian hero who safely negotiates the shoals of adolescence to the extent of becoming 'Captain' Hawkins (even if only to Israel Hands), *and* his own author. Nevertheless there are one or two clues scattered around to suggest that the carapace of adulthood may not, even by the end of the composition, be quite complete. One, already referred to, is the allusion to nightmares about the island in the last sentence of the book, but another, more significant one resides in the fact that there is one father-figure whom Jim never quite transcends, and that is, of course, Long John Silver. Hawkins senior dies, Billy Bones dies and so does Blind Pew, but Silver escapes. When Jim tells us that 'the formidable sea-faring man with one leg has gone clean out of my life' (219), it is clear that he has not gone clean out of his dreams. Unless we are to assume an unreasonable fear of psittacosis on Jim's part, the fact that the parrot is part of his nightmare testifies to its capacity to revive memories of Long John and all that he stands for. Telling one's secrets in recounting one's dreams becomes complicated when part of that secret is conveyed in a few seemingly unimportant words spoken by a parrot.

The relationship between Jim and Long John is at the very heart of the book and in its sophisticated nature shows us just how remiss it is to think of *Treasure Island* as a 'mere' adventure-story for children. Adventure there is, of course, and brilliantly constructed too, but we should never forget that in this case it feeds into the genre of the *Bildungsroman* (with which it is far from being incompatible) where a youth is subjected to a variety of experiences which will test his capacity and readiness for the sort of responsibilities that go with adulthood. It is in the hazard of this enterprise that the more substantial drama is played out and it involves the painful rupturing of relationships, the confrontation with unsuspected moral ambiguities which make choosing exceptionally difficult yet crucial to the growth-process, and the recognition that independence, though a prime objective, will bring with it loneliness and isolation. This drama begins in the second paragraph of the book with the arrival of Billy Bones and is so skilfully blended with the adventure that its existence has even been denied. The concentration of so many menacing authority figures does not succeed in crushing the boy's growing self-confidence, however, and he emerges with credit from the trial. He is helped in this by having already begun to distance himself from his father, clearly seeing himself as more able to cope with their unwelcome visitors. When his father's death duly occurs, it is something which he can then take in his stride.

The final step in this phase is taken when he decides to leave England with the squire and his companions in search of the treasure, but that decision is rendered irrevocable when, on returning to the inn after his brief stay in the squire's house, he discovers another boy—the new apprentice—in his place:

> It was on seeing that boy that I understood, for the first time, my situation. I had thought up to that moment of the adventures before me, not at all of the home that I was leaving; and now, at sight of this clumsy stranger, who was to stay here in my place beside my mother, I had my first attack of tears. I am afraid I led that boy a dog's life; for as he was new to the work, I had a hundred opportunities of setting him right and putting him down, and I was not slow to profit by them (46).

He is therefore already launched upon his voyage even before he reaches Bristol or sets his foot upon the deck of the *Hispaniola*.

Once on the ship Jim encounters yet another authority-figure in the person of Captain Smollett. The captain turns out to be as much a disciplinarian as Black Dog and declines to modify his authoritarian temper in any way in his dealings with Jim. Not only does he order him about very roughly—'Here, you ship's boy ... out of that! Off with you to the cook and get some work'—he also takes care to make his adjuration (addressed, as I have said, to Dr Livesey) audible to Jim: 'I'll have no favourites on my ship.' Jim is going to have to earn his passage as well as to accept unequivocally his subordination to an uncompromising ship's master.

It is a paradigm which this boy who has already glimpsed what lies beyond the adolescent's horizon is going to find it difficult to conform to, so it is unsurprising that he should tell us here (though in no very serious tone) that he 'hated the captain deeply' (59). In fact neither Jim nor the Captain gives ground and tension remains between them for the whole of the expedition. Twice Jim absents himself from the Captain's command and the Captain, on his part, makes it clear at the end that he will never permit Jim any privileges which would diminish his authority over him.

Jim does, however, get the last word—literally, for he becomes the author of the Captain in writing the account of their travels. Nor is one being arbitrary in crossing barriers in conflating the world of the book with the act of its inscription, for Stevenson has already set a precedent. Not only has he written one of his fables, 'The Persons of the Tale', in which the characters step outside their fictional world in order to talk about the author, but he has also given his Captain the name of Smollett.

Tobias Smollett was a Scottish writer who could have been predicted to attract Stevenson's interest. Having joined the navy at an early age, he rose to become surgeon's mate, sailed the Spanish Main and, as a young man of twenty, took part in an expedition against the Spaniards in the West Indies in 1741. He was a consumptive and because of his poor health and exiguous means took to spending substantial periods of time travelling in France and Italy, eventually dying at fifty in his home at Leghorn in 1771. Smollett was the author of, *inter alia*, *The Adventures of Roderick Random*, *The Expedition of Humphry Clinker* and *The Adventures of Peregrine Pickle*, and could be regarded as a contemporary of Long John Silver since the latter tells the gullible squire that he lost his leg in a naval action under the command of 'the immortal Hawke'. Hawke (1705–81), having first distinguished himself in action at Cape Finisterre in 1747, earned his 'immortality' by a celebrated victory at the battle of Quiberon Bay in 1759.[6] (Note 6 offers some speculations on the life and career of Long John Silver.)

It is impossible, therefore, to regard Smollett's name as accidental any more than is Herrick's in *The Ebb-Tide* or Hoseason's in *Kidnapped*.[7] Nor is it simply an example of Stevenson innocently sporting with the idea of reflexivity so that he can enjoy exposing the fictionality of his fictions (something which he *does* enjoy doing). As will become obvious, Stevenson has all the Modernists' disdain for the fathers of the tradition, which masks no small measure of Harold Bloom's anxiety of influence; so that Jim's refusal to knuckle down to 'Captain' Smollett and the latter's strenuous insistence that he will not abate a jot of Jim's apprentice-position as 'ship's boy', reflects a battle of literary generations. It is a battle Jim decisively wins when he has the privilege of 'inscribing' the Captain in his account of their voyage, but, arguably, the Captain has already lost it when he refuses to admit that Jim is privileged, whether he likes it or not—privileged, that is, by being the succeeding generation. Jim, therefore, establishes his maturity by becoming the author of the ship's master, thus indirectly affirming that, Kafka-like, one way *his* author could gain independence from *his* father was by becoming a writer.

   If this relationship shows Jim as achieving the independent status aspired to by the adolescent, that with Silver is a very different matter. From the start it is more intimate and more physical. Jim's dream of Silver's sexual potency is a mixture of fear and desire: fear of the castrating domination of this father-figure, desire for his potency (or, possibly, desire to submit to that potent sexuality). There is nothing outlandish in the suggestion that behind this particular fictional relationship can be discerned the complex relationship between Stevenson *père et fils*. In the last year of the author's life, his correspondence shows him as father-haunted as ever: 'He now haunts me, strangely enough, in two guises: as a man of fifty, lying on a hill-side and carving mottoes on a stick, strong and well; and as a younger man, running down the sands into the sea near North Berwick, myself—*aetat 11*— somewhat horrified at finding him so beautiful when stripped!'[8]

   No sooner is Silver mentioned on the third page of *Treasure Island* than he realises himself in Jim's subconscious awareness: 'How that personage haunted my dreams, I need scarcely tell you'; and, despite Jim's equivocation, he is there in the dreams of a much older Jim at the end of the tale. In between, Jim is subjected to the full range of attentions Stevenson allows his fictional fathers to visit upon their 'sons'—from assiduous wooing to an overt threat upon their lives. The first stage—the wooing—is highly successful, assisted as it is by Jim's naivety. Having been put on his guard against one-legged men by Billy Bones, his suspicions are roused at 'the very first mention of Long John in Squire Trelawney's letter' (48). When he sees him, however, his fears are at once allayed:

   one look at the man before me was enough. I had seen the
   captain, and Black Dog, and the blind man Pew, and I thought I

knew what a buccaneer was like—a very different creature, according to me, from this clean and pleasant-tempered landlord (49).

Clearly Jim has a long way to go before he learns the Stevensonian lesson implicit in this misreading of signs. Not that he can be blamed unduly, for Silver is one of the astutest in his class. The speed of his recovery and the quickness of his invention when Jim recognises Black Dog at the 'Spy-glass' is highly impressive, as is the way Stevenson judges the scene's potential for comedy to a hairsbreadth. The upshot of the whole incident, however, is that Silver, after flattering Jim ('You're a lad, you are, but you're smart as paint') puts himself on the same level, convincing Jim that 'here was one of the best of possible shipmates' (52). However it is as well to remember that Silver leaves Dr Livesey and the Squire with the same impression: '"The man's a perfect trump", declared the Squire' (53).

To Jim he is 'unweariedly kind', making much of him on his visits to the galley: 'Nobody more welcome than yourself, my son', he tells him and we see why the crew should respect and obey him as Jim has himself just observed them to do. When it suits him he can wear his authority very lightly even while reminding others of it in the most casual expressions—like 'my son' (62). What makes him an attractive figure, at least to Jim, is the way in which he relishes his own performance. Some of that was evident in the Black Dog incident, but even in introducing Jim to his parrot he indulges himself in a way that makes the youth think him 'the best of men' (63).

One of the most appealing things about Stevenson's writing is the manifest pleasure it gave him—and his almost provocative exposure of the fact. It is a point of some significance since it gives a fair indication of his refusal to endorse the established view that the objective of the art of fiction was to create a moral reality, structured on high principle and discriminating sensibilities, which would be capable of teaching life a lesson. In his essay, 'A Humble Remonstrance' Stevenson flatly rejects the Jamesean claim that literature can 'compete with life' and identify its essential truths. For him its product will remain the 'phantom reproductions of experience' which have little to do with factual experience which 'in the cockpit of life, can torture or slay'. When we are expressing our admiration of such reproductions what we are really doing is '[commending] the author's talent': that is, admiring artifice rather than 'real life'.

Though he is highly capable of giving us the illusion that what we are enjoying *is* like 'real life', Stevenson also enjoys deliberately showing his hand; he puts on a performance, and frequently has his characters do the same (James Durie, Alan Breck, as well as Long John Silver, come to mind). It is a sophisticated process of deconstruction: by all sorts of strategies of the narrative voice—inflections, wild extravagances (Dr Livesey's snuff-box full of parmesan), reflexivities—the text becomes a *soi-disant* performance. Stevenson draws our attention to his performance as author and has his characters frequently draw attention to *their* performance as characters. The later fable 'The Persons in the Tale' is, in this respect, entirely of a piece with the book to which it provides a coda.

Silver's performance in his introduction of 'Cap'n Flint' is a bravura piece of play-acting and Jim is captivated by it. At the conclusion of his performance 'John would touch his forelock with a solemn way he had' which delighted Jim and completely won him over (63). Silver's defence of his parrot's innocence and his respect for a theoretically outraged clergy—'Here's this poor old innocent bird o' mine swearing blue fire, and none the wiser, you may lay to that. She would swear the same, in a manner of speaking, before chaplain'—are alike tongue-in-cheek. Whether Jim relishes—or even recognises—the play-acting for what it is, is by no means clear, but achieving maturity has a great deal to do with *not* suspending one's disbelief too easily, and Jim's inexperience certainly allows him too readily to believe in Silver.

The degree to which he has read Silver as a man of sincerity, genuinely fond of him, and willing to talk to him 'like a man', comes out unequivocally in his reaction to his overhearing, Silver's wooing of another young man in precisely the same terms:

> You may imagine how I felt when I heard this abominable old rogue addressing another in the very same words of flattery as he had used to myself. I think, if I had been able, that I would have killed him through the barrel (67).

Jim's trust in words has been naive—despite the demolition-job done in his presence on the sanctity of inherent verbal meaning by a loquacious 200-year old parrot. As he goes through with the adventure he becomes much more aware of ambiguities until he can deal verbally in them himself. 'And now, Mr Silver,' he says when he becomes the pirates' prisoner, 'I believe you're the best man here ...', and Long John agrees: 'I'm cap'n here because I'm the best man by a long sea-mile' (78, 179). But what does Jim mean by 'best' now, and is it what Silver means? This is the dialogue which ends with Silver's famously enigmatic remark 'Ah you that's young—you and me might have done a power of good together!' Jim is the only one, it seems, who has not been surprised or puzzled by the remark for he makes no comment on it. While the 'power of good' will remain a mystery, the reason for Silver's show of favour to Jim is at least partly explained by his seeing in the youth a reflection of his younger self: 'I've always liked you, I have, for a lad of spirit, and the picter of my own self when I was young and handsome' (176). Even allowing for Silver's characteristically mocking flattery, the allusion merits attention for it is picked up again in 'Ah, you that's young...' Is this an expression of a sentiment much quoted by Stevenson—*si Jeunesse savait, si Vieillesse pouvait*—that is, the desire of the older man to yoke to his adult experience the vigour and drive of his youth? If so is it a way of empowering or emasculating surrogate youth? In exchange for the youth's potency he would give him his knowledge—but the 'power of good' they might do together remains Silver's to define, and *that* is a sinister degree of *dis*empowerment.

What I think this shows is how serious a threat to Jim's freedom and moral growth Silver has actually been. He has offered him power by talking to him 'like a man' and treating him as an equal, but he was always going to ensure that that power and that growth remained firmly circumscribed. The appeal in the offer has been almost dazzling to Jim—on his way to manhood but not observing the castrating knife in Long John's sleeve. What the latter has offered him has been a share in, or access to, his own mature sexual power as well as that residing in his whole mind and personality and Jim hasn't perceived that this is a trap which will, in the event, emasculate rather than empower him, for Silver is giving nothing up.

The high point of Silver's fascination for Jim is to be seen in an incident which seems to exceed the parameters of a boy's adventure story, though it is arguably the best piece of description in the whole book. This is that moment when Silver exerts his powers of seduction on another member of the crew to persuade him to join the pirates. His approach is the familiar one, and Jim, concealed close by, can hear it all:

> 'Mate', he was saying, 'it's because I thinks gold dust of you—gold
> dust, and you may lay to that. If I hadn't took to you like pitch,
> do you think I'd have been here a-warning of you?' (88)

As they argue, the sound of a scream from across the marsh signalling the death of another loyal seaman brings Tom to his feet, but Silver 'had not winked an eye. He stood where he was, resting lightly on his crutch, watching his companion like a snake about to spring. "John!" said the sailor, stretching out his hand.'

The appeal to this figure poised to strike (in the suggestive image of the snake) is ineffectual and when Tom defies Silver and turns to walk away, Silver strikes in a manner that is more like a sexual assault:

> With a cry, John seized the branch of a tree, whipped the crutch out of his armpit, and sent that uncouth missile hurtling through the air. It struck poor Tom, point foremost, and with stunning violence, right between the shoulders in the middle of his back. His hands flew up, he gave a sort of gasp, and fell.
>
> Whether he were injured much or little, none could ever tell. Like enough, to judge from the sound, his back was broken on the spot. But he had no time given him to recover. Silver, agile as a monkey, even without leg or crutch, was on top of him next moment, and had twice buried his knife up to the hilt in that defenceless body. From my place of ambush, I could hear him pant aloud as he struck the blows (89).

In many ways the description is a realisation of Jim's nightmare when he first dreamed of Silver: 'a monstrous kind of creature who had never had but the one leg, and that in the middle of his body', and who had pursued him 'over hedge and ditch'.

At the culmination of Silver's attack, Jim faints. Wallace Robson, a very astute (if reticent) commentator, has this to say: 'What makes this scene powerful is our intimate closeness to Silver during the murder: he is referred to twice as 'John'—unusually for *Treasure Island*.' He goes on to note that 'the older reader' will be struck by the moment when Silver twice buries his knife in Tom's body, and Jim says, 'I could hear him pant aloud as he struck the blows'. And Robson concludes:

> The *obvious* force of this scene lies in Jim's identification with the victim, its less obvious force is the secret participation of Jim (because of his *closeness* to Silver) and hence the reader.[9]

Nothing could be clearer than that Silver's enticement of Jim to share in his potency exerts an almost irresistible appeal for the adolescent (whose fainting may not be precisely what it seems). Nor could anything be clearer than the fact that it is, for this youth's development, a dead end in every sense of the term. It is no wonder, then, that Jim is ambiguous in his attachment to, and admiration of, Silver, even after the latter's exhibition of his brutal lust for murder. What he has to do is to escape Silver's powerful temptation and find his own way to the empowerment that goes with manhood.

In alluding to the saying, *si Jeunesse savait, si Vieillesse pouvait*, in his essay 'Crabbed Age and Youth', Stevenson takes issue with it for while he agrees that it is 'a very pretty sentiment', he believes that it is not always right: 'In five cases out of ten, it is not so much that the young people do not know, as that they do not choose.' Jim *does* choose, however, very publicly and at great risk to himself. Silver has presented him with an ultimatum to join the pirates or be killed: 'I always wanted you to jine and take your share, and die a gentleman, and now, my cock, you've got to ... you can't go back to your own lot, for they won't have you; and without you start a third ship's company all by yourself, which might be lonely, you'll have to jine with Cap'n Silver' (176).

Jim has apparently been excluded from 'the treaty' as Silver calls the deal he did with Dr Livesey and the others, so his back is to the wall:

> 'And now I am to choose?'
>
> 'And now you are to choose, and you may lay to that', said Silver.

Jim, of course, chooses to defy Silver which leads, interestingly, not to his death but to his life being saved by Silver. As a result they become, for the time being, genuinely dependent on each other and neither Jim's sympathy for Silver nor his appreciation of the clever game he sees him as playing is diminished. He even admits that his 'heart was sore for him, wicked as he was' when he considered 'the shameful gibbet that awaited him' (188)— which may, or may not, be an excuse for not facing up to the real source of his sympathy. Yet the completely unprincipled Silver remains an acute threat, for Jim knows that he cannot be trusted, particularly after having heard him tell the pirates of his brutal plan should they get the treasure and retake the *Hispaniola*. Silver reminds Jim of just how much he is at his mercy by tying the youth to him with a length of rope. As they approach the hiding-place of the treasure, Jim, tied to the rope's end, '[f]or all the world ... like a dancing bear', finds Silver directing 'murderous glances' towards him and is left in no doubt about his intentions: 'Certainly he took no pains to hide his thoughts; and certainly I read them like print' (207). However, after the discovery that the treasure has gone, Silver instantly changes sides again and this time, having no alternative, stays with the Squire's party until he makes his escape (presumably *confident* of making his escape).

Jim's lesson has been a substantial one. Essentially he has had to come to terms with the fact that growing up involves some painful and daunting discoveries—most notably that the world is characterised by the proliferation of misleading signs whereby duplicity and treachery (particularly from figures of authority) are initially concealed from the youth seeking access to the adult male world. He has to learn that moral categories are not clear-cut; that the same face can bespeak both affection and murder and render classification of its owner impossible.

As a psychological archetype the island is a lonely place, and those who venture upon it will either emerge from the trial triumphant against all the forces that would seek to deny selfhood and sustain the authority of the patriarchy; or, like David Balfour, be marooned in their sense of existential worthlessness, abject and malleable before the forces of authority. Jim does triumph—to the point where he can participate in the marooning of others. As the ship, that symbol of the resolved self, sails out through the narrows on its way home, its occupants catch a last sight of the pirates they had made castaways:

> we saw all three of them kneeling together on a spit of sand, with their arms raised in supplication. It went to all our hearts, I think, to leave them in that wretched state; but we could not risk another mutiny (217).

The island has been for Jim a challenge to his own nascent self-sufficiency and he must meet that challenge alone—hence his two desertions from the comforting support of the ship and the stockade, each of which is, of course, commanded by Captain Smollett.

In the iconography of *Treasure Island* knives play a considerable role making clear the nature of the trial facing Jim. On each occasion of desertion Jim is threatened by one: the first is wielded by Silver on the prostrate body of Tom, the second by yet another father-figure, the particularly disreputable Israel Hands (whom Stevenson also found in Defoe's *A General History of the Robberies and Murders of the Most Notorious Pyrates*). The knife that pins Jim to the mast is literally almost the last throw of the father-figures and it is altogether ineffectual. Predictably so, one might say, for Jim's authority has grown steadily in this his second desertion from Captain Smollett's command. He has himself used a knife to advantage, cutting the *Hispaniola*'s cable before taking command of the vessel. And take command he undoubtedly does: 'I've come aboard to take possession of this ship, Mr Hands; and you'll please regard me as your captain until further notice' (165), and Hands dutifully, if not without some irony, calls him 'Cap'n Hawkins' thenceforth.

It is easy to agree with Robson that 'In so far as the book describes the "growing up" of Jim, this is an important episode' (91). Jim himself is 'to the adult eye more experienced and psychologically secure in his handling of this new and grim anti-father'. But, as usual, this figure is not so easily disposed of. Even in Jim's moment of triumph when he makes his 'great conquest' of the ship, the baleful influence of the hostile father is felt: 'I should, I think, have had nothing left me to desire but for the eyes of the coxswain as they followed me derisively about the deck, and the odd smile that appeared continually on his face.' It might have been 'a haggard, old man's smile', but there was still danger in it: 'there was, besides that, a grain of derision, a shadow of treachery, in his expression, as he craftily watched, and watched, and watched me at my work' (158). The derision in Hands' expression is one of the many strategies of emasculation practised by the old upon the young in Stevenson, while treachery seems to be second nature to unideal fathers.

Jim wins this confrontation, too, however, though the menace in the father-figure seems never to be quite extirpated. The 'quivering' of the water above Hands' body makes him seem to move a little 'as if he were trying to rise' despite the fact that he has been 'both shot and drowned' (167). Jim sends the dead O'Brien over the side to join him and the internecine strife of fathers and sons is again mirrored in O'Brien—'still quite a young man'— finally resting on the bottom with his prematurely bald head 'across the knees of the [old] man who had killed him'. And the drama seems set to be enacted eternally as Jim looks down upon the bodies 'both wavering with the tremulous movement of the water' (168).

Through his integrity and resolution, Jim has vindicated himself triumphantly, thwarting the pirates by his rock-like steadfastness—'First and last we've split upon Jim Hawkins' (179)—and saving his friends: 'There is a kind of fate in this', we may recall Dr Livesey saying. 'Every step it's you that saves our lives' (194). From the start, however, Jim's readiness to shoulder responsibility and to act (or, Stevenson might say, to *choose*) has been obvious. Lying hidden in the apple-barrel he had realised after the first words from the pirates 'that the lives of all the honest men on board depended on me alone' (65). That 'alone' has singular force. To Jim, acting responsibly means, in these circumstances, acting alone, as though he is aware that the challenge confronting him is a deeply personal trial. Which is one reason why, despite his achievements, Treasure Island is still to him that 'accursed island' rather than Silver's 'sweet spot'.

Jim's revulsion is, however, evident even before he sets foot on the island. The sight of it, 'with its grey, melancholy woods, and wild stone spires', discomposes him to the extent that, he tells us, 'from that first look onward, I hated the very thought of Treasure Island' (81–2). It is not the reaction we expect from this adventurous youth and we won't find an explanation in the superficies of a boy's adventure-story. Stevenson's islands are, by and large, traps for the self-tormented where the traveller's moral adequacy (usually as that is reflected in his aspirations to manhood) is put under severe stress with results which are often less than flattering. The truth of this is obvious in, for example, *Kidnapped*, *The Ebb-Tide*, *Treasure Island* and even exotic tales like *The Isle of Voices*.

The active involvement of the sub-conscious is signalled in a number of such stories by the draining away of colour from the landscape and by the association of the landscape with dreaming. Jim first sees the island 'almost in a dream' (73) and then describes the 'grey, melancholy woods'. The dream-landscape runs strikingly true to psychoanalytical form and is heavily imbued with Freudian symbolism:

> Grey-coloured woods covered a large part of the surface. This even tint was indeed broken up by streaks of yellow sand-break in the lower lands, and by many tall trees of the pine family, out-topping the others—some singly, some in clumps; but the general colouring was uniform and sad. The hills ran up clear above the vegetation in spires of naked rock. All were strangely shaped, and the Spy-glass, which was by three or four hundred feet the tallest on the island, was likewise the strangest in configuration, running up sheer from almost every side, and then suddenly cut off at the top like a pedestal to put a statue on. (81)

In the manuscript draft (clearly a very early one) of the unfinished *The Castaways of Soledad*, another youth, the seventeen-year-old Walter Gillingly, awakes to catch his first glimpse of the Isle of Solitude 'through the break of the mist, up a sort of funnel of moonlit clouds'. But he, too, seems scarcely awake. 'Next moment a little flying shower had blurred it out, and I laid me down again to see the same peaks repeated in my dreams'. When the sun rises and Walter awakens again he finds no great improvement in the prospect before him. The island

> rose out of the sea in formidable cliffs, and it was topped by an incredible assembly of pinnacles, more like the ruin of some vast cathedral than the decay of natural hills; and these rocks were no less singular in colour than in shape; the most part black like coal,

some grey as ashes and the rest of a dull and yet deep red.
Nowhere was any green spot visible....

It strikes Walter as a 'quite dead and ruined lump of an island' and its 'infinitely dreary, desert and forbidding air' puts the castaways 'notably out of heart' and the reader in mind of Earraid.

If the sight of such islands as Soledad, Earraid and Treasure Island sends the hearts of these youths into their boots (which is how Jim puts it), it is because they instinctively realise that they are a tightly-contained theatre of action which they must enter if they are to prove their fitness for the adult world. Treasure Island, however, departs in one important particular from the accepted archetype. As a number of critics have noticed, there is—in Wallace Robson's words—'an absence of emotional pressure in the winning of the treasure'[10] and very little appearance of the meaning that is often held to accrue round the search for buried treasure, that is, the desirability of the mother's body. Nonetheless it is far from true to say, as Robson does, that 'its geography is purely functional, mere stage-setting'.[11] The last quoted extract, with its description of the almost painfully-truncated Spy-glass, suggests that Jim's anxiety has everything to do with his psychosexual development and bespeaks a troubled awareness of a highly vulnerable masculine identity. Though we should not dismiss out of hand the archetypal equation of buried treasure with the mother's body (Ben Gunn's cave where the treasure has been reburied accords well with the conventional delineations of the symbol—with the additional detail of Captain Smollett being already ensconced there), there is another latent meaning in buried treasure which alludes to 'selfhood, independence, identity'.[12] Thus while for the pirate-crew 'the very sight of the island had relaxed the cords of discipline' (82) for Jim it signals the need to establish his *own* discipline in defiance of that imposed by the father-figures. Yet their potency—concentrated in Silver—is formidable and Jim's reaction, as witnessed at the time of Tom's murder, for example, is an authentic mixture of half-pleasurable terror and envy.

The earlier nightmares which had been induced by the description of Long John Silver have a subterranean link to Jim's dream-like vision of the island. In fact, the island is to be the focus of the struggle presaged in the first dream and one which will be decisive for Jim's development and independence. As Fowler notes, 'Jim chose to face the terrible father.... And the reward for his boldness was not only that Silver kept him alive, but that the good father's party cut the tether of dependence and ratified the free self-hood that he had stolen.' Had Jim chosen as Silver wanted, 'he would indeed have become the son of a sea-cook'.[13]

The island thus becomes Jim's Peniel where he struggles, like Jacob, for a new identity. It is a life-and-death struggle for selfhood with the youth having to meet challenge after challenge. Not only does he surmount them, he also becomes hardened by them so that when the time comes for him to have to dispose of the dead O'Brien, he does so with some degree of equanimity:

> as the habit of tragical adventures had worn off almost all my terror for the dead, I took him by the waist as if he had been a sack of bran, and, with one good heave, tumbled him overboard (168).

He may well be surrounded by dogs and murderers as the quotation from Revelations on the back of the 'black spot' handed to Silver suggests; but that he has come safely through their 'dark and bloody sojourn on the island' (218) means that he has served out the adolescent's apprenticeship. As Ben Gunn promised (95), finding the treasure has made a man of him though his new status has been earned in the process, not bought by the proceeds.

But always there is a Long John Silver who will not be transcended. He is, if you like, both the residual self-doubt in Jim's mind and residual desire; sentiments which will persist long after the action even to the time when Jim is himself an author in command of his crew of characters. For though Jim assures us at the end that Silver has gone 'clean out of [his] life', he is indubitably present as a mocking echo in the voice of the parrot which invades Jim's dreams and ends his narrative.

By far the most insidious of the father-figures in *Treasure Island*, Long John Silver is also the most seductive. We recognise him as such, in part at least, because we have come to appreciate that Jim has reached a vulnerable and decisive stage of growth. His susceptibility to Silver's ingratiating tactics is therefore natural as is his response to the latter's self-command and command over others. ('All the crew respected and even obeyed him' [62].) What Silver *seems* to Jim to be offering him through his intimacy and confidences is a share in his power and a certain enfranchisement which comes with it. But the degree of freedom he offers is illusory for he is a far more ruthless defender of his authority than Captain Smollett ever was, with no scruples about invoking the supreme sanction against recalcitrants. Smollett will eventually cut Jim adrift, so to speak, in an act which mirrors Thomas Stevenson's repeated threat to disinherit his son. Silver would go about things with less equivocation: he would simply kill him.

Nonetheless, in Silver, there is unquestionably an appeal. His persuasive wooing is as confident as Lovelace's or Richard III's and for much the same reason: he knows that there is a response in the object of his attention. And Jim's behaviour confirms the accuracy of his perceptions. Even when he is expressing his 'horror' at Silver's planned treachery, the terms in which he does so are significant: he had acquired, he tells us, 'a horror of his cruelty, duplicity and power' (73). The third term is a little surprising and makes us look again at that rather ambiguous word 'horror', which Stevenson uses a lot. It is ambiguous because it often seems *not* to mean unalloyed revulsion but to include fascination or even desire as well. (He was 'somewhat horrified', we may recall, at finding his father 'so beautiful when stripped'.)

At this stage in the adolescent's growth, power is going to attract and Silver's seductive potency will prove particularly irresistible. Initially Jim, with a degree of conceit appropriate to his age, is inclined to interpret his apparent admission into Silver's confidences as a kind of power-sharing. A certain disingenuousness might be thought to be present in this, for no son ever thinks of this sort of access to power as remaining at the level of a mere share—any more than a father thinks to draw attention to the areas which are quarantined from such access and sequestrated in the small print of the patriarchal mind. A very good example of both 'father' and 'son' playing this game occurs in *Kidnapped* when David Balfour prides himself on his ability to 'smell out [Ebenezer's] secrets one after another, and grow to be that man's king and ruler', while his uncle, apparently willing to admit David's claims, is secretly planning his transportation.

It is not long before Jim realises that any such offer to share power is, contrary to what it first looks like, a ruse to *disarm* him. When he re-enters the stockade and is confronted by Silver instead of his friends, he soon realises that a crucial choice has to be made. The offer that Silver makes him is not without its attractions, nor has the affinity he has always felt for Silver lost all its potency. He would, for one thing, enjoy the Conradian solace of being one of a crew, particularly comforting when one is beginning to contemplate the problematics of manhood and the loneliness such an aspiration brings with it. Long John's temptation is real because the position it ascribes to Jim is accurate: he is at a cross-roads in his development, and his dilemma is a recognisable one for the growing adolescent, though it is not often realised in such a picturesque way. Silver's words deserve to be weighed well:

> 'the short and the long of the whole story is about here: you can't go back to your own lot, for they won't have you; and, without

you start a whole ship's company all by yourself, which might be
lonely, you'll have to jine with Cap'n Silver' (176).

In some ways the short and the long of the whole story is about here, for it
is Jim's moment of decision: whether to maroon himself like David Balfour,
in abject submissiveness, or to take arms against a sea of troubles and, in
transcending them, achieve independence and his own authority—or
oblivion. In fact, we have had a very good indication of what is likely to
happen in that Jim has, it could be argued, already started his own ship's
company *and*, as 'Cap'n Hawkins', put down his first mutiny in so capably
despatching O'Brien and Israel Hands (the latter characterised by his 'old
man's smile' and 'shadow of treachery').

It is, however, also true that loneliness is endemic in this situation as so
many of Conrad's characters found out, and isolation can destroy moral
integrity. So Jim may defy Silver and eventually see him bested—but he will
not be able to lay his ghost. The slightly mocking, paternalistic figure who
flatters him with compliments about his *savoir faire* as though he were already
a man ('I never saw a better boy than that. He's more a man than any pair of
rats of you in this here house ...' [180]) is a reminder that such a 'caring'
person (with, of course, an alternative game-plan) is not just a comfort but a
necessity, given that no one's integrity is quite proof against fears of its own
inadequacy.

Another, more substantial, reason for Silver's durability is to be found,
paradoxically, in his repeated acts of treachery and duplicity. In them lies
much of the secret of his power, for they are the product of a total and
shameless absence of any firm commitment or principle. Whatever lip-
service he may pay to such notions, it can be no more than this, for he is
prepared to sacrifice any or all of them on the instant should the *summum
bonum*, his own self-preservation, be threatened. 'Dooty is dooty' is a
sentiment he never tires of repeating but it is the stuff of his brazen
effrontery, for he is as far from believing in that fixed standard of conduct
which governs Conrad's mariners, for example, as it is possible for any man,
seafaring or landlubber, to be.

The net result, however, is that there inheres in him an irreducible
sense of his own being. Others may take seriously notions of duty, loyalty and
honest-dealing and agonise over them, espousing certain ethical and moral
principles in the process—all of which are capable of eroding their self-
certainty. For Silver, no compromise is necessary: struggle and conflict are
simplified and externalised under his Gloucester-like credo: 'I am myself
alone.'

The power which derives from the total absence of principle is, as the foregoing allusion reminds us, the power that animates some of Shakespeare's most charismatic villains—Iago, Edmund, Richard III—as well as Milton's Satan, to whom James Durie, for example, is frequently compared in *The Master of Ballantrae*. What gives this power additional glamour is the freedom it appears to bring with it, which is, in truth, its justification in the eyes of its exponents. It may, of course, be freedom to go to the devil as the penultimate paragraph of *Treasure Island* suggests (or freedom to *be* the devil, as Milton's Satan portrays it), but it is immensely attractive nonetheless and perhaps not least to those who believe that there is a higher order of society than the piratical and are prepared to accept certain constraints on their freedom in order to sustain it.

An important factor which adds to the charisma of the Shakespearian and Miltonic villains is their almost demonic energy. Their position demands it and so, in a similar way, does Silver's, for his sort of freedom depends on his mobility, on his repudiation of all fixed principle, even on a fluidity of personality which amounts to a constant reconstruction of 'self'. In the tale, perhaps the two most striking things about Silver are his remarkable physical agility, given his missing limb, and a parallel and equally notable mental agility which allows him to change his position in a flash, as he does when he discovers the treasure to be gone, or to exploit the unexpected to the full, as he does with Jim's return to the stockade. Power and mobility clearly go together, a nexus which receives its most dramatic rendering in the scene where Silver kills the loyal seaman, Tom. It is worth a moment's pause to reflect on Stevenson's imaginative achievement in the characterisation of Silver: to observe how the amputation of a leg and its substitution by a crutch actually *increases* the character's apparent mobility, power and dangerous unpredictability. Worth noting too, perhaps, is the fact that the most impressive of recent productions of *Richard III* had Anthony Sher play Richard on crutches, giving him a devastating speed of attack at any moment from the most unexpected quarter, confounding and cowing his opponents with his protean versatility.

For both these characters, their crippled condition is turned to advantage: their mobility and their freedom are, it seems, enhanced to a pitch which makes of their actions a relished performance. Free—indeed, conditioned by their unrelenting egotism—to manipulate every situation and to play a multiplicity of roles, however incompatible or extravagant they may be, they find themselves given natural access to the matter of comedy. So for Silver in his 'knowing' exchange with Jim on the very subject of mobility when they come in sight of the island. Jim is deeply apprehensive about what their landfall will mean to him whereas Silver, whose interest in it is very different, dilates enthusiastically on the attractions of this 'sweet spot':

> 'You'll bathe and you'll climb trees, and you'll hunt goats, you will; and you'll get aloft on them hills like a goat yourself. Why, it makes me young again. I was going to forget my timber leg, I was. It's a pleasant thing to be young, and have ten toes ...' (734).

Mobility is indeed the key, so that there is much irony in Silver solemnly telling the crew-member he is attempting to subvert that, with middle-age looming, he is going to settle down as a pillar of genteel society: 'I'm fifty, mark you; once back from this cruise, I set up gentleman in earnest' (67). For a middle-aged pirate to put out a prospectus offering superannuated security in good society as an inducement to recruits to sail under his skull-and-cross-bones flag adds a Gilbertian touch which everyone (including Silver) enjoys and no one believes. The fact is that his ethic makes movement essential and 'settling down' a fatal contradiction. Shark-like, when he stops swimming, he drowns. So it is appropriate that he quits the story in a shore boat having stolen some of the treasure 'to help him on his further wanderings' (219).

Stevenson's scepticism about the capacity of language to sort out moral categories and define truth ('words are for communication, not for judgement', he says in his essay on Walt Whitman) also gets ventilation in *Treasure Island*. For example, Long John's supposed surname serves too many functions for it to be taken simply as an inherited patronymic—he is quick-silver when we think of his agility, silver-tongued when we think of him as a persuasive talker, unredeemed bar-silver when we think of the treasure.[14] He masks his duplicity by a handling of language so adroit that it makes words his accomplices in the grossest deceptions. Thus when we hear that he could 'speak like a book when so minded' (62) or that Jim could 'read [his thoughts] like print' (207) we recognise Stevenson again indulging a mischievous taste for sly deconstructive jabs at his own text which, cumulatively, amount to something significant.

The realisation that words 'are all coloured and foresworn', as he says in the Whitman essay, that they are among the world's most *misleading* signs, is the beginning of wisdom for many a Stevenson character. When Silver lays outrageous claim to being *un homme de parole*—brazenly telling Dr Livesey not to trust the word of the other pirates—the doctor's sneer is justified: 'No ... you're the man to keep your word—we know that' (217). But Silver is, it appears, not at all discomfited for he is at one with James Durie and Captain

Hoseason in deriding the notion of inalienable verbal truth. It is quite fitting, therefore, that many years later when Jim is frightened out of his sleep, it is not by a voice which 'speaks sense' but by the gabbling of a parrot—*un perroquet des paroles*, one might say—whose voice burlesques the fundamentals of language and meaning yet still succeeds in summoning the ghost of Long John Silver.

There is no chance that Silver will disappear from Jim's dreams for he is bred in the bones of his adolescence. When this figure of the 'terrible father' receives the black spot from his crew, he tosses it derisively to Jim who reads the word 'Depposed' written in wood-ash. But we know that Silver will never be deposed, as an older Jim now occupied in constructing him anew in his memoir clearly indicates: 'I have that curiosity beside me at this moment; but not a trace of writing now remains beyond a single scratch, such as a man might make with his thumb-nail' (188). Texts which vanish are surprisingly frequent occurrences in Stevenson's work but on this occasion disappearance leaves the subject not less but more 'real'.

After so much evidence of duplicity and treachery, Jim's total condemnation of Silver would have been a foregone conclusion in a run-of-the-mill boy's adventure story.[15] That this doesn't happen challenges the reader to develop a more sophisticated explanation of the motivating psychology. That it has everything to do with the adolescent's struggle to escape the circumscribing edicts of paternal authority and arrive at a mature independence has been the ground of the foregoing argument. Jim has at first been won over by this, to him, powerful and attractive father-figure who seems to be there almost as a role-model to *help* him through the travails of adolescence. The discovery that even the trusted father-figure is irredeemably treacherous is something Jim has to learn as part of his own growth-process. However, though it is a lesson once learned, never forgotten, Silver will never be completely banished from the young man's mental impedimenta, nor even entirely from his affections. Had it been arranged otherwise, it would have suggested that the developing adolescent had completely vanquished the 'terrible father', whereas the symbolic figure of the father, with his quiver-full of prohibitions and anathemas, is a permanent fixture in psychic reality (as Stevenson's own life reveals all too clearly).

Stevenson has brilliantly sustained Silver's authenticity right to the end by mixing affectionate geniality with plentiful evidence of his capacity even for murder when his position is seriously under threat. When the 'son' defies him to his face he resorts to the full ferocity of the archetype, humiliating the rebellious adolescent by leading him on the end of a rope very possibly to his death. (The incident is a curious one, almost superfluous in fact, yet the intrinsically powerful image deployed in it graphically illustrates the savage and repressive discipline visited by the Stevensonian father-figure upon the son.) The authenticity is, however, further strengthened by having him not just escape but demonstrate his permanence by invading Jim's dreams as a mocking echo in the voice of the parrot.

The attractiveness of Silver's kind of power and freedom, though particularly magnetic for the late-adolescent, is universal, and were he to be extirpated the picture of the world left to us would be a false one. Silver may be primarily an authority-figure from the class of fathers, but, as has been shown, he is also an authority-figure from the class of Shakespearian villains. As such he is the reflection of that human desire for an unconstrained, amoral freedom coupled with—indeed premised on—an unachievable self-sufficiency:

> '... I am I, Antonio,
> By choice myself alone.'

Though the polychromatic Silver, so full of verbal panache, would never put the matter as baldly as Auden's Antonio, this is nonetheless the self-system at the root of all his actions.

It is a tribute to Jim's growing maturity that he recognises the ineradicability of Silver's appeal. To admit the attraction of such a figure is to recognise one's own limitations—or, rather, the limits within which one has elected to live—and at the same time to acknowledge one's secret desires. It is to admit that appearances are essentially deceptive and the drawing of moral distinctions hazardous. Jim does not seek to disown him, satisfied that the 'formidable seafaring man with one leg' has simply 'gone clean out of [his] life', but honest enough to allow that he has not disappeared from his dreams. It is the mature Jim, the author of the narrative, who tells us this, adding that 'oxen and wain-ropes would not bring [him] back to that accursed island'. As I said at the beginning such vehemence is initially surprising, for the island could be thought of as the scene of his most brilliant success; but then not everyone has Jim's—or Stevenson's—difficulty in escaping the father's gravitational pull.

NOTES

1. 'Parables of Adventure: the Debatable Novels of Robert Louis Stevenson' in *Nineteenth Century Scottish Fiction*, ed. Campbell (1979), p. 111.

2. 'The Sea Cook' in *The Definition of Literature and Other Essays* (Cambridge, 1984), p. 95.

3. The words are Dianne Sadoff's in *Monsters of Affection: Dickens, Eliot and Brontë on Fatherhood* (Baltimore, 1982), p. 2.

4. In *Son and Father: Before and Beyond the Oedipus Complex*, Peter Blos examines the workings of the libidinal attraction between son and father. Discussing the boy's 'search for the loving and loved father' (so intense at times that it is often described as 'father-hunger'), he writes: 'This facet of the boy's father–complex assumes in adolescence a libidinal ascendancy that impinges on every aspect of the son's emotional life.' The resolution of the isogender complex during male adolescence occupies 'the centre of the therapeutic stage on which the process of psychic restructuring is played out' (p. 33). This is when the adolescent boy faces the task 'of renouncing the libidinal bond that he had once formed and experienced in relation to the dyadic and triadic, i.e., preoedipal and oedipal, father' (p. 43).

For an acute analysis of 'the most prohibited of the incest taboos' see Jean-Michel Rabat's excellent essay, 'A Clown's Inquest into Paternity: Fathers Dead or Alive, in *Finnegans Wake*' in *The Fictional Father*, ed. Robert Con Davis, pp. 99ff.

5. Leonard F. Manheim, 'The Law as "Father"', *American Imago*, Vol. 12, 1955.

6. Silver, having lost his own leg, is pulling the Squire's. Later Jim hears him telling his co-conspirators that he lost his leg in 'the same broadside [where] old Pew lost his dead-lights'. And he adds the circumstantial detail that he was 'ampytated' by a surgeon— 'out of college and all'—who 'was hanged like a dog, and sun-dried like the rest at Corso Castle'. The surgeon was one of Roberts' men, he tells us, and their collective misfortune was the result of changing their ship's name (66). Undoubtedly Silver is referring to Peter Scudamore, surgeon to Bartholomew Roberts, the pirate captain whose ship had been re-christened the *Royal Fortune*. After his capture, Scudamore tried to persuade other members of the crew to attempt an escape, arguing that the alternative was to submit to being taken to Cape Corso 'and be hang'd like a dog, and be sun-dry'd'. They declined and Scudamore was sentenced to death at Corso Castle in March 1722, duly hanged and no doubt 'sun-dry'd'. (See Daniel Defoe's *A General History of the Robberies and Murders of the most Notorious Pyrates*, pp. 217ff.) Scudamore had been less than a year with Roberts so Silver's leg was 'ampytated' between October 1721 and March 1722! Further, unless he took up piracy at a precociously early age, Silver is also telling lies about his age when he takes occasion to tell his fellows that he is now fifty. Trelawney is clearly speaking *after* Quiberon Bay (1759) which means that Silver should indeed be concerned about his superannuation.

7. Or even Trelawney's perhaps: Edward John Trelawny's *Adventures of a Younger Son* (1831, 1835, 1856) had so much to do with piracy that Byron and Shelley took to calling its author 'The Pirate'. (I am indebted to Dr Robert Dingley for this reference.) After the publication of *Kidnapped*, Edmund Gosse wrote to Stevenson telling him that 'pages and pages might have come out of some lost book of Smollett's'. He adds: 'You are very close to the Smollett manner sometimes, but better, because you have none of Smollett's violence' (quoted by Frank McLynn, *Robert Louis Stevenson*, p. 268).

8. 14 July 1894 to Adelaide Boodle. Once again a parallel with Kafka suggests itself. Unlike Stevenson Kafka was deeply ashamed of his body, particularly when compared to his father's: 'I was, after all, depressed by your mere physical presence. I remember, for instance, how we often undressed together in the same bathing-hut. There was I, skinny, weakly, slight, you strong, tall, broad ... I was proud of my father's body'. *Letter to the Father*, pp. 163, 164.

9. Op. cit., p. 89.

10. Op. cit., p. 94.

11. Op. cit., p. 89.

12. Alastair Fowler, op. cit., p. 111.

13. Ibid., p. 113.

14. Fowler suggests also the 'reprobate silver' of Jeremiah 6:30, the wicked being so called because 'God hath rejected them'.

15. In an essay published in 1951 but still of great value, David Daiches makes a highly perceptive remark which admirably pinpoints both the nature of the difference between *Treasure Island* and run-of-the-mill adventure stories and the source of the book's literary distinction: 'There are ways of blocking off overtones of meaning which certain kinds of popular artists use when they are writing *mere* adventure stories or mere romances; such writers pose only problems that are soluble, or apparently soluble, and the pretence is kept up *throughout* that the final resolution does indeed solve the problem .... How different from all this is *Treasure Island*! The characters for whom our sympathies are enlisted go off after hidden treasure out of casual greed, and when their adventure is over have really achieved very little except a modicum of self-knowledge. And Silver, magnificent and evil, disappears into the unknown, the moral ambiguities of his character presented but unexplained'. (*Stevenson and the Art of Fiction*, New York, 1951, pp. 10–11).

JOHN HOLLANDER

On A Child's Garden of Verses

Robert Louis Stevenson is an author who has become newly interesting for the period of literary sensibility that some like to call postmodern. Certainly, as a writer of romance rather than novel (although *The Master of Ballantrae* is as much a novel—and as much a romance—as Scott's *Guy Mannering*) he could thereby seem more of a neglected precursor; and Jorge Luis Borges's profound admiration of Stevenson could itself propound, for readers of thirty-five years ago, a kind of puzzle in itself.

Except for the marginalized (male juvenile) *Treasure Island* and *Kidnapped*, the short fiction, considered as insufficiently modern thrillers, was not read much after World War II. But I have been continually surprised to discover how many college students among those who have taken writing courses from me at Yale remember the experience of encountering, and many of the texts themselves, of Stevenson's *Child's Garden of Verses*. It has remained canonical for three quarters of a century, although in a haunting sort of way; turning back to it recently has produced some unexpectedly spooky encounters for me. I had also been reading through Stevenson's considerable body of verse generally. This was not only to reacquaint myself with the few old favorites I had known before—the charming sonnet in couplets to Henry James, for example, or the fascinating if not wholly satisfying experiments in vers libre that may have come from his friendship

From *The Work of Poetry*. © 1997 by Columbia University Press.

with William Ernest Henley; it was also to explore the entire range of his verse, within which to consider the poems for children and the remarkable influence on subsequent writers I feel they have had. The spooky encounters included coming across such lines as the lovely rondeau-like reworking of Théodore de Banville's verses based on a children's game, "Nous n'irons plus aux bois" that I had known both in the original and in A.E. Housman's adaptation ("We'll to the woods no more, / The laurels all are cut"). It begins

> We'll walk to the woods no more
> But stay beside the fire
> To weep for old desire
> And things that are no more.
>   The woods are spoiled and hoar,
> The ways are full of mire;
> We'll walk the woods no more
> But stay beside the fire.

I had written a poem of my own, with the Banville in mind but diverging from it, only to find that it had been more traveled by than I had known. More determinedly spooky was the realization that other moments in my poetry of the past twenty years may have resounded with some of what I'd actually remembered from the children's verses—it now seemed, for example, that a bit from the rhyme called "The Swing" had certainly crept into my extended mad-song called "The Seesaw."

But going through *A Child's Garden of Verses*, Stevenson's remarkable volume of 1885, has produced some ghostly moments of another sort, reencounters with verses I had grown up with, some of them well remembered, some of them perhaps unread even then, some of them half remembered. And some, undoubtedly, fruitfully repressed under less than dire pressures, only to return unwittingly in my own writing. Moreover, the adult reader now reads them not, as the child had, for what in life he or she recognized, but for what the writer had been doing and, additionally, for what the reader found in prior reading. (A favorite example of this is rereading Hans Christian Andersen's *Mermaid* after you have known Blake's *Book of Thel*.) Robert Schumann composed his wonderful set of *Kinderscenen* (*Op*. 13) in 1838; they are romantic and thus somewhat ironic evocations of "scenes from childhood" for adults to play (and too hard for all but a few advanced children). His *Album für die Jugend* (*Op*. 68), published a decade later, was a much larger collection of pieces written for children to play. If we put "read" or "comprehendingly hear" for "play," we have the difference between the child-speakers in some of Blake's or Wordsworth's shorter poems, and Jane Taylor's rhymes written for children. I shall among other things consider here a wonderful Album for the Young reconsidered as the Scenes from Childhood they had become, and argue that, indeed, this is what they always were, the later adult poetry speaking in the children's verses.

My actual return to Stevenson's poems for children was perhaps heralded by my hearing one day last summer on my car radio an unannounced voice on NPR reading an unannounced text:

> Whenever the moon and stars are set,
>   Whenever the wind is high,
> All night long in the wind and the wet,
>   A man goes riding by.
> Late in the night when the fires are out,
> Why does he gallop and gallop about?
>
> Whenever the trees are crying aloud,
>   And ships are tossed at sea,
> By, on the highway, low and loud,
>   By at the gallop goes he.
> By at the gallop he goes, and then
> By he comes back at the gallop again.

I shivered somewhat, having forgotten the poem and the way it haunted me as a child with the all but erotic excitement that latency period is so full of, with its puzzling indeterminacy: who is the man? is he driven by the wind? driving it? I was too young for serious personifications, so the possibility that man might be the storm wind itself was deferred until, some years later, I read *The King of the Golden River* and encountered South-West Wind, Esq. (I do remember at the time—because my mother when I was quite young liked to sing, unprofessionally but with some understanding, Schubert *Lieder* while my father played them—vaguely associating the wind-rider with the opening of *Erlkönig: Wer reitet so spät / Durch Nacht und Wind*?)

The unidentified voice turned out to be that of Robert McNeil, of the PBS nightly news report, talking about his boyhood in Canada, and particularly about his reading. He had, both somewhat uncannily and, on present contemplation, unsurprisingly, wondered about the poem in some of the same ways I had. I can now recognize the particular moves of ars poetica that were responsible for some of these effects and the delight one could take in them without even realizing what one was noticing: the "Whenever ..."

quatrain, concluding in the three pounding dactyls of the couplet that reinforced the opening d'*dah* da rhythm of "Whenever"; and then, again, in the initially linked second stanza, the idiomatically innocent passing-move of "by" in the "riding by" of the first one becomes a major question. To "ride by" in the absolute (instead of, say, "riding by my house") is the essence of this windy spirit, and the "by" keeps coming up (as if the very word were like a bell to toll you back again outside the house) in insistent anaphoric repetition, throughout the stanza.

It was interesting to discover that Stevenson himself had previously dealt poetically with the matter of the storm rider in a more ambitious way. The first of two free verse poems, "Storm," is quite Whitmanian in tone— praising the sublime energies of the tempestuous seashore, and hailing the "big, strong, bullying, boisterous waves, / That are of all things in nature the nearest thoughts to human" but not in form (the free verse is of the short-lined mode, its line breaks marking clear syntactic periods). The second, "Stormy Nights," is a precursor of the later children's poem; it is a meditation on the gains and losses of maturity that comes right from Wordsworth's Immortality ode:

> I was then the Indian,
> Well and happy and full of glee and pleasure,
> Both hands full of life.
> And not without divine impulses
> Shot into me by the untried non-ego.

And indeed, at the end of the poem, he breaks out, again in the cadences of Whitman, "Why do you taunt my progress, / O green-spectacled Wordsworth! in beautiful verses, / You, the elderly poet?") The central scene from the childhood that he "Perfectly love[s], and keenly recollect[s]"—but that he interestingly remembers without wanting to "recall" even if he could—is the night-riding storm going

> ... by me like a cloak-wrapt horseman
> Stooping over the saddle—
> Go by and come again and yet again,
> Like some one riding with a pardon,
> And ever baffled, ever shut from passage.

The repetition is of import here, as it will be in the less violent and menacing *by*s of "Windy Nights," even as the more menacing storm has been transformed into the less violent wind, mysterious rather than directly terrifying.

It is not terror, but rather wonder, that marks *A Child's Garden of Verses*—a pastoral world (*et in arcadia vixi*, he later wrote of his own childhood days at Colinton Manse, and near the Water of Leith, whose remembered stream would emerge from time to time among its flowers). I myself recall encountering this in "Bed in Summer" the book's opening poem. It was my generation's own introduction, too, to the great problematics of reading. I didn't dress by yellow candlelight, but rather, electric light; on the other hand, in summer, I did indeed "have to go to bed by day"; and dealing with this puzzle in a very Emersonian sort of ad hoc way, I think I concluded that the winter part of the paradox covered fictional experience—from books, and requiring corrective historical adjustments—whereas the summer part spoke to my own experience in an unmediated way. I wonder now how it was to function as the introductory poem, with delicate allegory providing an argument for the book it led off—like Frost's "Pasture"—rather than explicitly, like Herrick's opening catalogue of what his Hesperides would be about or Ben Jonson's "Why I Write Not of Love." The speaker's wonder at a paradoxical reversal invites the reader to follow it into meditative reflection and projective imagination; as a child, I did not need to be told "you come, too." The book that follows deals with many objects of wonder: shadows inside a house at night, the totally different companion-cast shadow of the child himself; the domestic and the foreign; the fleeting vignettes through a railway carriage window; the fireplace-meditation.... Even more, though, the adult reader may see the poem's day–night reversal as figuring a complex dialectic of projected adulthood and recollected childhood that underlies the whole volume.

In the course of gently but firmly contradicting the perplexing casuistries of her adult interlocutor, the "simple child, / That lightly draws its breath" of Wordsworth's "We Are Seven" asserts that her two dead siblings are indeed pre-sent and accounted for: "Their graves are green, they may be seen" she says, and goes on to report that

> ... often after sun-set, Sir
> When it is light and fair,
> I take my little porringer,
> And eat my supper there.

We might feel that no child would say "my little porringer," any more than "my little shoes"—this is a normatively large adult talking. Yet in Stevenson's

"Land of Story-Books," the speaker can speak of his trek of escape from adult evening pursuits ("They sit at home and talk and sing, / And do not play at anything")

> Now, with my little gun, I crawl
> All in the dark along the wall,
> And follow round the forest track
> Away behind the sofa back

and, even more implausibly, can say of the imagined hunter's camp he reaches, "These are the hills, these are the woods, / These are my starry solitudes." And yet, in the case of this speaker, a post-Wordsworthian poet whose discourse we shall be examining, we may be less disturbed, partially because the rhetoric of Victorian adults, of English poets generally, of elegantly expressed feelings of acutely remembered childhood experiences, all come together in what I think is a unique poetic language that, I shall suggest, has had considerable consequence. Another, crucial matter is that Wordsworth wasn't writing for children to read and listen to; children spoken *for* in these lines respond directly and innocently to the adult language, and accept it as a representation of what they have noticed or felt.

The imagined voyage or trek is central to many of these poems. "Travel" has overtones of the imaginative nocturnal activities of "Il Penseroso." And I must call attention here only to its remarkable little episode in which the child, imagining his Asian and African travels, comes to a vision, in some fancied *Arabia deserta*, of a distant and later condition that is able to contemplate the realm of childhood only through souvenirs as images:

> Where among the desert sands
> Some deserted city stands,
> All its children, sweep and prince,
> Grown to manhood ages since,
> Not a foot in street or house,
> Not a stir of child or mouse,
> And when kindly falls the night,
> In all the town no spark of light.

The child reaches in his journey the house of childhood to find nobody home. (Whether this poem underlies Frost's "Directive" might be interesting to contemplate.)

The "North-West Passage" sequence, with its little journey upstairs to bed at night being mapped on a little pattern of quest-romance—I always remembered the stanza from it that I could only decades later come to feel as almost Marvellian:

> Now we behold the embers flee
> About the firelit hearth; and see
> Our faces painted as we pass,
> Like pictures, on the window-glass.

The hearth-meditation, so important in a line that runs from Coleridge through American poetry of the nineteenth and twentieth centuries, is further exemplified by "Armies in the Fire"; in its second stanza, the relation of literature to imagination—here, imagined armies moving among burning cities—is gently touched upon, through the agency of reflected firelight:

> Now in the falling of the gloom
> The red fire paints the empty room:
> And warmly on the roof it looks,
> And flickers on the backs of books.

And it is perhaps significant that this poem follows the one called "The Land of Story-Books." But it is the final stanza

> Blinking embers, tell me true
> Where are those armies marching to,
> And what the burning city is
> That crumbles in your furnaces!

The answer can only come to the adult writer, who has no doubt been thinking of the last quatrain of Shakespeare's great autumnal sonnet 73, "That time of year thou mayst in me behold"

> In me thou west the ashes of such fire
> That on the ashes of his youth doth lie.

If this is childhood itself, slowly being consumed "with that which it was nourished by," its name and nature are necessarily enwrapped in veils of the oracular for the child, who is still, as Ben Jonson would put it, a "spectator" rather than an "understander."

A variant of the overland trek is the sea voyage, as in "My Ship and I," in which the child is

> ... the captain of a tidy little ship,
>   Of a ship that goes a-sailing on the pond;
> And my ship it keeps a-turning all around and all about;
> But when I'm a little older, I shall find the secret out
>   How to send my vessel sailing on beyond.

The only sailor aboard is a doll figure; and the speaker resolves, in a marvelous inversion of growing up and being able to make adult journeys, one day to shrink to the size of the doll, now quickened to life. The two of them may then stop sailing around in circles in the narrow confines of the pond, "to voyage and explore." Pond-sailing and voyaging, circling and navigating, seem here to trope play and work—but the work is itself figured as higher play—the speaker will grow down in order to play better at the grown-up voyaging. The innocent speaker can't grasp some of the complexities of the experienced reading of such poems, but I think the figurative topoi—such as the voyage of life here—are better learned obliquely than when parable, proverb, or whatever plainly propound them.

There is also the "Pirate Story," with its meadow-as-sea, and the bed-boat, to which I shall return. I think in this connection of "Where Go the Boats?" with its introduction of the river of time topos

> Dark brown is the river,
>   Golden is the sand,
> It flows along for ever,
>   With trees on either hand

and the subtle but available music of the syntax itself that takes the young reader or listener sailing on a voyage accompanying the one made by the floating leaves construed as boats—

> On goes the river
>   And out past the mill,
> Away down the valley,
>   Away down the hill.
>
> Away down the river,
>   A hundred miles or more,

Other little children
　　Shall bring my boats ashore.

The passage from *On* through *away ... away* comes to rest at the final slightly different *away* (it is no longer where the river *goes*, but where it *is*). In another poem, "The Cow," the big hit for me as a child was the third line of stanza 1 "The friendly cow all red and white, / I love with all my heart: She gives me cream with all her might, / To eat on apple-tart"—all children must know there's something wonderfully and benignly strange about putting it *that* way, even if they're city children who don't know from direct observation that whatever might is expended in the process is that of the hands and arms of the milker.

　　This is not whimsy at all, I think. It marks one rhetorical point along an interesting range of attitudes and distances implied by what the child-poet of the book notices and cannot notice about what he is in fact saying. The poems are neither naive nor sentimental, as it were, but move across a spectrum of these. They are not arch, although Stevenson had indeed previously written, and designed some woodcuts for, arch, half self-mocking moral emblems whose tone prefigures that of Belloc's cautionary verses. Aside from instructive moral rhymes by Isaac Watts (and, indeed, some fine epigraphic poems by Jean Ingelow in her children's romance *Mopsa the Fairy* in 1869), *A Child's Garden of Verses* may be the first book of poems for children by an otherwise accomplished adult writer—in this sense, a parallel to Andersen, Hawthorne, Ruskin, and Kingsley. Perhaps James Hogg's "A Boy's Song" might be mentioned here; Stevenson echoes his fellow Scot in "The Dumb Soldier" about a toy soldier buried in a hole in the grass

When the grass is ripe like grain,
When the scythe is stoned again,
When the lawn is shaven clear,
Then my hole will reappear

(and there are Whitmanian overtones here as well, I think). More interestingly, as a book, *A Child's Garden of Verses* engages not so much the matter of whimsy, or of the cautionary, but of romance—in this, being akin to *Treasure Island* and *Kidnapped*. The speaker is the child himself throughout—and here perhaps is to raise the point about how this book is mostly *pueris sed non virginibusque*—(although John Bunyan had some two hundred years earlier produced a collection of moral emblems specifying

plainly in its title *A Book for Boys and Girls*). A sole exception, perhaps, is the
"Marching Song" with its bouncy trochaic rhythm:

> Bring the comb and play upon it!
>   Marching, here we come!
> Willie cocks his highland bonnet,
>   Johnnie beats the drum.
>
> Mary Jane commands the party,
>   Peter leads the rear.

And, in the last stanza

> Here's enough of fame and pillage,
>   Great commander Jane!
> Now that we've been round the village,
>   Let's go home again.

But it may be supposed that Jane gets to command by virtue of her age on
the one hand and the extreme youth of her valiant warriors on the other. (In
this regard, by the way, I note that Charles Robinson's first and canonical
1896 illustrations showed as many girls as possible when the lack of gender
specificity in a particular poem allowed it.)

At least one contemporary reviewer quoted the well-known couplet
called (with some delicate irony, perhaps) "Happy Thought" as instancing
puerile thought and puerile expression. You may remember that it goes "The
world is so full of a number of things, / I'm sure we should all be as happy as
kings." This is certainly not a simple matter. The pastoral dialectic of
childhood remembered and expressed in adult language breeds strong
ironies. James Thurber used the ultimate line in his own debunking moral to
one of his wonderful, adult fables for our time ("The world is so full of a
number of things, / I'm sure we should all be as happy as kings, and we all
know how happy kings are")—and, indeed, this is just the point: in an almost
Blakean way, the child of the poem doesn't know the darker side of what he
is saying; the adult reading it to a listening child does, and indeed may mutter
Thurber's addition as his or her own afterthought. But the child in the verse-
garden is saying something else as well: the plenitude he beholds is the
demesne of his attentiveness, not a realm over which he wields the kind of
repressive power that is the only sort that may be correctly addressed in
universities today. (I can't help but recount how my poetic contemporary,

Richard Howard, told me that in his first-grade class—in Cleveland in the mid-thirties—his teacher, remarking that many residual kings were currently being shoved into exile or otherwise attended to, asked them to memorize her emended text—"I'm sure we should all be as happy as birds." Such a devout literalist would be at home in most university English departments today.)

Stevenson's child is, in fact, as well as in figure, monarch of all he surveys only because he can notice it with active pleasure and control it benignly in his imagination. And thus "richer than untempted kings" he can indeed feel. It is for this inherent sense of the dialectic of childhood pastoral (which Empson first identifies with Alice, and which continues in another mode here), with Blake lurking at the borders, that one might recall Stevenson's remark in a letter to William Ernest Henley in March 1883, to the effect that "Poetry is not the strong point of the text, and I shrink from any title that might seem to claim that quality; otherwise we might have *Nursery Muses* or *New Songs of Innocence* (but that were a blasphemy)." But Stevenson indeed knew well what true poetry was. He entitles his collection of 1887 *Underwoods*, the title Ben Jonson gave to a selected portion of his oeuvre; in his epigraph to that volume, Stevenson acknowledges the borrowing, at the same time showing that he is eminently qualified to do so:

Of all my verse, like not a single line;
But like my title for it is not mine.
That title from a better man I stole:
Ah, how much better had I stol'n the whole!

which itself is a perfect pastiche of Ben Jonson. Many of his own poems have premonitions of Hardy—the Hardy he could probably not have read yet, *Wessex Poems* being first published in 1890, and certainly of many Georgian poets like de la Mare. What keeps surprising the adult reader of the poems in the *Child's Garden* is how full they are of the stuff of true poetry. One quick instance here: in "Escape at Bedtime," a poem about being outside one's house at night, a brief catalogue of the constellations certainly invites the young reader's reminders of his or her own wonder at the stars:

The Dog, and the Plough, and the Hunter, and all,
    And the star of the sailor, and Mars,
These shone in the sky, and the pail by the wall
    Would be half full of water and stars.

But a present delight at the hidden zeugma of the last line, ("of" being literal in the case of the water, figurative in the case of the stars, reduplicating another figurative "of" if the water is full of stars too—how we must labor to represent our intuitions! how free the child is of the need to do so!). And it is in the first apprehension of such patterns and devices that the young reader, unknowing of their names and identities—let alone their venerable literary history—can encounter them as found natural objects, like shells along a shore, and keep them among other treasured souvenirs.

Suffice it to say these verses have played a remarkable role in the education of writers in English since they first appeared. (They may even, for a brief while, continue to. In a Yale College verse-composition class one fall, seven out of sixteen students had grown up with some or all of them, although only two evinced any acquaintance whatsoever with either KJV or even the New English Bible.)

Earlier I quoted a line from Cowper's Alexander Selkirk poem ("I am monarch of all I survey"). It makes a kind of subliminal return in what is one of the central poems of the collection, "The Land of Counterpane." The child remembers an occasion when he "was sick and lay a-bed," his head propped up by pillows, and how he deployed his playthings—toy soldiers, houses and trees, ships—on the field of his bed's coverlet. It is, like a very few others, in the past tense, so that the child-narrator seems almost to double with the adult speaker (the verbs' past tense being perfect for the child, imperfect for the adult poet). It concludes:

> I was the giant, great and still
> That sits upon the pillow-hill
> And sees before him, dale and plain,
> The pleasant land of counterpane.

Joan Richardson, in her biography of Wallace Stevens (I:219) suggests the importance of this poem for the later poet, invoking "land of counterpane with its little, sick hero fantasizing himself 'atop a hill.'" Certainly the topos is a venerable one. The visionary prospect from a height, of what one cannot literally enter, stems from Moses on Pisgah at least through Adam on his high hill in *Paradise Lost*, combines in modernity with Petrarch's view of his own world—able to be reentered after having been seen from above—from the top of Mont Ventoux.

This seems to be one of the two central fables of the *Garden*, the other being the solitary trek. Let us consider some of its occasions; for example, these lines from "The Swing":

> Up in the air and over the wall,
>   Till I can see so wide,
> Rivers and trees and cattle and all
>   Over the countryside—

or "Foreign Lands," which begins

> Up into the cherry tree
> Who should climb but little me?

[and here, the Dorothy Parker (b. 1893) agenda? the smarty-pants send up of it—we wait for the smartass second couplet]

> I held the trunk with both my hands
> And looked abroad on foreign lands.

> I saw the next door garden lie,
> Adorned with flowers, before my eye,
> And many pleasant places more
> That I had never seen before.

> I saw the dimpling river pass
> And be the sky's blue looking-glass;
> The dusty roads go up and down
> With people tramping in to town.

One of the things this can do for an imaginative child reading it is to acknowledge and somehow license his or her own private fancy of just such a kind. The adult world is full of suppressions and restrictions of just such fancies and discoveries (admittedly, inventing the poetic wheel), as Wordsworth indeed understood. Poetry is an important bivalent connection between childhood and maturity, privileging neither, aware of the ways in which growing up can be a kind of growing down.

In poems presented to children, this link can often run along an axis of this kind of recognition. And it can talk to children, for themselves and for the poet's—or at least, the romantic and later poet's—reconstruction of his or her own childhood. What helps to make Stevenson's verses into true poetry of a kind is this dark conceit running through them: the book's child-poet speaks in the language of English poetry and, reciprocally, introduces his very young listeners/readers to poetic form and trope and mythology, so that in some way, for many generations of middle-class children (as well as working-class ones still fortunate enough to have been schooled before 1960 or so), future writers were being secretly educated. It would be amusing to search the compass of the *Garden* for subsequent echoes or even topoi, all the way from Wallace Stevens to the resonant last line of "Singing": "The organ with the organ man / Is singing in the rain; in Arthur Freed's (b. 1894) celebrated lyric of the popular song of 1929.

In *A Child's Garden of Verses* the visionary prospects need not always be revealed from a literal height. The child conjures up pageants and parades. One such poem chronicles a visionary parade of "every kind of beast and man," when

> All night long and every night,
> When my mama puts out the light,
> I see the people marching by,
> As plain as day, before my eye.

They start slowly, gather speed, and are followed by the child "Until we reach the town of Sleep." Children acknowledge such an experience—it is very common—and grasp that final conceit. The title, "Young Night-Thought," is half for them, and half—the allusively part-joking, part-serious half—for the adult, well-read reader, who, while not having gone through the ten thousand or so lines of Edward Young's *Night Thoughts on Life, Death, and Immortality*, would at least have known of it and its tediously extensive agenda.

Another actual height is that of "The Hayloft," with the mown grass piled up "in mountain tops / For mountaineers to roam"; these are named with great pleasure and seriousness

> Here is Mount Clear, Mount Rusty-Nail,
>   Mount Eagle and Mount High;-
> The mice that in these mountains dwell,
>   No happier are than I!

There is an echo here, incidentally, of Lovelace in "To Althea from Prison"—"The birds, that wanton in the air / Know no such liberty"; there lurks in Stevenson's poem the issue, although not the cadence, of the final occurrence of Lovelace's refrain "Angels alone, that soar above, / Enjoy such liberty." But indeed, seventeenth-century poetry resounds through *A Child's Garden of Verses*: "Auntie's Skirts" is Herrick's "Whenas in silks my Julia goes," with the substitution of the excitements of general sensuous wonder for those of eros:

> Whenever Auntie moves around,
> Her dresses make a curious sound,
> They trail behind her up the floor,
> And trundle after through the door.

And in another poem the eponymous gardener himself ("Far in the plots, I see him dig / Old and serious, brown and big")—perhaps a secret surrogate for the poet-gardener of the garden of verses—gets unwittingly likened to the Aesopian ant being rebuked by the Anacreontic grasshopper of Richard Lovelace's poem:

> Silly gardener! summer goes,
> And winter comes with pinching toes,
> When in the garden bare and brown
> You must lay your barrow down.
>
> Well now, and while the summer stays,
> To profit by these garden days
> O how much wiser you would be
> To play at Indian wars with me!

Lovelace's grasshopper suffers the Aesopian fate in winter ("Poor verdant fool, and now green ice"); he is a singer, not a provider. But the gardener, a worker, is for the young speaker—for whom play is serious and labor a distraction—frivolously improvident. There is perhaps something Blakean about this dialectic, and it appears in other places in the book. (One might consider, for example, a phrase in "At the Sea-Side" that seems to govern the rhetoric of the whole little poem: "When I was down beside the sea / A wooden spade they gave to me / To dig the sandy shore." The "they gave to me" momentarily turns the speaker into a strange kind of figure, half-emblematic, half a Blakean innocent speaker shadowed by the dark consciousness of the adult reader.)

I conclude by returning to a personal observation about the importance of this book for me. Tags and phrases from so many of these poems have rung in my head since the age of four or five, some as I first heard them, later as I began to read them. I know how I tried to live for a while myself in my own Land of Counterpane, even though I'd had to figure out dimly what sort of coverlet constituted it, and even though at first the final lines, "And sees before him, dale and plain / The pleasant land of counterpane," puzzled me in that dale and plain I wanted to hear both *dale* and *plain* as somehow adjectival—a "dale" vision being perhaps a clear or radiant one. My own night journeys were on shipboard—the "My bed is like, a little boat" was a very resonant topos for me, and I note the return of it in a prose poem from a sequence called "In Place"; "The Boat" begins, "It took him away on some nights, its low engine running silently on even until he was too far out to hear it himself. It was as dark as the elements of night and water through which it moved. It was built for one: he was helmsman and supercargo both." And it ends with what I now realize is a consideration not just of the bed-boat, but of the whole scene of childhood, and of the relation between memories of it and allusions to what was for me one of the great texts of childhood, as seen with what Wallace Stevens called "a later reason": "It was out of service for some years, after which he came to realize that his final ride on it, some night, would not be unaccompanied, that the boatman on that voyage would stay aboard, and that he himself would disembark at last."

VANESSA SMITH

Piracy and Exchange:
Stevenson's Pacific Fiction

In a series of unpublished Imaginary Dispatches, probably written in 1885, Stevenson adopted a variety of roles, including those of the explorer Henry Morton Stanley, of 'Banzaboo' (prime minister of 'the Cannibal Islands') and of a reporter at a meeting of 'The American Pirates Trades Union', in order to parody the hypocrisy of policy. The interleaving of satiric pieces on the topics of colonialism and copyright establishes a parallel between the ironies and inconsistencies of imperialist and literary exploitation, while the 'American Pirates' dispatch exposes the unstable association of republican sentiments with free-trade ethics:

> The chairman opened the meeting with an address in which he said 'Ladies and Gentlemen, the liberties of this free and mighty land are being interfered with. The greedy Britisher envious of our cuteness wishes to secure our birthright. (hisses and groans.) He says in a disgusting and insulting manner that if we want books we must pay for 'em (groans), but no gentlemen we won't stand it (applause). Shall the downtrodden and perfidious Briton trample on one of our Great Institutions?'[1]

The ludic dispatches were written some years before Stevenson placed himself at the periphery of print and of empire in the Pacific, yet they

From *Literary Culture and the Pacific: Nineteenth-Century Textual Encounters.* © 1998 by Vanessa Smith.

anticipate an intermeshing of concerns which is less heavy-handedly present in his late fiction. The novels and short stories that Stevenson published from and also set in the Pacific mediate anxieties about the material basis of literary production through an exploration of the narrative modes and forms of authority available in this peripheral context. These texts express a concern about those interconnections between discursive and commercial exchange that are implicit in their own production.

THE WRECKER AS BEACHCOMBER NARRATIVE

Writing to Will Low, the American painter to whom he dedicated *The Wrecker*, some time after the novel's publication, Stevenson posed a question about the value of artistic labour:

> And then the problem that Pinkerton laid down: why the artist can do nothing else? is one that continually exercises myself ... I think of the Renaissance fellows, and their all-round human sufficiency, and compare it with the ineffable smallness of the field in which we labour and in which we do so little. I think *David Balfour* a nice little book, and very artistic, and just the thing to occupy the leisure of a busy man; but for the top flower of a man's life it seems to me inadequate. Small is the word; it is a small age, and I am of it. I could have wished to be otherwise busy in this world. I ought to have been able to build lighthouses and write *David Balfours* too.[2]

Addressed to Low, such sentiments harbour an element of nostalgia. The pair had been members of the Barbizon artist's colony for periods during the years 1875 to 1877, at a time when, Low reminisced later, they 'were more intent upon learning our respective trades than in producing finished works of art'.[3] In those days, uncommitted to singularity of artistic endeavour and less concerned with the benefits of protectionism, they were part of a group who formed 'The Barbizon Free-Trading Company, Unlimited' whose planned activities included sailing a yacht and trading in sealskins.[4] Four of the company, including Stevenson, also bought shares in a barge, which was never used.[5] In his letter to Low, Stevenson goes on to compare himself unfavourably with Fielding the 'active magistrate' and Richardson the 'busy bookseller', and to wish that his own curriculum did not exclude the work of his father and grandfather, both engineers, whose lighthouse constructions guard the coasts of Scotland.[6] Yet perhaps more apposite than the activities of earlier canonical authors to Stevenson's ideal of the literary jack of all trades was the local example of the Pacific beachcomber. As I observed earlier, the beachcomber author is a figure defined by multiple projects, from the technical to the performative. In *The Wrecker* the beachcomber offers an implicit model for a sustained investigation of the modes of labour that accompany and define artistic production.

The Wrecker was the second of three novels that Stevenson wrote in collaboration with his stepson, Lloyd Osbourne.[7] Like the collaborative projects of the novel's protagonists, Loudon Dodd and Jim Pinkerton, Stevenson and Osbourne's joint authorship was a business venture. Osbourne's American citizenship gave their writing the protection of United States copyright laws prior to the International Copyright Act of July 1891. The profits of *The Wrecker* were intended to contribute to the purchase of a trading schooner that Stevenson and his family planned to operate between the islands of the South Pacific. Where Loudon Dodd's artistic pursuits are supported by Pinkerton's business activities, Stevenson's art was to finance an enterprise of trade. In a letter to Henry James he refers to the novel as 'a machine', but also as a piece of, possibly dubious, craftsmanship, in which he practises 'the curious (and perhaps unsound) technical manoeuvre of running the story together to a point as we go along, the narrative becoming more succinct and the details fining off with every page'.[8] Aspiring to a writing that is one of several ventures, Stevenson produces a text whose labour is a shifting term, neither simple mechanics nor pure artistry.

The Wrecker tells the story of Loudon Dodd's various attempts to find suitable employment on the spectrum between art and labour. His father, James Dodd, a millionaire businessman who finishes life a bankrupt, sends his son to Muskegon Commercial Academy. Here, in what amounts to an education in exchange-value, Dodd participates in gambling games with 'college paper' and ledgers, experiencing accelerated shifts of fortune which serve only to convince him that 'the whole traffic was illusory'.[9] His own ambitions are unspecifically 'artistic'. His father is involved in the planning of the new city of Muskegon, and, in a brief affiliation with paternal aspirations, Dodd engages in an autodidactic pursuit of architecture. This phase of the novel has echoes in Stevenson's biography: Stevenson had himself initially studied engineering in the tradition of his 'family of engineers', and then completed a law degree as a compromise between his literary aspirations and his father's professional ambitions for him. Dodd's description of his architectural pursuits could equally describe Stevenson engaged in the study of engineering: 'I threw myself headlong into my father's work, acquainted myself with all the plans, their merits and defects, read besides in special books, made myself a master of the theory of strains, studied the current prices of materials.' (23) (Stevenson acknowledged in a letter to Edward Burlingame that, although his protagonist was based primarily on Will Low, 'Much of the experience of Loudon Dodd is drawn from my own life.'[10])

Dodd's father agrees to send him to Paris to study sculpting, intending him to put artistic training to a practical purpose in designing the facades of public buildings in the city of Muskegon. On his way to the Continent, Dodd visits his maternal relatives in Edinburgh. He finds favour with his grandfather, Alexander Loudon, a former stonemason whose shoddy workmanship is, however, inimical to Dodd's artistic pretensions. When Alexander takes him on a tour of some houses he has fabricated, Dodd comments: 'I have rarely seen a more shocking exhibition: the brick seemed to be blushing to the walls, and the slates on the roof to have turned pale with shame; but I was careful not to communicate these impressions to the aged artificer at my side.' (29) After his father's bankruptcy and death, a gift of money and later posthumous bequest from his grandfather enable Dodd to escape the curse of labour in his Uncle Adam's grocery business. The paternity of a businessman who can only appreciate art as engineering and the legacy of an incompetent *bricoleur* provide an insecure foundation for Dodd's artistic pursuits. Jim Pinkerton, the combined businessman-*bricoleur* who takes over the burden of Dodd's maintenance, is in part a reincarnation of these father-figures.

Pinkerton, Dodd's closest friend in Paris and erstwhile benefactor, is a jack of all trades. Pinkerton cannot understand the exclusive devotion which characterises Dodd's artistic ambitions, while Dodd defines his singular pursuit against the multiplicity of Pinkerton's endeavours: 'this was not an artist who had been deprived of the practice of his single art; but only a business man of very extended interests' (46). Pinkerton has numerous 'irons in the fire' (98). He has been a 'tin-typer', or travelling photographer, with a sideline in ethnography:

> As he tramped the Western States and Territories, taking tintypes ... he was taking stock by the way, of the people, the products, and the country, with an eye unusually observant and a memory unusually retentive; and he was collecting for himself a body of magnanimous and semi-intellectual nonsense, which he supposed to be the natural thoughts and to contain the whole duty of the born American. (42–3)

He has found employment as a railroad-scalper, a trade whose essence, Dodd explains, 'appears to be to cheat the railroads out of their due fare' (43), and while in Paris acts as foreign correspondent for an American newspaper. Back in San Francisco, his projects multiply: he hawks brandy, keeps an advertising office, charters a boat for fishing parties, refurbishes condemned vessels, and has a tenth share in 'a certain agricultural engine'. (98) He promotes a public lecture upon Dodd's return to the United States from Paris, and organises what become notorious weekend picnics, with Dodd acting again as showman.

The portrait of Pinkerton, Stevenson's correspondence attests, was in fact based upon a figure from the world of metropolitan publishing: his American literary agent Samuel Sidney McClure.[11] Stevenson regarded McClure as something of a shyster, and worried about the risks he might have engendered by placing his literary fortunes partly in McClure's hands. In the year that *The Wrecker* was published, he wrote to Charles Baxter from Samoa: 'I fear the solvency of the Great McClure must be a-totter. This will leave me in a dreadful hole, for I have no idea my money will have been kept separate as he proposed; the being is too Pinkertonish for that.'[12] However Pinkerton's dubious 'irons in the fire' range beyond the literary, recalling the projects of the beachcomber William Diaper, who writes in his autobiography:

> I had about fifty irons in the fire at once, and not one of them burnt. I supplied as many as thirty or forty ships in the season during the year, with pork and vegetables at quite a thousand per cent. profit ... Even the red chilli-peppers which grew wild all round, I employed the boys and girls to gather them in bushels, and then bottled them up in vinegar which I made myself from the ripe bananas, and sold hundreds of bottles to the foremast hands of all these ships ... Another source of wealth or income was the way I used to receive the officers and crews of the ships when they came on shore for liberty. I always treated them to a picnic or '*al fresco*' meal under the nice shady branches of the tree which stood on the green where I used to spread the good things of the whole island.

There are certain immediate dissimilarities between the activities of the metropolitan and the Pacific *bricoleur*. Pinkerton's ventures are purely entrepreneurial, where Diaper accompanies promotion with manual labour. Diaper's profit margin is more arbitrary. Yet both are portrayed as engrossed in the romance of business venture, rather than in acquisition: in the narrative, rather than the artefacts, of enterprise. Pinkerton is described as 'representing to himself a highly coloured part in life's performance ... Reality was his romance; he gloried to be thus engaged' (97), while Diaper claims to have been absorbed by the process of accumulation rather than the question of profit: 'I neglected nothing with which I could make money, not so much for the love of it—as I did not at that time any more than now worship it—as for the amusement it gave me in accumulating it.' Pinkerton's funds are perpetually in circulation: 'No dollar slept in his possession; rather, he kept all simultaneously flying, like a conjurer with oranges.' (98–9) Diaper's profits change shape within the chameleon economy of barter: 'if not money, perhaps [payment was] a "hickery" shirt, worth to me quite two dollars, as I could convert all these things into pigs, which in the end meant money'.[13] Both Pinkerton and Diaper of course include textual production among their business ventures.

Pinkerton involves Dodd in the purchase of an exorbitantly priced wreck, the *Flying Scud*, which has come up for sale in San Francisco under mysterious circumstances, and which he suspects of containing an illicit cargo of opiate. Dodd is sent aboard another ship, the *Norah Creina*, to the Pacific island of Midway where the wreck lies abandoned, to endeavour to secure this anticipated treasure. Here, engaged in the anti-aesthetic labours of 'wrecker', taking apart the *Flying Scud*, Dodd attains manhood. Rather than single-minded and sedentary artistic pursuits, he comes to celebrate *bricolage*, and a masculine world of manual labour:

> if things had gone smooth with me, I should be now swollen like a prize-ox in body, and fallen in mind to a thing perhaps as low as many types of the *bourgeois*—the implicit or exclusive artist ... The dull man is made, not by the nature, but by the degree of his immersion in a single business ... The eternal life of man, spent under the sun and rain and in rude physical effort, lies upon one side, scarce changed since the beginning.
>
> I would I could have carried along to Midway Island with me all the writers and the prating artists of my time. Day after day of hope deferred, of heat, of unremitting toil; night after night of aching limbs, bruised hands, and a mind obscured with the grateful vacancy of physical fatigue. (232–3)

This speech recalls another eulogy to physical labour, within Stevenson's correspondence from Samoa. Writing to Sidney Colvin about his work weeding and path-breaking on the Vailima estate, he observes of himself:

To come down covered with mud and drenched with sweat and
rain after some hours in the bush, change, rub down, and take a
chair in the verandah, is to taste a quiet conscience. And the
strange thing that I remark is this: if I go out and make sixpence,
bossing my labourers and plying the cutlass or the spade, idiot
conscience applauds me: if I sit in the house and make twenty
pounds, idiot conscience wails over my neglect and the day
wasted.[14]

In a letter from which I quoted in my introduction, Oscar Wilde comments
acerbically on such relishing descriptions of physical exertion: 'To chop wood
with any advantage to oneself, or profit to others, one should not be able to
describe the process ... Stevenson merely extended the sphere of the artificial by
taking to digging.'[15] He suggests that the elevation of toil is the ultimate literary
illusion. Stevenson's self-conscious espousal of the benefits of manual labour
transforms the sought escape from literary dilettantism into a literary activity.

The Wrecker's questions about the material base of aesthetic pursuits and
the value of artistic enterprise as measured against forms of manual activity
surface repeatedly in Stevenson's meditations, published and private, on the
art of writing. Perhaps because he was conscious of having broken with the
practical tradition of his 'family of engineers', and of having been dependent
on his father's financial support to establish his literary career, Stevenson was
impelled to interrogate the validity of literature as labour. This concern had a
wider frame of reference, however, within later nineteenth-century literary
debate. There was, as Kenneth Graham has observed, a utilitarian emphasis
to Victorian defences of the novelist's art.[16] The image of the novelist as
craftsman, and of writing as technical labour, was a critical commonplace:
Trollope's *An Autobiography* famously referred to the novelist as a cobbler,
whose method was mechanical.[17] Such metaphors reflect anxieties about the
capacity of literature to function as a means of support for its producers.
Stevenson wrote, less solemnly, in a letter of July 1883:

you will never weary of an art at which you fervently and
superstitiously labour ... Forget the world in a technical trifle ...
Bow your head over technique. Think of technique when you rise
and when you go to bed. Forget purposes in the meanwhile; get
to love technical processes, to glory in technical successes; get to
see the world entirely through technical spectacles, to see it
entirely in terms of what you can do.[18]

The emphasis on the technical here is rhetorical, even incantatory, rather than a materialist critique. Repetition culminates in the aurally pleasurable but ludicrous 'technical spectacles': this is still playful, rather than laborious, writing. However Stevenson's subsequent experiences publishing texts from the Pacific served to defamiliarise the 'literature as labour' commonplace; his distance from metropolitan centres slowing down and rendering practically explicit the processes of literary production.

Rather than any materially valuable cargo, Dodd retrieves from the *Flying Scud* a wealth of story. He locates evidence that the crew who had been rescued from the ship was in fact a cast of interlopers. Ascertaining their true identities, Dodd uncovers the history of a fellow-dilettante, Norris Carthew, whom he recognises as, effectively, his double. Carthew has early in life been cast off by his father and sent to Australia as a remittance man. There he is redeemed, like Dodd, from an emasculated existence by entry into the communal, physical world of masculine labour. He takes up work on a railway gang, and then joins a group of friends aboard the ship *Currency Lass* on a trading venture in the Pacific. They begin with excellent fortune in Butaritari, where they are able to make an inflated profit on the sale of their cargo. However, luck changes when the mast of their ship splits in mid-ocean, and they are forced to take to the lifeboat and make for Midway. This island, which they have been misled by their ship's directory to believe supports an active coaling station, turns out to be a barren guano deposit. The appearance of the *Flying Scud* offers a conditional promise of rescue: the captain of the ship demands that the group hands over the huge spoils of its trading venture in return for removal from Midway. In an outbreak of extreme violence, the crew of the *Currency Lass* massacres the crew of the *Flying Scud*. This explains the substitution of identities which has taken place upon the ship's return to San Francisco. Dodd's attempts to uncover the true history of the wreck are initially motivated by a plan to blackmail Carthew, and thus to turn story directly into profit. However a growing sense of recognition encourages him to refigure his role as that of Carthew's ally. For Carthew, the achieved world of masculine activity has tipped over into violence. Dodd retrieves a balance by in turn converting the destructive activity of 'wrecker' into the reconstructive role of storyteller.

The interdependence of constructive and destructive forms of masculine physicality is an assumption that informs the collected literature of the Pacific beachcomber. And there are further echoes to suggest that the types of labour and alterity explored in *The Wrecker* are influenced by this local model. The two vessels upon which Dodd and Carthew achieve manhood, the *Norah Creina* and the *Currency Lass*, are both makeshift constructions: *bricolage*. The former has been rushed through overhauling in San Francisco, and the latter is precariously reassembled from a state of dilapidation: 'she sold ... a shade above her value as old junk; and the three adventurers had scarce been able to afford even the most vital repairs. The rigging, indeed, had been partly renewed, and the rest set up; [the] old canvas had been patched together into one decently serviceable suit of sails; [the] masts still stood, and might have wondered at themselves.' (357–8) Their respective crews are similarly cobbled together. The latter's includes a genuine *bricoleur* 'Richard Hemstead ... had an odd-job-man's handiness with tools.' (357) The crew members of the *Currency Lass* reappear in San Francisco like beachcombers returning to metropolitan society: under false names, telling a duplicitous story, the captain sustaining an injury which prevents him from signing authorship of his testimony. It is the *bricolage* nature of the typical ship's crew in the Pacific—its members material-to-hand, occupying a particular function for the space of a journey—which produces the narrative motivation of *The Wrecker*, enabling the perplexing substitution of one crew for another.

Dodd ultimately achieves a patronage less emasculating than those which he rejects during the course of the novel. In the prologue, he arrives in the Marquesas as the partner of his double, Carthew. In this role he continues to represent the supported dilettante: the ship he runs upon Carthew's capital is a floating gallery of *objets d'art*, rather than the beachcomber's *objets trouvés*, and he distinguishes himself from the beachcomber by its furnishings: '"His money, my taste," said Dodd. "The black walnut bookshelves are old English; the books all mine—mostly Renaissance French. You should see how the beachcombers wilt away when they go round them, looking for a change of seaside library novels. The mirrors are genuine Venice; that's a good piece in the corner. The daubs are mine—and his; the mudding mine."' (6) Unlike William Diaper's swap-library of refashioned books on handmade shelves, Dodd's books and bookshelves are collector's pieces. Nonetheless, this assemblage retains the character of *bricolage*. part the work of his hands, part appropriation, uniting artefacts from a variety of contexts. In the epilogue, Stevenson enters the frame of one of Dodd's projects. Like the editors of the beachcombers' 'mendicant' texts, he is represented as using his literary authority to bring Dodd's narrative into print. Yet neither Dodd's associations with Carthew nor with Stevenson are further instances of straightforward patronage. Once in possession of the narrative of *The Wrecker*, Dodd has attained a valuable item of exchange—Carthew's secret, and Stevenson's story—with which he can negotiate upon his own terms. In fact, Dodd successfully attains what

Stevenson and Osbourne hope to earn from the writing of the novel: a vessel for trade among the islands.

Dodd, like the beachcomber, has pursued a wide range of dubious types of employment, which provide the material for his narrative: wrecker, opium-smuggler, blackmailer, '"It's rather singular," said he, "but I seem to have practised all these means of livelihood."' (10) It is the multiplicity, rather than singularity, of Dodd's operations which characterises him as *bricoleur* rather than dilettante. His arrival in the prologue is viewed through the eyes of another type of beachcomber, reminiscent of Jean Cabri or James O'Connell: 'the famous tattooed white man, the living curiosity of Tai-o-hae' (2). This figure is an icon of alterity—tattooed, cannibal: 'he would hear again the drums beat for a man-eating festival; perhaps he would summon up the form of that island princess for the love of whom he had submitted his body to the cruel hands of the tattooer'. Yet this 'so strange a figure of a European' also defines Stevenson's authorial practice in *The Wrecker*. Like the tattooed man, whose 'memory would serve him with broken fragments of the past', Stevenson draws upon the different contexts of his varied experience—Paris, San Francisco, the Marquesas—to produce a narrative that is also a *bricolage*.

In the novel's epilogue, Stevenson explains to Will Low the 'genesis and growth' (425) of a book which is in fact less an organic production than an assemblage. In the early 1920s, Low was to develop into a major composition a sketch he had made of Stevenson while the pair were living in the artists' colony of Barbizon. One commentator referred to the painting as his 'affectionate answer, perhaps, to Stevenson's epilogue in "The Wrecker"'.[19] Low also published for private circulation a book describing the genesis and growth of this artwork. Ambiguously entitled 'Concerning a Painting of Robert Louis Stevenson', this text slips between representing Stevenson as subject and as implicit author of his portrait. Low's commentary is heavily conscious of his sitter's development from student into renowned literary figure, preceding the maturation of his sketch into a finished artwork. His painting is now a posthumous memorial, deriving interest and authority primarily from its subject, even as it, like Stevenson's epilogue, draws from a shared pool of memories that continue to situate the two artists as novices and equals. Yet Low's pamphlet also offers an exhaustive description of artistic composition: of the conceptualisation and realisation of a project of representation. The distinction between the aesthetics espoused by his text and *The Wrecker's* epilogue is effectively one between composition and *bricolage*. The epilogue describes a narrative developed from yarning. The task of writing is figured as manual craftsmanship: 'the scaffolding of the tale had been put together. But the question of treatment was as usual more obscure.' (425) Its finished product is a fabricated article, a piece of weaving, rather than a precious artwork:

> The tone of the age, its movement, the mingling of races and classes in the dollar hunt, the fiery and not quite unromantic struggle for existence with its changing trades and scenery, and two types in particular, that of the American handyman of business and that of the Yankee merchant sailor—we agreed to dwell on at some length, and make the woof to our not very precious warp. (426)

This plot summary incorporates a range of projects and contexts of activity familiar from beachcomber accounts. The authors also represent literary production as oral exchange, a depiction which somewhat belies facts. Stevenson and Osbourne's formal collaboration involved sequential writing and revision: much discussion of the project took place in correspondence while Lloyd was in Europe settling the family's affairs, Stevenson complaining at one time to Lloyd: 'This is the hell of collaboration half the world away.'[20] Commenting later on literary collaboration, Stevenson suggested that this type of authorship presses at the limits of oral communication: 'The great difficulty of collaboration is that you can't tell what you mean. I know what kind of an effect I mean a character to give—what kind of *tache* he is to make; but how am I to tell my collaborator in words.'[21] Nonetheless, in the epilogue the authors are keen to place the genesis of their story in a productive oral context. Here the beachcomber narrative offered an implicit answer to the problems of construction which the novel posed. The authors refer to their aim of uniting the complex plot of detective fiction with the detail of daily life: romance with realism. They succeed in creating an aleatory text, in which disparate narratives build into a story, simultaneously bringing a variety of contexts into play. As I argued in chapter 1, part of the appeal of the beachcomber narrative lay in the dubious status of the account, in the challenge it offered the reader of sifting true story from tall tale. In the conflicting and yet duplicate histories of Dodd and Carthew, two non-singular artists, or beachcomber—*bricoleurs*, Stevenson's longstanding preoccupation with the double, the *alter ego*, is remodelled at the periphery.

THE EBB-TIDE: CONVERTING BEACHCOMBER TO MISSIONARY

With the writing of *The Ebb-Tide*, the process of collaboration between Stevenson and Lloyd Osbourne broke down. Stevenson's account, in correspondence, of the construction of the novella stresses a division of labour. Osbourne drafted the first four chapters in 1889/90. Stevenson rewrote this section with little emendation, and then set the work aside until 1893, when he completed the story with 'The Quartet'. After serialisation in Britain in *Today* (11 November, 1893–3 February 1894), and in the United States in *McClure's Magazine* (February–July 1894), adverse reviews led Stevenson to consider deleting Osbourne's name from the book's cover: erasure, rather than signature of authorship seemed in this instance more likely to serve Osbourne's literary reputation. Stevenson described the writing of the novel as a debilitating labour, rather than the playful construction of a *bricolage*: 'it has been such a grind! ... I break down at every paragraph, I may observe, and lie here, and sweat, and curse over the blame thing, till I can get one sentence wrung out after another.'[22] Both Stevenson and his reviewers characterised the subject matter of *The Ebb-Tide* as waste material, a failed literary transaction: 'Of grace, virtue, beauty, we get no glimpse. All we have in exchange is a picture of the fag-ends of certain useless and degraded lives.'[23]

The writing of *The Ebb-Tide* was a failure of *bricolage*: a grinding labour, bringing together parts that failed to cohere, producing waste material, rather than a useful new object. *The Ebb-Tide* is the tale of the demise of the beachcomber narrative. Where *The Wrecker* represented the beachcomber, implicitly, as a figure of enterprise, *The Ebb-Tide* portrays the beachcomber explicitly as a figure of waste. Pinkerton, the archetypal *bricoleur* of the earlier novel, is a speculator with the projective energy of the New World citizen, the American democratic subject. *The Ebb-Tide* instead depicts the implication of the Pacific beachcomber within the class values of Old World society. The novel tells the stories of three beachcombers, each representing a different tier of the British class system. Robert Herrick is an Oxford-educated son of the prosperous middle classes, whose family has become bankrupt; Davis has been a merchant sea captain; and Huish is a Cockney who was once a clerk. The class origins which I argued earlier were temporarily suspended for Europeans in the pre-colonial context of the early nineteenth-century Pacific, are depicted in *The Ebb-Tide* as returning to subjugate the beachcomber during the colonial period.

The class status of the three beachcombers is defined, in the absence of material possessions 'on the beach', by the types of narration in which they engage. They shelter within the ruins of the old calaboose at Papeete in Tahiti, a building in which Herman Melville had earlier been held on the charge of mutiny.[24] Their context, then, links them to the production of the canonical beachcomber texts, *Typee* and *Omoo*. Yet despite their proximity to a literary heritage, the types of narration and writing in which the three beachcombers of *The Ebb-Tide* engage fail to achieve authority, and are fragmentary and self-enclosed. Huish, who is ill, demands to be entertained with a yarn. Herrick responds by invoking an *Arabian Nights* scenario, in which a magic carpet transports the beachcombers back to metropolitan society. As each takes up the tale, the backgrounds of the three are defined by their fantasies of home yarned at the periphery; by the metonymies, particularly of food, through which class represents itself as personal taste. In this version of the *Arabian Nights* the other is not the Oriental, but the returned beachcomber, gazing upon British society as outsider.

Davis remains the closest of the trio to the model of the enterprising beachcomber, and it is he who instigates the most practical of narrative activities. He earns breakfast by dancing and singing English musical favourites to a group of Polynesian sailors, a performance which is the residue of the beachcomber's earlier role as cross cultural translator. He also engages the other two beachcombers in a letter-writing project, begging writing implements from the British consul. Inspired by reminiscence, he suggests that they each write to loved ones at home in England. The letters that they produce are romanticised accounts of their present life: South Seas fictions. However only Huish is comfortable with the role of duplicitous narrator. Davis and Herrick, conscious of the gap between a fictional romance and the reality of their situation, are reluctant, guilty authors: 'Now they would write a word or two, now scribble it out; now they would sit biting at the pencil end and staring seaward; now their eyes would rest on the clerk, where he sat propped on the canoe, leering and coughing, his pencil racing glibly on the paper.'[25] Huish produces a generic romance tale in which he claims to have made his fortune: 'I wrote to her and told her 'ow I had got rich, and married a queen in the Hislands, and lived in a blooming palace.' (192) His pronunciation slurs the Pacific islands with the Scottish Highlands that were the setting of Stevenson's own romances. Huish's story reinvokes those of an earlier generation of beachcombers—of figures such as William Mariner, whose tale of adoption into the Tongan aristocracy is the material of romance. However, in the era of Pacific colonialism, romance is figured as degenerate. Huish's facility with this type of writing is indicative of his unredeemed nature, and his text is reviled and destroyed: 'the clerk reached out his hand, picked up the letter, which had fallen to the earth, and tore it into fragments, stamp and all' (192).

Herrick's productions, on the other hand, reflect a classical education, and are the antithesis of the beachcomber's *bricolage*. He lacks the 'gift of fabrication', so that his ventures into numerous professions have acquired for

him the name of 'incompetent' (175). He is distinguished by his library
rather than by his manual productions, carrying 'a tattered Virgil in his
pocket' (174). Herrick holds on to this artefact of a 'dead tongue', even while
he lives, surrounded by a double oral heritage, among yarning sailors in
Polynesia. Where Cannibal Jack's library was one of his many successful
enterprises, Herrick's book is a further testimony to his incompetence—a
text he is able neither to circulate nor to subsist upon:

> Certainly, if money could have been raised upon the book,
> Robert Herrick would long ago have sacrificed that last
> possession; but the demand for literature, which is so marked a
> feature in some parts of the South Seas, extends not so far as the
> dead tongues; and the Virgil, which he could not exchange
> against a meal, had often consoled him in his hunger. (174)

The name Robert Herrick alludes, of course, to the author of *Hesperides*
(1648), and like the verse of the Carolinean poet, Herrick's 'literary'
productions are effete, self-conscious pieces. He inscribes his own epitaph—
the 'famous phrase' from Beethoven's Fifth Symphony, and a line from the
Aeneid—on the calaboose walls that once housed Melville, and which have
since become decorated with the cave paintings of the other, Polynesian and
European: 'The crumbling whitewash was all full of them: Tahitian names,
and French, and English, and rude sketches of ships under sail and men at
fisticuffs.' (193) Where the *bricolage* productions of the beachcomber were
adaptive to context, Herrick's chosen form of writing, the epitaph, is static,
expressing a determination to endure, to leave a sign. He takes pleasure in
the incongruity of his inscription, in the social distinction his quotations
imply: '"So", thought he, "they will know that I loved music and had classical
tastes. They? He, I suppose: the unknown, kindred spirit that shall come
some day and read my *memor querela*. Ha, he shall have Latin too!"' (194)
The reader he fantasizes is singular, rather than communal: he prides himself
on writing a language of few initiates. But bathetically, his actual audience
turns out to be Davis, who incorporates Herrick's solipsistic, congealed
quotation into plot. By coincidence, the captain figures, Herrick's inscription
was made at the very time at which he himself succeeded in securing a new
venture for the three beachcombers: to crew the contaminated ship *Farallone*,
with its cargo of champagne, to Australia. Davis brings Herrick's dead
fragments of language into line with active enterprise, invoking the
providential thesis:

'About how long ago since you wrote *up* this truck?' he asked.

'What does it matter?' exclaimed Herrick. 'I daresay half an hour.'

'My God, its strange!' cried Davis. 'There's some men would call that accidental: not me. That...' and he drew his thick finger under the music—'that's what I call Providence.' (196)

Herrick's impotence marks a demise in the figure of the gentleman beachcomber, of whom Melville is the canonical precedent. Like Herrick, Melville was the son of a prosperous merchant who went bankrupt, forcing his son to seek employment on board whaling ships cruising the Pacific. T. Walter Herbert has argued that Melville's South Seas fictions betray 'the complex psychology of the failed patrician'.[26] In *Omoo*, Melville depicts a ship's crew comprised of similar types to the *Ebb-Tide's* three protagonists. The captain, an educated Cockney, is like Herrick, 'in no wise competent'. The mate Jermin prefigures Davis: a capable seaman with a weakness for strong drink. But the most authoritative figure aboard this vessel is Dr Long Ghost, a character in the model of the gentleman beachcomber, who carries similar cultural baggage to Herrick: 'he quoted Virgil, and talked of Hobbes of Malmsbury, beside repeating poetry by the canto, especially Hudibras'. Long Ghost converts literary fragment into active narrative, rather than the dead text of epitaph. He is a teller of stories and a singer of songs: 'he had more anecdotes than I can tell of. Then such mellow old songs he sang, in a voice so round and racy, the real juice of sound. How such notes came forth from his lank body was a constant marvel. Upon the whole, Long Ghost was as entertaining a companion as one could wish.'[27] For *The Ebb-Tide's* trio, by contrast, a general failure of enterprise is signalled by the exhaustion of narrative possibility that marks their aleatory or shallow creative endeavours.

Davis's proposal is an attempt to revive the beachcomber in a project of active speculation. The authors of *The Ebb-Tide* turn to the type of plot which motivated *Omoo* and *The Wrecker*, seeking to create a profitable story from the waste material of the three beached protagonists. In the prologue to *The Wrecker*, Loudon Dodd boasts of his involvements in a series of duplicitous speculations, as wrecker, smuggler, and blackmailer. The common product of these ventures is narrative. Dodd and Pinkerton gamble upon the story that lies hidden in the mysterious wreck of the *Flying Scud*, and the tale within their tale is the wealth that they eventually recover. In the first half of *The Ebb-Tide*, Davis proposes a parallel set of projects: to smuggle the *Farallone's* cargo of champagne, to wreck the ship and claim from the profits of insurance using blackmail, to intimidate the owner of the pearl island upon which they alight. Yet in this novel such ventures are ill-fated: the twists of plot offer only a series of dead-ends. As the only men in Papeete willing to sail the ship *Farallone* despite a risk of infection, the trio are marked as doomed subjects, gambling with death. Possibilities recede, like an ebb-tide, leaving the beachcomber washed up, a useless object rather than a fabricator. The novel Lloyd Osbourne begins by rewriting the plot of *The Wrecker* is laid aside, becomes waste material, exhausted like its protagonists. When Stevenson takes up the thread of narrative again in 'The Quartet', introducing the character of Attwater, the owner of the pearl island, he recycles this waste material in a new *bricolage*. However, it is the figure of the missionary as represented by Attwater, rather than of the beachcomber, who provides the authority for continuation: who offers to make something of the legacy of the beachcomber.

Each of the trio takes up the threads of narrative without success, grasping and then surrendering the reins of authorship. Herrick's 'incompetence' is indicated by his inability to assume control until the very conclusion of the story. The more resourceful plotting of Davis, already mentioned, meets its match in Attwater. He hands authority over to Huish, who formulates a desperate plan to destroy Attwater using a bottle of acid. The bottle is a significant image in *The Ebb-Tide*, emblematising the emptying out of meaning that accompanies closure of speculation. The cargo of champagne aboard the *Farallone* initially represents bounty to the three beachcombers. These bottles, however, contain wine turned to water.

> 'Illo!' said Huish. 'Ere's a bad bottle.'
>
> He poured some of the wine into the mug: it was colourless and still. He smelt and tasted it ... The mug passed round; each sipped, each smelt of it; each stared at the bottle in its glory of gold paper as Crusoe may have stared at the footprint; and their minds were swift to fix upon a common apprehension. The difference between a bottle of champagne and a bottle of water is not great; between a shipload of one or the other lay the whole scale from riches to ruin.
>
> A second bottle was broached ... Still with the same result: the contents were still colourless and tasteless, and dead as the rain in a beached fishing boat. (226-7)

Where Crusoe, the mythical beachcomber hero, encountered the sign of presence, the footprint on the sand, the three latter-day beachcombers are confronted by the sign of absence, water, the featurelessness of which is verified by each of their senses. The bottle of luxury becomes the bottle of despair, to be substituted by Huish's bottle of bile. In the stories of castaways on desert islands, bottles assume significance as bearing final messages; ultimate authorial statements. Huish's last-resort bottle of acid, on the other hand, serves a horrific project of erasure, signalling the expiration of the beachcomber plot.

Attwater's pearl island is a space replete with poetic possibilities: an appropriate setting for the figure who emerges as the dominant authorial presence within the narrative. Stevenson depicts the atoll landscape as one of deceptive minimalism and metaphoric abundance, recalling his description of the Tuamotus in *In the South Seas*. It exhausts Herrick's limited poetic capacities:

> He tortured himself to find analogies. The isle was like the rim of a great vessel sunken in the waters; it was like the embankment of an annular railway grown upon with wood: so slender it seemed amidst the outrageous breakers, so frail and pretty, he would scarce have wondered to see it sink and disappear without a sound, and the waves close smoothly over its descent. (237)

I suggested earlier that the atoll represents a feminine geography within Stevenson's island vocabulary. Herrick's poetic failure is perhaps due here to the attempt to impose masculine similes upon a feminine landscape. The atoll is both fertile, producing a wealth of pearls, and barren, its population recently annihilated by an epidemic, and it is this ambiguous signification that Attwater's own sermonising fails to reconcile. For of course his pearl island is not simply a physical space: it is also a missionary colony, and an exegetical text.

If Attwater's are the ascendent poetics of *The Ebb-Tide*, this development reflects a post-contact Pacific historical teleology. The missionary's authority and influence defeat the projects of the superseded beachcomber. Robert Irwin Hillier has compared the character of Attwater to those missionaries whom Stevenson lionized in his correspondence from the Pacific: George Brown of Samoa, Shirley Baker of Tonga, and James Chalmers of New Guinea. Hillier claims that 'the similarities between Attwater and actual missionary figures are sufficient to demonstrate that Stevenson regarded Attwater as heroic'.[28] Yet rather than simply endorsing the missionary as hero, Stevenson represents in the figure of Attwater the dominance of evangelical discourse: a discourse which, in the later nineteenth-century Pacific, prospered through association with colonial policy. Attwater's are the poetics of absolute authority. He is introduced just as the beachcombers' fund of invention becomes exhausted: 'They had no plan, no story prepared.' (240) He terrifies Herrick with his godlike omnipresence: '"He knows all, he sees through all; we only make him laugh with our pretences—he looks at us and laughs like God!"' (271) He refers to himself consistently using the indefinite pronoun *one*, describing his actions in the third person in a self-consciously writerly fashion. He claims to be 'a plain man and very literal' (259), but his speech is imbued with the classical education of the later nineteenth-century 'gentleman' missionary.

In Attwater's confrontation with Huish, the aristocrat defeats the proletarian, and literacy overcomes orality. Attwater prides himself on being a winnower of souls, on providing in his island colony a context in which both Polynesian and Western subjects may find an opportunity to prove their worth. However, his is the touchstone of class: 'The presence of the gentleman lighted up like a candle the vulgarity of the clerk.' (242) During his first encounter with Attwater, Huish reverts to an oral performance described as innately 'savage', but redolent of Cockney culture, singing 'a piece of the chorus of a comic song which he must have heard twenty years before in London: meaningless gibberish that, in that hour and that place, seemed hateful as a blasphemy: "Hikey, pikey, crikey, fikey, chillinga-wallaba dory."' (248) Huish's nonsense is a sound poem, an echo: it is blasphemous in its very non-literacy. Attwater, in turn, subtly denigrates Huish by reading rather than speaking his name. He titles Huish 'Mr Whish', pronouncing the Cockney self-nomination *Uish* as it might be written rather than as it must be heard. Attwater mimics orality by consciously over-articulating. By contrast, Huish's plan to destroy Attwater involves manufacturing a duplicitous letter of truce which is a piece of transcribed speech. It is distinguished within Stevenson's text by its typeface, which is further fractured by apostrophes marking verbal ellipses: 'I 'ave deputed my friend and partner, Mr J.L. Huish, to l'y before you my proposals, and w'ich by their moderytion, will, I trust, be found to merit your attention. Mr J.L. Huish is entirely unarmed, I swear to Gawd! and will 'old 'is 'ands over 'is 'ead from the moment he begins to approach you.' (290) Huish fetishises the unfamiliar written text: 'Huish read the letter with the innocent joy of amateurs, chuckled gustfully to himself, and reopened it more than once after it was refolded, to repeat the pleasure.' (290) The contest between beachcomber and missionary is depicted as one between two discursive modes: the beachcomber's linked to British working-class oral traditions, and the missionary's to the advent of literacy.

Attwater's literal-mindedness expresses his commitment to the Old

Testament paradigm of earthly vengeance and reward. However, his favoured mode of discourse is the New Testament poetics of parable. He offers the unnerving redemption of a place within sermon. The populace of his island, decimated by disease, are resurrected as the subjects of story. He tells the beachcombers a morality fable of opposite types, former inhabitants of the atoll to whom he refers as Obsequious and Sullens. The pair represent two colonial caricatures, the mimic and the silent slave. Their public faces have deceived Attwater: the subservient figure in fact proves duplicitous, while the silent native is revealed to be loyal in his motives. The discovery of their true identities comes too late to save the pair from their master's swift and destructive judgement. The fable depicts a regime of absolute power based on insufficient perception; however other aspects of Attwater's authority illustrate an alternative model of control, which finds explicit statement in Stevenson's public comments on missionary policy.

In the lecture from which I quoted earlier, entitled 'Missions in the South Seas', Stevenson focuses on the necessity of adaptation to context. He urges missionaries, in their encounters with Pacific cultures, 'to seek rather the point of agreement than the points of difference; to proceed rather by confirmation and extension than by iconoclasm'.[29] It is the ability to negotiate between the culture of his origins and that of his adopted context which renders Attwater an insurmountable force. At a dinner party for the beachcombers, he displays his authority through his masterful appropriation of Polynesian cuisine, serving dishes which utilise the island's natural delicacies:

> They sat down to an island dinner, remarkable for its variety and excellence: turtle-soup and steak, fish, fowls, a sucking-pig, a cocoanut salad, and sprouting cocoanut roasted for dessert. Not a tin had been opened; and save for the oil and vinegar in the salad, and some green spears of onion which Attwater cultivated and plucked with his own hand, not even the condiments were European. (261)

Attwater is a missionary liberated from dependence on the metropolitan article. In this context, his ability to manipulate that slippery signifier, the bottle, is only a supplementary sign of control: 'Sherry, hock, and claret succeeded each other, and the *Farallone* champagne brought up the rear with the dessert.' (261)

By appropriating the beachcomber's strategy of cultural interaction, once the beachcomber has become an exhausted force, the missionary in turn achieves ascendency in the Pacific. Attwater has stored up a treasure-trove of material for *bricolage* in a house on his island

> which stood gaping open on the afternoon, seiz[ing] on the mind of Herrick with its multiplicity and disorder of romantic things. Therein were cables, windlasses and blocks of every size and capacity; cabin windows and ladders; rusty tanks, a companion hatch; a binnacle with its brass mountings and its compass idly pointing, in the confusion and dusk of that shed, to a forgotten pole; ropes, anchors, harpoons, a blubber-dipper of copper, green with years, a steering-wheel, a tool-chest with the vessel's name upon the top, the *Asia*: a whole curiosity shop of sea-curios, gross and solid, heavy to lift, ill to break, bound with brass and shod with iron. (250)

Attwater goads Herrick to make metaphor from this material: '"only old junk! And does Mr Hay find a parable?"' (250) The beachcomber is conscious, however, of his poetic enervation. When Herrick eventually offers himself to Attwater it is as another object cast up by the tide, unable to fashion anything from himself, but hoping to serve as an element in the missionary's *bricolage*. '"Can you do anything with me? ... I am broken crockery; I am a burst drum; the whole of my life is gone to water; I have nothing left that I believe in, except my living horror of myself ... I put myself, helpless, in your hands."' (279)

The union of the beachcomber and the missionary represents a powerful force, and was espoused by Stevenson in his lecture on missions. There he recommends that the missionary attempt to recognise, rather than antagonise, the beachcomber:

> Too many missionaries make a mistake ... when they expect, not only from their native converts, but from white men (by no means of the highest class) shipwrecked or stranded at random in these islands, a standard of conduct which no parish minister in the world would dare to expect of his parishioners and church-members. There is here, in these despised whites, a second reservoir of moral power, which missionaries too often neglect and render nugatory ... The trader is therefore, at once by experience and by influence, the superior of the missionary. He is a person marked out to be made use of by an intelligent mission.

Stevenson's polemic describes Herrick's plot: 'Sometimes a very doubtful character, sometimes an exceedingly decent gentleman, he will almost invariably be made the better by some intelligent and kindly attention, for which he is often burning, and he will almost invariably be made the worse by neglect, by being ignored or by insult ... The missions and the traders have to be made more or less in unison.'[30]

The kind of redemption offered to the beachcomber by the missionary is not, however, represented within the fictional context of *The Ebb-Tide* as unambiguously positive. Davis, who becomes a cipher for Attwater's discourse, is an emasculated figure at the close of the novel, prepared to sacrifice the prospect of a return to wife and family in order to remain in a childlike role as 'Attwater's spoiled darling and pet penitent!' (301) Attwater's theology becomes, upon Davis's lips, a 'voluble and incoherent stream of prayer' (300): a form of nonsense, akin to the threatening gobbledegook of Huish's Cockney verbage. Herrick himself has earlier indicated an aptitude for Attwater's brand of redemption, which is discursive rather than ethical. His storytelling in the calaboose was already termed a 'parable' (179). Huish found it too redolent of sermon, commenting sarcastically: ' "It's like the rot there is in tracts" ' (180); ' "it's like *Ministering Children!*" ' (181) Indeed, Herrick's acquired sense of masculine purpose at the end of *The Ebb-Tide* reflects his resistance to complete conversion as much as it exemplifies the beachcomber's refashioning by the missionary.

'THE BEACH OF FALESĀ': TRADE SECRETS

Although Stevenson's lecture on missions discusses the potentially redemptive role of beachcombers—'white men (by no means of the highest class) shipwrecked or stranded at random in these islands', his specific reference is to 'traders'. This slip, perhaps made for the benefit of an audience unfamiliar with the term *beachcomber* (which H. E. Maude claims is of 'genuine island coinage') elides an important distinction between the two roles, which reflects their potential to serve, as Stevenson advocates, the missionary cause. According to Maude, 'what really differentiated the beachcombers from other immigrants was the fact that they were essentially integrated into, and dependent for their livelihood on, the indigenous communities ... To all intents and purposes they had voluntarily or perforce contracted out of the European monetary economy.'[31] Traders, on the other hand, were representatives of European and American commercial agendas. They operated at the nexus of Western and Pacific cultures, facilitating the two-way circulation of goods and produce. Traders manned the outposts of capitalist enterprise, and hence were more realistic candidates for appropriation to missionary colonialist agendas than the outcast beachcomber. They were not simply colluders, however; their role retained a certain ambivalence, falling in the unreliable territory between colonial representative and maverick entrepreneur.

'The Beach of Falesā', Stevenson's narrative of 'a South Seas Trader', is a story of divided allegiances. The trader, John Wiltshire, pits himself against and defeats his rival, the gentleman beachcomber Case, and in the process affirms his loyalty to the island community he has made his own. A text about the ethics of trade, 'The Beach of Falesā' is itself a product of transaction. It was published in book form in the volume *Island Nights' Entertainments*, with two other tales, 'The Bottle Imp' (originally published in the *New York Herald*, 8, 15, 22 February, 1 March 1891, and in *Black and White*, 28 March, 4 April 1891) and 'The Isle of Voices' (originally published in the *National Observer*, 4, 11, 18, 25 February 1893). Stevenson had wanted 'The Beach of Falesā' to be brought out as a single volume: the stories that came to accompany it were intended for a differently conceived 'Island Nights' Entertainments'. During preparation for printing, the 'Falesā' manuscript's idiosyncratic spellings and grammar were subject to correction by editors and proof-readers, and certain passages were censored. In his minutely documented study of these textual alterations, Barry Menikoff argues that editorial intervention effectively diluted the story's radical critique of colonial practice.[32] Menikoff draws attention to the subtle ways in which editors and publishers, aiming for the production of a smoothly literate text, ironed out disruptive effects that embodied Stevenson's attempt to transcribe the mixed language of his adopted context.

Stevenson's distance from metropolitan publishing centres slowed down negotiations over the text. The stages of publication become foregrounded in a dilatory series of questions, cross-decisions and re-evaluations, formulated in exchanges of letters across the Pacific. This slow-motion process provides a counterweight at the level of production to the readerly acceleration which, Menikoff argues, was edited into Stevenson's resistant text. He notes that 'the compositors and proof-readers ... supplied substitutes which insured that a reader, when he passed over a sentence, would not have to pause or give a special ear to sound and meaning because a familiar word appeared in an unorthodox context. Instead he could glide gracefully over the page, automatically filling out the words and, on occasion, the clichés.' Physical distance acted as an impediment to production. Nor did this dynamic simply reinforce a familiar opposition between metropolitan advancement and peripheral obstruction: the urge towards acceleration coming from technologically advanced publishing centres, and resisted by an author from the Pacific wishing to preserve, as artefact, an 'authentic' piece of cultural transcription. The ultimate objective of Menikoff's study is to recuperate 'The Beach of Falesā' as a modernist, writerly text, whose aesthetic of difficulty has been attenuated by the conservative emendations of the literary establishment. He argues that

> *Falesā* presented [compositors and proof-readers] with a more complex problem: it substituted ambiguity in language for certainty ... The ambiguity was not merely that of an occasional word or syntactical construction but that of method and manner ... It is as if the effort to communicate by mastering a clear style is contravened by the realisation that the style may not be a means for discovering any truth at all, except, paradoxically, that ambiguity and irresolution are the conditions of life.[33]

Despite his claims for 'The Beach of Falesā''s Modernism, Menikoff's project is essentially Romantic in its conception of authorship; motivated by a belief in the integrity of authorial creation that leads him back to the original, the signatory hand. His study describes the death of authorship that occurs when the sanctity of the text is violated by the philistine interventions of publishers. But while 'The Beach of Falesā' is clearly a product of transaction, there are alternative ways of interpreting the effects of negotiation. The editorial changes to Stevenson's manuscript disrupt a unified authorial intention, inscribing instead the process of the book's cross-cultural production. The negotiated printed text of 'The Beach of Falesā' makes manifest the contract implicit in all writing from oral cultural contexts, which may seek to remain faithful to the 'voice' of the exotic, but which remains financially dependent upon a metropolitan audience. The publishers' decision to print 'The Beach of Falesā' as part of *Island Nights' Entertainments* results in the production of a volume that makes explicit this dialogical impulse. The two halves of the book (the first story is novella length, and occupies slightly more than half the pages of the volume) demonstrate alternative traditions of storytelling. While the dedication of *Island Nights' Entertainments* to 'Three Old Shipmates Among the Islands'— friends from Stevenson's cruise aboard the *Janet Nichol*—explicitly situates the volume as a whole within the narrative context of the shipboard yarn, only 'The Beach of Falesā' actually exemplifies this mode of discourse. 'The Bottle Imp' and 'The Isle of Voices' have the aggregative format and rhythmical language of Polynesian oral compositions. Stevenson was an appreciative audience for, and a collector of, both these types of oral tradition. Graham Balfour observed that 'Well as Stevenson could himself tell a story, he was never tired of studying the methods of other men, and never failed to express his high appreciation of sailors' yarns.'[34]

Yet Stevenson opposed the combination of different narrative modes in a single volume, insisting in correspondence that 'The B. of F. is *simply not* to appear along with 'The Bottle Imp', a story of a totally different scope and intention, to which I have already made one fellow, and which I design for a substantive volume.'[35] A segregation was evident in the corpus of texts he produced from the Pacific, which can be divided between romances that retained a Scottish location, betraying only indirectly their context of production, and works of a local influence and setting. This discernible link between subject matter and genre reflects the fact that Stevenson's later writings were produced according to alternative criteria: on the one hand, continuing in the romance tradition, and on the other, offering Polynesian culture to the metropolitan reader as ethnographic artefact, a project which entailed an espousal of realism. He asserts that '['The Beach of Falesā'] is the first realistic South Sea story; I mean with real South Sea character and details of life; everybody else who has tried, that I have seen, got carried away by the romance and ended in a kind of sugar candy sham epic, and the whole effect was lost—there was no etching, no human grin, consequently no conviction.'[36] The contested juxtaposition of European and Polynesian oral narrative models in *Island Nights' Entertainments*, however, foregrounds implicit tensions and reciprocities between these traditions, reintroducing to the book as a whole the polyphonic and disjunctive structure that Menikoff seeks to recover for 'The Beach of Falesā'.

At the opening of 'The Beach of Falesā', Wiltshire arrives at a 'high island', after 'years on a low island near the line, living for the most part solitary among natives'.[37] The change of topographies offers him the promise of a cure: 'Here was a fresh experience; even the tongue would be quite strange to me; and the look of these woods and mountains, and the rare smell of them, renewed my blood.' (3) Like Stevenson making his first 'island landfall' in *In the South Seas*, Wiltshire has come to the high island in need of recuperation, but his illness is diagnosed as the lack of white society: 'I was sick for white neighbours after my four years at the line'. (5) This disablement is registered partly as a loss of technological dexterity. He spells out the effect of looking towards shore through a telescope, implying a defamiliarised relationship with the instrument: 'I took the glass; and the shores leapt nearer, and I saw the tangle of woods and the breach of the surf.' (3) This acquired technological naivete echoes representations of native wonderment from early European accounts of the Pacific—compare Kotzebue's description of a Samoan chief looking through a telescope for the first time:

> A telescope which I held in my hand attracted the observation of the chief, who took it for a gun. I directed him to look through it; but the sudden vision of the distant prospect brought so close to his eye that he could even distinguish the people on the strand, so terrified him, that nothing could induce him to touch the magic instrument again.[38]

As Wiltshire's story develops, technological facility is exposed as a force of exploitation.

The settler community that Wiltshire enters constitutes a predetermined narrative frame. It is populated by a cast of characters whose names have onomantic resonances. Wiltshire is not the first mercantile Adam to occupy this Edenic scene; his predecessor is 'old Adams'. The devil is represented by 'Black Jack', Case's accessory. 'Vigours', 'Whistling Jimmie' and 'Underhill' all meet apposite fates. This morality play cast also provides Stevenson with the opportunity for self-reflexive allusion. The villain of the piece, the gentleman beachcomber Case, offers an alternative model of the artist to Wiltshire, the plain-style storyteller. Case is a manipulator of devices and effects. His name signifies the subject both of detective fiction and, *avant la lettre*, of the psychoanalytic session.[39] These two discourses are, according to Walter Ong, typically literate. Ong claims that 'Detective plots are deeply interior ... by contrast with the old oral narrative. The oral narrator's protagonist, distinguished typically for his external exploits, has been replaced by the interior consciousness of the typographic protagonist', while 'It would appear that the advent of modern depth psychology parallels the development of the character in drama and the novel, both depending on the inward turning of the psyche produced by writing and intensified by print.'[40] The name *Case* may also of course allude to the bag of tricks with which he keeps the population of Falesā in thrall. In the figure of Case, Stevenson associates malign technological wizardry with literate discourse.

Case's features are mask-like—'He was yellow and smallish, had a hawk's nose to his face, pale eyes, and his beard trimmed with scissors' (5)— and he is a gifted actor and mimic—'He could speak, when he chose, fit for a drawing room; and when he chose he could blaspheme worse than a Yankee boatswain, and talk smart to sicken a Kanaka. The way he thought would pay best at the moment, that was Case's way, and it always seemed to come natural, and like as if he was born to it.' (5–6) His facility reflects Stevenson's own capacity to register a multitude of different voices within his tale. As Menikoff observes:

> In *Falesā* he possessed a subject that allowed him to meld the array of dialects and idioms that he had absorbed in his travels as an 'emigrant' across the continental United States, and on his cruises through the Pacific. At his command were American slang, Samoan, pidgin English (what the professional linguists call Beach-la-mar), and the ubiquitous sailor's talk, a range of terms and expressions that were commonplace at one extreme and required a glossary at the other.[41]

Case's authorship, however, produces a false text. He procures an attractive Falesān girl, Uma, for Wiltshire, and organises their 'marriage', writing the certificate, 'signatures and all, in a leaf out of the ledger'. (13) Case's document certifies that Uma 'is illegally married to Mr John Wiltshire for one week, and Mr John Wiltshire is at liberty to send her to hell when he pleases'. He manipulates a familiar scenario: the innocent native is duped by a writing that is fetishized without being comprehended. This section of the plot raises issues about the ethics of writing within which Stevenson is himself indirectly implicated. The marriage certificate can be contextualised by an episode from his travels. At church service in Butaritari, he observed a group of traders' wives, noting the 'unusually enviable' position they occupied within their community. He reports, however, that

> the certificate of one, when she proudly showed it, proved to run thus, that she was 'married for one night', and her gracious partner was at liberty to 'send her to hell' the next morning; but she was none the wiser or the worse for the dastardly trick. Another, I heard, was married on a work of mine in a pirated edition; it answered the purpose as well as a Hall Bible.[42]

Stevenson's own writing, then, had occupied the space of the false text in the instance of deception on which Case's document is modelled. He points out, however, that the book employed was 'a pirated edition', from which he derived no profit; distinguishing his own authorship from self-serving literate impositions upon Pacific populations, and implying that he and the trader's wife are the mutual victims of literary exploitation. Case's false document was in turn the focus of censorship by Stevenson's editors. It was excised from *The Illustrated London News* and the 1892 copyright versions of the tale, and subsequently modified for publication (in the manuscript, 'week' had read as 'night') in accordance with perceptions of audience sensibilities.[43] The latter tussle of terminology appears so arbitrary as to represent primarily a contest of authority between writer and editors, subsumed into an ethical agenda.

The marriage certificates Stevenson mentions in *In the South Seas* represent a contract which is mutually beneficial. The trader gains a sexual partner, and his wife obtains both unlimited access to foreign commodities, and immunity by association from the tabus and curfews that restrict other members of her community. The marriage certificate in 'The Beach of Falesā' is similarly mutually binding, but it represents the deception of both parties. By signing, Wiltshire becomes united with a bride who turns out to have been tabued by her own community. The morning after his wedding night, the locals register that the trader's cynically achieved domesticity is also a performance in their eyes, by forming an audience outside his house: 'Some dozen young men and children made a piece of a half-circle, flanking my house ... and they all sat silent, wrapped in their sheets, and stared at me and my house as straight as pointer dogs.' (17) Unable to speak their language, Wiltshire is at the mercy of Case as interpreter of this silent message. Case offers to discover from the village chiefs the story behind Wiltshire's alienation. The explanation he 'translates', however, is one of which he is in effect the author.

Case is not, then, simply a malign colonial exploiting a small island community. His success lies in his ability to negotiate between cultures, and to play upon mutual assumptions. His false certificate may manipulate Uma's innocent fetishisation of writing, but equally it plays upon Wiltshire's faith that, as a self-nominated 'British subject', writing will always be his tool, and, more broadly, on the trader's complacent ignorance of the codes and practices of his new community. Case accompanies his adoption of the role of Wiltshire's interpreter with the mimicked rhetoric of imperial duty: 'I count it the White Man's Quarrel.' (27) Wiltshire uncritically reiterates this discourse, instructing Case to declare to the chiefs: 'I'm a white man, and a British subject, and no end of a big chief at home; and I've come here to do them good, and bring them civilisation.... I demand the reason of this treatment as a white man and a British subject.' (29) Before he can overcome Case's treacherous influence, Wiltshire must cease to place confidence in false colonial kinship, and begin to identify with the interests of Falesā's indigenous community. In the early part of the story there is a clear division between the depiction of the Western settlers of Falesā', whose apposite names fix them, albeit grotesquely, in the mind of the reader, and the representation of the native population as inscrutably other, 'like graven images' (18), without individuated subjectivity. The exception here is of course Uma, who initially stands out among the 'Kanakas' of Falesā simply as the object of Wiltshire's voyeuristic sexual appraisal, but who forces her husband to recognise the integral humanity which is signalled by her own name (Uma is the core of the word *human*; in Samoan the word signifies wholeness and completeness).

Uma's affection for Wiltshire is prompted by her fetishisation of the written document. She believes the false marriage certificate to be authoritative: its textuality offers her a more substantial sign of her changed status than empty words. She tells Wiltshire: '"White man, he come here, I marry him all-e-same Kanaka; very well then, he marry me all-e-same white woman. Suppose he no marry, he go 'way, woman he stop. All-e-same thief, empty-hand, Tonga-heart—no can love! Now you come marry me. You big heart—you no shamed island girl. That thing I love you far too much. I proud."' (39)[44] Yet her naive faith in the deceptive document amounts also to a form of indirect authorship. Implicitly at Uma's dictation, Wiltshire transforms the false marriage certificate into the true sign that she believes it to be, and so begins his own course of redemption. He summons the local missionary, the Reverend Tarleton, to perform a genuine marriage ceremony, which is carried out in the language of the Polynesian bride rather than the English groom: '"And I guess you'd better do it in native"', Wiltshire orders the missionary, '"it'll please the old lady."' (44) Wiltshire gives way to an outburst of self-denigration that echoes and inverts his earlier, self-affirming imperialist rhetoric: '"I'm no missionary, nor missionary lover; I'm no Kanaka, nor favourer of Kanakas—I'm just a trader; I'm just a common low God-damned white man and British subject, the sort you would like to wipe your boots on."' (42) His recognition that British nationality does not guarantee authority coincides with the development of a more active role for his wife, who takes over the role of interpreter, becoming Wiltshire's accessory in unravelling the further plots of the villainous Case.

Although another Western character, the missionary, is required to bring the false marriage within the realm of law, his authority as guide and interpreter is simultaneously undermined. Tarleton, whose name (as well as being that of the most famous of the Elizabethan clowns), echoes 'charlatan', tells Wiltshire of his betrayal by a most promising convert, the teacher Namu. Namu's name signals to the English reader an inverted humanity, the reverse of Uma's. Tarleton has placed his faith in Namu as a genuine vessel of transcendent truth. He claims: 'All our islanders easily acquire a kind of eloquence, and can roll out and illustrate, with a great deal of vigour and fancy, second-hand sermons; but Namu's sermons are his own, and I cannot deny that I have found them means of grace.' (46) However Namu proves to be a mimic preacher. Under Case's influence, his discourse evolves into a pastiche of Protestant, Catholic and Polynesian superstition, undermining the claims of each religion to the status of absolute truth. Its form remains indistinguishable from genuine Christian sermon, but its content is blasphemous, creating a tension that has been well analysed, in another context, by Homi Bhabha: 'A discourse at the crossroads of what is known and permissible and that which though known must be kept concealed; a discourse uttered between the lines and as such both against the rules and within them.'[45] Namu's false teaching recalls the destabilising mimicry practised by those Pacific cult leaders discussed earlier, and similarly incorporates a self-reflexive turn. In the following speech, reported by Tarleton, he explicitly professes the relative value of the sign:

> 'I reasoned thus: if this sign of the cross were used in a Popey manner it would be sinful, but when it is used only to protect men from a devil, which is a thing harmless in itself, the sign too must be harmless. For the sign is neither good nor bad. But if the bottle be full of gin, the gin is bad; and if the sign made in idolatry be bad, so is the idolatry.' And, very like a native pastor, he had a text apposite about the casting out of devils. (47)

Tarleton resists for too long the acknowledgement of Namu's defection, and with it the provisionality of his own discourse. He thus becomes implicated in a horror story of economic rivalry. Case has achieved ascendency as local trader by disposing of his rivals with the collusion of Namu. Old Adams is suspected of having been poisoned, Vigours survives, but is driven out, and Underhill is buried alive while paralysed by palsy, with Namu officiating. Tarleton has nonetheless determined upon a policy of wilful ignorance: 'At that moment, with Namu's failure fresh in my view, the work of my life appeared a mockery; hope was dead in me ... Right or wrong, then, I determined on a quiet course.' (49) He resorts to commentary only in the indirect and contested language of scriptural allusion: 'On Sunday I took the pulpit in the morning, and preached from First Kings, nineteenth, on the fire, the earthquake and the voice, distinguishing the true spiritual power, and referring with such plainness as I dared to recent events in Falesā.' (50) His textual exegesis is undermined by a performance which purports to expose the complicity between the discourse of the missionary and commercial profit. After the service, Case practices a simple magic trick, making believe to pluck a dollar out of Tarleton's head, and thus providing his local audience with apparent material evidence that the missionary's words are tainted at their source with lucre. Tarleton punningly recognises his text-bound impotence, in an oral cultural context in which such performances achieve immediate authority: 'I wish I had learnt legerdemain instead of Hebrew, that I might have paid the fellow out with his own coin.' (51)

Case creates a performance that turns to account the symbolic imagination of cargo cult. Manipulating Polynesian modes of understanding, he offers a critique of Western economic motivations: he is a two-faced mimic of settler and indigenous practices. Earlier, when responding to Wiltshire's inquiries as to why the islanders avoided his trade, Case feigned a respect for the uncanny which gave way to the rhetoric of relativism: '" In short, I'm afraid," says he. "... The Kanakas won't go near you, that's all. And who's to make 'em? We traders have a lot of gall, I must say; we make these poor Kanakas take back their laws, and take up their taboos, and that, whenever it happens to suit us."' (32) In Case, anti-colonialist critique, as well as imperialist rhetoric, is destabilised. Perhaps the only discourse that is redeemed within this story is the transcendent discourse of love, as it is represented in the union between the trader Wiltshire and the Polynesian woman Uma. Stevenson's faith in such cross-cultural coupling did not extend, however, to the production of his own text: he objected to the mismatching of a sailor's yarn, 'The Beach of Falesá', with his island tales 'The Bottle Imp' and 'The Isle of Voices' in the *Island Nights' Entertainments* volume.

Case's 'legerdemain' goes beyond sleight of hand. He successfully manipulates the myth of Western technological supremacy, managing a personal cargo cult as theatre. In the woods behind Falesá he has created a 'temple' of special effects with which he keeps the village awed. He moves between the insider community of the beach and this uncanny peripheral zone with the confidence of an actor stepping on to and off stage. Wiltshire's description of Case returning from a visit to the woods portrays him emerging from behind curtains into a spotlight, in costume: 'I saw the hanging front of the woods pushed suddenly open, and Case, with a gun in his hand, step forth into the sunshine on the black beach. He was got up in light pyjamas.' (56) Wiltshire's task becomes, in turn, to expose the workings of Case's theatre. He identifies Case's sham effects as they are shown up by the genuinely uncanny natural landscape. Exploring the woods, Wiltshire encounters fantastical growth: 'lots of sensitive ... ropes of liana hanging down like a ship's rigging, and nasty orchids growing in the forks like funguses' (61–2). Case's 'tyrolean harps', instruments which produce an eerie whistling sound, stand out among the rank fertility as non-organic in form. They are makeshift assemblages, incorporating identifiable items of trade: 'A box it was, sure enough, and a candle-box at that, with the brand upon the side of it; and it had banjo strings stretched so as to sound when the wind blew.' (64) Wiltshire pays a grudging tribute to Case's gift of fabrication: 'I must say I rather admired the man's ingenuity. With a box of tools and a few mighty simple contrivances he had made out to have a devil of a temple.' (66) Yet Case's theatre is also represented as a shoddy imposition. He has set up a gallery of masks on what appear to be the relics of a real 'temple'. This genuinely unearthly construction dwarfs the impact of his trademarked fright show:

> There was a wall in front of me, the path passing it by a gap; it was tumbledown and plainly very old, but built of big stones very well laid; and there is no native alive today upon that island that could dream of such a piece of building! Along all the top of it was a line of queer figures, idols or scarecrows, or what not ... And the singular thing was that all these bogies were as fresh as toys out of a shop. (65)

Local tales have also invested the landscape surrounding Falesā with uncanny resonances. Unlike Case's productions, these stories effectively incorporate the natural, and thus acquire a potency that remains undiminished at the end of Wiltshire's narrative. Uma tries to prevent her husband from entering the woods by recounting traditional superstitions. She tells of devil women who seduce the most promising Falesān youths, and of a boar 'with a man's thoughts' (61) that once chased her; two versions of the erotic turned horrific which invert the trajectory of Wiltshire's own love story, where the erotic is redeemed by law. The successful dénouement of Wiltshire's narrative depends implicitly upon this suppression, but Uma's stories, which reinvoke the threat of the erotic, are an unresolved moment within that narrative, describing a magic whose workings are never exposed. Her fantastic tales are incorporated directly into Wiltshire's narrative, rather than quoted as Uma's speech, implying his internalisation of a mode of belief which he explicitly rejects.

Before he can defeat Case's wizardry, Wiltshire must perform a task which gives him a practical insight into labour value. As he explains:

> Of course we could get no labour, being all as good as tabooed, and the two women and I turned to and made copra with our own hands. It was copra to make your mouth water when it was done—I never understood how much natives cheated me till I had made that four hundred pounds of my own hand—and it weighed so light I felt inclined to take and water it myself. (53)

Once he has manufactured the genuine product, he is equipped not only to recognise 'native' duplicity, but to expose Case's false technologies. He approaches Case's sanctuary indirectly, from backstage: 'Digging off the earth with my hands, I found underneath tarpaulin stretched on boards, so that this was plainly the roof of a cellar.... The entrance was on the far side' (66). Evading the specular logic imposed by the architecture of Case's 'museum', Wiltshire is able to uncover its mode of construction, the workings by which its magical effects are produced. He exposes the material base of his rival's symbolic performance, the tools of his trade.

Having mastered Case's stagecraft, Wiltshire can declare himself exempt from the allegorical fate that has determined the histories of his predecessors. He warns Case: '"My name ain't Adams, and it ain't Vigours; and I mean to show you that you've met your match."' (68) He plans a nocturnal return visit to Case's sanctuary in order to explode Case's special effects in a triumphant spectacle of his own. When Uma tries to prevent him departing, he slips strategically into missionary rhetoric, claiming that he will be protected by the authority of the Bible: 'I turned to the title-page, where I thought there would likely be some English, and so there was. "There!" said I. "Look at that! 'London: Printed for the British and Foreign Bible Society, Blackfriars,' and the date, which I can't read, owing to its being in three X's. There's no devil in hell can look near the Bible Society, Blackfriars."' (73) Uma responds with a scepticism which Wiltshire interprets as naive literalism, and he is eventually compelled to substantiate his claims for the book by carrying it with him as a safeguard: 'I took to the road, laden like a donkey. First there was that Bible, a book as big as your head, which I had let myself in for by my own tomfoolery.' (74) Uma subsequently learns that Case has discovered Wiltshire's plan. She abandons her superstitious qualms to follow her husband into the woods and warn him of his danger. Wiltshire mines Case's temple, transforming the woods into an infernal landscape: 'the whole wood was scattered with red coals and brands from the explosion; they were all round me on the flat, some had fallen below in the valley, and some stuck and flared in the tree-tops' (80). In this appropriate setting, the devilish Case meets his end.

Wiltshire's narrative concludes in pointed obfuscation. In his sermon at the burial of Case, the Reverend Tarleton refuses to acknowledge the incompatibility between practices of exploitation and the discourse of salvation. Wiltshire complains: 'what he ought to have done was to up like a man and tell the Kanakas plainly Case was damned, and a good riddance; but I never could get him to see it my way.' (84) Case leaves behind him a simple account, the pure economic subtext of his symbolic theatre: 'All they found was a bit of a diary, kept for a good many years, and all about the price of copra, and chickens being stolen, and that; and the books of the business and the will I told you of in the beginning.' (85) Wiltshire's grudging conversion to fair dealing is limited to his interaction with the community of Falesā, and fails to translate into general practice: 'I was half glad when the firm moved me on to another station, where I was under no kind of a pledge and could look my balances in the face.' (86) Uma's physical transformation, from the seductive feminine slightness which distinguishes her at the opening of the story, to a figure of bulk, disproportionate by English standards: 'She's turned a powerful big woman, and could throw a London bobby over her shoulder' (86), marks the successful integration of the erotic. Yet it is the problem posed by his half-caste daughters, the product of his legal union with Uma, which converts Wiltshire's paternalist conclusion into a question:

> But what bothers me is the girls. They're only half-castes, of course; I know that as well as you do, and there's nobody thinks less of half-castes than I do, but they're mine, and about all I've got. I can't reconcile my mind to their taking up with Kanakas, and I'd like to know where I'm to find the whites?[46]

'THE BOTTLE IMP': DIMINISHING RETURNS

'The Bottle Imp' is a tale of fluctuating value. It has a certain mythical status within Stevenson's *oeuvre*, but its originality has also been contested on several fronts. Biographers and scholars have repeatedly claimed that the story was first published in Samoan, as 'O Le Fagu Aitu', in the missionary journal *O le Sulu Samoa*.[47] In fact, the translation that came out in the May to December editions of the *Sulu* was preceded by the English original that appeared in the *New York Herald* and in *Black and White*. Nonetheless, copies of the relevant issues of the Samoan journal have subsequently acquired a greater value than the first English versions, since, as Isobel Strong explained in a letter to an inquirer, primitive printing conditions in Samoa rendered 'O Le Fagu Aitu' a particularly ephemeral text: 'I believe there are no copies extant. It was printed on paper of such particular vileness and flimsiness that we weren't even able to preserve our own set.'[48] The Samoan missionary J. E. Newell found, when he advertised for copies of the periodical shortly after Stevenson's death, that only two sets were forthcoming. He interpreted this reticence as follows: 'Apparently the Samoans who are the happy possessors of the first piece of foreign fiction they ever saw are reluctant to part with it.'[49] This depiction of blithe proprietorship contrasts, of course, with the anxieties produced by possession of the bottle within Stevenson's tale.

The confusion over initial publication reflects the tale's iconic status, as sign of the author's happy creative synthesis with Samoan culture. Newell notes that 'O Le Fagu Aitu' has a special status in Samoan literary history, as the first serial story to become available to a Samoan readership. According to Albert Lee, Newell's correspondent, it was the source of Stevenson's authorial reputation among the Samoans: 'as a result of its publication the natives ever afterwards called Stevenson "Tusitala"—the teller of tales'. In preparing the translation of the tale, Stevenson was able to test and extend his knowledge of the Samoan language. He worked with the missionary Arthur Claxton at drafting of the Samoan text: Claxton recalled that Stevenson 'seemed to enjoy the balancing of rival expressions in the Samoan idiom'.[50] The reminiscences of his tutor, the Reverend S. J. Whitmee, provide a fuller account of the legacies of Stevenson's ventures into Samoan. Referring to another of the author's projects—this time a full composition in Samoan—Whitmee emphasises Stevenson's appreciation of the nuances of the tongue:

> Mr Stevenson wished to write a story in Samoan for the natives, and I suggested that he should bring a portion of his MS. for me to read. This exactly suited him. Those points in grammar and idiom, also the appropriateness of words, about which he was almost fastidious, could be discussed. I found him to be a keen student; and the peculiarities and niceties of the language greatly interested him. He thought the language was wonderful, and quite agreed with me that the Samoans must have descended from a much higher condition of intellectual culture, to possess such a tongue. The extent of the vocabulary, the delicate differences of form and expressive shades of meaning, the wonderful varieties of the pronouns and particles, astonished him.[51]

The history of a mutually productive and affirming exchange between the author and his peripheral literary audience, however, is undermined by alternative accounts of the tale's genesis and reception. In a prefatory note, Stevenson suggests that 'the fact that the tale has been designed and written for a Polynesian audience may lend it some extraneous interest nearer home'. Yet this 'extraneous interest' is clearly ethnographic rather than critical. Stevenson figured his Samoan audience as naively literalist, unable to distinguish between fantasy and history. In a letter to Arthur Conan Doyle, he digressed on the type of reception offered to fiction by a Samoan audience:

> You might perhaps think that, were you to come to Samoa, you might be introduced as the Author of 'The Engineer's Thumb'. Disabuse yourself. They do not know what it is to make up a story. 'The Engineer's Thumb' (God forgive me) was narrated as a piece of actual and factual history. Nay, and more, I who write to you have had the indiscretion to perpetrate a trifling piece of fiction entitled 'The Bottle Imp'. Parties who come up to visit my unpretentious mansion, after having admired the ceilings by Vanderputty and the tapestry by Gobbling, manifest towards the end a certain uneasiness which proves them to be fellows of an infinite delicacy. They may be seen to shrug a brown shoulder, to roll up a speaking eye, and at last the secret bursts from them: 'Where is the bottle?'[52]

Stevenson jests patronisingly about life in a context without connoisseurship. Yet his acknowledgement of the spirit of delicacy that restrains the 'secret' question recognises a connection his Samoan audience has made between the wealth exhibited within Stevenson's colonial mansion and the magical bottle of his fiction. Effectively, the Bottle Imp of the story has been conflated with the story of 'The Bottle Imp'. Stevenson's literary output, the real source of his fortune, is elided with the immoral exchange represented by the fantastical bottle.

Attentiveness to sources has led 'sophisticated', as well as 'naive' readers of 'The Bottle Imp' to interrogate the tale. Where Stevenson credits the source of his story in a deprecating manner—'Any student of that very unliterary product, the English drama of the early part of the century, will here recognise the name and the root idea of a piece once rendered popular by the redoubtable B. Smith' (88)—his critics have suggested that a more substantial literary background informed the writing of 'The Bottle Imp'. In an article in *Modern Language Notes* for January 1910, Joseph Beach traced the authorship of the original plot, first to a romance drama by the misremembered O. Smith, then to a volume entitled 'Popular Tales and Romances of the Northern Nations', published in 1823, and specifically to the tale of 'Das Galgenmännlein', by the Baron de Lamotte-Fouqué. Beach is concerned to emphasize, nonetheless, that the circulation of the tale ceases with Stevenson, who has rendered it all his own: 'In all details of the narrative, Stevenson is his own inimitable self.'[53] However, a more aggressive editorial in the New York *Sun* some years later questioned the originality of the 'Bottle Imp' narrative. This article referred to the same sources, the volume of northern tales and the tale by Lamotte-Fouqué, ironically failing to acknowledge the precedence of Beach's literary researches. The novelty of the editorial lies rather in the insistent pressure it places upon the issue of literary debt. The writer claims that Stevenson's effective plagiarism raises questions regarding 'the canons of artistic conscience, the ethics of appropriation and adaptation, and the equities of ownership'.[54] He is concerned to reclaim the story from its Pacific adaptation to its northern origin. His comments betray that sense of affront which recurs in European responses to Pacific appropriations of European culture, evidencing a comparable slippage between the discourses of aesthetics and economics. The easy shift from references to 'canons of artistic conscience' to questions of 'equities of ownership' suggests that the metropolitan writer, and not just the purportedly naive Samoan, has confused real with fictional coinage.

A literalist reader is in fact constructed by the narration of 'The Bottle Imp', which repeatedly alludes to the non-fictional status of events and characters within the tale. The protagonist, for instance, is introduced under a pseudonym, as though to protect a living citizen from the imputations of fiction: 'There was a man of the island of Hawaii, whom I shall call Keawe; for the truth is, he still lives, and his name must be kept secret' (89). As the story progresses, the narrator continually avoids naming recipients of the bottle, who are implicated in its cycle of immoral gain: '(I must not tell his name)'; 'the name of a man, which, again, I had better not repeat.' (107) It appears that those who have had dealings with the bottle have magically attained, in addition to wished-for wealth, a historical, rather than fictional, status.

The pseudonym Stevenson chooses for his protagonist is 'Keawe', a name resonant within Hawaiian heroic tradition. The story displays the hallmarks of oral composition. Sentences are rhythmically constructed, with the aggregative, repetitive, syntactically inverted format of oral discourse: 'This is a fine town, with a fine harbour, and rich people uncountable; and in particular, there is one hill which is covered with palaces.' Similes invoke a

Pacific frame of reference: 'Keawe could see him as you see a fish in a pool upon the reef.' (89) Yet Keawe is also a product of the acquired culture of literacy: 'he could read and write like a schoolmaster'. A hero between oral and literate traditions, he represents the cultural moment at which his story is produced in the Pacific. He is a traveller between cultures, a sailor who, at the beginning of the tale, is on furlough in San Francisco. He journeys from California back to Hawaii and later between Polynesian islands, following the trajectory of Stevenson's own Pacific travels. The tale that critics have attempted to reclaim to northern European origins is shaped in both its form and content by the historical and geographical context of its production.

Keawe is strolling through the town of San Francisco, enjoying a tourist's taste of a foreign culture, when he espies a luxurious mansion, whose owner looks despondently from the window. The man invites Keawe into his home, and shows him the bottle which is the source of his enviable fortune. An imp dwells within the bottle, who will grant all its owner's wishes. If he or she dies with it in their possession, however, they are damned. The bottle can be sold, but only for less than its purchasing price; otherwise, it cannot be disposed of. The educated Keawe is sceptical of the man's claims, and is invited to put them to the test. He is thus tricked into purchasing the bottle. He attempts to sell it at a profit to a merchant of exotic items, whose wares include 'shells from the wild islands, old heathen deities, old coined money, pictures from China and Japan, and all manner of things that sailors bring in their sea-chests'. (94) The bottle cannot, of course, be assimilated upon advantageous terms among those cultural artefacts—themselves the relics of Pacific trade's uneven exchange. So Keawe returns to Hawaii with the imp still in his possession. The Polynesian has acquired a metropolitan article whose magical powers are not simply a figment of naive imagination.

'The Bottle Imp' is in part a commentary on the representation of the gullible native, duped and over-impressed by foreign material culture, familiar from the early literature of the Pacific, and even from certain passages in Stevenson's own Pacific travel account. In Hawaii, Keawe uses the bottle to create a house furnished with remarkable objects:

> As for the house, it was three stories high, with great chambers and broad balconies on each. The windows were of glass, so excellent that it was as clear as water and as bright as day. All manner of furniture adorned the chambers. Pictures hung upon the wall in golden frames—pictures of ships, and men fighting, and of the most beautiful women and singular places; nowhere in the world are there pictures of so bright a colour as those Keawe

found hanging in his house. As for the knick-knacks, they were extraordinary fine: chiming clocks and musical boxes, little men with nodding heads, books filled with pictures, weapons of price from all quarters of the world, and the most elegant puzzles to entertain the leisure of a solitary man. And as no one would care to live in such chambers, only to walk through and view them, the balconies were made so broad that a whole town might have lived upon them in delight. (98)

The Pacific islander is depicted here, no longer as ethnographic object, but as the curator of a museum stocked with the artefacts of other cultures. Fascination with items of imported manufacture has graduated to connoisseurship. But such magnificence is for display rather than use, and the reality of Keawe's domestic existence shifts to the margins (or rather the balconies). This house recalls the many-windowed 'eidolon' on the Kona coast, which Stevenson described in *In the South Seas*. Where that mansion was depicted as epitomising a superficial display of foreign style that proved empty within, Keawe's rooms are replete with valuable acquisitions. Stevenson had felt that his own travels in Hawaii were overshadowed by the precedent of the deified Cook.[55] In 'The Bottle Imp', Keawe is told of the ways in which the bottle has shaped the course of European history: 'Napoleon had this bottle, and by it he grew to be king of the world; but he sold it at the last and fell. Captain Cook had this bottle, and by it he found his way to so many islands; but he, too, sold it, and was slain upon Hawaii.' (91) In this reconciliation of myth with history, Cook's achievement becomes devil-work: he is less an overreacher than a fortunate recipient of magical assistance.

If the bottle embodies the ambivalent transactions of Western capitalism, it provides a reflection of other relationships of exchange. Like the reciprocal contract of Pacific gift-giving, it binds recipients even as it endows them. And like the object of tabu, it combines blessings with dangerous powers. The bottle represents a mixed blessing for the narrative itself. It precipitates action, creating scenarios of accelerated change, but in its offer of instant gratification, fails to satisfy that desire for the perpetuation of desire that motivates the act of storytelling. Instead, that particular desire is accommodated by a romantic plot which is interwoven with, and eventually transcends, those complex economic relationships motivating the tale of the bottle. Keawe falls in love with a beautiful woman named Kokua. Like Uma in 'The Beach of Falesá', Kokua is initially perceived voyeuristically, performing a reverse strip-tease: 'he was aware of a woman bathing at the edge of the sea; and she seemed a well-grown girl, but he thought no more of it. Then he saw her white shift flutter as she put it on, and then her red holoku, and she was all freshened with the bath, and her eyes shone and were kind.' (101) After wooing Kokua, Keawe notices that he is in the first stage of leprous infection. He decides to seek out the bottle once again, in order to heal himself, and become a fit husband. He travels to Honolulu, where he traces the bottle to its current owner, following a trail of duplicated luxury: '"No doubt I am upon the track," thought Keawe. "These new clothes and carriages are all the gifts of the little imp, and these glad faces are the faces of men who have taken their profit and got, rid of the accursed thing in safety. When I see pale cheeks and hear sighing, I shall know that I am near the bottle."' (107–8) The value of the bottle has depreciated to a single cent. It lies in the possession of a man whose damnation is signalled by excessive whiteness: he is 'white as a corpse'. Keawe purchases it. believing that further exchange has been precluded; willingly condemning himself in order to save his love for Kokua. The bottle thus serves as agent, not of material gain, but of sacrifice, and so begins to be transformed from a symbol of acquisitiveness into a touchstone of genuine emotion.

Kokua's qualities of humanity and intelligence are, like Uma's, quick to emerge. Her name signifies helper and comforter in Hawaiian.[56] Yet she is also the modern, literate Pacific islander: 'I was educated in a school in Honolulu; I am no common girl.' (112) Once she becomes aware of Keawe's plight, her education enables her to find a way of exploiting those very laws of circulation that seem to entrap him: '"What is this you say about a cent? But all the world is not America ... Come, Keawe, let us go to the French islands; let us go to Tahiti, as fast as ships can bear us. There we have four centimes, three centimes, two centimes, one centime; four possible sales to come and go; and two of us to push the bargain."' Even from within the map of empire, Kokua is aware, exploitation can be delegated. The couple travel to Tahiti, equipped with costumes and props, and put on a calculated performance. Kokua packs 'the richest of their clothes and the bravest of the knick-knacks in the house. "For", said she, "we must seem to be rich folks, or who would believe in the bottle?"' (113) Their display is an investment in advertising, designed to create a market for their product. Yet they are regarded with suspicion, and fail to dispose of the bottle.

They resort, in turn, to self-sacrifice. Kokua secretly buys the bottle back from her husband, using as her agent a poor old man. Freed from the burden of damnation, Keawe succumbs to drunkenness. His companion in his lapse is a beachcomber: 'Now there was an old brutal Haole drinking with

him, one that had been a boatswain of a whaler—a runaway, a digger in gold
mines, a convict in prisons. He had a low mind and a foul mouth; he loved
to drink and see others drunken; and he pressed the glass upon Keawe.' (120)
The Haole (white man) encourages Keawe to suspect his wife of infidelity. In
an attempt to prove her false, Keawe spies on Kokua, and finds her alone, not
with a man, but with the feminine bottle, 'milk-white ..., with a round belly
and a long neck', now an object of virtue, the touchstone of her loyalty. He
employs the beachcomber to buy the bottle back for him. However, the man
subsequently refuses to return the bottle to Keawe, claiming '"I reckon I'm
going anyway ... and this bottle's the best thing to go with I've struck yet."'
(124) In the beachcomber, the bottle locates its appropriate owner: a figure
inhabiting the space between Western and Pacific systems of exchange; the
unredeemed subject of the narrative.

'THE ISLE OF VOICES': COINED PHRASES

In 'The Isle of Voices', Hawaiian materialism is once again depicted as
sourced in magic. This is a magician's nephew story, whose protagonist is
Keola, son-in-law of the wizard Kalamake. Kalamake has legendary stature:
'It was rumoured that he had the art or the gift of the old heroes. Men had
seen him at night upon the mountains, stepping from one cliff to the next;
they had seen him walking in the high forest, and his head and shoulders
were above the trees.' (127) He is represented as a figure deeply enshrined
within Hawaiian oral tradition: '"Blind as Kalamake that can see across
tomorrow" was a byword in the islands' (127); '"Bright as Kalamake's
dollars" was another saying in the Eight Isles' (128). His powers, however,
resemble those of the white settler in Hawaii rather than those of a
Polynesian. He is a figure of civic authority and financial influence: 'no man
was more consulted in all the Kingdom of Hawaii. Prudent people bought,
sold and married, and laid out their lives by his counsels.' His enemies suffer
a fate comparable to the genocide that followed European contact with
Pacific societies: 'of his enemies, some had dwindled in sickness by virtue of
his incantations, and some had been spirited away, the life and the clay both,
so that folk looked in vain for so much as a bone of their bodies.' His house
is built 'in the European style' (129), and he hides his wealth in a locked
writing desk 'under the print of Kamehameha the fifth, and a portrait of
Queen Victoria with her crown' (128). He is, indeed, 'more white to look
upon than any foreigner'. (127)

Keola is fascinated by Kalamake's wealth, which materialises without
apparent labour: 'he neither sold, nor planted, nor took hire—only now and

then for his societies—and there was no source conceivable for so much silver coin'. As the internal rhyme here betrays, sorcery is the source of this mysterious fortune. Kalamake eventually takes Keola into his confidence. He requires his son-in-law's assistance in a magical ritual: a process of minting. Keola is transported on a woven mat front the high Hawaiian island of Molokai to a low Pacific atoll. Here he is instructed to burn a fire of leaves upon the mat's surface, while Kalamake gathers shells upon the beach. These transform to coins at the wizard's touch. As the flame expires, he jumps back upon the mat, and the pair return home, laden with money. This abundant production in a reduced and alien landscape perhaps recalls Stevenson's own account of his stay on the barren atoll of Fakarava, a setting which yielded the author a wealth of fantastical narratives. In the transformation of factual into fictional atoll landscape, the location of subject matter becomes an act of false coinage.

Kalamake's magic is, like that of the bottle imp, the apotheosis of cargo cult: the material object proves self-replicating. Like Keawe, Keola functions as a Pacific empiricist, submitting to trial a powerful system of circulation. But where Keawe had the heroic capacity to transform the significance of the bottle, Keola is an anti-hero, in the mould of the sorcerer's apprentice. His usurpation of power reflects merely a desire to occupy the position of his master, while maintaining an iniquitous structure of production. Keola falls under the misapprehension that his father-in-law's authority is transferable, and can be used to serve himself-a delusion he shares with Hawaiians who seek a stake in the power of government. His wife Lehua recalls the fates of apparently influential figures within the Hawaiian administration, which illustrate the consequences of dissent: '"Think of this person and that person; think of Hua, who was a noble of the House of Representatives, and went to Honolulu every year; and not a bone or a hair of him was found. Remember Kamau, and how he wasted to a thread, so that his wife lifted him with one hand."' (134) In this parable of post-contact Hawaii, an imported mode of civil government is shown to be accompanied by a legacy of physical decline. The Oedipal interactions of the father-in-law Kalamake and the son-in-law Keola are paradigmatic of colonial relations. The son is offered a partial entry into power, but in attempting to usurp authority provokes the castrating wrath of the father. Kalamake pretends to acquiesce to Keola's demand for a share of his power, and invites him on a sea voyage that quickly becomes a nightmare. Initially Kalamake affects phallic equality: 'the two sat in the stern and smoked cigars' (135), but then, in a horrific tumescence, the wizard reveals his authoritative stature, swelling to giant-size: 'behold-as he drew his finger from the ring, the finger stuck and the ring was burst' (136), and mocking Keola's desire to appropriate the phallus: '"are you sure you would not rather have a flute?"' He looms away across the ocean, and at once a trading vessel of similar proportions appears, figuring the interchangeability of the wizard's castrating power and that of capitalist venture.

Keola is rescued, and joins the boat's crew. He absconds at an atoll which turns out to be that same 'isle of voices' where the wizard gathers his coins. Keola joins a cannibalistic nomadic tribe whose members are making their annual sojourn upon the island. On his initial trip to the atoll, invisible and inviolable, he had observed the tribe with the immunity of an ethnographic field-worker, recording novel practices: '"they are not very particular about dress in this part of the country"'; '"these are strange manners."' (131) Now, however, visiting the island as flesh rather than spirit, he becomes aware that he is under physical threat. The atoll landscape is the space of the Pacific other: the reverse face of that Westernised Polynesia which is most successfully represented by Hawaiian civil society. The tribe's cannibalism renders its members the objects of a fearful fascination to Keola, the Hawaiian citizen. They belong to the mythical elsewhere of travellers' tales: 'He had heard tell of eaters of men in the South islands, and the thing had always been a fear to him; and here it was knocking at his door. He had heard besides, by travellers, of their practices.' (145) In fact the members of the tribe are themselves also model colonial subjects, whose annual reversion to traditional practices upon the atoll constitutes a return of the repressed:

> 'to tell you the truth, my people are eaters of men; but this they keep secret. And the reason they will kill you before we leave is because in our island ships come, and Donat-Kimiran comes and talks for the French, and there is a white trader there in a house with a verandah, and a catechist. Oh, that is a fine place indeed! The trader has barrels filled with flour; and a French warship once came in the lagoon and gave everybody wine and biscuit.'

The Eucharist of empire is only the public face of cannibalistic consumption—its 'civil' guise: '[Keola] judged they were too civil to be wholesome'. (142)

As anti-hero, Keola remains, unlike the protagonists of 'The Beach of Falesā' and 'The Bottle Imp', unredeemed by a unique love relationship. He is instead strategically assisted by two wives during the course of the story. His second wife, chosen for him by the tribe, alerts him to his physical danger. He departs for the ocean beach of the atoll, the fleshless realm of voice, where he dwells plagued by the whisperings of the invisible wizards. The tribe represents corporeal threat, disguised behind an accomplished discursive façade: 'The people of the tribe were very civil, as their way was. They were elegant speakers, and they made beautiful poetry, and jested at meals, so that a missionary must have died laughing. It was little enough that Keola cared for their fine ways; all he saw was the white teeth shining in their months—' (145) The other side of the atoll is, by contrast, a realm of disembodied tongues: 'All tongues of the earth were spoken there: the French, the Dutch, the Russian, the Tamil, the Chinese. Bodiless voices called to and fro; unseen hands poured sand upon the flames.' (146) For Keola, the Pacific subject, this intangibility represents the ungraspable power of global economics, to be explained as magical production, according to a logic of cargo cult: '"And to think how they have fooled me with their talk of mints," says he, "and that money was made there, when it is clear that all the new coin in all the world is gathered on these sands."' (147) The divided geography of the atoll landscape maps the split subjectivity of the Pacific anti-hero: on the one side consumed by a heritage of otherness, with its discourses of primitivity, cannibalism and savagery, and, on the other, absorbed within a system of economic circulation whose power and profit lie in foreign hands. In a final battle, wizards and tribe are left to their mutual destruction: the binary oppositions of flesh and spirit, savage and civilised, lock in annihilating contest.

Keola is rescued by his first wife, Lehua, who returns him to Molokai on the magic mat. Like 'The Beach of Falesā', 'The Isle of Voices' concludes with overt recantation. Keola consults the atlas and reassures himself that the wizard Kalamake has been safely relegated to a distant space: 'Keola knew by this time where that island was—and that is to say, in the Low or Dangerous Archipelago. So they fetched the atlas and looked upon the distance in the map, and by what they could make of it, it seemed a long way for an old gentleman to walk.' (150) He finds his appetite unaffected by recollections of his brush with cannibalism: 'he was mighty pleased to be home again in Molokai and sit down beside a bowl of poi—for ... there was none in the Isle of Voices.' (149–50) The couple consult the local missionary, who admits, punningly, that he 'could make neither head nor tail' of the magical coinage. He willingly implicates his own endeavours, nonetheless, in the tainted transaction of its production, advising Keola 'to give some of it to the lepers and some of it to the missionary fund' as absolution. At the same time, he betrays the pair to the Hawaiian civil authorities, on the contradictory conviction that the money he has accepted is counterfeit: 'he warned the police at Honolulu that, by all he could make out, Kalamake and Keola had been coining false money, and it would not be amiss to watch them'. The coins thus retain their duplicitous status. Ambiguous signifiers, both true and false, valuable donation and worthless forgery, they expose the missionary's divided colonial loyalties.

NOTES

1. Robert Louis Stevenson, Autograph Manuscript of Imaginary Dispatches [1885], Beinecke Library, ms 5957.

2. Letter to Will H. Low, 15 January [1894], Bradford A. Booth and Finest Mehew (eds.), *The Letters of Robert Louis Stevenson*, New Haven: Yale University Press, 1995, vol. VIII, p. 235.

3. Will H. Low, *Concerning a Painting of Robert Louis Stevenson*, Bronxville, New York: Bronx Valley Press, 1924.

4. Robert Louis Stevenson, 'The Barbizon Free-Trading Company, unlimited', typescript, 3 pp., Beinecke Library, ms 6002.

5. George L. McKay, *A Stevenson Library Catalogue of a collection of writings by and about Robert Louis Stevenson formed by Edwin J. Beinecke*, New Haven: Yale University Press, 1961, vol. V, p. 1729.

6. Stevenson pays tribute to his paternal heritage in *Records of a Family of Engineers*, London: William Heinemann, 1924.

7. These Were *The Wrong Box* (1889), *The Wrecker* (1892), and *The Ebb-Tide* (1884). The pair had been involved in 'literary' collaboration since Osbourne's childhood. James D. Hart, *The Private Press Ventures of Samuel Lloyd Osbourne and R. L. S.*, Los Angeles: Book Club of California, 1966.

8. 'It's a machine, you know; don't expect aught else: a machine, and a police machine.' Letter to Henry James [?25 May 1892], Booth and Mehew (eds.), *Letters*, vol. VII, p. 292.

9. Robert Louis Stevenson and Lloyd Osbourne, *The Wrecker*, London: Cassell and Company, 1893, p. 17. Subsequent references are to this edition.

10. Letter to Burlingame, 11 March [1890], Booth and Mehew (eds.), *Letters*, vol. VI, p. 375.

11. Letter to Lloyd Osbourne, [5 November 1890], ibid., vol. VII, p. 35; compare Colvin to Baxter, 26 May 1893, Beinecke Library, ms 4247.

12. Letter to Charles Baxter, [30 March 1892], Booth and Mehew (eds.), *Letters*, vol. VII, p. 258.

13. William Diapea, *Cannibal Jack*, London: Faber and Gwyer, 1928, pp. 232–3.

14. Letter to Sidney Colvin, [3] November 1890, Booth and Mehew (eds.), *Letters*, vol. VII, p. 20.

15. Oscar Wilde to Robert Ross, 6 April 1897, Rupert Hart Davis (ed.), *Selected Letters of Oscar Wilde*, Oxford University Press, 1979, p. 24.

16. Kenneth Graham, *English Criticism of the Novel, 1865–1900*, Oxford: Clarendon Press, 1965, pp. 4–5.

17. Peter Keating, *The Haunted Study: a social history of the English novel, 1875–1914*, London: Fontana, 1989, pp. 11–12.

18. Letter to A. Trevor Haddon, 5 July 1883, Booth and Mehew (eds.), *Letters*, vol. IV, pp. 140–1.

19. Christopher Morley, 'Notes on a Painting', reprinted from the *New York Evening Post*, 18 October 1923, in Low, *Concerning a Painting*, p. 7.

20. Letter to Lloyd Osbourne, 29 September 1890, Booth and Mehew (eds.), *Letters*, vol. VII, p. 9.

21. Letter to Robert Alan Mowbray Stevenson, [*c.* g September 1894], ibid., vol. VIII, p. 364.

22. Letter to Sidney Colvin, 16 May 1893; compare letter to Colvin, 27 May–18 June 1893; ibid., vol. VIII, pp. 68; 87–94.

23. Review in the *Speaker*, 29 September 1894, quoted in Paul Maixner (ed.), *Robert Louis Stevenson: the critical heritage*, London: Routledge, 1981, p. 450.

24. Alastair Fowler, 'Parable of Adventure: the debatable novels of Robert Louis Stevenson', in Ian Campbell (ed.), *Nineteenth-Century Scottish Fiction: critical essays*, Manchester: Carcanet, 1979, p. 116.

25. Robert Louis Stevenson, 'The Ebb-Tide', in *Dr. Jekyll and Mr. Hyde and other stories*, London: Penguin, 1987, pp. 188–9. All subsequent references are to this text.

26. T. Walter Herbert, *Marquesan Encounters*, Cambridge, Mass.: Harvard University Press, 1980, p. 155.

27. Herman Melville, *Omoo*, New York: Library of America, 1982, pp. 334, 336, 337.

28. Robert Hillier, *The South Seas Fiction of Robert Louis Stevenson*, New York: Peter Lang, 1989, p. 137.

29. Stevenson, 'Missions in the South Seas', Sydney: State Library of N.S.W., AS25/19, p. 1.

30. Ibid., p, 4.

31. H.E. Maude, *Of Islands and Men*, Oxford University Press, 1968, p. 135.

32. Barry Menikoff, *Robert Louis Stevenson and 'The Beach of Falesá'*, Edinburgh University Press, 1984, p. 59.

33. Ibid., pp. 72, 64–5.

34. Graham Balfour, 'A South Sea Trader', *Macmillan's* (November 1896), p. 67.

35. Letter to Charles Baxter, 11 August 1892, Booth and Mehew (eds.), *Letters*, vol. VII, p. 350.

36. Letter to Sidney Colvin, 28 September 1891, ibid., p. 161.

37. Stevenson, *Island Nights' Entertainments*, London: Hogarth Press, 1987, p. 3. Subsequent references are to this edition.

38. Otto von Kotzebue, *A New Voyage Round the World in the Years 1823, 24, 25, and 26*, London: Colburn and Bentley, 1830, vol. I, pp. 282–3.

39. Stephen Heath, 'Psychopathic sexualis': Stevenson's *Strange Case*, in *Futures for English* (ed. Colin MacCabe), Manchester University Press, 1988, explores the nuances of the term 'case' in Stevenson's *Strange Case of Dr Jekyll and Mr Hyde*. Recent critics have focused on the psychology of the narrator in attempting to recuperate 'The Beach of Falesá' for modernity and post-modernity. Menikoff represents Wiltshire's narrative as a failed psychoanalytic session: 'This, of course, is the underlying quest of Wiltshire throughout the novel—to discover meaning and order, and to find some vindication for his own life. That he cannot is one of the basic ironies of the story', while Lisa St Aubin de Terán claims that: 'Stevenson is quick to show that he is offering us an adventure story which is the mask for a case study in neurosis.' Case is, in a practical sense, Wiltshire's object of study. Menikoff, *Robert Louis Stevenson and 'The Beach of Falesá'*, p. 69; Lisa St Aubin de Terán, introduction to *Island Nights' Entertainments*, p. ii.

306   Vanessa Smith

40. Walter J. Ong, *Orality and Literacy: the technologizing of the word*, London: Methuen, 1982, pp. 149–50, 154.

41. Menikoff, *Robert Louis Stevenson and 'The Beach of Falesā'*, p. 58.

42. Stevenson, *In the South Seas*, p. 267; compare Menikoff, *Robert Louis Stevenson and 'The Beach of Falesā'*, p. 85.

43. Menikoff, Robert. *Louis Stevenson and 'The Beach of Falesā'*, pp. 83–90.

44. According to Stevenson's Samoan vocabulary lists, *Fa'alototoga*, or 'to have the heart of a Tongan' means 'to be without love, greedy, revengeful'.

45. Homi Bhabha, 'Of Mimicry and Man', *The Location of Culture*, London: Routledge, 1994, p. 89.

46. The problem of the half-caste daughter is playfully developed in a manuscript of an unpublished drama written at Vailima. In this fragment, which gestures towards a reversal of the typical scenario of South Seas seduction, a sailor, Henderson, turns up in Samoa to claim the adopted baby daughter of his wealthy uncle. The girl, Fanua, who has reached an attractive puberty, is repelled by the idea of removing to England, where women are forced to wear stays and spend their time idly making calls. She is only convinced of the appeal of the idea once Henderson has presented himself as a suitor, with 'no use for corsets.' Play (untitled). Portion. New Haven, Beinecke Library, ms 6722, p. 8.

47. For instance Balfour, *The Life of Robert Louis Stevenson*, vol. II, p. 130; Joseph Beach, 'The Sources of Stevenson's "Bottle Imp"', *Modern Language Notes* 25 (1910), p. 12.

48. Quoted in Albert Lee, '"Black and White" and "O Le Sulu Samoa"', *Black and While*, 6 February 1897, p. 175.

49. Ibid. Original ms in Beinecke Library.

50. Revd A.E. Claxton, 'Stevenson as I Knew Him in Samoa', in Rosaline Masson (ed.), *I Can Remember Robert Louis Stevenson*, Edinburgh: W. and R. Chambers, 1922, p. 249; reprinted from *Chambers's Journal* (October 1922).

51. Revd S.J. Whitmee, 'Tusitala: A New Reminiscence of R.L.S.', in Masson (ed.), *I Can Remember Robert Louis Stevenson*, p. 232.

52. Letter to Arthur Conan Doyle, 23 August 1893, Booth and Mehew (eds.), *Letters*, vol. VIII, p. 155; compare Beach, 'The Sources of Stevenson's "Bottle Imp"', p. 12; H. J. Moors, *With Stevenson in Samoa*, London: T. Fisher Unwin, 1911, p. 97.

53. Beach, 'The Sources of Stevenson's "Bottle Imp"', p. 17.

54. The editorial is summarised and quoted under the title 'Stevenson's Borrowed Plot' in *The Literary Digest*, 18 July 1914, pp. 105–6.

55. *In the South Seas*, pp. 191, 183.

56. Mary Kawena Pukui and Samuel H. Elbert (eds.), *Hawaiian-English Dictionary*, Honolulu: University of Hawaii Press, 1957.

Chronology

1850	Robert Louis Stevenson is born November 13 in Edinburgh, Scotland to Thomas and Margaret Isabella Balfour Stevenson.
1862	Travels with his parents to Europe.
1867	Begins to study engineering at Edinburgh University.
1871	Abandons engineering to study law.
1873	Goes to Suffolk to stay with cousins after a bout of ill health and arguments with his father over his agnosticism; meets Frances Sitwell; becomes friends with Sidney Colvin; travels to France after experiencing more health problems;
1874	returns to Edinburgh and resumes study of law; contributes to *Cornhill Magazine*.
1875	Is called to the Bar but does not practice; contributes to *Vanity Fair*; meets W.E. Henley; joins his cousin, Bob Stevenson, in France at the artists' colony at Barbizon, Fontainebleau.
1876	Canoes the canals of northern France, a trip which is later recounted in *An Inland Voyage*; meets Fanny Osbourne, an American woman who is married with two children.
1878	Fanny returns to her husband in California and initiates divorce proceedings; publication of *An Inland Voyage* and *Edinburgh: Picturesque Notes*.

1879	*Travels with a Donkey* is published; spends time in England, Scotland, and France; starts on his way to join Fanny in the United States.
1880	Marries Fanny in San Francisco; publishes *Deacon Brodie*, a play written in collaboration with W.E. Henley; Stevenson and his wife return to Scotland.
1881	Completes *Treasure Island*, which is serialized in *Young Folks*; publishes *Virginibus Puerisque*.
1882	Moves with Fanny to Hyères, France; publishes *Familiar Studies of Men and Books* and *New Arabian Nights*.
1883	Publication of *Treasure Island* and *The Silverado Squatters*.
1884	Suffers ill health throughout winter and spring; the couple moves to England, to Bournemouth, which will remain their home until 1887; publishes two collaborations with W.E. Henley: *Austin Guinea* and *Beau Austin*; also publishes "A Humble Remonstrance" in response to Henry James' "The Art of Fiction."
1885	Receives Henry James at Bournemouth; publishes *A Child's Garden of Verses*, *Prince Otto*, and *More New Arabian Nights*, as well as *The Dynamiter* (in collaboration with Fanny) and *Macaire* (in collaboration with W.E. Henley).
1886	Publishes *The Strange Case of Dr. Jekyll and Mr. Hyde*, Stevenson's first big success, and *Kidnapped*.
1887	Thomas Stevenson, Robert's father, dies in May; journeys to America with his mother, wife, and stepson Lloyd; stays in Saranac in the Adirondack Mountains; publishes *The Merry Men and Other Tales and Fables*, *Underwoods*, *Memories and Portraits*, and *A Memoir of Fleeming Jenkin*.
1888	Stevenson is commissioned to produce a series of travel sketches on the South Seas for newspapers; sails with family on the *Casco* to the Marquesas, Paumotus, Tahiti, and Hawaii; publishes *The Black Arrow*.
1889	Mother returns to Scotland; Stevenson travels with Fanny and Lloyd from Honolulu to Samoa; starts work on *A Footnote to History*.
1890	Buys estate on the island of Upolu in Samoa; Robert's ill health leads the family to the conclusion that he will never be able to leave the tropics.

1891   Publishes "The Bottle Imp" serially, both in English and Samoan.

1892   British High Commissioner for the Western Pacific issues *A Regulation for the Maintenance of Peace and Good Order in Samoa*, an attempt to put a stop to Stevenson's activities in Samoan politics and affairs.

1893   "The Isle of Voices" appears in the *National Observer*; war breaks out in Samoa; publishes *Island Nights' Entertainments* and *Catriona*; begins to publish *The Ebb-Tide* serially.

1894   Followers of Mataafa, whom Stevenson had supported during the war, build "The Road of Loving Hearts" to thank Stevenson for aiding their cause; publishes *The Ebb-Tide*; on December 3, Stevenson dies of cerebral hemorrhage.

Contributors

HAROLD BLOOM is Sterling Professor of the Humanities at Yale University. He is the author of over 20 books, including *Shelley's Mythmaking* (1959), *The Visionary Company* (1961), *Blake's Apocalypse* (1963), *Yeats* (1970), *A Map of Misreading* (1975), *Kabbalah and Criticism* (1975), *Agon: Toward a Theory of Revisionism* (1982), *The American Religion* (1992), *The Western Canon* (1994), and *Omens of Millennium: The Gnosis of Angels, Dreams, and Resurrection* (1996). *The Anxiety of Influence* (1973) sets forth Professor Bloom's provocative theory of the literary relationships between the great writers and their predecessors. His most recent books include *Shakespeare: The Invention of the Human* (1998), a 1998 National Book Award finalist, *How to Read and Why* (2000), *Genius: A Mosaic of One Hundred Exemplary Creative Minds* (2002), and *Hamlet: Poem Unlimited* (2003). In 1999, Professor Bloom received the prestigious American Academy of Arts and Letters Gold Medal for Criticism, and in 2002 he received the Catalonia International Prize.

G.K. CHESTERTON (1874–1936), renowned British man of letters, wrote poetry, novels, criticism and essays. Among his books are studies of Charles Dickens, Robert Browning, St. Thomas Aquinas, Geoffrey Chaucer, and William Cobbett.

LESLIE FIEDLER has taught at the State University of New York, Buffalo. His many books include *Love and Death in the American Novel, Waiting for the End, What Was Literature?* and *Tyranny of the Normal*.

ROBERT KIELY is Professor of English at Harvard University. He is the author of *The Romantic Novel in England, Beyond Egotism: The Fiction of James Joyce, Virginia Woolf, and D.H. Lawrence*, and a memoir entitled *Still Learning: Spiritual Sketches from a Professor's Life*.

DOUGLAS GIFFORD teaches at the University of Glasgow. He is the author of *James Hogg: A Critical Study* and editor of the *History of Scottish Literature in the Nineteenth Century*.

K.G. SIMPSON is Lecturer in English at Strathclyde University and has published work on Tobias Smollett, Robert Burns, Laurence Sterne, and Robert Louis Stevenson.

WILLIAM VEEDER is Professor of English at the University of Chicago. He is the author of *Mary Shelley and* Frankenstein: *The Fate of Androgyny*, and *Henry James, the Lessons of the Master: Popular Fiction and Personal Style in the Nineteenth Century*.

GEORGE DEKKER is Joseph S. Atha Professor in Humanities at Stanford University. His works include *The American Historical Romance, James Fenimore Cooper: The Novelist*, and *Sailing After Knowledge: The Cantos of Ezra Pound*.

STEPHEN ARATA is Associate Professor of English at the University of Virginia. He has edited William Morris's *News From Nowhere* and has written articles on Joseph Conrad, Oscar Wilde, and Walter Scott.

ALAN SANDISON is Emeritus Professor of English at the University of New England. He is the author of *The Wheel of Empire*.

JOHN HOLLANDER, poet, editor, and critic, teaches English at Yale University. He is the author of *The Figure of Echo, Melodious Guile, The Untuning of the Sky*, and many collections of poetry, including, most recently, *Figurehead* and *Picture Window*.

VANESSA SMITH is a Research Fellow in the English Department at University of Sydney. She is co-editor of *Exploration and Exchange: a South Seas Anthology, 1680–1900* and also of *Islands in History and Representation*.

Bibliography

Arata, Stephen D. *Fictions of Loss in the Victorian Fin de Siecle*. Cambridge: Cambridge University Press, 1966.

Balfour, Graham. *The Life of Robert Louis Stevenson*. London: Methuen, 1915.

Buckton, Oliver. "Reanimating Stevenson's Corpus." *Nineteenth-Century Literature* 55 (June 2000): 22–58.

Butts, Dennis. *R.L. Stevenson*. London: Bodley Head, 1966

Calder, Jenni. *RLS: A Life Study*. London: Hamish Hamilton, 1980.

———, ed. *The Robert Louis Stevenson Companion*. Edinburgh: Paul Harris, 1980.

———, ed. *Stevenson and Victorian Scotland*. Edinburgh: Edinburgh University Press, 1981

Chesterton, G.K. *Robert Louis Stevenson*. London: Hodder and Stoughton, 1927.

Clemens, Valdine. *The Return of the Repressed: Gothic Horror from* The Castle of Otranto *to* Alien. New York: New York University Press, 1999.

Daiches, David. *Robert Louis Stevenson*. Norfolk, CT: New Directions, 1947.

———. *Robert Louis Stevenson and His World*. London: Thames and Hudson, 1973.

———. *Stevenson and the Art of Fiction*. New York: Privately printed, 1951.

Edmond, Rod. *Representing the South Pacific: Colonial Discourse from Cooke to Gauguin*. New York: Cambridge University Press, 1999.

Egan, Joseph J. "Dark in the Poet's Corner: Stevenson's 'A Lodging for the Night.'" *Studies in Short Fiction* 7 (1970): 402–8.

————. "'Markheim': A Drama of Moral Psychology." *Nineteenth-Century Fiction* 20 (1966): 377–84.

Eigner, Edwin. *Robert Louis Stevenson and Romantic Tradition*. Princeton: Princeton University Press, 1966.

Furnas, J.C. *Voyage to Windward: The Life of Robert Louis Stevenson*. New York: William Sloane Assoc., 1951.

Gates, Barbara T. *Victorian Suicide: Mad Crimes and Sad Histories*. Princeton: Princeton University Press, 1988.

Goh, Robbie. "Textual Hyde and Seek: 'Gentility,' Narrative Play, and Prescription in Stevenson's *Dr. Jekyll and Mr. Hyde*." *Journal of Narrative Theory* 29 (1999): 158–83.

Good, Graham. "Rereading Robert Louis Stevenson." *Dalhousie Review* 62 (1982): 44–59.

Gosse, Edmund. *Robert Louis Stevenson: His Work and Personality*. London: Hodder and Stoughton, 1924.

Gray, William. "Stevenson's 'Auld Alliance': France, Art Theory, and the Breath of Money in *The Wrecker*." *Scottish Studies Review* 3 (2002): 54–65.

Hammond, J.R. *A Robert Louis Stevenson Companion*. New York: Macmillan, 1984.

Hart, James A. *Robert Louis Stevenson: From Scotland to Silverado*. Cambridge: Harvard University Press, 1966.

Heath, Stephen. "Psychopathia Sexualis: Stevenson's Strange Case." *Critical Quarterly* 28 (1986): 93–108.

Hellman, George S. *The True Stevenson: A Study in Clarification*. Boston: Little, Brown, 1925.

Hennessy, James Pope. *Robert Louis Stevenson*. London: Jonathan Cape, 1974.

Herdman, John. *The Double in Nineteenth-Century Fiction*. Basingstoke: Macmillan, 1990.

Hillier, Robert Irwin. *The South Seas Fiction of Robert Louis Stevenson*. New York: Peter Lang, 1989.

Hollander, John. *The Work of Poetry*. New York: Columbia University Press, 1997.

Johnstone, Aruthur. *Recollections of Robert Louis Stevenson in the Pacific*. London: Chatto and Windus, 1905.

Kiely, Robert. *Robert Louis Stevenson and the Fiction of Adventure*. Cambridge: Harvard University Press, 1964.

Lascelles, Mary. *The Story-Teller Retrieves the Past*. Oxford: Oxford University Press, 1980.

Linehan, Katherine Bailey. "Taking Up With Kanakas: Stevenson's Complex Social Criticism in 'The Beach of Falesā.'" *English Literature in Transition 1880–1920* 33 (1990): 407–22.

Mackay, Margaret. *The Violent Friend: The Story of Mrs. Robert Louis Stevenson*. Garden City, New York: Doubleday, 1968.

Maixner, Paul, ed. *Robert Louis Stevenson: The Critical Heritage*. London: Routledge and Kegan Paul, 1981.

McGaw, Martha Mary. *Stevenson in Hawaii*. Honolulu: University of Hawaii Press, 1950.

Miller, Karl. *Doubles: Studies in Literary History*. Oxford: Oxford University Press, 1985.

Nabokov, Vladimir. "The Strange Case of Dr. Jekyll and Mr. Hyde." In *Lectures on Literature*, ed. Fredson Bowers. New York: Harcourt Brace Jovanovich, 1980.

Noble, Andrew, ed. *Robert Louis Stevenson*. Totowa: Barnes and Noble, 1983.

Punter, David. *The Literature of Terror: A History of Gothic Fictions from 1765 to the present day*. London: Longman, 1980.

Saposnik, Irving S. *Robert Louis Stevenson*. New York: Twayne, 1974.

Shearer, Tom. "A Strange Judgement of God's? Stevenson's *The Merry Men*." *Studies in Scottish Literature* 20 (1985): 71–87.

Simpson, K.G. "Realism and Romance: Stevenson and Scottish Values." *Studies in Scottish Literature* 20 (1985): 231–47.

Smith, Andrew. *Gothic Radicalism*. New York: St. Martin's, 2000.

Smith, Janet Adams. *Henry James and Robert Louis Stevenson: A Record of Friendship and Criticism*. London: Rupert Hart-Davis, 1948.

Stern, G.B. *Robert Louis Stevenson*. London: Longman, 1952.

Swearingen, Roger G. *The Prose Writings of Robert Louis Stevenson: A Guide*. London: Macmillan, 1980.

Thorpe, Douglas. "Calvin, Darwin, and the Double: The Problem of Divided Nature in Hogg, MacDonald, and Stevenson." *Newsletter of the Victorian Studies Association of Western Canada* 11 (1985): 6–22.

Veeder, William, and Hirsh, Gordon, eds. *Dr. Jekyll and Mr. Hyde: After One Hundred Years*. Chicago: University of Chicago Press, 1988.

Woolf, Leonard, "The Fall of Stevenson." In *Essays on Literature, History, Politics, Etc.* London: Hogarth, 1927.

Acknowledgments

"The Style of Stevenson" from *The Collected Works of G.K. Chesterton XVIII: Thomas Carlyle, Leo Tolstoy, Robert Louis Stevenson, Chaucer* with an introduction and notes by Russell Kirk. 95–102. © 1991 by Ignatius Press, San Francisco. Reprinted by permission of A P Watt Ltd. on behalf of The Royal Literary Fund.

"R.L.S. Revisited" from *No! in Thunder: Essays on Myth and Literature* by Leslie A. Fiedler. 77–91. © 1960 by Leslie A. Fiedler. Reprinted by permission.

"The Aesthetics of Adventure" from *Robert Louis Stevenson and the Fiction of Adventure* by Robert Kiely. 19–57. © 1964 by the President and Fellows of Harvard College. Reprinted by permission.

"Stevenson and Scottish Fiction: The Importance of *The Master of Ballantrae*" by Douglas Gifford from *Stevenson and Victorian Scotland* edited by Jenni Calder. 62–86. © by Edinburgh University Press and individual contributors 1981. Reprinted by permission.

"Author and Narrator in *Weir of Hermiston*" by K.G. Simpson from *Robert Louis Stevenson* edited by Andrew Noble. 202–226. © 1983 by Vision Press Ltd. Reprinted by permission.

"Children of the Night: Stevenson and Patriarchy" by William Veeder from

Dr. Jekyll and Mr. Hyde: After One Hundred Years edited by William Veeder and Gordon Hirsch. 107–156. © 1988 by The University of Chicago. Reprinted by permission.

"James and Stevenson: The Mixed Current of Realism and Romance" by George Dekker from *Critical Recontructions: The Relationship of Fiction and Life* edited by Robert M. Polhemus and Roger B. Henkle. 127–149. © 1994 by the Board of Trustees of the Leland Stanford Junior University. Reprinted by permission.

"The sedulous ape: atavism, professionalism, and Stevenson's *Jeykyll and Hyde*" from *Fictions of Loss in the Victorian Fin de Siecle* by Stephen Arata. 33–53. © 1996 by Cambridge University Press. Reprinted by permission.

"*Treasure Island*: The Parrot's Tale" from *Robert Louis Stevenson and the Appearance of Modernism: A Future Feeling* by Alan Sandison. 48–80. © 1996 by Alan Sandison. Reprinted by permission.

"*On A Child's Garden of Verses*" from *The Work of Poetry* by John Hollander. 129–141. © 1997 by Columbia University Press. Reprinted by permission.

"Piracy and exchange: Stevenson's Pacific fiction" from Literary Culture and the Pacific: Nineteenth-century textual encounters by Vanessa Smith. 145–191. © 1998 by Vanessa Smith. Reprinted by permission.

Index